PLUTARCH'S LIVES

VOLUME TWO

ACROPOLIS AND TEMPLE OF THESEUS

PLUTARCH'S LIVES

The Translation Called Dryden's

Corrected from the Greek and Revised by

A. H. CLOUGH

Sometime Fellow and Tutor of the Oriel College, Oxford, and Late Professor of the English Language and Literature at University College, London

With
Dr. William Smith's Historical Notes

IN FIVE VOLUMES

VOLUME TWO

Illustrated

WILDSIDE PRESS

CONTENTS

Vol. II

	PAGE
ALCIBIADES	3
CORIOLANUS	59
COMPARISON OF ALCIBIADES WITH CORIOLANUS	112
TIMOLEON	118
ÆMILIUS PAULUS	170
COMPARISON OF TIMOLEON WITH ÆMILIUS PAULUS	217
PELOPIDAS	220
MARCELLUS	262
COMPARISON OF PELOPIDAS WITH MARCELLUS	303
ARISTIDES	308
MARCUS CATO	347
COMPARISON OF ARISTIDES WITH MARCUS CATO	388
PHILOPŒMEN	395
FLAMININUS	422
COMPARISON OF PHILOPŒMEN WITH FLAMININUS	454

ILLUSTRATIONS

Vol. II

Acropolis and Temple of Theseus	*Frontispiece*
	FACING PAGE
Lictors	102
Naval Fight During the First Punic War . .	190
The Macedonian Phalanx in the Defiles of Thracia	264

PLUTARCH'S LIVES

ALCIBIADES [1]

Translated by Mr. John Somers (Lord Somers), the Statesman

ALCIBIADES, as it is supposed, was anciently descended from Eurysaces, the son of Ajax, by his father's side; and by his mother's side from Alcmæon. Dinomache, his mother, was the daughter of Megacles. His father, Clinias, having fitted out a galley at his own expense, gained great honor in the sea-fight at Artemisium, and was afterwards slain in the battle of Coronea, fighting against the Bœotians. Pericles and Ariphron, the sons of Xanthippus, nearly related to him, became the guardians of Alcibiades. It has been said not untruly that the friendship which Socrates felt for him has much contributed to his fame; and certain it is, that, though we have no account from any writer concerning the mother of Nicias or Demosthenes, of Lamachus or Phormion, of Thrasybulus or Theramenes, notwithstanding these were all illustrious men of the same period, yet we know even the nurse of Alcibiades, that her country was Lacedæmon, and her name Amycla; and that Zopyrus was his teacher and attendant; the one being recorded by Antisthenes, and the other by Plato.[2]

It is not, perhaps, material to say any thing of the beauty of Alcibiades, only that it bloomed with him in all the ages of his life, in his infancy, in his youth, and

---

[1] Alcibiades was born about 450 B.C. He possessed a beautiful person, transcendent abilities, and great wealth. His youth was disgraced by his amours and debaucheries, which indeed continued for the most part throughout his life. He was assassinated in 404 B.C.—Dr. WILLIAM SMITH.

[2] Plato records it in the First Alcibiades.

in his manhood; and, in the peculiar character becoming to each of these periods, gave him, in every one of them, a grace and a charm. What Euripides says, that

> "Of all fair things the autumn, too, is fair,"[3]

is by no means universally true. But it happened so with Alcibiades, amongst few others, by reason of his happy constitution and natural vigor of body. It is said that his lisping, when he spoke, became him well, and gave a grace and persuasiveness to his rapid speech. Aristophanes takes notice of it in the verses in which he jests at Theorus; "How like a *colax* he is," says Alcibiades, meaning a *corax*;[4] on which it is remarked,

> "How very happily he lisped the truth."

Archippus also alludes to it in a passage where he ridicules the son of Alcibiades;

> "That people may believe him like his father,
> He walks like one dissolved in luxury,

[3] *Of all fair things the autumn is most fair* is Lord Somers's verse, going a little beyond the original. It seems probable, however, that the critics, who reduced the original words to the form of an iambic line, put themselves to unnecessary trouble. Plutarch quotes it elsewhere as said *viva voce* by Euripides at a supper party, when he was laughed at for putting his arms round Agathon, a bearded man, and kissing him. See Matthiæ's Euripides (*Fragm. Incert.*, 124). The passage from Aristophanes, just below, is from the Wasps, 44th and following verses.

[4] This fashionable Attic lisp, or slovenly articulation, turned the sound *r* into *l*. *Colax*, a flatterer; *Corax*, a crow.

> Lets his robe trail behind him on the ground,
> Carelessly leans his head, and in his talk
> Affects to lisp."

His conduct displayed many great inconsistencies and variations, not unnaturally, in accordance with the many and wonderful vicissitudes of his fortunes; but among the many strong passions of his real character, the one most prevailing of all was his ambition and desire of superiority, which appears in several anecdotes told of his sayings whilst he was a child. Once being hard pressed in wrestling, and fearing to be thrown, he got the hand of his antagonist to his mouth, and bit it with all his force; and when the other loosed his hold presently, and said, "You bite, Alcibiades, like a woman." "No," replied he, "like a lion." Another time as he played at dice in the street, being then but a child, a loaded cart came that way, when it was his turn to throw; at first he called to the driver to stop, because he was to throw in the way over which the cart was to pass; but the man giving him no attention and driving on, when the rest of the boys divided and gave way, Alcibiades threw himself on his face before the cart, and, stretching himself out, bade the carter pass on now if he would; which so startled the man, that he put back his horses, while all that saw it were terrified, and, crying out, ran to assist Alcibiades. When he began to study, he obeyed all his other masters fairly well, but refused to learn upon the flute, as a sordid thing, and not becoming a free citizen; saying, that to play on the lute or the harp does not in any way disfigure a man's body or face, but one is hardly to be known by the most intimate friends, when playing on the flute. Besides, one who plays on the harp may speak or sing at the same time; but the use of the flute stops the mouth, intercepts the voice, and prevents all articulation. "Therefore," said he, "let the Theban youths pipe, who do not know how to speak, but we Athenians, as our ancestors have told us, have Minerva for our patroness, and Apollo for our protector, one of whom threw away the flute, and the other stripped the Flute-player of his skin." Thus, between raillery and good earnest, Alcibiades kept not only himself but others from learning, as it presently became the talk of the young boys, how Alcibiades despised playing on the flute, and ridiculed those who studied it. In consequence of which, it ceased to be reckoned amongst the liberal accomplishments, and became generally neglected.

It is stated in the invective which Antiphon wrote against Alcibiades, that once, when he was a boy, he ran away to the house of Democrates, one of those who made a favorite of him, and that Ariphron had determined to cause proclamation to be made for him, had not Pericles diverted him from it, by saying, that if he were dead, the proclaiming of him could only cause it to be discovered one day sooner, and if he were safe, it would be a reproach to him as long as he lived. Antiphon also says, that he killed one of his own servants with the blow of a staff in Sibyrtius's wrestling ground. But it is unreasonable to give credit to all that is objected by an enemy, who makes open profession of his design to defame him.

It was manifest that the many well-born persons who were continually seeking his company, and making their court to him, were attracted and captivated by his brilliant and extraordinary beauty only. But the affection which Socrates entertained for him is a great evidence of the natural noble qualities and good disposition of the boy, which Socrates, indeed, detected both in and under his personal beauty; and, fearing that his wealth and station and the great number both of strangers and Athenians who flattered and caressed him, might at last corrupt him, resolved, if possible, to interpose, and preserve so hopeful a plant from perishing in the flower, before its fruit came to perfection. For never did fortune surround and enclose a man with so many of those things which we vulgarly call goods, or so protect him from every weapon of philosophy, and fence him from every access of free and searching words, as she did Alcibiades; who, from the beginning, was exposed to the flatteries of those who sought merely his gratification, such as might well unnerve him, and indispose him to listen to any real adviser or instructor. Yet such was the happiness of his genius, that he discerned Socrates from the rest, and admitted him, whilst he drove away the wealthy and the noble who made court to him. And, in a little time, they grew intimate, and Alcibiades, listening now to language entirely free from every thought of unmanly fondness and silly displays of affection, finding himself with one who sought to lay open to him the deficiencies of his mind, and repress his vain and foolish arrogance,

"Dropped like the craven cock his conquered wing." [5]

He esteemed these endeavors of Socrates as most truly a means which the gods made use of for the care and preservation of youth,[6] and began to think

[5] *Dropped like the craven cock his conquered wing* is quoted again in the life of Pelopidas, but is otherwise unknown. The words in the Phædrus of Plato, alluded to presently, are simply *Anteros the image of love,* and admit of more than one interpretation. Plutarch, however, seems to take them to mean *the reciprocation* and return *of love.*

[6] In allusion to the philosophical theory which he quoted in

meanly of himself, and to admire him; to be pleased with his kindness, and to stand in awe of his virtue; and, unawares to himself, there became formed in his mind that reflex image and reciprocation of Love, or Anteros,[7] that Plato talks of. It was a matter of general wonder, when people saw him joining Socrates in his meals and his exercises, living with him in the same tent, whilst he was reserved and rough to all others who made their addresses to him, and acted, indeed, with great insolence to some of them. As in particular to Anytus, the son of Anthemion, one who was very fond of him, and invited him to an entertainment which he had prepared for some strangers. Alcibiades refused the invitation; but, having drunk to excess at his own house with some of his companions, went thither with them to play some frolic; and, standing at the door of the room where the guests were enjoying themselves, and seeing the tables covered with gold and silver cups, he commanded his servants to take away the one half of them, and carry them to his own house; and then, disdaining so much as to enter into the room himself, as soon as he had done this, went away. The company was indignant, and exclaimed at his rude and insulting conduct; Anytus, however, said, on the contrary he had shown great consideration and tenderness in taking only a part, when he might have taken all.

He behaved in the same manner to all others who courted him, except only one stranger, who, as the story is told, having but a small estate, sold it all for about a hundred staters, which he presented to Al-

the life of Theseus, that love is a divine provision for the care of the young.

[7] Eros and Anteros, Love and Love-again.

cibiades, and besought him to accept. Alcibiades, smiling and well pleased at the thing, invited him to supper, and, after a very kind entertainment, gave him his gold again, requiring him, moreover, not to fail to be present the next day, when the public revenue was offered to farm, and to outbid all others. The man would have excused himself, because the contract was so large, and would cost many talents; but Alcibiades, who had at that time a private pique against the existing farmers of the revenue, threatened to have him beaten if he refused. The next morning, the stranger, coming to the market-place, offered a talent more than the existing rate; upon which the farmers, enraged and consulting together, called upon him to name his sureties, concluding that he could find none. The poor man, being startled at the proposal, began to retire; but Alcibiades, standing at a distance, cried out to the magistrates, " Set my name down, he is a friend of mine; I will be security for him." When the other bidders heard this, they perceived that all their contrivance was defeated; for their way was, with the profits of the second year to pay the rent for the year preceding; so that, not seeing any other way to extricate themselves out of the difficulty, they began to entreat the stranger, and offered him a sum of money. Alcibiades would not suffer him to accept of less than a talent; but when that was paid down, he commanded him to relinquish the bargain, having by this device relieved his necessity.

Though Socrates had many and powerful rivals, yet the natural good qualities of Alcibiades gave his affection the mastery. His words overcame him so much, as to draw tears from his eyes, and to disturb his very soul. Yet sometimes he would abandon himself to flatterers, when they proposed to him varieties of pleasure, and would desert Socrates; who, then, would pursue him, as if he had been a fugitive slave. He despised every one else, and had no reverence or awe for any but him. Cleanthes the philosopher, speaking of one to whom he was attached, says his only hold on him was by his ears, while his rivals had all the others offered them; and there is no question that Alcibiades was very easily caught by pleasures; and the expression used by Thucydides[3] about the excesses of his habitual course of living gives occasion to believe so. But those who endeavored to corrupt Alcibiades took advantage chiefly of his vanity and ambition, and thrust him on unseasonably to undertake great enterprises, persuading him, that as soon as he began to concern himself in public affairs, he would not only obscure the rest of the generals and statesmen, but outdo the authority and the reputation which Pericles himself had gained in Greece. But in the same manner as iron which is softened by the fire grows hard with the cold, and all its parts are closed again; so, as often as Socrates observed Alcibiades to be misled by luxury or pride, he reduced and corrected him by his addresses, and made him humble and modest, by showing him in how many things he was deficient, and how very far from perfection in virtue.

[3] *The expression used by Thucydides* occurs in his account of one of Alcibiades's orations on the Sicilian War (*VI.*, 15), where he speaks of it as one of the chief causes which ultimately led to the disasters of the city, that people, in alarm at the excessiveness of his personal licentiousness and scorn of all legal restrictions in his habits of life, would not trust themselves to his guidance, which was the best and wisest, in matters of public policy.

When he was past his childhood, he went once to a grammar-school, and asked the master for one of Homer's books; and he making answer that he had nothing of Homer's, Alcibiades gave him a blow with his fist, and went away. Another schoolmaster telling him that he had Homer corrected by himself; "How?" said Alcibiades, "and do you employ your time in teaching children to read? You, who are able to amend Homer, may well undertake to instruct men." Being once desirous to speak with Pericles, he went to his house, and was told there that he was not at leisure, but busied in considering how to give up his accounts to the Athenians; Alcibiades, as he went away, said, "It were better for him to consider how he might avoid giving up his accounts at all."

Whilst he was very young, he was a soldier in the expedition against Potidæa, where Socrates lodged in the same tent with him, and stood next him in battle. Once there happened a sharp skirmish, in which they both behaved with signal bravery; but Alcibiades receiving a wound, Socrates threw himself before him to defend him, and beyond any question saved him and his arms from the enemy, and so in all justice might have challenged the prize of valor. But the generals appearing eager to adjudge the honor to Alcibiades, because of his rank, Socrates, who desired to increase his thirst after glory of a noble kind, was the first to give evidence for him, and pressed them to crown him, and to decree to him the complete suit of armor. Afterwards, in the battle of Delium, when the Athenians were routed and Socrates with a few others was retreating on foot, Alcibiades, who was on horseback, observing it, would not pass on, but stayed to shelter him from the danger, and brought him safe off, though the enemy pressed hard upon them, and cut off many. But this happened some time after.

He gave a box on the ear to Hipponicus, the father of Callias, whose birth and wealth made him a person of great influence and repute. And this he did unprovoked by any passion or quarrel between them, but only because, in a frolic, he had agreed with his companions to do it. People were justly offended at this insolence, when it became known through the city; but early the next morning, Alcibiades went to his house and knocked at the door, and, being admitted to him, took off his outer garment, and, presenting his naked body, desired him to scourge and chastise him as he pleased. Upon this Hipponicus forgot all his resentment, and not only pardoned him, but soon after gave him his daughter Hipparete in marriage. Some say that it was not Hipponicus, but his son Callias, who gave Hipparete to Alcibiades, together with a portion of ten talents, and that after, when she had a child, Alcibiades forced him to give ten talents more, upon pretence that such was the agreement if she brought him any children. Afterwards, Callias, for fear of coming to his death by his means, declared, in a full assembly of the people, that if he should happen to die without children, the state should inherit his house and all his goods. Hipparete was a virtuous and dutiful wife, but, at last, growing impatient of the outrages done to her by her husband's continual entertaining of courtesans, as well strangers as Athenians, she departed from him and retired to her brother's house. Alcibiades seemed not at all concerned at this, and lived on still in the same luxury; but the law requiring that she should deliver to the archon in person, and not by proxy, the instrument by which she claimed a divorce, when, in obedience to the law, she presented herself before him to perform this, Alcibiades came in, caught her up, and carried her home through the market-place, no one daring to oppose him, nor to take her from him. She continued with him till her death, which happened not long after, when Alcibiades had gone to Ephesus. Nor is this violence to be thought so very enormous or unmanly. For the law, in making her who desires to be divorced appear in public, seems to design to give her husband an opportunity of treating with her, and of endeavoring to retain her.

Alcibiades had a dog which cost him seventy minas, and was a very large one, and very handsome. His tail, which was his principal ornament, he caused to be cut off, and his acquaintance exclaiming at him for it, and telling him that all Athens was sorry for the dog, and cried out upon him for this action, he laughed, and said, "Just what I wanted has happened, then. I wished the Athenians to talk about this, that they might not say something worse of me."

It is said that the first time he came into the assembly was upon occasion of a largess of money which he made to the people. This was not done by design, but as he passed along he heard a shout, and inquiring the cause, and having learned that there was a donative making to the people, he went in amongst them and gave money also. The multitude thereupon applauding him, and shouting, he was so transported at it, that he forgot a quail which he had under his robe, and the bird, being frightened by the noise, flew off; upon which the people made louder acclamations than before, and many of them started up to pursue the bird; and one

Antiochus, a pilot, caught it and restored it to him, for which he was ever after a favorite with Alcibiades.

He had great advantages for entering public life; his noble birth, his riches, the personal courage he had shown in divers battles, and the multitude of his friends and dependents, threw open, so to say, folding doors for his admittance. But he did not consent to let his power with the people rest on any thing, rather than on his own gift of eloquence. That he was a master in the art of speaking, the comic poets bear him witness; and the most eloquent of public speakers, in his oration against Midias,[9] allows that Alcibiades, among other perfections, was a most accomplished orator. If, however, we give credit to Theophrastus, who of all philosophers was the most curious inquirer, and the greatest lover of history, we are to understand that Alcibiades had the highest capacity for inventing, for discerning what was the right thing to be said for any purpose, and on any occasion; but, aiming not only at saying what was required, but also at saying it well, in respect, that is, of words and phrases, when these did not readily occur, he would often pause in the middle of his discourse for want of the apt word, and would be silent and stop till he could recollect himself, and had considered what to say.

His expenses in horses kept for the public

---

[9] *Demosthenes in his oration against Midias,* whom he prosecuted for an assault upon himself, has a long passage about the way in which Alcibiades, in former times, in spite of all his great pretensions, high birth and wealth, capacity as a general, and skill as an orator, had not been tolerated in his insolence to private persons.

games, and in the number of his chariots, were matter of great observation; never did any one but he, either private person or king, send seven chariots to the Olympic games. And to have carried away at once the first, the second, and the fourth prize, as Thucydides says, or the third, as Euripides relates it, outdoes far away every distinction that ever was known or thought of in that kind. Euripides celebrates his success in this manner:—

> "—But my song to you,
> Son of Clinias, is due.
> Victory is noble; how much more
> To do as never Greek before;
> To obtain in the great chariot race
> The first, the second, and third place;
> With easy step advanced to fame,
> To bid the herald three times claim
> The olive for one victor's name."

The emulation displayed by the deputations of various states, in the presents which they made to him, rendered this success yet more illustrious. The Ephesians erected a tent for him, adorned magnificently; the city of Chios furnished him with provender for his horses and with great numbers of beasts for sacrifice; and the Lesbians sent him wine and other provisions for the many great entertainments which he made. Yet in the midst of all this he escaped not without censure, occasioned either by the ill-nature of his enemies or by his own misconduct. For it is said, that one Diomedes, an Athenian, a worthy man and a friend to Alcibiades, passionately desiring to obtain the victory at the Olympic games, and having heard much of a chariot which belonged to the state at Argos, where he knew that Alcibiades had great power and many friends, prevailed with him to undertake to buy the chariot. Alcibiades did indeed buy it, but then claimed it for his own, leaving Diomedes to rage at him, and to call upon the gods and men to bear witness to the injustice. It would seem there was a suit at law commenced upon this occasion, and there is yet extant an oration concerning the chariot, written by Isocrates in defence of the son of Alcibiades. But the plaintiff in this action is named Tisias, and not Diomedes.

As soon as he began to intermeddle in the government, which was when he was very young, he quickly lessened the credit of all who aspired to the confidence of the people, except Phæax, the son of Erasistratus, and Nicias, the son of Niceratus, who alone could contest it with him. Nicias was arrived at a mature age, and was esteemed their first general. Phæax was but a rising statesman like Alcibiades; he was descended from noble ancestors, but was his inferior, as in many other things, so, principally, in eloquence. He possessed rather the art of persuading in private conversation than of debate before the people, and was, as Eupolis said of him,

"The best of talkers, and of speakers worst."

There is extant an oration written by Phæax against Alcibiades, in which, amongst other things, it is said, that Alcibiades made daily use at his table of many gold and silver vessels, which belonged to the commonwealth, as if they had been his own.

There was a certain Hyperbolus, of the township of Perithœdæ, whom Thucydides also speaks of as a man of bad character, a general butt for the mockery of all the comic writers of the time, but quite unconcerned at the worst things they could say, and, being careless of glory, also insensible of shame; a temper which some people call boldness and courage, whereas it is indeed impudence and recklessness. He was liked by nobody, yet the people made frequent use of him, when they had a mind to disgrace or calumniate any persons in authority. At this time, the people, by his persuasions, were ready to proceed to pronounce the sentence of ten years' banishment, called ostracism. This they made use of to humiliate and drive out of the city such citizens as outdid the rest in credit and power, indulging not so much perhaps their apprehensions as their jealousies in this way. And when, at this time, there was no doubt but that the ostracism would fall upon one of those three, Alcibiades contrived to form a coalition of parties, and, communicating his project to Nicias, turned the sentence upon Hyperbolus himself. Others say, that it was not with Nicias, but Phæax, that he consulted, and, by help of his party, procured the banishment of Hyperbolus, when he suspected nothing less. For, before that time, no mean or obscure person had ever fallen under that punishment, so that Plato, the comic poet, speaking of Hyperbolus, might well say,

> "The man deserved the fate; deny 't who can?
> Yes, but the fate did not deserve the man;
> Not for the like of him and his slave-brands
> Did Athens put the sherd into our hands."

But we have given elsewhere a fuller statement of what is known to us of the matter.

Alcibiades was not less disturbed at the distinctions which Nicias gained amongst the enemies of Athens, than at the honors which the Athenians themselves paid to him. For though Alcibiades was the proper appointed person[10] to receive all Lacedæmonians when they came to Athens, and had taken particular care of those that were made prisoners at Pylos, yet, after they had obtained the peace and restitution of the captives, by the procurement chiefly of Nicias, they paid him very special attentions. And it was commonly said in Greece, that the war was begun by Pericles, and that Nicias made an end of it, and the peace was generally called the peace of Nicias. Alcibiades was extremely annoyed at this, and, being full of envy, set himself to break the league. First, therefore, observing that the Argives, as well out of fear as hatred to the Lacedæmonians, sought for protection against them, he gave them a secret assurance of alliance with Athens. And communicating, as well in person as by letters, with the chief advisers of the people there, he encouraged them not to fear the Lacedæmonians, nor make concessions to them, but to wait a little, and keep their eyes on the Athenians, who, already, were all but sorry they had made peace, and would soon give it up. And, afterwards, when the Lacedæmonians had made a league with the Bœotians, and had not delivered up Panactum entire, as they ought to have done by the treaty, but only after first destroying it, which gave great offence to the people of Athens, Alcibiades laid hold of that opportunity to exasperate them more highly. He exclaimed fiercely against Nicias, and accused him of many things, which seemed

---

[10] The Proxĕnus, that is, who in the ancient cities exercised, in a private station, and as a matter of private magnificence and splendid hospitality (he being always a citizen of the state in which he resided), many of the duties of protection now officially committed to consuls and resident ministers.

probable enough; as that, when he was general, he made no attempt himself to capture their enemies that were shut up in the isle of Sphacteria, but, when they were afterwards made prisoners by others, he procured their release and sent them back to the Lacedæmonians, only to get favor with them; that he would not make use of his credit with them to prevent their entering into this confederacy with the Bœotians and Corinthians, and yet, on the other side, that he sought to stand in the way of those Greeks who were inclined to make an alliance and friendship with Athens, if the Lacedæmonians did not like it.

It happened, at the very time when Nicias was by these arts brought into disgrace with the people, that ambassadors arrived from Lacedæmon, who, at their first coming, said what seemed very satisfactory, declaring that they had full powers to arrange all matters in dispute upon fair and equal terms. The council received their propositions, and the people was to assemble on the morrow to give them audience. Alcibiades grew very apprehensive of this, and contrived to gain a secret conference with the ambassadors. When they were met, he said: " What is it you intend, you men of Sparta? Can you be ignorant that the council always act with moderation and respect towards ambassadors, but that the people are full of ambition and great designs? So that, if you let them know what full powers your commission gives you, they will urge and press you to unreasonable conditions. Quit, therefore, this indiscreet simplicity, if you expect to obtain equal terms from the Athenians, and would not have things extorted from you contrary to your inclinations, and begin to treat with the people upon some reasonable articles, not avowing yourselves plenipotentiaries;

and I will be ready to assist you, out of good-will to the Lacedæmonians." When he had said thus, he gave them his oath for the performance of what he promised, and by this way drew them from Nicias to rely entirely upon himself, and left them full of admiration of the discernment and sagacity they had seen in him. The next day, when the people were assembled and the ambassadors introduced, Alcibiades, with great apparent courtesy, demanded of them, With what powers they were come? They made answer that they were not come as plenipotentiaries.

Instantly upon that, Alcibiades, with a loud voice, as though he had received and not done the wrong, began to call them dishonest prevaricators, and to urge that such men could not possibly come with a purpose to say or do any thing that was sincere. The council was incensed, the people were in a rage, and Nicias, who knew nothing of the deceit and the imposture, was in the greatest confusion, equally surprised and ashamed at such a change in the men. So thus the Lacedæmonian ambassadors were utterly rejected, and Alcibiades was declared general, who presently united the Argives, the Eleans, and the people of Mantinea, into a confederacy with the Athenians.

No man commended the method by which Alcibiades effected all this, yet it was a great political feat thus to divide and shake almost all Peloponnesus, and to combine so many men in arms against the Lacedæmonians in one day before Mantinea; and, moreover, to remove the war and the danger so far from the frontier of the Athenians, that even success would profit the enemy but little, should they be conquerors, whereas, if they were defeated, Sparta itself was hardly safe.

After this battle at Mantinea, the select thousand of the army of the Argives attempted to overthrow the government of the people in Argos, and make themselves masters of the city; and the Lacedæmonians came to their aid and abolished the democracy. But the people took arms again, and gained the advantage, and Alcibiades came in to their aid and completed the victory, and persuaded them to build long walls, and by that means to join their city to the sea, and so to bring it wholly within the reach of the Athenian power. To this purpose, he procured them builders and masons from Athens, and displayed the greatest zeal for their service, and gained no less honor and power to himself than to the commonwealth of Athens. He also persuaded the people of Patræ to join their city to the sea, by building long walls; and when some one told them, by way of warning, that the Athenians would swallow them up at last, Alcibiades made answer, "Possibly it may be so, but it will be by little and little, and beginning at the feet, whereas the Lacedæmonians will begin at the head and devour you all at once." Nor did he neglect either to advise the Athenians to look to their interests by land, and often put the young men in mind of the oath which they had made at Agraulos,[11] to the effect that they would account wheat and barley, and vines and olives, to be the limits of Attica; by which they were taught

---

[11] *At Agraulos* is the old reading, but *in* [the temple] *of Agraulos* is the early and certain correction. Agraulos, or Agraule, from whom the township of Agraule took its name, was one of the daughters of Cecrops, who, to fulfil an oracle which promised victory on such a condition, threw herself from the rocks of the Acropolis. The people built her a temple, and here the young Athenians, on first assuming arms, took this oath.

to claim a title to all land that was cultivated and productive.

But with all these words and deeds, and with all this sagacity and eloquence, he intermingled exorbitant luxury and wantonness in his eating and drinking and dissolute living; wore long purple robes like a woman, which dragged after him as he went through the market-place; caused the planks of his galley to be cut away, that so he might lie the softer, his bed not being placed on the boards, but hanging upon girths. His shield, again, which was richly gilded, had not the usual ensigns of the Athenians, but a Cupid, holding a thunderbolt in his hand, was painted upon it. The sight of all this made the people of good repute in the city feel disgust and abhorrence, and apprehension also, at his free-living, and his contempt of law, as things monstrous in themselves, and indicating designs of usurpation. Aristophanes has well expressed the people's feeling towards him:—

"They love, and hate, and cannot do without him."[12]

And still more strongly, under a figurative expression,

"Best rear no lion in your state, 't is true;
But treat him like a lion if you do."

The truth is, his liberalities, his public shows, and other munificence to the people, which were such as nothing could exceed, the glory of his ancestors, the force of his eloquence, the grace of his person, his strength of body, joined with his great courage and

[12] The quotations from Aristophanes are lines 1445, 1452 of the Frogs.

knowledge in military affairs, prevailed upon the
Athenians to endure patiently his excesses, to in-
dulge many things to him, and, according to their
habit, to give the softest names to his faults, at-
tributing them to youth and good nature. As, for
example, he kept Agatharcus, the painter, a prisoner
till he had painted his whole house, but then dismissed him with a reward. He publicly struck
Taureas, who exhibited certain shows in opposition
to him and contended with him for the prize. He
selected for himself one of the captive Melian women,
and had a son by her, whom he took care to educate.
This the Athenians styled great humanity; and yet
he was the principal cause of the slaughter of all the
inhabitants of the isle of Melos who were of age to
bear arms, having spoken in favor of that decree.
When Aristophon, the painter, had drawn Nemea
sitting and holding Alcibiades in her arms, the multitude seemed pleased with the piece, and thronged
to see it, but older people disliked and discredited it,
and looked on these things as enormities, and movements towards tyranny. So that it was not said
amiss by Archestratus, that Greece could not support a second Alcibiades. Once, when Alcibiades
succeeded well in an oration which he made, and the
whole assembly attended upon him to do him honor,
Timon the misanthrope did not pass slightly by him,
nor avoid him, as he did others, but purposely met
him, and, taking him by the hand, said, "Go on
boldly, my son, and increase in credit with the
people, for thou wilt one day bring them calamities
enough." Some that were present laughed at the
saying, and some reviled Timon; but there were
others upon whom it made a deep impression; so
various was the judgment which was made of him,
and so irregular his own character.

The Athenians, even in the lifetime of Pericles, had already cast a longing eye upon Sicily; but did not attempt any thing till after his death. Then, under pretence of aiding his confederates, they sent succors upon all occasions to those who were oppressed by the Syracusans, preparing the way for sending over a greater force. But Alcibiades was the person who inflamed this desire of theirs to the height, and prevailed with them no longer to proceed secretly, and by little and little, in their design, but to sail out with a great fleet, and undertake at once to make themselves masters of the island. He possessed the people with great hopes, and he himself entertained yet greater; and the conquest of Sicily, which was the utmost bound of their ambition, was but the mere outset of his expectation. Nicias endeavored to divert the people from the expedition, by representing to them that the taking of Syracuse would be a work of great difficulty; but Alcibiades dreamed of nothing less than the conquest of Carthage and Libya, and by the accession of these conceiving himself at once made master of Italy and of Peloponnesus, seemed to look upon Sicily as little more than a magazine for the war. The young men were soon elevated with these hopes, and listened gladly to those of riper years, who talked wonders of the countries they were going to; so that you might see great numbers sitting in the wrestling grounds and public places, drawing on the ground the figure of the island and the situation of Libya and Carthage. Socrates the philosopher and Meton the astrologer are said, however, never to have hoped for any good to the commonwealth from this war; the one, it is to be supposed, presaging what would ensue, by the intervention of his attendant Genius; and the other, either upon rational consideration of the project, or by use of the art of divination, conceived fears for its issue, and, feigning madness, caught up a burning torch, and seemed as if he would have set his own house on fire. Others report that he did not take upon him to act the madman, but secretly in the night set his house on fire, and the next morning besought the people, that for his comfort, after such a calamity, they would spare his son from the expedition. By which artifice, he deceived his fellow-citizens, and obtained of them what he desired.

Together with Alcibiades, Nicias, much against his will, was appointed general; and he endeavored to avoid the command, not the less on account of his colleague. But the Athenians thought the war would proceed more prosperously, if they did not send Alcibiades free from all restraint, but tempered his heat with the caution of Nicias. This they chose the rather to do, because Lamachus, the third general, though he was of mature years, yet in several battles had appeared no less hot and rash than Alcibiades himself. When they began to deliberate of the number of forces, and of the manner of making the necessary provisions, Nicias made another attempt to oppose the design, and to prevent the war; but Alcibiades contradicted him, and carried his point with the people. And one Demostratus, an orator, proposing to give the generals absolute power over the preparations and the whole management of the war, it was presently decreed so. When all things were fitted for the voyage, many unlucky omens appeared. At that very time the feast of Adonis happened, in which the women were used to expose, in all parts of the city, images resembling dead men carried out to their burial, and to represent funeral solemnities by lamentations and mournful songs.

The mutilation, however, of the images of Mercury, most of which, in one night, had their faces all disfigured, terrified many persons who were wont to despise most things of that nature. It was given out that it was done by the Corinthians, for the sake of the Syracusans, who were their colony, in hopes that the Athenians, by such prodigies, might be induced to delay or abandon the war. But the report gained no credit with the people, nor yet the opinion of those who would not believe that there was any thing ominous in the matter, but that it was only an extravagant action, committed, in that sort of sport which runs into license, by wild young men coming from a debauch. Alike enraged and terrified at the thing, looking upon it to proceed from a conspiracy of persons who designed some commotions in the state, the council, as well as the assembly of the people, which was held frequently in a few days' space, examined diligently every thing that might administer ground for suspicion. During this examination, Androcles, one of the demagogues, produced certain slaves and strangers before them, who accused Alcibiades and some of his friends of defacing other images in the same manner, and of having profanely acted the sacred mysteries at a drunken meeting, where one Theodorus represented the herald, Polytion the torch-bearer, and Alcibiades the chief priest, while the rest of the party appeared as candidates for initiation, and received the title of Initiates. These were the matters contained in the articles of information,[13] which Thessalus, the son of Cimon, exhibited against Alcibiades, for his impious

---

[13] *Eisangĕlia*, the technical term for an indictment before the legislature for misdemeanors not coming strictly under the letter of any written law.

mockery of the goddesses, Ceres and Proserpine. The people were highly exasperated and incensed against Alcibiades upon this occasion, which, being aggravated by Androcles, the most malicious of all his enemies, at first disturbed his friends exceedingly. But when they perceived that all the seamen designed for Sicily were for him, and the soldiers also, and when the Argive and Mantinean auxiliaries, a thousand men at arms, openly declared that they had undertaken this distant maritime expedition for the sake of Alcibiades, and that, if he was ill-used, they would all go home, they recovered their courage, and became eager to make use of the great opportunity for justifying him. At this his enemies were again discouraged, fearing lest the people should be more gentle to him in their sentence, because of the occasion they had for his service. Therefore, to obviate this, they contrived that some other orators, who did not appear to be enemies to Alcibiades, but really hated him no less than those who avowed it, should stand up in the assembly and say, that it was a very absurd thing that one who was created general of such an army with absolute power, after his troops were assembled, and the confederates were come, should lose the opportunity, whilst the people were choosing his judges by lot, and appointing times for the hearing of the cause. And, therefore, let him set sail at once; good fortune attend him; and when the war should be at an end, he might then in person make his defence according to the laws.

Alcibiades perceived the malice of this postponement, and, appearing in the assembly, represented that it was monstrous for him to be sent with the command of so large an army, when he lay under such accusations and calumnies; that he deserved to die, if he could not clear himself of the crimes objected to him; but when he had so done, and had proved his innocence, he should then cheerfully apply himself to the war, as standing no longer in fear of false accusers. But he could not prevail with the people, who commanded him to sail immediately. So he departed, together with the other generals, having with them near 140 galleys, 5,100 men at arms, and about 1,300 archers, slingers, and light-armed men, and all the other provisions corresponding.

Arriving on the coast of Italy, he landed at Rhegium, and there stated his views of the manner in which they ought to conduct the war. He was opposed by Nicias; but Lamachus being of his opinion, they sailed for Sicily forthwith, and took Catana. This was all that was done while he was there, for he was soon after recalled by the Athenians to abide his trial. At first, as we before said, there were only some slight suspicions advanced against Alcibiades, and accusations by certain slaves and strangers. But afterwards, in his absence, his enemies attacked him more violently, and confounded together the breaking the images with the profanation of the mysteries, as though both had been committed in pursuance of the same conspiracy for changing the government. The people proceeded to imprison all that were accused, without distinction, and without hearing them, and repented now, considering the importance of the charge, that they had not immediately brought Alcibiades to his trial, and given judgment against him. Any of his friends or acquaintance who fell into the people's hands, whilst they were in this fury, did not fail to meet with very severe usage. Thucydides has omitted to name the informers, but others mention Dioclides and Teucer. Amongst whom is Phrynichus, the comic poet, in whom we find the following:—

> "O dearest Hermes! only do take care,
> And mind you do not miss your footing there;
> Should you get hurt, occasion may arise
> For a new Dioclides to tell lies."

To which he makes Mercury return this answer:—

> "I will so, for I feel no inclination
> To reward Teucer for more information."

The truth is, his accusers alleged nothing that was certain or solid against him. One of them, being asked how he knew the men who defaced the images, replying, that he saw them by the light of the moon, made a palpable mis-statement, for it was just new moon when the fact was committed. This made all men of understanding cry out upon the thing; but the people were as eager as ever to receive further accusations, nor was their first heat at all abated, but they instantly seized and imprisoned every one that was accused. Amongst those who were detained in prison for their trials was Andocides the orator, whose descent the historian Hellanicus deduces from Ulysses. He was always supposed to hate popular government, and to support oligarchy. The chief ground of his being suspected of defacing the images was because the great Mercury, which stood near his house, and was an ancient monument of the tribe Ægeïs, was almost the only statue of all the remarkable ones, which remained entire. For this cause, it is now called the Mercury of Andocides, all men giving it that name, though the inscription is evidence to the contrary. It happened that Andocides, amongst the rest who were prisoners upon the same account, contracted particular acquaintance and intimacy with one Timæus, a person inferior to him in repute, but of remarkable dexterity and boldness. He persuaded Andocides to accuse himself and some few others of this crime, urging to him that, upon his confession, he would be, by the decree of the people, secure of his pardon, whereas the event of judgment is uncertain to all men, but to great persons, such as he was, most formidable. So that it was better for him, if he regarded himself, to save his life by a falsity, than to suffer an infamous death, as really guilty of the crime. And if he had regard to the public good, it was commendable to sacrifice a few suspected men, by that means to rescue many excellent persons from the fury of the people. Andocides was prevailed upon, and accused himself and some others, and, by the terms of the decree, obtained his pardon, while all the persons named by him, except some few who had saved themselves by flight, suffered death. To gain the greater credit to his information, he accused his own servants amongst others. But notwithstanding this, the people's anger was not wholly appeased; and being now no longer diverted by the mutilators, they were at leisure to pour out their whole rage upon Alcibiades. And, in conclusion, they sent the galley named the Salaminian, to recall him. But they expressly commanded those that were sent, to use no violence, nor seize upon his person, but address themselves to him in the mildest terms, requiring him to follow them to Athens in order to abide his trial, and clear himself before the people. For they feared mutiny and sedition in the army in an enemy's country, which indeed it would have been easy for Alcibiades to effect, if he had wished it. For the soldiers were dispirited upon his departure,

ALCIBIADES

expecting for the future tedious delays, and that the war would be drawn out into a lazy length by Nicias, when Alcibiades, who was the spur to action, was taken away. For though Lamachus was a soldier, and a man of courage, poverty deprived him of authority and respect in the army. Alcibiades, just upon his departure, prevented Messena from falling into the hands of the Athenians. There were some in that city who were upon the point of delivering it up, but he, knowing the persons, gave information to some friends of the Syracusans, and so defeated the whole contrivance. When he arrived at Thurii, he went on shore, and, concealing himself there, escaped those who searched after him. But to one who knew him, and asked him if he durst not trust his own native country, he made answer, " In every thing else, yes; but in a matter that touches my life, I would not even my own mother, lest she might by mistake throw in the black ball instead of the white." When, afterwards, he was told that the assembly had pronounced judgment of death against him, all he said was " I will make them feel that I am alive."

The information against him was conceived in this form:—

"Thessalus, the son of Cimon, of the township of Lacia, lays information that Alcibiades, the son of Clinias, of the township of the Scambonidæ, has committed a crime against the goddesses Ceres and Proserpine, by representing in derision the holy mysteries, and showing them to his companions in his own house. Where being habited in such robes as are used by the chief priest when he shows the holy things, he named himself the chief priest, Polytion the torch-bearer, and Theodorus, of the township of Phegæa, the herald; and saluted the rest of his company as Initiates and Novices. All which was done contrary to the laws and institutions of the Eumolpidæ, and the heralds and priests of the temple at Eleusis."

He was condemned as contumacious upon his not appearing, his property confiscated, and it was decreed that all the priests and priestesses should solemnly curse him. But one of them, Theano, the daughter of Menon, of the township of Agraule, is said to have opposed that part of the decree, saying that her holy office obliged her to make prayers, but not execrations.

Alcibiades, lying under these heavy decrees and sentences, when first he fled to Thurii, passed over into Peloponnesus, and remained some time at Argos. But being there in fear of his enemies, and seeing himself utterly hopeless of return to his native country, he sent to Sparta, desiring safe conduct, and assuring them that he would make them amends by his future services for all the mischief he had done them while he was their enemy. The Spartans giving him the security he desired, he went eagerly, was well received, and, at his very first coming, succeeded in inducing them, without any further caution or delay, to send aid to the Syracusans; and so roused and excited them, that they forthwith despatched Gylippus into Sicily, to crush the forces which the Athenians had in Sicily. A second point was, to renew the war upon the Athenians at home. But the third thing, and the most important of all, was to make them fortify Decelea, which above every thing reduced and wasted the resources of the Athenians.

The renown which he earned by these public services was equalled by the admiration he attracted to his private life; he captivated and won over everybody by his conformity to Spartan habits. People

who saw him wearing his hair close cut, bathing in
cold water, eating coarse meal, and dining on black
broth, doubted, or rather could not believe, that he
ever had a cook in his house, or had ever seen a perfumer, or had worn a mantle of Milesian purple.
For he had, as it was observed, this peculiar talent
and artifice for gaining men's affections, that he
could at once comply with and really embrace and
enter into their habits and ways of life, and change
faster than the chameleon. One color, indeed, they
say the chameleon cannot assume; it cannot make
itself appear white; but Alcibiades, whether with
good men or with bad, could adapt himself to his
company, and equally wear the appearance of virtue
or vice. At Sparta, he was devoted to athletic exercises, was frugal and reserved; in Ionia, luxurious,
gay, and indolent; in Thrace, always drinking; in
Thessaly, ever on horseback; and when he lived with
Tisaphernes, the Persian satrap, he exceeded the
Persians themselves in magnificence and pomp. Not
that his natural disposition changed so easily, nor
that his real character was so very variable, but,
whenever he was sensible that by pursuing his own
inclinations he might give offence to those with
whom he had occasion to converse, he transformed
himself into any shape, and adopted any fashion,
that he observed to be most agreeable to them. So
that to have seen him at Lacedæmon, a man, judging
by the outward appearance, would have said, " 'Tis
not Achilles's son, but he himself, the very man " [14]

[14] *'Tis not Achilles's son, but he himself, the very man*, is
quoted elsewhere by Plutarch, but is otherwise unknown. *'Tis
the same woman still* is said of Helen by Electra in the Orestes
of Euripides (129), when, in making a funeral offering, she
had, to save her beauty, cut off only the very ends of her hair.

that Lycurgus designed to form; while his real feelings and acts would have rather provoked the exclamation, " 'Tis the same woman still." For while King Agis was absent, and abroad with the army, he corrupted his wife Timæa, and had a child born by her. Nor did she even deny it, but when she was brought to bed of a son, called him in public Leotychides, but, amongst her confidants and attendants, would whisper that his name was Alcibiades. To such a degree was she transported by her passion for him. He, on the other side, would say, in his vain way, he had not done this thing out of mere wantonness of insult, nor to gratify a passion, but that his race might one day be kings over the Lacedæmonians.

There were many who told Agis that this was so, but time itself gave the greatest confirmation to the story. For Agis, alarmed by an earthquake, had quitted his wife, and, for ten months after, was never with her; Leotychides, therefore, being born after those ten months, he would not acknowledge him for his son; which was the reason that afterwards he was not admitted to the succession.

After the defeat which the Athenians received in Sicily, ambassadors were despatched to Sparta at once from Chios and Lesbos and Cyzicus, to signify their purpose of revolting from the Athenians. The Bœotians interposed in favor of the Lesbians, and Pharnabazus of the Cyzicenes, but the Lacedæmonians, at the persuasion of Alcibiades, chose to assist Chios before all others. He himself, also, went instantly to sea, procured the immediate revolt of almost all Ionia, and coöperating with the Lacedæmonian generals, did great mischief to the Athenians. But Agis was his enemy, hating him for having dishonored his wife, and also impatient of his glory, as almost every enterprise and every success was ascribed to Alcibiades. Others, also, of the most powerful and ambitious amongst the Spartans, were possessed with jealousy of him, and, at last, prevailed with the magistrates in the city to send orders into Ionia that he should be killed. Alcibiades, however, had secret intelligence of this, and in apprehension of the result, while he communicated all affairs to the Lacedæmonians, yet took care not to put himself into their power. At last he retired to Tisaphernes, the king of Persia's satrap, for his security, and immediately became the first and most influential person about him. For this barbarian, not being himself sincere, but a lover of guile and wickedness, admired his address and wonderful subtlety. And, indeed, the charm of daily intercourse with him was more than any character could resist or any disposition escape. Even those who feared and envied him could not but take delight, and have a sort of kindness for him, when they saw him and were in his company. So that Tisaphernes, otherwise a cruel character, and, above all other Persians, a hater of the Greeks, was yet so won by the flatteries of Alcibiades, that he set himself even to exceed him in responding to them. The most beautiful of his parks, containing salubrious streams and meadows, where he had built pavilions, and places of retirement royally and exquisitely adorned, received by his direction the name of Alcibiades, and was always so called and so spoken of.

Thus Alcibiades, quitting the interests of the Spartans, whom he could no longer trust, because he stood in fear of Agis, endeavored to do them ill offices, and render them odious to Tisaphernes, who, by his means, was hindered from assisting them vigorously, and from finally ruining the Athenians.

For his advice was to furnish them but sparingly with money, and so wear them out, and consume them insensibly; when they had wasted their strength upon one another, they would both become ready to submit to the king. Tisaphernes readily pursued his counsel, and so openly expressed the liking and admiration which he had for him, that Alcibiades was looked up to by the Greeks of both parties, and the Athenians, now in their misfortunes, repented them of their severe sentence against him. And he, on the other side, began to be troubled for them, and to fear lest, if that commonwealth were utterly destroyed, he should fall into the hands of the Lacedæmonians, his enemies.

At that time the whole strength of the Athenians was in Samos. Their fleet maintained itself here, and issued from these head-quarters to reduce such as had revolted, and protect the rest of their territories; in one way or other still contriving to be a match for their enemies at sea. What they stood in fear of, was Tisaphernes and the Phœnician fleet of one hundred and fifty galleys, which was said to be already under sail; if those came, there remained then no hopes for the commonwealth of Athens. Understanding this, Alcibiades sent secretly to the chief men of the Athenians, who were then at Samos, giving them hopes that he would make Tisaphernes their friend; he was willing, he implied, to do some favor, not to the people, nor in reliance upon them, but to the better citizens, if only, like brave men, they would make the attempt to put down the insolence of the people, and, by taking upon them the government, would endeavor to save the city from ruin. All of them gave a ready ear to the proposal made by Alcibiades, except only Phrynichus, of the township of Dirades, one of the generals, who suspected, as the truth was, that Alcibiades concerned not himself whether the government were in the people or the better citizens, but only sought by any means to make way for his return into his native country, and to that end inveighed against the people, thereby to gain the others, and to insinuate himself into their good opinion. But when Phrynichus found his counsel to be rejected, and that he was himself become a declared enemy of Alcibiades, he gave secret intelligence to Astyochus, the enemy's admiral, cautioning him to beware of Alcibiades, and to seize him as a double dealer, unaware that one traitor was making discoveries to another. For Astyochus, who was eager to gain the favor of Tisaphernes, observing the credit Alcibiades had with him, revealed to Alcibiades all that Phrynichus had said against him. Alcibiades at once despatched messages to Samos, to accuse Phrynichus of the treachery. Upon this, all the commanders were enraged with Phrynichus, and set themselves against him, and he, seeing no other way to extricate himself from the present danger, attempted to remedy one evil by a greater. He sent to Astyochus to reproach him for betraying him, and to make an offer to him at the same time, to deliver into his hands both the army and the navy of the Athenians. This occasioned no damage to the Athenians, because Astyochus repeated his treachery, and revealed also this proposal to Alcibiades. But this again was foreseen by Phrynichus, who, expecting a second accusation from Alcibiades, to anticipate him, advertised the Athenians beforehand that the enemy was ready to sail in order to surprise them, and therefore advised them to fortify their camp, and to be in readiness to go aboard their ships. While the Athenians were intent upon doing these things, they received other letters from Alcibiades, admonishing them to beware of Phrynichus, as one who designed to betray their fleet to the enemy, to which they then gave no credit at all, conceiving that Alcibiades who knew perfectly the counsels and preparations of the enemy, was merely making use of that knowledge, in order to impose upon them in this false accusation of Phrynichus. Yet, afterwards, when Phrynichus was stabbed with a dagger in the market-place by Hermon, one of the guard, the Athenians, entering into an examination of the cause, solemnly condemned Phrynichus of treason, and decreed crowns to Hermon and his associates. And now the friends of Alcibiades, carrying all before them at Samos, despatched Pisander to Athens, to attempt a change of government, and to encourage the aristocratical citizens to take upon themselves the government, and overthrow the democracy, representing to them, that, upon these terms, Alcibiades would procure them the friendship and alliance of Tisaphernes.

This was the color and pretence made use of by those who desired to change the government of Athens to an oligarchy. But as soon as they prevailed, and had got the administration of affairs into their hands, under the name of the Five Thousand (whereas, indeed, they were but four hundred), they slighted Alcibiades altogether, and prosecuted the war with less vigor; partly because they durst not yet trust the citizens, who secretly detested this change, and partly because they thought the Lacedæmonians, who always befriended the government of the few, would be inclined to give them favorable terms.

The people in the city were terrified into submission, many of those who had dared openly to oppose the four hundred having been put to death. But those who were at Samos, indignant when they heard this news, were eager to set sail instantly for the Piræus; and, sending for Alcibiades, they declared him general, requiring him to lead them on to put down the tyrants. He, however, in that juncture, did not, as it might have been thought a man would, on being suddenly exalted by the favor of a multitude, think himself under an obligation to gratify and submit to all the wishes of those who, from a fugitive and an exile, had created him general of so great an army, and given him the command of such a fleet. But, as became a great captain, he opposed himself to the precipitate resolutions which their rage led them to, and, by restraining them from the great error they were about to commit, unequivocally saved the commonwealth. For if they then had sailed for Athens, all Ionia and the islands and the Hellespont would have fallen into the enemies' hands without opposition, while the Athenians, involved in civil war, would have been fighting with one another within the circuit of their own walls. It was Alcibiades alone, or, at least, principally, who prevented all this mischief; for he not only used persuasion to the whole army, and showed them the danger, but applied himself to them, one by one, entreating some, and constraining others. He was much assisted, however, by Thrasybulus of Stiria, who, having the loudest voice, as we are told, of all the Athenians, went along with him, and cried out to those who were ready to be gone. A second great service which Alcibiades did for them was, his undertaking that the Phœnician fleet, which the Lacedæmonians expected to be sent to them by the king of Persia, should either come in aid of the Athenians, or otherwise should not come at all. He sailed off with all expedition in order to perform this, and the ships, which had already been seen as near as Aspendus, were not brought any further by Tisaphernes, who thus deceived the Lacedæmonians; and it was by both sides believed that they had been diverted by the procurement of Alcibiades. The Lacedæmonians, in particular, accused him, that he had advised the Barbarian to stand still, and suffer the Greeks to waste and destroy one another, as it was evident that the accession of so great a force to either party would enable them to take away the entire dominion of the sea from the other side.

Soon after this, the four hundred usurpers were driven out, the friends of Alcibiades vigorously assisting those who were for the popular government. And now the people in the city not only desired, but commanded Alcibiades to return home from his exile. He, however, desired not to owe his return to the mere grace and commiseration of the people, and resolved to come back, not with empty hands, but with glory, and after some service done. To this end, he sailed from Samos with a few ships, and cruised on the sea of Cnidos, and about the isle of Cos; but receiving intelligence there that Mindarus, the Spartan admiral, had sailed with his whole army into the Hellespont, and that the Athenians had followed him, he hurried back to succor the Athenian commanders, and, by good fortune, arrived with eighteen galleys at a critical time. For both the fleets having engaged near Abydos, the fight between them had lasted till night, the one side having the advantage on one quarter, and the other on another. Upon his first appearance, both sides formed a false impression; the enemy was encouraged, and the Athenians terrified. But Alcibiades suddenly raised the Athenian ensign in the admiral ship, and fell upon those galleys of the Peloponnesians which had the advantage and were in pursuit. He soon put these to flight, and followed them so close that he forced them on shore, and broke the ships in pieces, the sailors abandoning them and swimming away, in spite of all the efforts of Pharnabazus, who had come down to their assistance by land, and did what he could to protect them from the shore. In fine, the Athenians, having taken thirty of the enemy's ships, and recovered all their own, erected a trophy. After the gaining of so glorious a victory, his vanity made him eager to show himself to Tisaphernes, and, having furnished himself with gifts and presents, and an equipage suitable to his dignity, he set out to visit him. But the thing did not succeed as he had imagined, for Tisaphernes had been long suspected by the Lacedæmonians, and was afraid to fall into disgrace with his king upon that account, and therefore thought that Alcibiades arrived very opportunely, and immediately caused him to be seized, and sent away prisoner to Sardis; fancying, by this act of injustice, to clear himself from all former imputations.

But about thirty days after, Alcibiades escaped from his keepers, and, having got a horse, fled to Clazomenæ, where he procured Tisaphernes additional disgrace by professing he was a party to his escape. From there he sailed to the Athenian camp, and, being informed there that Mindarus and Pharnabazus were together at Cyzicus, he made a speech to the soldiers, telling them that sea-fighting, land-fighting, and, by the gods, fighting against fortified cities too, must be all one for them, as, unless they conquered everywhere, there was no money for them. As soon as ever he got them on ship-board, he hasted to Proconnesus, and gave command to seize all the small vessels they met, and guard them safely in the interior of the fleet, that the enemy might have no notice of his coming; and a great storm of rain, accompanied with thunder and darkness, which happened at the same time, contributed much to the concealment of his enterprise. Indeed, it was not only undiscovered by the enemy, but the Athenians themselves were ignorant of it, for he commanded them suddenly on board, and set sail when they had abandoned all intention of it. As the darkness presently passed away, the Peloponnesian fleet were seen riding out at sea in front of the harbor of Cyzicus. Fearing, if they discovered the number of his ships, they might endeavor to save themselves by land, he commanded the rest of the captains to slacken, and follow him slowly, whilst he, advancing with forty ships, showed himself to the enemy, and provoked them to fight. The enemy, being deceived as to their numbers, despised them, and, supposing they were to contend with those only, made themselves ready and began the fight. But as soon as they were engaged, they perceived the other part of the fleet coming down upon them, at which they were so terrified that they fled immediately. Upon that, Alcibiades, breaking through the midst of them with twenty of his best ships, hastened to the shore, disembarked, and pursued those who abandoned their ships and fled to land, and made a great slaughter of them. Mindarus and Pharnabazus, coming to their succor, were utterly defeated. Mindarus was slain upon the place, fighting valiantly; Pharnabazus saved himself by flight. The Athenians slew great numbers of their enemies, won much spoil, and took all their ships. They also made themselves masters of Cyzicus, which was deserted by Pharnabazus, and destroyed its Peloponnesian garrison, and thereby not only secured to themselves the Hellespont, but by force drove the Lacedæmonians from out of all the rest of the sea. They intercepted some letters written to the ephors, which gave an account of this fatal overthrow, after their short laconic manner. "Our hopes are at an end. Mindarus is slain. The men starve. We know not what to do."

The soldiers who followed Alcibiades in this last fight were so exalted with their success, and felt that degree of pride, that, looking on themselves as invincible, they disdained to mix with the other soldiers, who had been often overcome. For it happened not long before, Thrasyllus had received a defeat near Ephesus, and, upon that occasion, the Ephesians erected their brazen trophy to the disgrace of the Athenians. The soldiers of Alcibiades reproached those who were under the command of Thrasyllus with this misfortune, at the same time magnifying themselves and their own commander, and it went so far that they would not exercise with them, nor lodge in the same quarters. But soon after, Pharnabazus, with a great force of horse and foot, falling upon the soldiers of Thrasyllus, as they were laying waste the territory of Abydos, Alcibiades came to their aid, routed Pharnabazus, and, together with Thrasyllus, pursued him till it was night; and in this action the troops united, and returned together to the camp, rejoicing and congratulating one another. The next day he erected a trophy, and then proceeded to lay waste with fire and sword the whole province which was under Pharnabazus, where none ventured to resist; and he took divers priests and priestesses, but released them without ransom. He prepared next to attack the Chalcedonians, who had revolted from the Athenians, and had received a Lacedæmonian governor and garrison. But having intelligence that they had removed their corn and cattle out of the fields, and were conveying it all to the Bithynians, who were their friends, he drew down his army to the frontier of the Bithynians, and then sent a herald to charge them with this proceeding. The Bithynians, terrified at his approach, delivered up to him the booty, and entered into alliance with him.

Afterwards he proceeded to the siege of Chalcedon, and enclosed it with a wall from sea to sea. Pharnabazus advanced with his forces to raise the siege, and Hippocrates, the governor of the town, at the same time, gathering together all the strength he had, made a sally upon the Athenians. Alcibiades divided his army so as to engage them both at once, and not only forced Pharnabazus to a dishonorable flight, but defeated Hippocrates, and killed him and a number of the soldiers with him. After this he sailed into the Hellespont, in order to raise supplies of money, and took the city of Selymbria, in which action, through his precipitation, he exposed himself to great danger. For some within the town had undertaken to betray it into his hands, and, by agreement, were to give him a signal by a lighted torch about midnight. But one of the conspirators beginning to repent himself of the design, the rest, for fear of being discovered, were driven to give the signal before the appointed hour. Alcibiades, as soon as he saw the torch lifted up in the air, though his army was not in readiness to march, ran instantly towards the walls, taking with him about thirty men only, and commanding the rest of the army to follow him with all possible speed. When he came thither, he found the gate opened for him, and entered with his thirty men, and about

ALCIBIADES

twenty more light-armed men, who were come up to them. They were no sooner in the city, but he perceived the Selymbrians all armed, coming down upon him; so that there was no hope of escaping if he stayed to receive them; and, on the other hand, having been always successful till that day, wherever he commanded, he could not endure to be defeated and fly. So, requiring silence by sound of a trumpet, he commanded one of his men to make proclamation that the Selymbrians should not take arms against the Athenians. This cooled such of the inhabitants as were fiercest for the fight, for they supposed that all their enemies were within the walls, and it raised the hopes of others who were disposed to an accommodation. Whilst they were parleying, and propositions making on one side and the other, Alcibiades's whole army came up to the town. And now, conjecturing rightly, that the Selymbrians were well inclined to peace, and fearing lest the city might be sacked by the Thracians, who came in great numbers to his army to serve as volunteers, out of kindness for him, he commanded them all to retreat without the walls. And upon the submission of the Selymbrians, he saved them from being pillaged, only taking of them a sum of money, and, after placing an Athenian garrison in the town, departed.

During this action, the Athenian captains who besieged Chalcedon concluded a treaty with Pharnabazus upon these articles: That he should give them a sum of money; that the Chalcedonians should return to the subjection of Athens; and that the Athenians should make no inroad into the province whereof Pharnabazus was governor; and Pharnabazus was also to provide safe conducts for the Athenian ambassadors to the king of Persia. Afterwards, when Alcibiades returned thither, Pharnabazus required that he also should be sworn to the treaty; but he refused it, unless Pharnabazus would swear at the same time. When the treaty was sworn to on both sides, Alcibiades went against the Byzantines, who had revolted from the Athenians, and drew a line of circumvallation about the city. But Anaxilaus and Lycurgus, together with some others, having undertaken to betray the city to him upon his engagement to preserve the lives and property of the inhabitants, he caused a report to be spread abroad, as if, by reason of some unexpected movement in Ionia, he should be obliged to raise the siege. And, accordingly, that day he made a show to depart with his whole fleet; but returned the same night, and went ashore with all his men at arms, and, silently and undiscovered, marched up to the walls. At the same time, his ships rowed into the harbor with all possible violence, coming on with much fury, and with great shouts and outcries. The Byzantines, thus surprised and astonished, while they all hurried to the defence of their port and shipping, gave opportunity to those who favored the Athenians, securely to receive Alcibiades into the city. Yet the enterprise was not accomplished without fighting, for the Peloponnesians, Bœotians, and Megarians not only repulsed those who came out of the ships, and forced them on board again, but, hearing that the Athenians were entered on the other side, drew up in order, and went to meet them. Alcibiades, however, gained the victory after some sharp fighting, in which he himself had the command of the right wing, and Theramenes of the left, and took about three hundred, who survived of the enemy, prisoners of war. After the battle, not one of the Byzantines was slain, or driven out of the city, according to the terms upon which the city was put into his hands, that they should receive no prejudice in life or property. And thus Anaxilaus, being afterwards accused at Lacedæmon for this treason, neither disowned nor professed to be ashamed of the action; for he urged that he was not a Lacedæmonian, but a Byzantine, and saw not Sparta, but Byzantium, in extreme danger; the city so blockaded that it was not possible to bring in any new provisions, and the Peloponnesians and Bœotians, who were in garrison, devouring the old stores, whilst the Byzantines, with their wives and children, were starving; that he had not, therefore, betrayed his country to enemies, but had delivered it from the calamities of war, and had but followed the example of the most worthy Lacedæmonians, who esteemed nothing to be honorable and just, but what was profitable for their country. The Lacedæmonians, upon hearing his defence, respected it, and discharged all that were accused.

And now Alcibiades began to desire to see his native country again, or rather to show his fellow-citizens a person who had gained so many victories for them. He set sail for Athens, the ships that accompanied him being adorned with great numbers of shields and other spoils, and towing after them many galleys taken from the enemy, and the ensigns and ornaments of many others which he had sunk and destroyed; all of them together amounting to two hundred. Little credit, perhaps, can be given to what Duris the Samian, who professed to be descended from Alcibiades, adds, that Chrysogonus, who had gained a victory at the Pythian games, played upon his flute for the galleys, whilst the oars kept time with the music; and that Callippides, the tragedian, attired in his buskins, his purple robes, and other ornaments used in the theatre, gave the word to the rowers, and that the admiral galley entered into the port with a purple sail. Neither Theopompus, nor Ephorus, nor Xenophon, mention them. Nor, indeed, is it credible, that one who returned from so long an exile, and such variety of misfortunes, should come home to his countrymen in the style of revellers breaking up from a drinking-party. On the contrary, he entered the harbor full of fear, nor would he venture to go on shore, till, standing on the deck, he saw Euryptolemus, his cousin, and others of his friends and acquaintance, who were ready to receive him, and invited him to land. As soon as he was landed, the multitude who came out to meet him scarcely seemed so much as to see any of the other captains, but came in throngs about Alcibiades, and saluted him with loud acclamations, and still followed him; those who could press near him crowned him with garlands, and they who could not come up so close yet stayed to behold him afar off, and the old men pointed him out, and showed him to the young ones. Nevertheless, this public joy was mixed with some tears, and the present happiness was allayed by the remembrance of the miseries they had endured. They made reflections, that they could not have so unfortunately miscarried in Sicily, or been defeated in any of their other expectations, if they had left the management of their affairs formerly, and the command of their forces, to Alcibiades, since, upon his undertaking the administration, when they were in a manner driven from the sea, and could scarce defend the suburbs of their city by land, and, at the same time, were miserably distracted with intestine factions, he had raised them up from this low and deplorable condition, and had not only restored them to their ancient dominion of the sea, but had also made them everywhere victorious over their enemies on land.

There had been a decree for recalling him from his banishment already passed by the people, at the instance of Critias, the son of Callæschrus, as appears by his elegies, in which he puts Alcibiades in mind of this service:—

> From my proposal did that edict come,
> Which from your tedious exile brought you home;
> The public vote at first was moved by me,
> And my voice put the seal to the decree.

The people being summoned to an assembly, Alcibiades came in amongst them, and first bewailed and lamented his own sufferings, and, in gentle terms complaining of the usage he had received, imputed all to his hard fortune, and some ill genius that attended him; then he spoke at large of their prospects, and exhorted them to courage and good hope. The people crowned him with crowns of gold, and created him general, both at land and sea, with absolute power. They also made a decree that his estate should be restored to him, and that the Eumolpidæ and the holy heralds should absolve him from the curses which they had solemnly pronounced against him by sentence of the people. Which when all the rest obeyed, Theodorus, the high-priest, excused himself, "For," said he, "if he is innocent, I never cursed him."

But notwithstanding the affairs of Alcibiades went so prosperously, and so much to his glory, yet many were still somewhat disturbed, and looked upon the time of his arrival to be ominous. For on the day that he came into the port, the feast of the goddess Minerva, which they call the Plynteria, was kept. It is the twenty-fifth day of Thargelion, when the Praxiergidæ solemnize their secret rites, taking all the ornaments from off her image, and keeping the part of the temple where it stands close covered. Hence the Athenians esteem this day most inauspicious, and never undertake any thing of importance upon it; and, therefore, they imagined that the goddess did not receive Alcibiades graciously and propitiously, thus hiding her face and rejecting him. Yet, notwithstanding, every thing succeeded according to his wish. When the one hundred galleys, that were to return with him, were fitted out and ready to sail, an honorable zeal detained him till the celebration of the mysteries was over. For ever since Decelea had been occupied, as the enemy commanded the roads leading from Athens to Eleusis, the procession, being conducted by sea, had not been performed with any proper solemnity; they were forced to omit the sacrifices and dances and other holy ceremonies, which had usually been performed in the way, when they led forth Iacchus. Alcibiades, therefore, judged it would be a glorious action, which would do honor to the gods and gain him esteem with men, if he restored the ancient splendor to these rites, escorting the procession again by land, and protecting it with his army in the face of the enemy. For either, if Agis stood still and did not oppose, it would very much diminish and obscure his reputation, or, in the other alternative, Alcibiades would engage in a holy war, in the cause of the gods, and in defence of the most sacred and solemn ceremonies; and this in the sight of his country, where he should have all his fellow-citizens witnesses of his valor. As soon as he had resolved upon this design, and had communicated it to the Eumolpidæ and heralds, he placed sentinels on the tops of the hills, and at the break of day sent forth his scouts. And then taking with him the priests and Initiates [15] and the Initiators, and encompassing them with his soldiers, he conducted them with great order and profound silence; an august and venerable procession, wherein all who did not envy him said, he performed at once the office of a high-priest and of a general. The enemy did not dare to attempt any thing against them, and thus he brought them back in safety to the city. Upon which, as he was exalted in his own thought, so the opinion which the people had of his conduct was raised to that degree, that they looked upon their armies as irresistible and invincible while he commanded them; and he so won, indeed, upon the lower and meaner sort of people, that they passionately desired to have him "tyrant" over them, and some of them did not scruple to tell him so, and to advise him to put himself out of the reach of envy, by abolishing the laws and ordinances of the people, and suppressing the idle talkers that were ruining the state, that so he might act and take upon him the management of affairs, without standing in fear of being called to an account.

How far his own inclinations led him to usurp sovereign power, is uncertain, but the most considerable persons in the city were so much afraid of it, that they hastened him on ship-board as speedily as they could, appointing the colleagues whom he chose, and allowing him all other things as he desired. Thereupon he set sail with a fleet of one hundred ships, and, arriving at Andros, he there fought with and defeated as well the inhabitants as the Lacedæmonians who assisted them. He did not, however, take the city; which gave the first occasion to his enemies for all their accusations against him.

[15] Mystæ and Mystagogi.

Certainly, if ever man was ruined by his own glory, it was Alcibiades. For his continual success had produced such an idea of his courage and conduct, that, if he failed in any thing he undertook, it was imputed to his neglect, and no one would believe it was through want of power. For they thought nothing was too hard for him, if he went about it in good earnest. They fancied, every day, that they should hear news of the reduction of Chios, and of the rest of Ionia, and grew impatient that things were not effected as fast and as rapidly as they could wish for them. They never considered how extremely money was wanting, and that, having to carry on war with an enemy who had supplies of all things from a great king, he was often forced to quit his armament, in order to procure money and provisions for the subsistence of his soldiers. This it was which gave occasion for the last accusation which was made against him. For Lysander, being sent from Lacedæmon with a commission to be admiral of their fleet, and being furnished by Cyrus with a great sum of money, gave every sailor four obols a day, whereas before they had but three. Alcibiades could hardly allow his men three obols, and therefore was constrained to go into Caria to furnish himself with money. He left the care of the fleet, in his absence, to Antiochus, an experienced seaman, but rash and inconsiderate, who had express orders from Alcibiades not to engage, though the enemy provoked him. But he slighted and disregarded these directions to that degree, that, having made ready his own galley and another, he stood for Ephesus, where the enemy lay, and, as he sailed before the heads of their galleys, used every provocation possible, both in words and deeds. Lysander at first manned out a few ships, and pursued him.

But all the Athenian ships coming in to his assistance, Lysander, also, brought up his whole fleet, which gained an entire victory. He slew Antiochus himself, took many men and ships, and erected a trophy.

As soon as Alcibiades heard this news, he returned to Samos, and loosing from thence with his whole fleet, came and offered battle to Lysander. But Lysander, content with the victory he had gained, would not stir. Amongst others in the army who hated Alcibiades, Thrasybulus, the son of Thrason, was his particular enemy, and went purposely to Athens to accuse him, and to exasperate his enemies in the city against him. Addressing the people, he represented that Alcibiades had ruined their affairs and lost their ships by mere self-conceited neglect of his duties, committing the government of the army, in his absence, to men who gained his favor by drinking and scurrilous talking, whilst he wandered up and down at pleasure to raise money, giving himself up to every sort of luxury and excess amongst the courtesans of Abydos and Ionia, at a time when the enemy's navy were on the watch close at hand. It was also objected to him, that he had fortified a castle near Bisanthe in Thrace, for a safe retreat for himself, as one that either could not, or would not, live in his own country. The Athenians gave credit to these informations, and showed the resentment and displeasure which they had conceived against him, by choosing other generals.

As soon as Alcibiades heard of this, he immediately forsook the army, afraid of what might follow; and, collecting a body of mercenary soldiers, made war upon his own account against those Thracians who called themselves free, and acknowledged no king. By this means he amassed to himself a considerable treasure, and, at the same time, secured the bordering Greeks from the incursions of the barbarians.

Tydeus, Menander, and Adimantus, the newmade generals, were at that time posted at Ægospotami, with all the ships which the Athenians had left. From whence they were used to go out to sea every morning, and offer battle to Lysander, who lay near Lampsacus; and when they had done so, returning back again, lay, all the rest of the day, carelessly and without order, in contempt of the enemy. Alcibiades, who was not far off, did not think so slightly of their danger, nor neglect to let them know it, but, mounting his horse, came to the generals, and represented to them that they had chosen a very inconvenient station, where there was no safe harbor, and where they were distant from any town; so that they were constrained to send for their necessary provisions as far as Sestos. He also pointed out to them their carelessness in suffering the soldiers, when they went ashore, to disperse and wander up and down at their pleasure, while the enemy's fleet, under the command of one general, and strictly obedient to discipline, lay so very near them. He advised them to remove the fleet to Sestos. But the admirals not only disregarded what he said, but Tydeus, with insulting expressions, commanded him to be gone, saying, that now not he, but others, had the command of the forces. Alcibiades, suspecting something of treachery in them, departed, and told his friends, who accompanied him out of the camp, that if the generals had not used him with such insupportable contempt, he would within a few days have forced the Lacedæmonians, however unwilling, either to have fought the Athenians at sea, or to have deserted their ships. Some looked upon this as a piece of ostentation only; others said, the thing was probable, for that he might have brought down by land great numbers of the Thracian cavalry and archers, to assault and disorder them in their camp. The event, however, soon made it evident how rightly he had judged of the errors which the Athenians committed. For Lysander fell upon them on a sudden, when they least suspected it, with such fury that Conon alone, with eight galleys, escaped him; all the rest, which were about two hundred, he took and carried away, together with three thousand prisoners, whom he put to death. And within a short time after, he took Athens itself, burnt all the ships which he found there, and demolished their long walls.

After this, Alcibiades, standing in dread of the Lacedæmonians, who were now masters both at sea and land, retired into Bithynia. He sent thither great treasure before him, took much with him, but left much more in the castle where he had before resided. But he lost great part of his wealth in Bithynia, being robbed by some Thracians who lived in those parts, and thereupon determined to go to the court of Artaxerxes, not doubting but that the king, if he would make trial of his abilities, would find him not inferior to Themistocles, besides that he was recommended by a more honorable cause. For he went, not as Themistocles did, to offer his service against his fellow-citizens, but against their enemies, and to implore the king's aid for the defence of his country. He concluded that Pharnabazus would most readily procure him a safe conduct, and therefore went into Phrygia to him, and continued to dwell there some time, paying him great respect, and being honorably treated by him. The Athenians, in the mean time, were miserably afflicted at

their loss of empire, but when they were deprived of
liberty also, and Lysander set up thirty despotic
rulers in the city, in their ruin now they began to
turn to those thoughts which, while safety was yet
possible, they would not entertain; they acknowledged and bewailed their former errors and follies,
and judged this second ill-usage of Alcibiades to be
of all the most inexcusable. For he was rejected,
without any fault committed by himself; and only
because they were incensed against his subordinate
for having shamefully lost a few ships, they much
more shamefully deprived the commonwealth of its
most valiant and accomplished general. Yet in this
sad state of affairs, they had still some faint hopes
left them, nor would they utterly despair of the
Athenian commonwealth, while Alcibiades was safe.
For they persuaded themselves that if before, when
he was an exile, he could not content himself to live
idly and at ease, much less now, if he could find any
favorable opportunity, would he endure the insolence of the Lacedæmonians, and the outrages of
the Thirty. Nor was it an absurd thing in the people to entertain such imaginations, when the Thirty
themselves were so very solicitous to be informed
and to get intelligence of all his actions and designs. In fine, Critias represented to Lysander that
the Lacedæmonians could never securely enjoy the
dominion of Greece, till the Athenian democracy was
absolutely destroyed; and though now the people of
Athens seemed quietly and patiently to submit to so
small a number of governors, yet so long as Alcibiades lived, the knowledge of this fact would never
suffer them to acquiesce in their present circumstances.

Yet Lysander would not be prevailed upon by
these representations, till at last he received secret

orders from the magistrates of Lacedæmon, expressly requiring him to get Alcibiades despatched; whether it was that they feared his energy and boldness in enterprising what was hazardous, or that it was done to gratify king Agis. Upon receipt of this order, Lysander sent away a messenger to Pharnabazus, desiring him to put it in execution. Pharnabazus committed the affair to Magæus, his brother, and to his uncle Susamithres. Alcibiades resided at that time in a small village in Phrygia, together with Timandra, a mistress of his. As he slept, he had this dream: he thought himself attired in his mistress's habit, and that she, holding him in her arms, dressed his head and painted his face as if he had been a woman; others say, he dreamed that he saw Magæus cut off his head and burn his body; at any rate, it was but a little while before his death that he had these visions. Those who were sent to assassinate him had not courage enough to enter the house, but surrounded it first, and set it on fire. Alcibiades, as soon as he perceived it, getting together great quantities of clothes and furniture, threw them upon the fire to choke it, and, having wrapped his cloak about his left arm, and holding his naked sword in his right, he cast himself into the middle of the fire, and escaped securely through it, before his clothes were burnt. The barbarians, as soon as they saw him, retreated, and none of them durst stay to expect him, or to engage with him, but, standing at a distance, they slew him with their darts and arrows. When he was dead, the barbarians departed, and Timandra took up his dead body, and, covering and wrapping it up in her own robes, she buried it as decently and as honorably as her circumstances would allow. It is said, that the famous Lais, who was called the Corinthian, though she was a native of Hyccara, a small town in Sicily, from whence she was brought a captive, was the daughter of this Timandra. There are some who agree with this account of Alcibiades's death in all points, except that they impute the cause of it neither to Pharnabazus, nor Lysander, nor the Lacedæmonians; but, they say, he was keeping with him a young lady of a noble house, whom he had debauched, and that her brothers, not being able to endure the indignity, set fire by night to the house where he was living, and, as he endeavored to save himself from the flames, slew him with their darts, in the manner just related.

CORIOLANUS[1]

Translated by Thomas Blomer, D.D.

The patrician house of the Marcii in Rome produced many men of distinction, and among the rest, Ancus Marcius, grandson to Numa by his daughter, and king after Tullus Hostilius. Of the same family were also Publius and Quintus Marcius, which two conveyed into the city the best and most abundant supply of water they have at Rome. As likewise Censorinus, who, having been twice chosen censor by the people, afterwards himself induced them to make a law that nobody should bear that office twice. But Caius Marcius, of whom I now write, being left an orphan, and brought up under the widowhood of his mother, has shown us by experience, that, although the early loss of a father may be attended with other disadvantages, yet it can hinder none from being either virtuous or eminent in the world, and that it is no obstacle to true goodness and excellence; however bad men may be pleased to lay the blame of their corruptions upon that misfortune and the neglect of them in their minority. Nor is he less an evidence to the truth of their opinion, who conceive that a generous and worthy nature without proper discipline, like a rich soil without culture, is apt, with its better fruits to produce also much that is bad and faulty. While the force and vigor of his soul and a persevering constancy in all he undertook, led him successfully into many noble achievements, yet, on the other side,

---

[1] Coriolanus, the hero of one of the most beautiful of the early Roman legends.—Dr. William Smith.

Shakespeare's play Coriolanus was directly derived from Plutarch's Coriolanus (North's version).—Israel Gollancz.

also, by indulging the vehemence of his passion, and through an obstinate reluctance to yield or accommodate his humors and sentiments to those of people about him, he rendered himself incapable of acting and associating with others. Those who saw with admiration how proof his nature was against all the softnesses of pleasure, the hardships of service, and the allurements of gain, while allowing to that universal firmness of his the respective names of temperance, fortitude, and justice, yet, in the life of the citizen and the statesman, could not choose but be disgusted at the severity and ruggedness of his deportment, and with his overbearing, haughty, and imperious temper. Education and study, and the favors of the muses, confer no greater benefit on those that seek them, than these humanizing and civilizing lessons, which teach our natural qualities to submit to the limitations prescribed by reason, and to avoid the wildness of extremes.

Those were times at Rome in which that kind of worth was most esteemed which displayed itself in military achievements; one evidence of which we find in the Latin word for virtue, which is properly equivalent to manly courage. As if valor and all virtue had been the same thing, they used as the common term the name of the particular excellence. But Marcius, having a more passionate inclination than any of that age for feats of war, began at once, from his very childhood, to handle arms; and feeling that adventitious implements and artificial arms would effect little, and be of small use to such as have not their native and natural weapons well fixed and prepared for service, he so exercised and inured his body to all sorts of activity and encounter, that, besides the lightness of a racer, he had a weight in close seizures and wrestling with an enemy, from which it was hard for any to disengage himself; so that his competitors at home in displays of bravery, loath to own themselves inferior in that respect, were wont to ascribe their deficiencies to his strength of body, which they said no resistance and no fatigue could exhaust.

The first time he went out to the wars, being yet a stripling, was when Tarquinius Superbus, who had been king of Rome and was afterwards expelled, after many unsuccessful attempts, now entered upon his last effort, and proceeded to hazard all as it were upon a single throw. A great number of the Latins and other people of Italy joined their forces, and were marching with him toward the city, to procure his restoration; not, however, so much out of a desire to serve and oblige Tarquin, as to gratify their own fear and envy at the increase of the Roman greatness, which they were anxious to check and reduce. The armies met and engaged in a decisive battle in the vicissitudes of which, Marcius, while fighting bravely in the dictator's presence, saw a Roman soldier struck down at a little distance, and immediately stepped in and stood before him, and slew his assailant. The general, after having gained the victory, crowned him for this act, one of the first, with a garland of oaken branches; it being the Roman custom thus to adorn those who had saved the life of a citizen; whether that the law intended some special honor to the oak, in memory of the Arcadians, a people the oracle had made famous by the name of acorn-eaters;[2] or whether the reason of it was because they might easily, and in all places

---

[2] "You ask me for Arcadia," said the oracle to the Spartans, when designing their early invasion. "You ask a great thing, I will not grant it. There are in Arcadia many acorn-eaters

where they fought, have plenty of oak for that purpose; or, finally, whether the oaken wreath, being sacred to Jupiter, the guardian of this city, might, therefore, be thought a proper ornament for one who preserved a citizen. And the oak, in truth, is the tree which bears the most and the prettiest fruit of any that grow wild, and is the strongest of all that are under cultivation; its acorns were the principal diet of the first mortals, and the honey found in it gave them drink. I may say, too, it furnished fowl and other creatures as dainties, in producing mistletoe for birdlime to ensnare them. In this battle, meantime, it is stated that Castor and Pollux appeared, and, immediately after the battle, were seen at Rome just by the fountain where their temple now stands, with their horses foaming with sweat, and told the news of the victory to the people in the Forum. The fifteenth of July, being the day of this conquest, became consequently a solemn holiday sacred to the Twin Brothers.

It may be observed, in general, that when young men arrive early at fame and repute, if they are of a nature but slightly touched with emulation, this early attainment is apt to extinguish their thirst and satiate their small appetite; whereas the first distinctions of more solid and weighty characters do but stimulate and quicken them and take them away, like a wind, in the pursuit of honor; they look upon these marks and testimonies to their virtue not as a recompense received for what they have already done, but as a pledge given by themselves of what they will perform hereafter, ashamed now to forsake

ready to prevent you. I, however, grudge you nothing. I grant you to dance about Tegea, and measure out the fair plain by the line."

or underlive the credit they have won, or, rather, not to exceed and obscure all that is gone before by the lustre of their following actions. Marcius, having a spirit of this noble make, was ambitious always to surpass himself, and did nothing, how extraordinary soever, but he thought he was bound to outdo it at the next occasion; and ever desiring to give continual fresh instances of his prowess, he added one exploit to another, and heaped up trophies upon trophies, so as to make it matter of contest also among his commanders, the later still vying with the earlier, which should pay him the greatest honor and speak highest in his commendation. Of all the numerous wars and conflicts in those days, there was not one from which he returned without laurels and rewards. And, whereas others made glory the end of their daring, the end of his glory was his mother's gladness; the delight she took to hear him praised and to see him crowned, and her weeping for joy in his embraces, rendered him, in his own thoughts, the most honored and most happy person in the world. Epaminondas is similarly said to have acknowledged his feeling, that it was the greatest felicity of his whole life that his father and mother survived to hear of his successful generalship and his victory at Leuctra. And he had the advantage, indeed, to have both his parents partake with him, and enjoy the pleasure of his good fortune. But Marcius, believing himself bound to pay his mother Volumnia all that gratitude and duty which would have belonged to his father, had he also been alive, could never satiate himself in his tenderness and respect for her. He took a wife, also, at her request and wish, and continued, even after he had children, to live still with his mother, without parting families.

The repute of his integrity and courage had, by

this time, gained him a considerable influence and authority in Rome, when the senate, favoring the wealthier citizens, began to be at variance with the common people, who made sad complaints of the rigorous and inhuman usage they received from the money-lenders. For as many as were behind with them, and had any sort of property, they stripped of all they had, by the way of pledges and sales; and such as through former exactions were reduced already to extreme indigence, and had nothing more to be deprived of, these they led away in person and put their bodies under restraint, notwithstanding the scars and wounds that they could show in attestation of their public services in numerous campaigns; the last of which had been against the Sabines, which they undertook upon a promise made by their rich creditors that they would treat them with more gentleness for the future, Marcus Valerius, the consul, having, by order from the senate, engaged also for the performance of it. But when, after they had fought courageously and beaten the enemy, there was, nevertheless, no moderation or forbearance used, and the senate also professed to remember nothing of that agreement, and sat without testifying the least concern to see them dragged away like slaves and their goods seized upon as formerly, there began now to be open disorders and dangerous meetings in the city; and the enemy, also, aware of the popular confusion, invaded and laid waste the country. And when the consuls now gave notice, that all who were of an age to bear arms should make their personal appearance, but found no one regard the summons, the members of the government, then coming to consult what course should be taken, were themselves again divided in opinion: some thought it most advisable to comply a little in favor of the poor, by relaxing their overstrained rights, and mitigating the extreme rigor of the law, while others withstood this proposal; Marcius in particular, with more vehemence than the rest, alleging that the business of money on either side was not the main thing in question, urged that this disorderly proceeding was but the first insolent step towards open revolt against the laws, which it would become the wisdom of the government to check at the earliest moment.

There had been frequent assemblies of the whole senate, within a small compass of time, about this difficulty, but without any certain issue; the poor commonalty, therefore, perceiving there was likely to be no redress of their grievances, on a sudden collected in a body, and, encouraging each other in their resolution, forsook the city with one accord, and seizing the hill which is now called the Holy Mount, sat down by the river Anio, without committing any sort of violence or seditious outrage, but merely exclaiming, as they went along, that they had this long time past been, in fact, expelled and excluded from the city by the cruelty of the rich; that Italy would everywhere afford them the benefit of air and water and a place of burial, which was all they could expect in the city, unless it were, perhaps, the privilege of being wounded and killed in time of war for the defence of their creditors. The senate, apprehending the consequences, sent the most moderate and popular men of their own order to treat with them.

Menenius Agrippa, their chief spokesman, after much entreaty to the people, and much plain speaking on behalf of the senate, concluded, at length, with the celebrated fable. "It once happened," he said, "that all the other members of a man mutinied against the stomach, which they accused as the only idle, uncontributing part in the whole body, while the rest were put to hardships and the expense of much labor to supply and minister to its appetites. The stomach, however, merely ridiculed the silliness of the members, who appeared not to be aware that the stomach certainly does receive the general nourishment, but only to return it again, and redistribute it amongst the rest. Such is the case," he said, "ye citizens, between you and the senate. The counsels and plans that are there duly digested, convey and secure to all of you, your proper benefit and support."

A reconciliation ensued, the senate acceding to the request of the people for the annual election of five protectors for those in need of succor, the same that are now called the tribunes of the people; and the first two they pitched upon were Junius Brutus and Sicinnius Vellutus, their leaders in the secession.

The city being thus united, the commons stood presently to their arms, and followed their commanders to the war with great alacrity. As for Marcius, though he was not a little vexed himself to see the populace prevail so far, and gain ground of the senators, and might observe many other patricians have the same dislike of the late concessions, he yet besought them not to yield at least to the common people in the zeal and forwardness they now showed for their country's service, but to prove that they were superior to them, not so much in power and riches, as in merit and worth.

The Romans were now at war with the Volscian nation, whose principal city was Corioli; when, therefore, Cominius the consul had invested this important place, the rest of the Volscians, fearing it would be taken, mustered up whatever force they could from all parts, to relieve it, designing to give the

Romans battle before the city, and so attack them on both sides. Cominius, to avoid this inconvenience, divided his army, marching himself with one body to encounter the Volscians on their approach from without, and leaving Titus Lartius, one of the bravest Romans of his time, to command the other and continue the siege. Those within Corioli, despising now the smallness of their number, made a sally upon them, and prevailed at first, and pursued the Romans into their trenches. Here it was that Marcius, flying out with a slender company, and cutting those in pieces that first engaged him, obliged the other assailants to slacken their speed; and then, with loud cries, called upon the Romans to renew the battle. For he had, what Cato thought a great point in a soldier, not only strength of hand and stroke, but also a voice and look that of themselves were a terror to an enemy. Divers of his own party now rallying and making up to him, the enemies soon retreated; but Marcius, not content to see them draw off and retire, pressed hard upon the rear, and drove them, as they fled away in haste, to the very gates of their city; where, perceiving the Romans to fall back from their pursuit, beaten off by the multitude of darts poured in upon them from the walls, and that none of his followers had the hardiness to think of falling in pellmell among the fugitives and so entering a city full of enemies in arms, he, nevertheless, stood and urged them to the attempt, crying out, that fortune had now set open Corioli, not so much to shelter the vanquished, as to receive the conquerors. Seconded by a few that were willing to venture with him, he bore along through the crowd, made good his passage, and thrust himself into the gate through the midst of them, nobody at first daring to resist him. But when the citizens, on looking about, saw that a very small number had entered, they now took courage, and came up and attacked them. A combat ensued of the most extraordinary description, in which Marcius, by strength of hand, and swiftness of foot, and daring of soul, overpowering every one that he assailed, succeeded in driving the enemy to seek refuge, for the most part, in the interior of the town, while the remainder submitted, and threw down their arms; thus affording Lartius abundant opportunity to bring in the rest of the Romans with ease and safety.

Corioli being thus surprised and taken, the greater part of the soldiers employed themselves in spoiling and pillaging it, while Marcius indignantly reproached them, and exclaimed that it was a dishonorable and unworthy thing, when the consul and their fellow-citizens had now perhaps encountered the other Volscians, and were hazarding their lives in battle, basely to misspend the time in running up and down for booty, and, under a pretence of enriching themselves, keep out of danger. Few paid him any attention, but, putting himself at the head of these, he took the road by which the consul's army had marched before him, encouraging his companions, and beseeching them, as they went along, not to give up, and praying often to the gods, too, that he might be so happy as to arrive before the fight was over, and come seasonably up to assist Cominius, and partake in the peril of the action.

It was customary with the Romans of that age, when they were moving in battle array, and were on the point of taking up their bucklers, and girding their coats about them, to make at the same time an unwritten will, or verbal testament, and to name who should be their heirs in the hearing of three or four witnesses. In this precise posture Marcius found them at his arrival, the enemy being advanced within view.

They were not a little disturbed by his first appearance, seeing him covered with blood and sweat, and attended with a small train; but when he hastily made up to the consul with gladness in his looks, giving him his hand, and recounting to him how the city had been taken, and when they saw Cominius also embrace and salute him, every one took fresh heart; those that were near enough hearing, and those that were at a distance guessing, what had happened; and all cried out to be led to battle. First, however, Marcius desired to know of him how the Volscians had arrayed their army and where they had placed their best men, and on his answering that he took the troops of the Antiates in the centre to be their prime warriors, that would yield to none in bravery, "Let me then demand and obtain of you," said Marcius, "that we may be posted against them." The consul granted the request, with much admiration of his gallantry. And when the conflict began by the soldiers darting at each other, and Marcius sallied out before the rest, the Volscians opposed to him were not able to make head against him; wherever he fell in, he broke their ranks, and made a lane through them; but the parties turning again, and enclosing him on each side with their weapons, the consul, who observed the danger he was in, despatched some of the choicest men he had for his rescue. The conflict then growing warm and sharp about Marcius, and many falling dead in a little space, the Romans bore so hard upon the enemies, and pressed them with such violence, that they forced them at length to abandon their ground, and to quit the field. And, going now to prosecute the victory, they besought Marcius, tired out with his toils, and faint and heavy through the loss of blood, that he would retire to the camp. He replied, however, that weariness was not for conquerors, and joined with them in the pursuit. The rest of the Volscian army was in like manner defeated, great numbers killed and no less taken captive.

The day after, when Marcius, with the rest of the army, presented themselves at the consul's tent, Cominius rose, and having rendered all due acknowledgment to the gods for the success of that enterprise, turned next to Marcius, and first of all delivered the strongest encomium upon his rare exploits, which he had partly been an eye-witness of himself, in the late battle, and had partly learned from the testimony of Lartius. And then he required him to choose a tenth part of all the treasure and horses and captives that had fallen into their hands, before any division should be made to others; besides which, he made him the special present of a horse with trappings and ornaments, in honor of his actions. The whole army applauded; Marcius, however, stepped forth, and declaring his thankful acceptance of the horse, and his gratification at the praises of his general, said, that all other things, which he could only regard rather as mercenary advantages than any significations of honor, he must waive, and should be content with the ordinary proportion of such rewards. "I have only," said he, "one special grace to beg, and this I hope you will not deny me. There was a certain hospitable friend of mine among the Volscians, a man of probity and virtue, who is become a prisoner, and from former wealth and freedom is now reduced to servitude. Among his many misfortunes let my intercession redeem him from the one of being sold as a common slave." Such a refusal and such a request on the part of Marcius were followed with yet louder acclamations; and he had many more admirers of this generous superiority to avarice, than of the bravery he had shown in battle. The very persons who conceived some envy and despite to see him so specially honored, could not but acknowledge, that one who so nobly could refuse reward, was beyond others worthy to receive it; and were more charmed with that virtue which made him despise advantage, than with any of those former actions that had gained him his title to it. It is the higher accomplishment to use money well than to use arms; but not to need it is more noble than to use it.

When the noise of approbation and applause ceased, Cominius, resuming, said, "It is idle, fellow-soldiers, to force and obtrude those other gifts of ours on one who is unwilling to accept them; let us, therefore, give him one of such a kind that he cannot well reject it; let us pass a vote, I mean, that he shall hereafter be called Coriolanus, unless you think that his performance at Corioli has itself anticipated any such resolution." Hence, therefore, he had his third name of Coriolanus, making it all the plainer that Caius was a personal proper name, and the second, or surname, Marcius, one common to his house and family; the third being a subsequent addition which used to be imposed either from some particular act or fortune, bodily characteristic, or good quality of the bearer. Just as the Greeks, too, gave additional names in old time, in some cases from some achievement, Soter, for example, and Callinicus; or personal appearance, as Physcon and Grypus; good qualities, Euergetes and Philadelphus; good fortune,

Eudæmon, the title of the second Battus.[8] Several monarchs have also had names given them in mockery, as Antigonus was called Doson, and Ptolemy, Lathyrus. This sort of title was yet more common among the Romans. One of the Metelli was surnamed Diadematus, because he walked about for a long time with a bandage on his head, to conceal a scar; and another, of the same family, got the name of Celer, from the rapidity he displayed in giving a funeral entertainment of gladiators within a few days after his father's death, his speed and energy in doing which was thought extraordinary. There are some, too, who even at this day take names from certain casual incidents at their nativity; a child that is born when his father is away from home is called Proculus; or Postumus, if after his decease; and when twins come into the world, and one dies at the birth, the survivor has the name of Vopiscus. From bodily peculiarities they derive not only their Syllas and Nigers, but their Cæci and Claudii; wisely endeavoring to accustom their people not to reckon either the loss of sight, or any other bodily misfortune, as a matter of disgrace to them, but to answer to such names without shame, as if they were really their own. But this discussion better befits another place.

The war against the Volscians was no sooner at an end, than the popular orators revived domestic troubles, and raised another sedition, without any new cause of complaint or just grievance to proceed upon, but merely turning the very mischiefs that un-

---

[8] Sotēr, Saviour; Callinīcus, Victorious; Physcon, Fatpaunch; Grypus, Hook-nose; Euergĕtes, Benefactor; Philadelphus, Brotherly; Eudæmon, Fortunate; Doson, Going-to-give; Lathyrus is not certain.

avoidably ensued from their former contests into a pretext against the patricians. The greatest part of their arable land had been left unsown and without tillage, and the time of war allowing them no means or leisure to import provision from other countries, there was an extreme scarcity. The movers of the people then observing, that there was no corn to be bought, and that, if there had been, they had no money to buy it, began to calumniate the wealthy with false stories, and whisper it about, as if they, out of malice, had purposely contrived the famine. Meanwhile, there came an embassy from the Velitrani, proposing to deliver up their city to the Romans, and desiring they would send some new inhabitants to people it, as a late pestilential disease had swept away so many of the natives, that there was hardly a tenth part remaining of their whole community. This necessity of the Velitrani was considered by all more prudent people as most opportune in the present state of affairs; since the dearth made it needful to ease the city of its superfluous members, and they were in hope also, at the same time, to dissipate the gathering sedition by ridding themselves of the more violent and heated partisans, and discharging, so to say, the elements of disease and disorder in the state. The consuls, therefore, singled out such citizens to supply the desolation at Velitræ, and gave notice to others, that they should be ready to march against the Volscians, with the politic design of preventing intestine broils by employment abroad, and in the hope, that when rich as well as poor, plebeians and patricians, should be mingled again in the same army and the same camp, and engage in one common service for the public it would mutually dispose them to reconciliation and friendship.

But Sicinnius and Brutus, the popular orators, interposed, crying out, that the consuls disguised the most cruel and barbarous action in the world under that mild and plausible name of a colony, and were simply precipitating so many poor citizens into a mere pit of destruction, bidding them settle down in a country where the air was charged with disease, and the ground covered with dead bodies, and expose themselves to the evil influence of a strange and angered deity. And then, as if it would not satisfy their hatred to destroy some by hunger, and offer others to the mercy of a plague, they must proceed to involve them also in a needless war of their own making, that no calamity might be wanting to complete the punishment of the citizens for refusing to submit to that of slavery to the rich.

By such addresses, the people were so possessed, that none of them would appear upon the consular summons to be enlisted for the war; and they showed entire aversion to the proposal for a new plantation; so that the senate was at a loss what to say or do. But Marcius, who began now to bear himself higher and to feel confidence in his past actions, conscious, too, of the admiration of the best and greatest men of Rome, openly took the lead in opposing the favorers of the people. The colony was despatched to Velitræ, those that were chosen by lot being compelled to depart upon high penalties; and when they obstinately persisted in refusing to enroll themselves for the Volscian service, he mustered up his own clients, and as many others as could be wrought upon by persuasion, and with these made an inroad into the territories of the Antiates, where, finding a considerable quantity of corn, and collecting much booty, both of cattle and prisoners, he reserved nothing for himself in private, but returned safe to Rome, while those that ventured out with him were seen laden with pillage, and driving their prey before them. This sight filled those that had stayed at home with regret for their perverseness, with envy at their fortunate fellow-citizens, and with feelings of dislike to Marcius, and hostility to his growing reputation and power, which might probably be used against the popular interest.

Not long after he stood for the consulship; when, however, the people began to relent and incline to favor him, being sensible what a shame it would be to repulse and affront a man of his birth and merit, after he had done them so many signal services. It was usual for those who stood for offices among them to solicit and address themselves personally to the citizens, presenting themselves in the forum with the toga on alone, and no tunic under it; either to promote their supplications by the humility of their dress, or that such as had received wounds might more readily display those marks of their fortitude. Certainly, it was not out of suspicion of bribery and corruption that they required all such petitioners for their favor to appear ungirt and open, without any close garment; as it was much later, and many ages after this, that buying and selling crept in at their elections, and money became an ingredient in the public suffrages; proceeding thence to attempt their tribunals, and even attack their camps, till, by hiring the valiant, and enslaving iron to silver, it grew master of the state, and turned their commonwealth into a monarchy. For it was well and truly said that the first destroyer of the liberties of a people is he who first gave them bounties and largesses. At Rome the mischief seems to have stolen secretly in, and by little and little, not being at once discerned and taken notice of. It is not certainly known who the man was that did there first either bribe the citizens or corrupt the courts; whereas, in Athens, Anytus, the son of Anthemion, is said to have been the first that gave money to the judges, when on his trial, toward the latter end of the Peloponnesian war, for letting the fort of Pylos fall into the hands of the enemy; in a period while the pure and golden race of men were still in possession of the Roman forum.

Marcius, therefore, as the fashion of candidates was, showing the scars and gashes that were still visible on his body, from the many conflicts in which he had signalized himself during a service of seventeen years together, they were, so to say, put out of countenance at this display of merit, and told one another that they ought in common modesty to create him consul. But when the day of election was now come, and Marcius appeared in the forum, with a pompous train of senators attending him, and the patricians all manifested greater concern, and seemed to be exerting greater efforts, than they had ever done before on the like occasion, the commons then fell off again from the kindness they had conceived for him, and in the place of their late benevolence, began to feel something of indignation and envy; passions assisted by the fear they entertained, that if a man of such aristocratic temper, and so influential among the patricians, should be invested with the power which that office would give him, he might employ it to deprive the people of all that liberty which was yet left them. In conclusion, they rejected Marcius. Two other names were announced, to the great mortification of the senators, who felt as if the indignity reflected rather upon themselves than on Marcius. He, for his part, could not bear the affront with any patience. He had always indulged his temper, and had regarded the proud and contentious element of human nature as a sort of nobleness and magnanimity; reason and discipline had not imbued him with that solidity and equanimity which enters so largely into the virtues of the statesman. He had never learned how essential it is for any one who undertakes public business, and desires to deal with mankind, to avoid above all things that self-will, which, as Plato says, belongs to the family of solitude;[4] and to pursue, above all things, that capacity so generally ridiculed, of submission to ill-treatment. Marcius, straightforward and direct, and possessed with the idea that to vanquish and overbear all opposition is the true part of bravery, and never imagining that it was the weakness and womanishness of his nature that broke out, so to say, in these ulcerations of anger, retired, full of fury and bitterness against the people. The young patricians, too, all that were proudest and most conscious of their noble birth, had always been devoted to his interest, and, adhering to him now, with a fidelity that did him no good, aggravated his resentment with the expression of their indignation and condolence. He had been their captain, and their willing instructor in the arts of war, when out upon expeditions, and their model in that true emulation and love of excellence which makes men extol, without envy or jealousy, each other's brave achievements.

In the midst of these distempers, a large quantity of corn reached Rome, a great part bought up in Italy, but an equal amount sent as a present from Syracuse, from Gelo, then reigning there. Many began now to hope well of their affairs, supposing the

[4] To beware of *self-will, which belongs to the family of solitude,* is Plato's phrase of caution to Dion. See the life of Dion, where it is repeated more than once.

city, by this means, would be delivered at once, both of its want and discord. A council, therefore, being presently held, the people came flocking about the senate-house, eagerly awaiting the issue of that deliberation, expecting that the market-prices would now be less cruel, and that what had come as a gift, would be distributed as such. There were some within who so advised the senate; but Marcius, standing up, sharply inveighed against those who spoke in favor of the multitude, calling them flatterers of the rabble. traitors to the nobility, and alleging, that, by such gratifications, they did but cherish those ill seeds of boldness and petulance that had been sown among the people, to their own prejudice, which they should have done well to observe and stifle at their first appearance, and not have suffered the plebeians to grow so strong, by granting them magistrates of such authority as the tribunes. They were, indeed, even now formidable to the state, since every thing they desired was granted them; no constraint was put on their will; they refused obedience to the consuls, and, overthrowing all law and magistracy, gave the title of magistrate to their private factious leaders. "When things are come to such a pass, for us to sit here and decree largesses and bounties for them, like those Greeks where the populace is supreme and absolute, what would it be else," said he, " but to take their disobedience into pay, and maintain it for the common ruin of us all? They certainly cannot look upon these liberalities as a reward of public service, which they know they have so often deserted; nor yet of those secessions, by which they openly renounced their country; much less of the calumnies and slanders they have been always so ready to entertain against the senate; but will rather conclude that a bounty which seems to have no other visible cause or reason, must needs be the effect of our fear and flattery; and will, therefore, set no limit to their disobedience, nor ever cease from disturbances and sedition. Concession is mere madness; if we have any wisdom and resolution at all, we shall, on the contrary, never rest till we have recovered from them that tribunician power they have extorted from us; as being a plain subversion of the consulship, and a perpetual ground of separation in our city, that is no longer one, as heretofore, but has in this received such a wound and rupture, as is never likely to close and unite again, or suffer us to be of one mind, and to give over inflaming our distempers, and being a torment to each other."

Marcius, with much more to this purpose, succeeded, to an extraordinary degree, in inspiring the younger men with the same furious sentiments, and had almost all the wealthy on his side, who cried him up as the only person their city had, superior alike to force and flattery; some of the older men, however, opposed him, suspecting the consequences. As, indeed, there came no good of it; for the tribunes, who were present, perceiving how the proposal of Marcius took, ran out into the crowd with exclamations, calling on the plebeians to stand together, and come in to their assistance. The assembly met, and soon became tumultuous. The sum of what Marcius had spoken, having been reported to the people, excited them to such fury, that they were ready to break in upon the senate. The tribunes prevented this, by laying all the blame on Coriolanus, whom, therefore, they cited by their messengers to come before them, and defend himself. And when he contemptuously repulsed the officers who brought him the summons, they came themselves, with the Ædiles, or overseers of the market, proposing to carry him away by force,

and, accordingly, began to lay hold on his person.
The patricians, however, coming to his rescue, not
only thrust off the tribunes, but also beat the Ædiles,
that were their seconds in the quarrel; night, approaching,
put an end to the contest. But, as soon
as it was day, the consuls, observing the people to be
highly exasperated, and that they ran from all quarters
and gathered in the forum, were afraid for the
whole city, so that, convening the senate afresh, they
desired them to advise how they might best compose
and pacify the incensed multitude by equitable
language and indulgent decrees; since, if they wisely
considered the state of things, they would find that it
was no time to stand upon terms of honor, and a
mere point of glory; such a critical conjuncture called
for gentle methods, and for temperate and humane
counsels. The majority, therefore, of the senators,
giving way, the consuls proceeded to pacify the
people in the best manner they were able, answering
gently to such imputations and charges as had been
cast upon the senate, and using much tenderness and
moderation in the admonitions and reproofs they
gave them. On the point of the price of provisions,
they said, there should be no difference at all between
them. When a great part of the commonalty
was grown cool, and it appeared from their orderly
and peaceful behavior that they had been very much
appeased by what they had heard, the tribunes,
standing up, declared, in the name of the people, that
since the senate was pleased to act soberly and do
them reason, they, likewise, should be ready to yield
in all that was fair and equitable on their side; they
must insist, however, that Marcius should give in his
answer to the several charges as follows: first, could
he deny that he instigated the senate to overthrow
the government and annul the privileges of the

people? and, in the next place, when called to account for it, did he not disobey their summons? and, lastly, by the blows and other public affronts to the Ædiles, had he not done all he could to commence a civil war?

These articles were brought in against him, with a design either to humble Marcius, and show his submission, if, contrary to his nature, he should now court and sue the people; or, if he should follow his natural disposition, which they rather expected from their judgment of his character, then that he might thus make the breach final between himself and the people.

He came, therefore, as it were, to make his apology, and clear himself; in which belief the people kept silence, and gave him a quiet hearing. But when, instead of the submissive and deprecatory language expected from him, he began to use not only an offensive kind of freedom, seeming rather to accuse than apologize, but, as well by the tone of his voice as the air of his countenance, displayed a security that was not far from disdain and contempt of them, the whole multitude then became angry, and gave evident signs of impatience and disgust; and Sicinnius, the most violent of the tribunes, after a little private conference with his colleagues, proceeded solemnly to pronounce before them all, that Marcius was condemned to die by the tribunes of the people, and bid the Ædiles take him to the Tarpeian rock, and without delay throw him headlong from the precipice. When they, however, in compliance with the order, came to seize upon his body, many, even of the plebeian party, felt it to be a horrible and extravagant act; the patricians, meantime, wholly beside themselves with distress and horror, hurried up with cries to the rescue; and while some made actual use of their hands to hinder the arrest, and, surrounding Marcius, got him in among them, others, as in so great a tumult no good could be done by words, stretched out theirs, beseeching the multitude that they would not proceed to such furious extremities; and, at length, the friends and acquaintance of the tribunes, wisely perceiving how impossible it would be to carry off Marcius to punishment without much bloodshed and slaughter of the nobility, persuaded them to forbear every thing unusual and odious; not to despatch him by any sudden violence, or without regular process, but refer the cause to the general suffrage of the people. Sicinnius then, after a little pause, turning to the patricians, demanded what their meaning was, thus forcibly to rescue Marcius out of the people's hands, as they were going to punish him; when it was replied by them, on the other side, and the question put, "Rather, how came it into your minds, and what is it you design, thus to drag one of the worthiest men of Rome, without trial, to a barbarous and illegal execution?" "Very well," said Sicinnius, "you shall have no ground in this respect for quarrel or complaint against the people. The people grant your request, and your partisan shall be tried. We appoint you, Marcius," directing his speech to him, "the third market-day ensuing, to appear and defend yourself, and to try if you can satisfy the Roman citizens of your innocence, who will then judge your case by vote." The patricians were content with such a truce and respite for that time, and gladly returned home, having for the present brought off Marcius in safety.

During the interval before the appointed time (for the Romans hold their sessions every ninth day, which from that cause are called *nundinæ* in Latin), a war fell out with the Antiates, likely to be of some continuance, which gave them hope they might one way or other elude the judgment. The people, they presumed, would become tractable, and their indignation lessen and languish by degrees in so long a space, if occupation and war did not wholly put it out of their minds. But when, contrary to expectation, they made a speedy agreement with the people of Antium, and the army came back to Rome, the patricians were again in great perplexity, and had frequent meetings to consider how things might be arranged, without either abandoning Marcius, or yet giving occasion to the popular orators to create new disorders. Appius Claudius, whom they counted among the senators most averse to the popular interest, made a solemn declaration, and told them beforehand, that the senate would utterly destroy itself and betray the government, if they should once suffer the people to assume the authority of pronouncing sentence upon any of the patricians; but the oldest senators and most favorable to the people maintained, on the other side, that the people would not be so harsh and severe upon them, as some were pleased to imagine, but rather become more gentle and humane upon the concession of that power, since it was not contempt of the senate, but the impression of being contemned by it, which made them pretend to such a prerogative. Let that be once allowed them as a mark of respect and kind feeling, and the mere possession of this power of voting would at once dispossess them of their animosity.

When, therefore, Marcius saw that the senate was in pain and suspense upon his account, divided, as it were, betwixt their kindness for him and their apprehensions from the people, he desired to know of the tribunes what the crimes were they intended to charge him with, and what the heads of the indictment they would oblige him to plead to before the people; and being told by them that he was to be impeached for attempting usurpation, and that they would prove him guilty of designing to establish arbitrary government, stepping forth upon this, " Let me go then," he said, " to clear myself from that imputation before an assembly of them; I freely offer myself to any sort of trial, nor do I refuse any kind of punishment whatsoever; only," he continued, " let what you now mention be really made my accusation, and do not you play false with the senate." On their consenting to these terms, he came to his trial. But when the people met together, the tribunes, contrary to all former practice, extorted first, that votes should be taken, not by centuries, but tribes; a change, by which the indigent and factious rabble, that had no respect for honesty and justice, would be sure to carry it against those who were rich and well known, and accustomed to serve the state in war. In the next place, whereas they had engaged to prosecute Marcius upon no other head but that of tyranny, which could never be made out against him, they relinquished this plea, and urged instead, his language in the senate against an abatement of the price of corn, and for the overthrow of the tribunician power; adding further, as a new impeachment, the distribution that was made by him of the spoil and booty he had taken from the Antiates, when he overran their country, which he had divided among those that had followed him, whereas it ought rather to have been brought into the public treasury; which last accusation did, they say, more discompose Marcius than all the rest, as he had not anticipated he should ever be questioned on that subject, and, therefore, was less provided with any satisfactory answer to it on the sudden. And when, by way of excuse, he began to magnify the merits of those who had been partakers with him in the action, those that had stayed at home, being more numerous than the other, interrupted him with outcries. In conclusion, when they came to vote, a majority of three tribes condemned him; the penalty being perpetual banishment. The sentence of his condemnation being pronounced, the people went away with greater triumph and exultation than they had ever shown for any victory over enemies; while the senate was in grief and deep dejection, repenting now and vexed to the soul that they had not done and suffered all things rather than give way to the insolence of the people, and permit them to assume and abuse so great an authority. There was no need then to look at men's dresses, or other marks of distinction, to know one from another; any one who was glad was, beyond all doubt, a plebeian; any one who looked sorrowful, a patrician.

Marcius alone, himself, was neither stunned nor humiliated. In mien, carriage, and countenance, he bore the appearance of entire composure, and while all his friends were full of distress, seemed the only man that was not touched with his misfortune. Not that either reflection taught him, or gentleness of temper made it natural for him, to submit; he was wholly possessed, on the contrary, with a profound and deep-seated fury, which passes with many for no pain at all. And pain, it is true, transmuted, so to say, by its own fiery heat into anger, loses every appearance of depression and feebleness; the angry man makes a show of energy, as the man in a high fever does of natural heat, while, in fact, all this action of the soul is but mere diseased palpitation, distention, and inflammation. That such was his distempered state appeared presently plainly enough in his actions. On his return home, after saluting his mother and his wife, who were all in tears and full of loud lamentations, and exhorting them to moderate the sense they had of his calamity, he proceeded at once to the city gates, whither all the nobility came to attend him; and so, not so much as taking any thing with him, or making any request to the company, he departed from them, having only three or four clients with him. He continued solitary for a few days in a place in the country, distracted with a variety of counsels, such as rage and indignation suggested to him; and proposing to himself no honorable or useful end, but only how he might best satisfy his revenge on the Romans, he resolved at length to raise up a heavy war against them from their nearest neighbors. He determined, first to make trial of the Volscians, whom he knew to be still vigorous and flourishing, both in men and treasure, and he imagined their force and power was not so much abated, as their spite and anger increased by the late overthrows they had received from the Romans.

There was a man of Antium, called Tullus Aufidius, who, for his wealth and bravery and the splendor of his family, had the respect and privilege of a king among the Volscians, but whom Marcius knew to have a particular hostility to himself, above all other Romans. Frequent menaces and challenges had passed in battle between them, and those exchanges of defiance to which their hot and eager emulation is apt to prompt young soldiers had added private animosity to their national feelings of opposition. Yet for all this, considering Tullus to have a certain generosity of temper, and knowing that no Volscian, so much as he, desired an occasion to requite upon the Romans the evils they had done, he did what much confirms the saying, that

> Hard and unequal is with wrath the strife,
> Which makes us buy its pleasure with our life.[5]

Putting on such a dress as would make him appear to any whom he might meet most unlike what he really was, thus, like Ulysses,—

> The town he entered of his mortal foes.

His arrival at Antium was about evening, and though several met him in the streets, yet he passed along without being known to any, and went directly to the house of Tullus, and, entering undiscovered, went up to the fire-hearth, and seated himself there without speaking a word, covering up his head. Those of the family could not but wonder, and yet they were afraid either to raise or question him, for there was a certain air of majesty both in his posture and silence, but they recounted to Tullus, being then at supper, the strangeness of this accident. He immediately rose from table and came in, and asked him who he was, and for what business he came thither; and then Marcius, unmuffling himself, and pausing awhile, "If," said he, "you cannot yet call me to mind, Tullus, or do not believe your eyes concerning me, I must of necessity be my own accuser. I am Caius Marcius, the author of so much mischief

---

[5] The adage about wealth is from Heraclitus, and is quoted in two other places by Plutarch, as also by Aristotle. I have let the couplet stand, but the original, though it has the run of an iambic verse, was probably prose. The line from Homer is from Helen's description, in the fourth book of the Odyssey (*IV.*, 246).

to the Volscians; of which, were I seeking to deny it, the surname of Coriolanus I now bear would be a sufficient evidence against me. The one recompense I received for all the hardships and perils I have gone through, was the title that proclaims my enmity to your nation, and this is the only thing which is still left me. Of all other advantages, I have been stripped and deprived by the envy and outrage of the Roman people, and the cowardice and treachery of the magistrates and those of my own order. I am driven out as an exile, and become an humble suppliant at your hearth, not so much for safety and protection (should I have come hither, had I been afraid to die?), as to seek vengeance against those that expelled me; which, methinks, I have already obtained, by putting myself into your hands. If, therefore, you have really a mind to attack your enemies, come then, make use of that affliction you see me in to assist the enterprise, and convert my personal infelicity into a common blessing to the Volscians; as, indeed, I am likely to be more serviceable in fighting for than against you, with the advantage, which I now possess, of knowing all the secrets of the enemy that I am attacking. But if you decline to make any further attempts, I am neither desirous to live myself, nor will it be well in you to preserve a person who has been your rival and adversary of old, and now, when he offers you his service, appears unprofitable and useless to you."

Tullus, on hearing this, was extremely rejoiced, and giving him his right hand, exclaimed, "Rise, Marcius, and be of good courage; it is a great happiness you bring to Antium, in the present you make us of yourself; expect every thing that is good from the Volscians." He then proceeded to feast and entertain him with every display of kindness, and for several days after they were in close deliberation together on the prospects of a war.

While this design was forming, there were great troubles and commotions at Rome, from the animosity of the senators against the people, heightened just now by the late condemnation of Marcius. Besides that, their soothsayers and priests, and even private persons, reported signs and prodigies not to be neglected; one of which is stated to have occurred as follows: Titus Latinus,[6] a man of ordinary condition, but of a quiet and virtuous character, free from all superstitious fancies, and yet more from vanity and exaggeration, had an apparition in his sleep, as if Jupiter came and bade him tell the senate, that it was with a bad and unacceptable dancer that they had headed his procession. Having beheld the vision, he said, he did not much attend to it at the first appearance; but after he had seen and slighted it a second and third time, he had lost a hopeful son, and was himself struck with a palsy. He was brought into the senate on a litter to tell this, and the story goes, that he had no sooner delivered his message there, but he at once felt his strength return, and got upon his legs, and went home alone, without need of any support. The senators, in wonder and surprise, made a diligent search into the matter. That which his dream alluded to was this: some citizen had, for some heinous offence, given up a servant of his to the rest of his fellows, with charge to whip him first through the market, and then to kill him; and while they were executing this command, and scourging the wretch, who screwed and turned himself into all manner of shapes and unseemly motions, through the

[6] The correct name is probably Titus Latinius, for which Tiberius Atinius, in Livy, is merely a misreading.

pain he was in, the solemn procession in honor of Jupiter chanced to follow at their heels. Several of the attendants on which were, indeed, scandalized at the sight, yet no one of them interfered, or acted further in the matter than merely to utter some common reproaches and execrations on a master who inflicted so cruel a punishment. For the Romans treated their slaves with great humanity in these times, when, working and laboring themselves, and living together among them, they naturally were more gentle and familiar with them. It was one of the severest punishments for a slave who had committed a fault, to have to take the piece of wood which supports the pole of a wagon, and carry it about through the neighborhood; a slave who had once undergone the shame of this, and been thus seen by the household and the neighbors, had no longer any trust or credit among them, and had the name of *furcifer; furca* being the Latin word for a prop, or support.

When, therefore, Latinus had related his dream, and the senators were considering who this disagreeable and ungainly dancer could be, some of the company, having been struck with the strangeness of the punishment, called to mind and mentioned the miserable slave who was lashed through the streets and afterward put to death. The priests, when consulted, confirmed the conjecture; the master was punished; and orders given for a new celebration of the procession and the spectacles in honor of the god. Numa, in other respects also a wise arranger of religious offices, would seem to have been especially judicious in his direction, with a view to the attentiveness of the people, that, when the magistrates or priests performed any divine worship, a herald should go before and proclaim with a loud voice, *Hoc age,* Do this you are about, and so warn them to mind whatever sacred action they were engaged in, and not suffer any business or worldly avocation to disturb and interrupt it; most of the things which men do of this kind, being in a manner forced from them, and effected by constraint. It is usual with the Romans to recommence their sacrifices and processions and spectacles, not only upon such a cause as this, but for any slighter reason. If but one of the horses which drew the chariots called Tensæ, upon which the images of their gods were placed, happened to fail or falter, or if the driver took hold of the reins with his left hand, they would decree that the whole operation should commence anew; and, in latter ages, one and the same sacrifice was performed thirty times over, because of the occurrence of some defect or mistake or accident in the service. Such was the Roman reverence and caution in religious matters.

Marcius and Tullus were now secretly discoursing of their project with the chief men of Antium, advising them to invade the Romans while they were at variance among themselves. And when shame appeared to hinder them from embracing the motion, as they had sworn to a truce and cessation of arms for the space of two years, the Romans themselves soon furnished them with a pretence, by making proclamation, out of some jealousy or slanderous report, in the midst of the spectacles, that all the Volscians who had come to see them should depart the city before sunset. Some affirm that this was a contrivance of Marcius, who sent a man privately to the consuls, falsely to accuse the Volscians of intending to fall upon the Romans during the games, and to set the city on fire. This public affront roused and inflamed their hostility to the Romans; and Tullus, perceiving it, made his advantage of it, aggravating the fact, and working on their indignation till he persuaded them, at last, to despatch ambassadors to Rome, requiring the Romans to restore that part of their country and those towns which they had taken from the Volscians in the late war. When the Romans heard the message they indignantly replied, that the Volscians were the first that took up arms, but the Romans would be the last to lay them down. This answer being brought back, Tullus called a general assembly of the Volscians; and the vote passing for a war, he then proposed that they should call in Marcius, laying aside the remembrance of former grudges, and assuring themselves that the services they should now receive from him as a friend and associate, would abundantly outweigh any harm or damage he had done them when he was their enemy. Marcius was accordingly summoned, and having made his entrance, and spoken to the people, won their good opinion of his capacity, his skill, counsel, and boldness, not less by his present words than by his past actions. They joined him in commission with Tullus, to have full power as general of their forces in all that related to the war. And he, fearing lest the time that would be requisite to bring all the Volscians together in full preparation might be so long as to lose him the opportunity of action, left order with the chief persons and magistrates of the city to provide other things, while he himself, prevailing upon the most forward to assemble and march out with him as volunteers without staying to be enrolled, made a sudden inroad into the Roman confines, when nobody expected him, and possessed himself of so much booty, that the Volscians found they had more than they could either carry away or use in the camp. The abundance of provision which he gained, and the waste and havoc of the country which he made, were, however, of themselves and in his account, the smallest results of that invasion; the great mischief he intended, and his special object in all, was to increase at Rome the suspicions entertained of the patricians, and to make them upon worse terms with the people. With this view, while spoiling all the fields and destroying the property of other men, he took special care to preserve their farms and lands untouched, and would not allow his soldiers to ravage there, or seize upon any thing which belonged to them. From hence their invectives and quarrels against one another broke out afresh, and rose to a greater height than ever; the senators reproaching those of the commonalty with their late injustice to Marcius; while the plebeians, on their side, did not hesitate to accuse them of having, out of spite and revenge, solicited him to this enterprise, and thus, when others were involved in the miseries of a war by their means, they sat like unconcerned spectators, as being furnished with a guardian and protector abroad of their wealth and fortunes, in the very person of the public enemy. After this incursion and exploit, which was of great advantage to the Volscians, as they learned by it to grow more hardy and to contemn their enemy, Marcius drew them off, and returned in safety.

But when the whole strength of the Volscians was brought together into the field, with great expedition and alacrity, it appeared so considerable a body, that they agreed to leave part in garrison, for the security of their towns, and with the other part to march against the Romans. Marcius now desired Tullus to choose which of the two charges would be most agreeable to him. Tullus answered, that since he knew Marcius to be equally valiant as himself, and far more fortunate, he would have him take the command of those that were going out to the war, while he made it his care to defend their cities at home and provide all conveniences for the army abroad. Marcius thus reinforced, and much stronger than before, moved first towards the city called Circæum, a Roman colony. He received its surrender, and did the inhabitants no injury; passing thence, he entered and laid waste the country of the Latins, where he expected the Romans would meet him, as the Latins were their confederates and allies, and had often sent to demand succors from them. The people, however, on their part, showing little inclination for the service, and the consuls themselves being unwilling to run the hazard of a battle, when the time of their office was almost ready to expire, they dismissed the Latin ambassadors without any effect; so that Marcius, finding no army to oppose him, marched up to their cities, and, having taken by force Toleria, Lavici, Peda, and Bola,[7] all of which offered resistance, not only plundered their houses, but made a prey likewise of their persons. Meantime, he showed particular regard for all such as came over to his party, and, for fear they might sustain any damage against his will, encamped at the greatest distance he could, and wholly abstained from the lands of their property.

After, however, that he had made himself master of Bola, a town not above ten miles from Rome, where he found great treasure, and put almost all

[7] *Bola,* in the list with *Toleria, Lavici, and Peda* (or Pedum), is obviously meant for a different town from *Bola,* a few lines below,—*a town not above ten miles from Rome.* The spelling in the Greek differs, and there is little doubt that in the latter place *Bolla,* so written in the Greek, should be turned into *Boïlla,* the equivalent used for the Latin *Bovillæ.*

the adults to the sword; and when, on this, the other Volscians that were ordered to stay behind and protect their cities, hearing of his achievements and success, had not patience to remain any longer at home, but came hastening in their arms to Marcius, saying that he alone was their general and the sole commander they would own; with all this, his name and renown spread throughout all Italy, and universal wonder prevailed at the sudden and mighty revolution in the fortunes of two nations which the loss and the accession of a single man had effected.

All at Rome was in great disorder; they were utterly averse from fighting, and spent their whole time in cabals and disputes and reproaches against each other; until news was brought that the enemy had laid close siege to Lavinium, where were the images and sacred things of their tutelar gods, and from whence they derived the origin of their nation, that being the first city which Æneas built in Italy. These tidings produced a change as universal as it was extraordinary in the thoughts and inclinations of the people, but occasioned a yet stranger revulsion of feeling among the patricians. The people now were for repealing the sentence against Marcius, and calling him back into the city; whereas the senate, being assembled to preconsider the decree, opposed and finally rejected the proposal, either out of the mere humor of contradicting and withstanding the people in whatever they should desire, or because they were unwilling, perhaps, that he should owe his restoration to their kindness; or having now conceived a displeasure against Marcius himself, who was bringing distress upon all alike, though he had not been ill treated by all, and was become a declared enemy to his whole country, though he knew well enough that the principal and all the better men condoled with him, and suffered in his injuries.

This resolution of theirs being made public, the people could proceed no further, having no authority to pass any thing by suffrage, and enact it for a law, without a previous decree from the senate. When Marcius heard of this, he was more exasperated than ever, and, quitting the siege of Lavinium, marched furiously towards Rome, and encamped at a place called the Cluilian ditches, about five miles from the city. The nearness of his approach did, indeed, create much terror and disturbance, yet it also ended their dissensions for the present; as nobody now, whether consul or senator, durst any longer contradict the people in their design of recalling Marcius; but, seeing their women running affrighted up and down the streets, and the old men at prayer in every temple with tears and supplications, and that, in short, there was a general absence among them both of courage and wisdom to provide for their own safety, they came at last to be all of one mind, that the people had been in the right to propose as they did a reconciliation with Marcius, and that the senate was guilty of a fatal error to begin a quarrel with him when it was a time to forget offences, and they should have studied rather to appease him. It was, therefore, unanimously agreed by all parties, that ambassadors should be despatched, offering him return to his country, and desiring he would free them from the terrors and distresses of the war. The persons sent by the senate with this message were chosen out of his kindred and acquaintance, who naturally expected a very kind reception at their first interview, upon the score of that relation and their old familiarity and friendship with him; in which, however, they were much mistaken. Being led through the enemy's camp, they found him sitting in state amidst the chief men of the Volscians, looking insupportably proud and arrogant. He bade them declare the cause of their coming, which they did in the most gentle and tender terms, and with a behavior suitable to their language. When they had made an end of speaking, he returned them a sharp answer, full of bitterness and angry resentment, as to what concerned himself, and the ill usage he had received from them; but as general of the Volscians, he demanded restitution of the cities and the lands which had been seized upon during the late war, and that the same rights and franchises should be granted them at Rome, which had been before accorded to the Latins; since there could be no assurance that a peace would be firm and lasting, without fair and just conditions on both sides. He allowed them thirty days to consider and resolve.

The ambassadors being departed, he withdrew his forces out of the Roman territory. This, those of the Volscians who had long envied his reputation, and could not endure to see the influence he had with the people, laid hold of, as the first matter of complaint against him. Among them was also Tullus himself, not for any wrong done him personally by Marcius, but through the weakness incident to human nature. He could not help feeling mortified to find his own glory thus totally obscured, and himself overlooked and neglected now by the Volscians, who had so great an opinion of their new leader, that he alone was all to them, while other captains, they thought, should be content with that share of power, which he might think fit to accord. From hence the first seeds of complaint and accusation were scattered about in secret, and the malcontents met and heightened each other's indignation, saying, that to retreat as he did, was in effect to betray and deliver up, though not their cities and their arms, yet what was as bad, the critical times and opportunities for action, on which depend the preservation or the loss of every thing else; since in less than thirty days' space, for which he had given a respite from the war, there might happen the greatest changes in the world. Yet Marcius spent not any part of the time idly, but attacked the confederates of the enemy, ravaged their land, and took from them seven great and populous cities in that interval. The Romans, in the meanwhile, durst not venture out to their relief; but were utterly fearful, and showed no more disposition or capacity for action, than if their bodies had been struck with a palsy, and become destitute of sense and motion. But when the thirty days were expired, and Marcius appeared again with his whole army, they sent another embassy to beseech him that he would moderate his displeasure, and would withdraw the Volscian army, and then make any proposals he thought best for both parties; the Romans would make no concessions to menaces, but if it were his opinion that the Volscians ought to have any favor shown them, upon laying down their arms they might obtain all they could in reason desire.

The reply of Marcius was, that he should make no answer to this as general of the Volscians, but, in the quality still of a Roman citizen, he would advise and exhort them, as the case stood, not to carry it so high, but think rather of just compliance, and return to him, before three days were at an end, with a ratification of his previous demands; otherwise, they must understand that they could not have any further freedom in passing through his camp upon idle errands.

When the ambassadors were come back, and had

acquainted the senate with the answer, seeing the whole state now threatened as it were by a tempest, and the waves ready to overwhelm them, they were forced, as we say in extreme perils, to let down the sacred anchor. A decree was made, that the whole order of their priests, those who initiated in the mysteries or had the custody of them, and those who, according to the ancient practice of the country, divined from birds, should all and every one of them go in full procession to Marcius with their pontifical array, and the dress and habit which they respectively used in their several functions, and should urge him, as before, to withdraw his forces, and then treat with his countrymen in favor of the Volscians. He consented so far, indeed, as to give the deputation an admittance into his camp, but granted nothing at all, nor so much as expressed himself more mildly; but, without capitulating or receding, bade them once for all choose whether they would yield or fight, since the old terms were the only terms of peace. When this solemn application proved ineffectual, the priests, too, returning unsuccessful, they determined to sit still within the city, and keep watch about their walls, intending only to repulse the enemy, should he offer to attack them, and placing their hopes chiefly in time and in extraordinary accidents of fortune; as to themselves, they felt incapable of doing any thing for their own deliverance; mere confusion and terror and ill-boding reports possessed the whole city; till at last a thing happened not unlike what we so often find represented, without, however, being accepted as true by people in general, in Homer. On some great and unusual occasion we find him say:—

But him the blue-eyed goddess did inspire;[8]

[8] *But him the blue-eyed goddess did inspire* is the first line of the 21st book of the Odyssey, only that for *him*, we should

and elsewhere:—

> But some immortal turned my mind away,
> To think what others of the deed would say;

and again:—

> Were 't his own thought or were 't a god's command.

People are apt, in such passages, to censure and disregard the poet, as if, by the introduction of mere impossibilities and idle fictions, he were denying the action of a man's own deliberate thought and free choice; which is not, in the least, the case in Homer's representation, where the ordinary, probable, and

have *her;* Minerva inspires Penelope with the thought of the trial by the bow. Plutarch no doubt quoted from memory. The next two lines are wholly different from any thing now to be found in Homer. The third quotation is from the ninth Odyssey (339), where the Cyclops is described coming home at evening to his cave, and *were it some thought of his own, or so ordered him by a god, he left none of his flock outside, but drove them all into his hollow fold.* In the same book (*IX.*, 299), is also the line: *But I consulted with my own great soul;* Ulysses consulted with himself whether he should kill the Cyclops as he lay drunk and asleep, but reflected that there would then be no one to move away the stone from the door and let them out. *He spoke; Achilles, with quick pain possessed,* is from Iliad I., 188, and the lines about Bellerophon from Iliad VI., 161. Coray in his notes compares the doctrine given at the end of the first paragraph of the following page (91) with a passage in Plato's Critias (p. 109), where it is said, that *we in our several tribes and cities are the flocks whom the divine beings severally tend, not by any bodily compulsion applied to our bodies, but by an intellectual agency operating on the rudder, to which all living things most aptly answer, of the soul.*

habitual conclusions that common reason leads to are continually ascribed to our own direct agency. He certainly says frequently enough:—

> But I consulted with my own great soul;

or, as in another passage:—

> He spoke. Achilles, with quick pain possessed,
> Revolved two purposes in his strong breast;

and in a third:—

> —Yet never to her wishes won
> The just mind of the brave Bellerophon.

But where the act is something out of the way and extraordinary, and seems in a manner to demand some impulse of divine possession and sudden inspiration to account for it, here he does introduce divine agency, not to destroy, but to prompt the human will; not to create in us another agency, but offering images to stimulate our own; images that in no sort or kind make our action involuntary, but give occasion rather to spontaneous action, aided and sustained by feelings of confidence and hope. For either we must totally dismiss and exclude divine influences from every kind of causality and origination in what we do, or else what other way can we conceive in which divine aid and coöperation can act? Certainly we cannot suppose that the divine beings actually and literally turn our bodies and direct our hands and our feet this way or that, to do what is right; it is obvious that they must actuate the practical and elective element of our nature, by certain initial occasions, by images presented to the imagination, and thoughts suggested to the mind, such either as to excite it to, or avert and withhold it from, any particular course.

In the perplexity which I have described, the Roman women went, some to other temples, but the greater part, and the ladies of highest rank, to the altar of Jupiter Capitolinus. Among these suppliants was Valeria, sister to the great Poplicola, who did the Romans eminent service both in peace and war. Poplicola himself was now deceased, as is told in the history of his life; but Valeria lived still, and enjoyed great respect and honor at Rome, her life and conduct no way disparaging her birth. She, suddenly seized with the sort of instinct or emotion of mind which I have described, and happily lighting, not without divine guidance, on the right expedient, both rose herself, and bade the others rise, and went directly with them to the house of Volumnia, the mother of Marcius. And coming in and finding her sitting with her daughter-in-law, and with her little grandchildren on her lap, Valeria, then surrounded by her female companions, spoke in the name of them all:—

"We that now make our appearance, O Volumnia, and you, Vergilia, are come as mere women to women, not by direction of the senate, or an order from the consuls, or the appointment of any other magistrate; but the divine being himself, as I conceive, moved to compassion by our prayers, prompted us to visit you in a body, and request a thing on which our own and the common safety depends, and which, if you consent to it, will raise your glory above that of the daughters of the Sabines, who won over their fathers and their husbands from mortal enmity to peace and friendship. Arise and come with us to Marcius; join in our supplication, and bear for your country this true and just testimony on her behalf; that, notwithstanding the many mischiefs that have been done her, yet she has never outraged

LICTORS

you, nor so much as thought of treating you ill, in all her resentment, but does now restore you safe into his hands, though there be small likelihood she should obtain from him any equitable terms." [9]

The words of Valeria were seconded by the acclamations of the other women, to which Volumnia made answer:—

"I and Vergilia, my countrywoman, have an equal share with you all in the common miseries, and we have the additional sorrow, which is wholly ours, that we have lost the merit and good fame of Marcius, and see his person confined, rather than protected, by the arms of the enemy. Yet I account this the greatest of all misfortunes, if indeed the affairs of Rome be sunk to so feeble a state as to have their last dependence upon us. For it is hardly imaginable he should have any consideration left for us, when he has no regard for the country which he was wont to prefer before his mother and wife and children. Make use, however, of our service; and lead us, if you please, to him; we are able, if nothing more, at least to spend our last breath in making suit to him for our country."

Having spoken thus, she took Vergilia by the hand, and the young children, and so accompanied them to the Volscian camp. So lamentable a sight much affected the enemies themselves, who viewed them in respectful silence. Marcius was then sitting in his place, with his chief officers about him, and seeing the party of women advance toward them, wondered what should be the matter; but perceiving at length, that his mother was at the head of them,

[9] Through all this narrative Plutarch appears to have made a mistake. The mother of Coriolanus was Veturia, and his wife Volumnia.

he would fain have hardened himself in his former inexorable temper, but, overcome by his feelings, and confounded at what he saw, he did not endure they should approach him sitting in state, but came down hastily to meet them, saluting his mother first, and embracing her a long time, and then his wife and children, sparing neither tears nor caresses, but suffering himself to be borne away and carried headlong, as it were, by the impetuous violence of his passion.

When he had satisfied himself, and observed that his mother Volumnia was desirous to say something, the Volscian council being first called in, he heard her to the following effect: " Our dress and our very persons, my son, might tell you, though we should say nothing ourselves, in how forlorn a condition we have lived at home since your banishment and absence from us; and now consider with yourself, whether we may not pass for the most unfortunate of all women, to have that sight, which should be the sweetest that we could see, converted, through I know not what fatality, to one of all others the most formidable and dreadful,—Volumnia to behold her son, and Vergilia her husband, in arms against the walls of Rome. Even prayer itself, whence others gain comfort and relief in all manner of misfortunes, is that which most adds to our confusion and distress; since our best wishes are inconsistent with themselves, nor can we at the same time petition the gods for Rome's victory and your preservation, but what the worst of our enemies would imprecate as a curse, is the very object of our vows. Your wife and children are under the sad necessity, that they must either be deprived of you, or of their native soil. As for myself, I am resolved not to wait till war shall determine this alternative for me; but if I cannot prevail with you to prefer amity and concord to quarrel and hostility, and to be the benefactor to both parties, rather than the destroyer of one of them, be assured of this from me, and reckon steadfastly upon it, that you shall not be able to reach your country, unless you trample first upon the corpse of her that brought you into life. For it will be ill in me to wait and loiter in the world till the day come wherein I shall see a child of mine, either led in triumph by his own countrymen, or triumphing over them. Did I require you to save your country by ruining the Volscians, then, I confess, my son, the case would be hard for you to solve. It is base to bring destitution on our fellow-citizens; it is unjust to betray those who have placed their confidence in us. But, as it is, we do but desire a deliverance equally expedient for them and us; only more glorious and honorable on the Volscian side, who, as superior in arms, will be thought freely to bestow the two greatest of blessings, peace and friendship, even when they themselves receive the same. If we obtain these, the common thanks will be chiefly due to you as the principal cause; but if they be not granted, you alone must expect to bear the blame from both nations. The chance of all war is uncertain, yet thus much is certain in the present, that you, by conquering Rome, will only get the reputation of having undone your country; but if the Volscians happen to be defeated under your conduct, then the world will say, that, to satisfy a revengeful humor, you brought misery on your friends and patrons."

Marcius listened to his mother while she spoke, without answering her a word, and Volumnia, seeing him stand mute also for a long time after she had ceased, resumed: "O my son," said she, "what is the meaning of this silence? Is it a duty to postpone every thing to a sense of injuries, and wrong to gratify a mother in a request like this? Is it the characteristic of a great man to remember wrongs that have been done him, and not the part of a great and good man to remember benefits such as those that children receive from parents, and to requite them with honor and respect? You, methinks, who are so relentless in the punishment of the ungrateful, should not be more careless than others to be grateful yourself. You have punished your country already; you have not yet paid your debt to me. Nature and religion, surely, unattended by any constraint, should have won your consent to petitions so worthy and so just as these; but if it must be so, I will even use my last resource." Having said this, she threw herself down at his feet, as did also his wife and children; upon which Marcius, crying out, "O mother! what is it you have done to me?" raised her up from the ground, and pressing her right hand with more than ordinary vehemence, "You have gained a victory," said he, " fortunate enough for the Romans, but destructive to your son; whom you, though none else, have defeated." After which, and a little private conference with his mother and his wife, he sent them back again to Rome, as they desired of him.

The next morning, he broke up his camp, and led the Volscians homeward, variously affected with what he had done; some of them complaining of him and condemning his act, others, who were inclined to a peaceful conclusion, unfavorable to neither. A third party, while much disliking his proceedings, yet could not look upon Marcius as a treacherous person, but thought it pardonable in him to be thus shaken and driven to surrender at last, under such compulsion. None, however, opposed his commands; they all obediently followed him, though rather from admiration of his virtue, than any regard they now had to his authority. The Roman people, meantime, more effectually manifested how much fear and danger they had been in while the war lasted, by their deportment after they were freed from it. Those that guarded the walls had no sooner given notice that the Volscians were dislodged and drawn off, but they set open all their temples in a moment, and began to crown themselves with garlands and prepare for sacrifice, as they were wont to do upon tidings brought of any signal victory. But the joy and transport of the whole city was chiefly remarkable in the honors and marks of affection paid to the women, as well by the senate as the people in general; every one declaring that they were, beyond all question, the instruments of the public safety. And the senate having passed a decree that whatsoever they would ask in the way of any favor or honor should be allowed and done for them by the magistrates, they demanded simply that a temple might be erected to Female Fortune, the expense of which they offered to defray out of their own contributions, if the city would be at the cost of sacrifices, and other matters pertaining to the due honor of the gods, out of the common treasury. The senate, much commending their public spirit, caused the temple to be built and a statue set up in it at the public charge; they, however, made up a sum among themselves, for a second image of Fortune, which the Romans say uttered, as it was putting up, words to this effect, "Blessed of the gods, O women, is your gift."

These words they profess were repeated a second time, expecting our belief for what seems pretty nearly an impossibility. It may be possible enough, that statues may seem to sweat, and to run with tears, and to stand with certain dewy drops of a sanguine color; for timber and stones are frequently known to contract a kind of scurf and rottenness, productive of moisture; and various tints may form on the surfaces, both from within and from the action of the air outside; and by these signs it is not absurd to imagine that the deity may forewarn us. It may happen, also, that images and statues may sometimes make a noise not unlike that of a moan or groan, through a rupture or violent internal separation of the parts; but that an articulate voice, and such express words, and language so clear and exact and elaborate, should proceed from inanimate things, is, in my judgment, a thing utterly out of possibility. For it was never known that either the soul of man, or the deity himself, uttered vocal sounds and language, alone, without an organized body and members fitted for speech. But where history seems in a manner to force our assent by the concurrence of numerous and credible witnesses, we are to conclude that an impression distinct from sensation affects the imaginative part of our nature, and then carries away the judgment, so as to believe it to be a sensation: just as in sleep we fancy we see and hear, without really doing either. Persons, however, whose strong feelings of reverence to the deity, and tenderness for religion, will not allow them to deny or invalidate any thing of this kind, have certainly a strong argument for their faith, in the wonderful and transcendent character of the divine power; which admits no manner of comparison with ours, either in its nature or its action, the modes or the strength of its operations. It is no contradiction to reason that it should do things that we cannot do, and effect what for us is impracticable: differing from us in all respects,[10] in its acts yet more than in other points we may well believe it to be unlike us and remote from us. Knowledge of divine things for the most part, as Heraclitus says, is lost to us by incredulity.

When Marcius came back to Antium, Tullus, who thoroughly hated and greatly feared him, proceeded at once to contrive how he might immediately despatch him; as, if he escaped now, he was never likely to give him such another advantage. Having therefore, got together and suborned several partisans against him, he required Marcius to resign his charge, and give the Volscians an account of his administration. He, apprehending the danger of a private condition, while Tullus held the office of general and exercised the greatest power among his fellow-citizens, made answer, that he was ready to lay down his commission, whenever those from whose common authority he had received it, should think fit to recall it, and that in the mean time he was ready to give the Antiates satisfaction, as to all particulars of his conduct, if they were desirous of it.

An assembly was called, and popular speakers, as had been concerted, came forward to exasperate and incense the multitude; but when Marcius stood up to answer, the more unruly and tumultuous part of the people became quiet on a sudden, and out of reverence allowed him to speak without the least

---

[10] The divine nature, *differing from us in all respects,* may very well be conceived to differ in its acts and mode of agency yet more than in any thing else. The sense of the passage from Heraclitus, which is quoted also by Clement of Alexandria (*Stromata V., cxiii*), is very uncertain. It may merely mean that divine things transcend our powers of belief and knowledge.

disturbance; while all the better people, and such as were satisfied with a peace, made it evident by their whole behavior, that they would give him a favorable hearing, and judge and pronounce according to equity.

Tullus, therefore, began to dread the issue of the defence he was going to make for himself; for he was an admirable speaker, and the former services he had done the Volscians had procured and still preserved for him greater kindness than could be outweighed by any blame for his late conduct. Indeed, the very accusation itself was a proof and testimony of the greatness of his merits, since people could never have complained or thought themselves wronged, because Rome was not brought into their power, but that by his means they had come so near to taking it. For these reasons, the conspirators judged it prudent not to make any further delays, nor to test the general feeling; but the boldest of their faction, crying out that they ought not to listen to a traitor, nor allow him still to retain office and play the tyrant among them, fell upon Marcius [11] in a body, and slew him there, none of those that were present offering to defend him. But it quickly appeared that the action was in nowise approved by the majority of the

---

[11] "Marcius was a man too full of passion and choler, and too much given over to self-will and opinion, as one of a high mind and great courage, that lacked the gravity and affability that is gotten with judgment of learning and reason, which only is to be looked for in a governor of State: and that remembered not how wilfulness is the thing of the world, which a governor of a commonwealth, for pleasing, should shun, being that which Plato called 'solitariness'; as in the end, all men that are wilfully given to a self-opinion and obstinate mind, and who will never yield to other's reason but to their own, remain without

Volscians, who hurried out of their several cities to show respect to his corpse; to which they gave honorable interment, adorning his sepulchre with arms and trophies, as the monument of a noble hero and a famous general. When the Romans heard tidings of his death, they gave no other signification either of honor or of anger towards him, but simply granted the request of the women, that they might put themselves into mourning and bewail him for ten months, as the usage was upon the loss of a father or a son or a brother; that being the period fixed for the longest lamentation by the laws of Numa Pompilius, as is more amply told in the account of him.

Marcius was no sooner deceased, but the Volscians felt the need of his assistance. They quarrelled first with the Æquians, their confederates and their friends, about the appointment of the general of their joint forces, and carried their dispute to the length of bloodshed and slaughter; and were then defeated by the Romans in a pitched battle, where not only Tullus lost his life, but the principal flower of their whole army was cut in pieces; so that they were forced to submit and accept of peace upon very dishonorable terms, becoming subjects of Rome, and pledging themselves to submission.

company, and forsaken of all men. For a man that will live in the world must needs have patience, which lusty bloods make but a mock at. So Marcius, being a stout man of nature, that never yielded in any respect, as one thinking that to overcome always and to have the upper hand in all matters, was a token of magnanimity and of no base and faint courage, which spitteth out anger from the most weak and passioned part of the beast, much like the matter of an impostume: went home to his house, full freighted with spite and malice against the people."—NORTH's PLUTARCH: *Life of Coriolanus.*

COMPARISON OF ALCIBIADES WITH CORIOLANUS

HAVING described all their actions that seem to deserve commemoration, their military ones, we may say, incline the balance very decidedly upon neither side. They both, in pretty equal measure, displayed on numerous occasions the daring and courage of the soldier, and the skill and foresight of the general; unless, indeed, the fact that Alcibiades was victorious and successful in many contests both by sea and land, ought to gain him the title of a more complete commander. That so long as they remained and held command in their respective countries, they eminently sustained, and when they were driven into exile, yet more eminently damaged the fortunes of those countries, is common to both. All the sober citizens felt disgust at the petulance, the low flattery, and base seductions which Alcibiades, in his public life, allowed himself to employ with the view of winning the people's favor; and the ungraciousness, pride, and oligarchical haughtiness which Marcius, on the other hand, displayed in his, were the abhorrence of the Roman populace. Neither of these courses can be called commendable; but a man who ingratiates himself by indulgence and flattery, is hardly so censurable as one who, to avoid the appearance of flattering, insults. To seek power by servility to the people is a disgrace, but to maintain it by terror, violence, and oppression, is not a disgrace only, but an injustice.

Marcius, according to our common conceptions of his character, was undoubtedly simple and straightforward; Alcibiades, unscrupulous as a public man, and false. He is more especially blamed for

ALCIBIADES AND CORIOLANUS

the dishonorable and treacherous way in which, as Thucydides relates, he imposed upon the Lacedæmonian ambassadors, and disturbed the continuance of the peace. Yet this policy, which engaged the city again in war, nevertheless placed it in a powerful and formidable position, by the accession, which Alcibiades obtained for it, of the alliance of Argos and Mantinea. And Coriolanus also, Dionysius relates, used unfair means to excite war between the Romans and the Volscians, in the false report which he spread about the visitors at the Games; and the motive of this action seems to make it the worse of the two; since it was not done, like the other, out of ordinary political jealousy, strife, and competition. Simply to gratify anger from which, as Ion says, no one ever yet got any return, he threw whole districts of Italy into confusion, and sacrificed to his passion against his country numerous innocent cities. It is true, indeed, that Alcibiades also, by his resentment, was the occasion of great disasters to his country, but he relented as soon as he found their feelings to be changed; and after he was driven out a second time, so far from taking pleasure in the errors and inadvertencies of their commanders, or being indifferent to the danger they were thus incurring, he did the very thing that Aristides is so highly commended for doing to Themistocles: he came to the generals who were his enemies, and pointed out to them what they ought to do. Coriolanus, on the other hand, first of all attacked the whole body of his countrymen, though only one portion of them had done him any wrong, while the other, the better and nobler portion, had actually suffered, as well as sympathized, with him. And, secondly, by the obduracy with which he resisted numerous embassies and supplications, addressed in propitiation of his single anger and offence, he showed that it had been to destroy and overthrow, not to recover and regain his country, that he had excited bitter and implacable hostilities against it. There is, indeed, one distinction that may be drawn. Alcibiades, it may be said, was not safe among the Spartans, and had the inducements at once of fear and of hatred to lead him again to Athens; whereas Marcius could not honorably have left the Volscians, when they were behaving so well to him: he, in the command of their forces and the enjoyment of their entire confidence, was in a very different position from Alcibiades, whom the Lacedæmonians did not so much wish to adopt into their service, as to use, and then abandon. Driven about from house to house in the city, and from general to general in the camp, the latter had no resort but to place himself in the hands of Tisaphernes; unless, indeed, we are to suppose that his object in courting favor with him was to avert the entire destruction of his native city, whither he wished himself to return.

As regards money, Alcibiades, we are told, was often guilty of procuring it by accepting bribes, and spent it ill in luxury and dissipation. Coriolanus declined to receive it, even when pressed upon him by his commanders as an honor; and one great reason for the odium he incurred with the populace in the discussions about their debts was, that he trampled upon the poor, not for money's sake, but out of pride and insolence.

Antipater, in a letter written upon the death of Aristotle the philosopher, observes, " Amongst his other gifts he had that of persuasiveness;" and the absence of this in the character of Marcius made all his great actions and noble qualities unacceptable to those whom they benefited: pride, and self-will, the consort, as Plato calls it, of solitude, made him insufferable. With the skill which Alcibiades, on the contrary, possessed to treat every one in the way most agreeable to him, we cannot wonder that all his successes were attended with the most exuberant favor and honor; his very errors, at times, being accompanied by something of grace and felicity. And so, in spite of great and frequent hurt that he had done the city, he was repeatedly appointed to office and command; while Coriolanus stood in vain for a place which his great services had made his due. The one, in spite of the harm he occasioned, could not make himself hated, nor the other, with all the admiration he attracted, succeed in being beloved by his countrymen.

Coriolanus, moreover, it should be said, did not as a general obtain any successes for his country, but only for his enemies against his country. Alcibiades was often of service to Athens, both as a soldier and as a commander. So long as he was personally present, he had the perfect mastery of his political adversaries; calumny only succeeded in his absence. Coriolanus was condemned in person at Rome; and in like manner killed by the Volscians, not indeed with any right or justice, yet not without some pretext occasioned by his own acts; since, after rejecting all conditions of peace in public, in private he yielded to the solicitations of the women, and, without establishing peace, threw up the favorable chances of war. He ought, before retiring, to have obtained the consent of those who had placed their trust in him; if indeed he considered their claims on him to be the strongest. Or, if we say that he did not care about the Volscians, but merely had prosecuted the war, which he now abandoned, for the satisfaction of his own resentment, then the

noble thing would have been, not to spare his country
for his mother's sake, but his mother in and with his
country; since both his mother and his wife were
part and parcel of that endangered country. After
harshly repelling public supplications, the entreaties
of ambassadors, and the prayers of priests, to con-
cede all as a private favor to his mother was less an
honor to her than a dishonor to the city which thus
escaped, in spite, it would seem, of its own demerits,
through the intercession of a single woman. Such
a grace could, indeed, seem merely invidious, un-
gracious, and unreasonable in the eyes of both parties; he retreated without listening to the persuasions
of his opponents, or asking the consent of his friends.
The origin of all lay in his unsociable, supercilious,
and self-willed disposition, which, in all cases, is
offensive to most people; and when combined with a
passion for distinction, passes into absolute savageness and mercilessness. Men decline to ask favors
of the people, professing not to need any honors
from them; and then are indignant if they do not
obtain them. Metellus, Aristides, and Epaminondas
certainly did not beg favors of the multitude; but
that was because they, in real truth, did not value
the gifts which a popular body can either confer or
refuse; and when they were more than once driven
into exile, rejected at elections, and condemned in
courts of justice, they showed no resentment at the
ill-humor of their fellow-citizens, but were willing
and contented to return and be reconciled when the
feeling altered and they were wished for. He who
least likes courting favor, ought also least to think
of resenting neglect; to feel wounded at being refused a distinction can only arise from an overween-
ing appetite to have it.

Alcibiades never professed to deny that it was

pleasant to him to be honored, and distasteful to him to be overlooked; and, accordingly, he always tried to place himself upon good terms with all that he met; Coriolanus's pride forbade him to pay attentions to those who could have promoted his advancement, and yet his love of distinction made him feel hurt and angry when he was disregarded. Such are the faulty parts of his character, which in all other respects was a noble one. For his temperance, continence, and probity, he might claim to be compared with the best and purest of the Greeks; not in any sort or kind with Alcibiades, the least scrupulous and most entirely careless of human beings in all these points.

TIMOLEON[1]

Translated by Thomas Blomer, D.D.

It was for the sake of others that I first commenced writing biographies; but I find myself proceeding and attaching myself to it for my own; the virtues of these great men serving me as a sort of looking-glass, in which I may see how to adjust and adorn my own life. Indeed, it can be compared to nothing but daily living and associating together; we receive, as it were, in our inquiry, and entertain each successive guest, view

> Their stature and their qualities,[2]

and select from their actions all that is noblest and worthiest to know.

---

[1] The wisdom of Timoleon's rule in Sicily is attested by the flourishing condition of the island for several years even after his death. He assumed no title or office but lived as a private citizen among the Syracusans. He died in 337 B.C.—Dr. William Smith.

[2] As they sat at meat in the tent, after Achilles had consented to give Priam Hector's body, *Priam, son of Dardanus, eyed Achilles, admiring* his stature and his qualities, *and his appearance, as it were of a god, and Achilles in turn looked with admiration upon Priam* (Iliad, XXIV., 629). The line that follows is from a lost play, the Tympanistæ of Sophocles, a fragment found at great length elsewhere:—

> Ah, and what greater pleasure can one have,
> Landed from sea, safe in one's home, to list
> With slumbering sense the swift descending rain?

(*Dindorf, fragment* 563.)

> Ah, and what greater pleasure could one have?

or, what more effective means to one's moral improvement? Democritus tells us we ought to pray that of the phantasms appearing in the circumambient air, such may present themselves to us as are propitious, and that we may rather meet with those that are agreeable to our natures and are good, than the evil and unfortunate; which is simply introducing into philosophy a doctrine untrue in itself, and leading to endless superstitions. My method, on the contrary, is, by the study of history, and by the familiarity acquired in writing, to habituate my memory to receive and retain images of the best and worthiest characters. I thus am enabled to free myself from any ignoble, base, or vicious impressions, contracted from the contagion of ill company that I may be unavoidably engaged in, by the remedy of turning my thoughts in a happy and calm temper to view these noble examples. Of this kind are those of Timoleon the Corinthian, and Paulus Æmilius, to write whose lives is my present business; men equally famous, not only for their virtues, but success; insomuch that they have left it doubtful whether they owe their greatest achievements to good fortune, or their own prudence and conduct.

The affairs of the Syracusans, before Timoleon was sent into Sicily, were in this posture: after Dion had driven out Dionysius the tyrant, he was slain by treachery, and those that had assisted him in delivering Syracuse were divided among themselves; and thus the city, by a continual change of governors, and a train of mischiefs that succeeded each other, became almost abandoned, while of the rest of Sicily, part was now utterly depopulated and desolate through long continuance of war, and most of the cities that had been left standing were in the hands of barbarians and soldiers out of employment, that were ready to embrace every turn of government. Such being the state of things, Dionysius takes the opportunity, and in the tenth year of his banishment, by the help of some mercenary troops he had got together, forces out Nysæus, then master of Syracuse, recovers all afresh, and is again settled in his dominion; and as at first he had been strangely deprived of the greatest and most absolute power that ever was, by a very small party, so now in a yet stranger manner, when in exile and of mean condition, he became the sovereign of those who had ejected him. All, therefore, that remained in Syracuse, had to serve under a tyrant, who at the best was of an ungentle nature and exasperated now to a degree of savageness by the late misfortunes and calamities he had suffered. The better and more distinguished citizens having timely retired thence to Hicetes, ruler of the Leontines, put themselves under his protection, and chose him for their general in the war; not that he was much preferable to any open and avowed tyrant; but they had no other sanctuary at present, and it gave them some ground of confidence, that he was of a Syracusan family, and had forces able to encounter those of Dionysius.

In the mean time, the Carthaginians appeared before Sicily with a great navy, watching when and where they might make a descent upon the island; and terror at this fleet made the Sicilians incline to send an embassy into Greece to demand succors from the Corinthians, whom they confided in rather than others, not only upon the account of their near kindred and the great benefits they had often received by trusting them, but because Corinth had ever shown herself attached to freedom and averse from tyranny, and had engaged in many noble wars, not for empire or aggrandizement, but for the sole liberty of the Greeks. But Hicetes, who made it the business of his command not so much to deliver the Syracusans from other tyrants, as to enslave them to himself, had already entered into some secret conferences with those of Carthage, while in public he commended the design of his Syracusan clients, and despatched ambassadors from himself, together with theirs, into Peloponnesus; not that he really desired any relief to come from there, but, in case the Corinthians, as was likely enough, on account of the troubles of Greece and occupation at home, should refuse their assistance, hoping then he should be able with less difficulty to dispose and incline things for the Carthaginian interest, and so make use of these foreign pretenders, as instruments and auxiliaries for himself, either against the Syracusans or Dionysius, as occasion served. This was discovered a while after.

The ambassadors being arrived, and their request known, the Corinthians, who had always a great concern for all their colonies and plantations, but especially for Syracuse, since by good fortune there was nothing to molest them in their own country, where they were enjoying peace and leisure at that time, readily and with one accord passed a vote for their assistance. And when they were deliberating about the choice of a captain for the expedition, and the magistrates were urging the claims of various aspirants for reputation, one of the crowd stood up and named Timoleon, son of Timodemus, who had long absented himself from public business, and had neither any thoughts of, nor the least pretension to, an employment of that nature. Some god or other, it might rather seem, had put it in the man's heart to mention him; such favor and good-will on the part of Fortune seemed at once to be shown in his election, and to accompany all his following actions, as though it were on purpose to commend his worth, and add grace and ornament to his personal virtues. As regards his parentage, both Timodemus his father, and his mother Demariste, were of high rank in the city; and as for himself, he was noted for his love of his country, and his gentleness of temper, except in his extreme hatred to tyrants and wicked men. His natural abilities for war were so happily tempered, that while a rare prudence might be seen in all the enterprises of his younger years, an equal courage showed itself in the last exploits of his declining age. He had an elder brother, whose name was Timophanes, who was every way unlike him, being indiscreet and rash, and infected by the suggestions of some friends and foreign soldiers, whom he kept always about him, with a passion for absolute power. He seemed to have a certain force and vehemence in all military service, and even to delight in dangers, and thus he took much with the people, and was advanced to the highest charges, as a vigorous and effective warrior; in the obtaining of which offices and promotions, Timoleon much assisted him, helping to conceal or at least to extenuate his errors, embellishing by his praise whatever was commendable in him, and setting off his good qualities to the best advantage.

It happened once in the battle fought by the Corinthians against the forces of Argos and Cleonæ, that Timoleon served among the infantry, when Timophanes, commanding their cavalry, was brought into extreme danger; as his horse being wounded fell forward, and threw him headlong amidst the enemies, while part of his companions dispersed at once in a panic, and the small number that remained, bearing up against a great multitude, had much ado to maintain any resistance. As soon, therefore, as Timoleon was aware of the accident, he ran hastily in to his brother's rescue, and covering the fallen Timophanes with his buckler, after having received abundance of darts, and several strokes by the sword upon his body and his armor, he at length with much difficulty obliged the enemies to retire, and brought off his brother alive and safe. But when the Corinthians, for fear of losing their city a second time, as they had once before, by admitting their allies, made a decree to maintain four hundred mercenaries for its security, and gave Timophanes the command over them, he, abandoning all regard to honor and equity, at once proceeded to put into execution his plans for making himself absolute, and bringing the place under his own power; and having cut off many principal citizens, uncondemned and without trial, who were most likely to hinder his design, he declared himself tyrant of Corinth; a procedure that infinitely afflicted Timoleon, to whom the wickedness of such a brother appeared to be his own reproach and calamity. He undertook to persuade him by reasoning, that, desisting from that wild and unhappy ambition, he would bethink himself how he should make the Corinthians some amends, and find out an expedient to remedy and correct the evils he had done them. When his single admonition was rejected and contemned by him he makes a second attempt, taking with him Æschylus his kinsman, brother to the wife of Timophanes, and a certain diviner, that was his friend, whom Theopompus in his history calls Satyrus, but Ephorus and Timæus mention in theirs by the name of Orthagoras. After a few days, then, he returns to his brother with this company, all three of them surrounding and earnestly importuning him upon the same subject, that now at length he would listen to reason, and be of another mind. But when Timophanes began first to laugh at the men's simplicity, and presently broke out into rage and indignation against them, Timoleon stepped aside from him and stood weeping with his face covered, while the other two, drawing out their swords, despatched him in a moment.

On the rumor of this act being soon scattered about, the better and more generous of the Corinthians highly applauded Timoleon for the hatred of wrong and the greatness of soul that had made him, though of a gentle disposition and full of love and kindness for his family, think the obligations to his country stronger than the ties of consanguinity, and prefer that which is good and just before gain and interest and his own particular advantage. For the same brother, who with so much bravery had been saved by him when he fought valiantly in the cause of Corinth, he had now as nobly sacrificed for enslaving her afterward by a base and treacherous usurpation. But then, on the other side, those that knew not how to live in a democracy, and had been used to make their humble court to the men of power, though they openly professed to rejoice at the death of the tyrant, nevertheless, secretly reviling Timoleon, as one that had committed an impious and abominable act, drove him into melancholy and dejection. And when he came to understand how heavily his mother took it, and that she likewise uttered the saddest complaints and most terrible imprecations against him, he went to satisfy and comfort her as to what had happened; and finding that she would not endure so much as to look upon him, but caused her doors to be shut, that he might

have no admission into her presence, with grief at
this he grew so disordered in his mind and so disconsolate, that he determined to put an end to his perplexity with his life, by abstaining from all manner
of sustenance. But through the care and diligence
of his friends, who were very instant with him, and
added force to their entreaties, he came to resolve
and promise at last, that he would endure living,
provided it might be in solitude, and remote from
company; so that, quitting all civil transactions and
commerce with the world, for a long while after his
first retirement he never came into Corinth, but
wandered up and down the fields, full of anxious
and tormenting thoughts, and spent his time in
desert places, at the farthest distance from society
and human intercourse. So true it is that the minds
of men are easily shaken and carried off from their
own sentiments through the casual commendation or
reproof of others, unless the judgments that we
make, and the purposes we conceive, be confirmed by
reason and philosophy, and thus strength and steadiness. An action must not only be just and laudable
in its own nature, but it must proceed likewise from
solid motives and a lasting principle, that so we may
fully and constantly approve the thing, and be perfectly satisfied in what we do; for otherwise, after
having put our resolution into practice, we shall out
of pure weakness come to be troubled at the performance, when the grace and goodliness, which rendered it before so amiable and pleasing to us, begin
to decay and wear out of our fancy; like greedy
people, who, seizing on the more delicious morsels
of any dish with a keen appetite, are presently disgusted when they grow full, and find themselves oppressed and uneasy now by what they before so
greedily desired. For a succeeding dislike spoils the

best of actions, and repentance makes that which was never so well done, become base and faulty; whereas the choice that is founded upon knowledge and wise reasoning, does not change by disappointment, or suffer us to repent, though it happen perchance to be less prosperous in the issue. And thus Phocion, of Athens, having always vigorously opposed the measures of Leosthenes, when success appeared to attend them, and he saw his countrymen rejoicing and offering sacrifice in honor of their victory, " I should have been as glad," said he to them, "that I myself had been the author of what Leosthenes has achieved for you, as I am that I gave you my own counsel against it." A more vehement reply is recorded to have been made by Aristides the Locrian, one of Plato's companions, to Dionysius the elder, who demanded one of his daughters in marriage: " I had rather," said he to him, " see the virgin in her grave, than in the palace of a tyrant." And when Dionysius, enraged at the affront, made his sons be put to death a while after, and then again insultingly asked, whether he were still in the same mind as to the disposal of his daughters, his answer was, " I cannot but grieve at the cruelty of your deeds, but am not sorry for the freedom of my own words." Such expressions as these may belong perhaps to a more sublime and accomplished virtue.

The grief, however, of Timoleon at what had been done, whether it arose from commiseration of his brother's fate, or the reverence he bore his mother, so shattered and broke his spirits, that for the space of almost twenty years, he had not offered to concern himself in any honorable or public action. When, therefore, he was pitched upon for a general, and joyfully accepted as such by the suffrages of the people, Teleclides, who was at that time the most powerful and distinguished man in Corinth, began to exhort him that he would act now like a man of worth and gallantry: "For," said he, "if you do bravely in this service, we shall believe that you delivered us from a tyrant; but if otherwise, that you killed your brother." While he was yet preparing to set sail, and enlisting soldiers to embark with him, there came letters to the Corinthians from Hicetes, plainly disclosing his revolt and treachery. For his ambassadors were no sooner gone for Corinth, but he openly joined the Carthaginians, negotiating that they might assist him to throw out Dionysius, and become master of Syracuse in his room. And fearing he might be disappointed of his aim, if troops and a commander should come from Corinth before this were effected, he sent a letter of advice thither, in all haste, to prevent their setting out, telling them they need not be at any cost and trouble upon his account, or run the hazard of a Sicilian voyage, especially since the Carthaginians, alliance with whom against Dionysius the slowness of their motions had compelled him to embrace, would dispute their passage, and lay in wait to attack them with a numerous fleet. This letter being publicly read, if any had been cold and indifferent before as to the expedition in hand, the indignation they now conceived against Hicetes so exasperated and inflamed them all, that they willingly contributed to supply Timoleon, and endeavored, with one accord, to hasten his departure.

When the vessels were equipped, and his soldiers every way provided for, the female priests of Proserpina had a dream or vision, wherein she and her mother Ceres appeared to them in a travelling garb, and were heard to say that they were going to sail with Timoleon into Sicily; whereupon the Corinthians, having built a sacred galley, devoted it to them and called it the galley of the goddesses. Timoleon went in person to Delphi, where he sacrificed to Apollo, and, descending into the place of prophecy, was surprised with the following marvellous occurrence. A riband with crowns and figures of victory embroidered upon it, slipped off from among the gifts that were there consecrated and hung up in the temple, and fell directly down upon his head; so that Apollo seemed already to crown him with success, and send him thence to conquer and triumph. He put to sea only with seven ships of Corinth, two of Corcyra, and a tenth which was furnished by the Leucadians; and when he was now entered into the deep by night, and carried with a prosperous gale, the heaven seemed all on a sudden to break open, and a bright spreading flame to issue forth from it, and hover over the ship he was in; and, having formed itself into a torch, not unlike those that are used in the mysteries, it began to steer the same course, and run along in their company, guiding them by its light to that quarter of Italy where they designed to go ashore. The soothsayers affirmed, that this apparition agreed with the dream of the holy women, since the goddesses were now visibly joining in the expedition, and sending this light from heaven before them: Sicily being thought sacred to Proserpina, as poets feign that the rape was committed there, and that the island was given her in dowry when she married Pluto.

These early demonstrations of divine favor greatly encouraged his whole army; so that, making all the speed they were able, by a voyage across the open sea, they were soon passing along the coast of Italy. But the tidings that came from Sicily much perplexed Timoleon, and disheartened his soldiers. For

Hicetes, having already beaten Dionysius out of the field, and reduced most of the quarters of Syracuse itself, now hemmed him in and besieged him in the citadel and what is called the Island, whither he was fled for his last refuge; while the Carthaginians, by agreement, were to make it their business to hinder Timoleon from landing in any port of Sicily; so that he and his party being driven back, they might with ease and at their own leisure divide the island among themselves. In pursuance of which design, the Carthaginians sent away twenty of their galleys to Rhegium, having aboard them certain ambassadors from Hicetes to Timoleon, who carried instructions suitable to these proceedings, specious amusements and plausible stories, to color and conceal dishonest purposes. They had order to propose and demand that Timoleon himself, if he liked the offer, should come to advise with Hicetes, and partake of all his conquests, but that he might send back his ships and forces to Corinth, since the war was in a manner finished, and the Carthaginians had blocked up the passage, determined to oppose them if they should try to force their way towards the shore. When, therefore, the Corinthians met with these envoys at Rhegium, and received their message, and saw the Phœnician vessels riding at anchor in the bay, they became keenly sensible of the abuse that was put upon them, and felt a general indignation against Hicetes, and great apprehensions for the Siceliots, whom they now plainly perceived to be as it were a prize and recompense to Hicetes on one side for his perfidy, and to the Carthaginians on the other for the sovereign power they secured to him. For it seemed utterly impossible to force and overbear the Carthaginian ships that lay before them and were double their number, as also to vanquish the victorious troops which Hicetes had with him in Syracuse, to take the lead of which very troops they had undertaken their voyage.

The case being thus, Timoleon, after some conference with the envoys of Hicetes and the Carthaginian captains, told them he should readily submit to their proposals (to what purpose would it be to refuse compliance?): he was desirous only, before his return to Corinth, that what had passed between them in private might be solemnly declared before the people of Rhegium, a Greek city, and a common friend to the parties; this, he said, would very much conduce to his own security and discharge; and they likewise would more strictly observe articles of agreement, on behalf of the Syracusans, which they had obliged themselves to in the presence of so many witnesses. The design of all which was, only to divert their attention, while he got an opportunity of slipping away from their fleet: a contrivance that all the principal Rhegians were privy and assisting to, who had a great desire that the affairs of Sicily should fall into Corinthian hands, and dreaded the consequences of having barbarian neighbors. An assembly was therefore called, and the gates shut, that the citizens might have no liberty to turn to other business; and a succession of speakers came forward, addressing the people at great length, to the same effect, without bringing the subject to any conclusion, making way each for another and purposely spinning out the time, till the Corinthian galleys should get clear of the haven; the Carthaginian commanders being detained there without any suspicion, as also Timoleon still remained present and gave signs as if he were just preparing to make an oration. But upon secret notice that the rest of the galleys were already gone off, and that his alone remained waiting for him, by the help and concealment of those Rhegians that were about the hustings and favored his departure, he made shift to slip away through the crowd, and, running down to the port, set sail with all speed; and having reached his other vessels, they came all safe to Tauromenium in Sicily, whither they had been formerly invited, and where they were now kindly received by Andromachus, then ruler of the city. This man was father of Timæus the historian, and incomparably the best of all those that bore sway in Sicily at that time, governing his citizens according to law and justice, and openly professing an aversion and enmity to all tyrants; upon which account he gave Timoleon leave to muster up his troops there, and to make that city the seat of war, persuading the inhabitants to join their arms with the Corinthian forces, and assist them in the design of delivering Sicily.

But the Carthaginians who were left in Rhegium perceiving, when the assembly was dissolved, that Timoleon had given them the go by, were not a little vexed to see themselves outwitted, much to the amusement of the Rhegians, who could not but smile to find Phœnicians complain of being cheated. However, they despatched a messenger aboard one of their galleys to Tauromenium, who, after much blustering in the insolent barbaric way, and many menaces to Andromachus if he did not forthwith send the Corinthians off, stretched out his hand with the inside upward, and then turning it down again, threatened he would handle their city even so, and turn it topsy-turvy in as little time, and with as much ease. Andromachus, laughing at the man's confidence, made no other reply, but, imitating his gesture, bid him hasten his own departure, unless he had a mind to see that kind of dexterity practised first upon the galley which brought him thither.

Hicetes, informed that Timoleon had made good his passage, was in great fear of what might follow, and sent to desire the Carthaginians that a large number of galleys might be ordered to attend and secure the coast. And now it was that the Syracusans began wholly to despair of safety, seeing the Carthaginians possessed of their haven, Hicetes master of the town, and Dionysius supreme in the citadel; while Timoleon had as yet but a slender hold of Sicily, as it were by the fringe or border of it, in the small city of the Tauromenians, with a feeble hope and a poor company; having but a thousand soldiers at the most, and no more provisions, either of corn or money, than were just necessary for the maintenance and the pay of that inconsiderable number. Nor did the other towns of Sicily confide in him, overpowered as they were with violence and outrage, and embittered against all that should offer to lead armies, by the treacherous conduct chiefly of Callippus, an Athenian, and Pharax, a Lacedæmonian captain, both of whom, after giving out that the design of their coming was to introduce liberty and depose tyrants, so tyrannized themselves, that the reign of former oppressors seemed to be a golden age in comparison, and the Sicilians began to consider those more happy who had expired in servitude, than any that had lived to see such a dismal freedom.

Looking, therefore, for no better usage from the Corinthian general, but imagining that it was only the same old course of things once more, specious pretences and false professions to allure them by fair hopes and kind promises into the obedience of a new master, they all, with one accord, unless it were the people of Adranum, suspected the exhortations, and rejected the overtures that were made them in his name. These were inhabitants of a small city, consecrated to Adranus, a certain god that was in high veneration throughout Sicily, and, as it happened, they were then at variance among themselves, insomuch that one party called in Hicetes and the Carthaginians to assist them, while the other sent proposals to Timoleon. It so fell out that these auxiliaries, striving which should be soonest, both arrived at Adranum about the same time; Hicetes bringing with him at least five thousand fighting men, while all the force Timoleon could make did not exceed twelve hundred. With these he marched out of Tauromenium, which was about three hundred and forty furlongs distant from that city. The first day he moved but slowly, and took up his quarters betimes after a short journey; but the day following he quickened his pace, and, having passed through much difficult ground, towards evening received advice that Hicetes was just approaching Adranum, and pitching his camp before it; upon which intelligence, his captains and other officers caused the vanguard to halt, that the army being refreshed, and having reposed a while, might engage the enemy with better heart. But Timoleon, coming up in haste, desired them not to stop for that reason, but rather use all possible diligence to surprise the enemy, whom probably they would now find in disorder, as having lately ended their march, and being taken up at present in erecting tents and preparing supper; which he had no sooner said, but laying hold of his buckler and putting himself in the front, he led them on as it were to certain victory. The braveness of such a leader made them all follow him with like courage and assurance. They were now within less than thirty furlongs of Adranum, which they quickly traversed, and immediately fell in upon the enemy, who were seized with confusion, and began to retire at their first approaches; one consequence of which was that, amidst so little opposition, and so early and general a flight, there were not many more than three hundred slain, and about twice the number made prisoners. Their camp and baggage, however, was all taken. The fortune of this onset soon induced the Adranitans to unlock their gates, and embrace the interest of Timoleon, to whom they recounted, with a mixture of affright and admiration, how, at the very minute of the encounter the doors of their temple flew open of their own accord, that the javelin also, which their god held in his hand, was observed to tremble at the point, and that drops of sweat had been seen running down his face: prodigies that not only presaged the victory then obtained, but were an omen, it seems, of all his future exploits, to which this first happy action gave the occasion.

For now the neighboring cities and potentates sent deputies one upon another, to seek his friendship and make offer of their service. Among the rest, Mamercus, the tyrant of Catana, an experienced warrior and a wealthy prince, made proposals of alliance with him, and, what was of greater importance still, Dionysius himself being now grown desperate, and wellnigh forced to surrender, despising Hicetes who had been thus shamefully baffled, and admiring the valor of Timoleon, found means to advertise him and his Corinthians that he should be content to deliver up himself and the citadel into their hands. Timoleon, gladly embracing this unlooked for advantage, sends away Euclides and Telemachus, two Corinthian captains, with four hundred men, for the seizure and custody of the castle, with directions to enter not all at once, or in open view, that being impracticable so long as the enemy kept guard, but by stealth, and in small companies. And so they took possession of the fortress, and the palace of Dionysius, with all the stores and ammunition he had prepared and laid up to maintain the war. They found a good number of horses, every variety of engines, a multitude of darts, and weapons to arm seventy thousand men (a magazine that had been formed from ancient time), besides two thousand soldiers that were then with him, whom he gave up with the rest for Timoleon's service. Dionysius himself, putting his treasure aboard, and taking a few friends, sailed away unobserved by Hicetes, and being brought to the camp of Timoleon, there first appeared in the humble dress of a private person, and was shortly after sent to Corinth with a single ship and a small sum of money. Born and educated in the most splendid court and the most absolute monarchy that ever was, which he held and kept up for the space of ten years succeeding his father's death, he had, after Dion's expedition, spent twelve other years in a continual agitation of wars and contests, and great variety of fortune, during which time all the mischiefs he had committed in his former reign were more than repaid by the ills he himself then suffered; since he lived to see the deaths of his sons in the prime and vigor of their age, and the rape of his daughters in the flower of their virginity, and the wicked abuse of his sister and his wife, who, after being first exposed to all the lawless insults of the soldiery, was then murdered with her children, and cast into the sea; the particulars of which are more exactly given in the life of Dion.

Upon the news of his landing at Corinth, there was hardly a man in Greece who had not the curiosity to come and view the late formidable tyrant, and say some words to him; part, rejoicing at his disasters, were led thither out of mere spite and hatred, that they might have the pleasure of trampling, as it were, on the ruins of his broken fortune; but others, letting their attention and their sympathy turn rather to the changes and revolutions of his life, could not but see in them a proof of the strength and potency with which divine and unseen causes operate amidst the weakness of human and visible things. For neither art nor nature did in that age produce any thing comparable to this work and wonder of fortune, which showed the very same man, that was not long before supreme monarch of Sicily, loitering about perhaps in the fish-market, or sitting in a perfumer's shop, drinking the diluted wine of taverns, or squabbling in the street with common women, or pretending to instruct the singing women of the theatre, and seriously disputing with them about the measure and harmony of pieces of music that were performed there. Such behavior on his part was variously criticized. He was thought by many to act thus out of pure compliance with his own natural indolent and vicious inclinations; while finer judges were of opinion, that in all this he was playing a politic part, with a design to be contemned among them, and that the Corinthians might not feel any apprehension or suspicion of his being uneasy under his reverse of fortune, or solicitous to retrieve it; to avoid which dangers, he purposely and against his true nature affected an appearance of folly and want of spirit in his private life and amusements.

However it be, there are sayings and repartees

of his left still upon record, which seem to show that he not ignobly accommodated himself to his present circumstances; as may appear in part from the ingenuousness of the avowal he made on coming to Leucadia, which, as well as Syracuse, was a Corinthian colony, where he told the inhabitants, that he found himself not unlike boys who have been in fault, who can talk cheerfully with their brothers, but are ashamed to see their father; so, likewise, he, he said, could gladly reside with them in that island, whereas he felt a certain awe upon his mind, which made him averse to the sight of Corinth, that was a common mother to them both. The thing is further evident from the reply he once made to a stranger in Corinth, who deriding him in a rude and scornful manner about the conferences he used to have with philosophers, whose company had been one of his pleasures while yet a monarch, and demanding, in fine, what he was the better now for all those wise and learned discourses of Plato, "Do you think," said he, "I have made no profit of his philosophy, when you see me bear my change of fortune as I do?" And when Aristoxenus the musician, and several others, desired to know how Plato offended him, and what had been the ground of his displeasure with him, he made answer, that, of the many evils attaching to the condition of sovereignty, the one greatest infelicity was that none of those who were accounted friends would venture to speak freely, or tell the plain truth; and that by means of such he had been deprived of Plato's kindness. At another time, when one of those pleasant companions that are desirous to pass for wits, in mockery to Dionysius, as if he were still the tyrant, shook out the folds of his cloak, as he was entering into the room where he was, to show there were no concealed weapons about him, Dionysius, by way of retort, observed, that he would prefer he would do so on leaving the room, as a security that he was carrying nothing off with him. And when Philip of Macedon, at a drinking party, began to speak in banter about the verses and tragedies which his father, Dionysius the elder, had left behind him, and pretended to wonder how he could get any time from his other business to compose such elaborate and ingenious pieces, he replied, very much to the purpose, " It was at those leisurable hours, which such as you and I, and those we call happy men, bestow upon our cups." Plato had not the opportunity to see Dionysius at Corinth, being already dead before he came thither; but Diogenes of Sinope, at their first meeting in the street there, saluted him with the ambiguous expression, " O Dionysius, how little you deserve your present life!" Upon which Dionysius stopped and replied, " I thank you, Diogenes, for your condolence." " Condole with you!" replied Diogenes; " do you not suppose that, on the contrary, I am indignant that such a slave as you, who, if you had your due, should have been let alone to grow old, and die in the state of tyranny, as your father did before you, should now enjoy the ease of private persons, and be here to sport and frolic it in our society?" So that when I compare those sad stories of Philistus, touching the daughters of Leptines, where he makes pitiful moan on their behalf, as fallen from all the blessings and advantages of powerful greatness to the miseries of an humble life, they seem to me like the lamentations of a woman who has lost her box of ointment, her purple dresses, and her golden trinkets. Such anecdotes will not, I conceive, be thought either foreign to my purpose of writing Lives, or unprofitable in themselves, by such readers as are not in too much haste, or busied and taken up with other concerns.

But if the misfortune of Dionysius appear strange and extraordinary, we shall have no less reason to wonder at the good fortune of Timoleon, who, within fifty days after his landing in Sicily, both recovered the citadel of Syracuse, and sent Dionysius an exile into Peloponnesus. This lucky beginning so animated the Corinthians, that they ordered him a supply of two thousand foot and two hundred horse, who, reaching Thurii, intended to cross over thence into Sicily; but finding the whole sea beset with Carthaginian ships, which made their passage impracticable, they were constrained to stop there, and watch their opportunity: which time, however, was employed in a noble action. For the Thurians, going out to war against their Bruttian enemies, left their city in charge with these Corinthian strangers, who defended it as carefully as if it had been their own country, and faithfully resigned it up again.

Hicetes, in the interim, continued still to besiege the castle of Syracuse, and hindered all provisions from coming in by sea to relieve the Corinthians that were in it. He had engaged also, and despatched towards Adranum, two unknown foreigners to assassinate Timoleon, who at no time kept any standing guard about his person, and was then altogether secure, diverting himself, without any apprehension, among the citizens of the place, it being a festival in honor of their gods. The two men that were sent, having casually heard that Timoleon was about to sacrifice, came directly into the temple with poniards under their cloaks, and pressing in among the crowd, by little and little got up close to the altar; but, as they were just looking for a sign from each other to begin the attempt, a third person struck one of them over the head with a sword, upon whose sudden fall, neither he that gave the blow, nor the partisan of him that received it, kept their stations any longer; but the one, making way with his bloody sword, put no stop to his flight, till he gained the top of a certain lofty precipice, while the other, laying hold of the altar, besought Timoleon to spare his life, and he would reveal to him the whole conspiracy. His pardon being granted, he confessed that both himself and his dead companion were sent thither purposely to slay him. While this discovery was made, he that killed the other conspirator had been fetched down from his sanctuary of the rock, loudly and often protesting, as he came along, that there was no injustice in the fact, as he had only taken righteous vengeance for his father's blood, whom this man had murdered before in the city of Leontini; the truth of which was attested by several there present, who could not choose but wonder too at the strange dexterity of fortune's operations, the facility with which she makes one event the spring and motion to something wholly different, uniting every scattered accident and lose particular and remote action, and interweaving them together to serve her purposes; so that things that in themselves seem to have no connection or interdependence whatsoever, become in her hands, so to say, the end and the beginning of each other. The Corinthians, satisfied as to the innocence of this seasonable feat, honored and rewarded the author with a present of ten pounds in their money,[3] since he had, as it were, lent the use of his just resentment to the tutelar genius that

[3] Ten Minas.

seemed to be protecting Timoleon, and had not preexpended this anger, so long ago conceived, but had reserved and deferred, under fortune's guidance, for his preservation, the revenge of a private quarrel.

But this fortunate escape had effects and consequences beyond the present, as it inspired the highest hopes and future expectations of Timoleon, making people reverence and protect him as a sacred person sent by heaven to avenge and redeem Sicily. Hicetes, having missed his aim in this enterprise, and perceiving, also, that many went off and sided with Timoleon, began to chide himself for his foolish modesty, that, when so considerable a force of the Carthaginians lay ready to be commanded by him, he had employed them hitherto by degrees and in small numbers, introducing their reinforcements by stealth and clandestinely, as if he had been ashamed of the action. Therefore, now laying aside his former nicety, he calls in Mago, their admiral, with his whole navy, who presently set sail, and seized upon the port with a formidable fleet of at least a hundred and fifty vessels, landing there sixty thousand foot, which were all lodged within the city of Syracuse; so that, in all men's opinion, the time anciently talked of and long expected, wherein Sicily should be subjugated by barbarians, was now come to its fatal period. For in all their preceding wars and many desperate conflicts with Sicily, the Carthaginians had never been able, before this, to take Syracuse; whereas Hicetes now receiving them, and putting the city into their hands, you might see it become now as it were a camp of barbarians. By this means, the Corinthian soldiers that kept the castle found themselves brought into great danger and hardship; as, besides that their provision grew scarce, and they began to be in want, because the havens were strictly guarded and blocked up, the enemy exercised them still with skirmishes and combats about their walls, and they were not only obliged to be continually in arms, but to divide and prepare themselves for assaults and encounters of every kind, and to repel every variety of the means of offence employed by a besieging army.

Timoleon made shift to relieve them in these straits, sending corn from Catana by small fishing-boats and little skiffs, which commonly gained a passage through the Carthaginian galleys in times of storm, stealing up when the blockading ships were driven apart and dispersed by the stress of weather; which Mago and Hicetes observing, they agreed to fall upon Catana, from whence these supplies were brought in to the besieged, and accordingly put off from Syracuse, taking with them the best soldiers in their whole army. Upon this, Neon the Corinthian, who was captain of those that kept the citadel, taking notice that the enemies who stayed there behind were very negligent and careless in keeping guard, made a sudden sally upon them as they lay scattered, and, killing some and putting others to flight, he took and possessed himself of that quarter which they call Acradina, and was thought to be the strongest and most impregnable part of Syracuse, a city made up and compacted, as it were, of several towns put together. Having thus stored himself with corn and money, he did not abandon the place, nor retire again into the castle, but fortifying the precincts of Acradina, and joining it by works to the citadel, he undertook the defence of both. Mago and Hicetes were now come near to Catana, when a horseman, despatched from Syracuse, brought them tidings that Acradina was taken; upon which they returned, in all haste, with great disorder and confusion, having neither been able to reduce the city they went against, nor to preserve that they were masters of.

These successes, indeed, were such as might leave foresight and courage a pretence still of disputing it with fortune, which contributed most to the result. But the next following event can scarcely be ascribed to any thing but pure felicity. The Corinthian soldiers who stayed at Thurii, partly for fear of the Carthaginian galleys which lay in wait for them under the command of Hanno, and partly because of tempestuous weather which had lasted for many days, and rendered the sea dangerous, took a resolution to march by land over the Bruttian territories, and, what with persuasion and force together, made good their passage through those barbarians to the city of Rhegium, the sea being still rough and raging as before. But Hanno, not expecting the Corinthians would venture out, and supposing it would be useless to wait there any longer, bethought himself, as he imagined, of a most ingenious and clever stratagem apt to delude and ensnare the enemy; in pursuance of which he commanded the seamen to crown themselves with garlands, and, adorning his galleys with bucklers both of the Greek and Carthaginian make, he sailed away for Syracuse in this triumphant equipage, and using all his oars as he passed under the castle with much shouting and laughter, cried out, on purpose to dishearten the besieged, that he was come from vanquishing and taking the Corinthian succors, which he fell upon at sea as they were passing over into Sicily. While he was thus trifling and playing his tricks before Syracuse, the Corinthians, now come as far as Rhegium, observing the coast clear, and that the wind

was laid as it were by miracle, to afford them in all
appearance a quiet and smooth passage, went immediately aboard on such little barks and fishing-boats
as were then at hand, and got over to Sicily with
such complete safety and in such an extraordinary
calm, that they drew their horses by the reins, swimming along by them as the vessels went across.

When they were all landed, Timoleon came to
receive them, and by their means at once obtained
possession of Messena, from whence he marched in
good order to Syracuse, trusting more to his late
prosperous achievements than his present strength,
as the whole army he had then with him did not
exceed the number of four thousand; Mago, however,
was troubled and fearful at the first notice of his
coming, and grew more apprehensive and jealous
still upon the following occasion. The marshes
about Syracuse, that receive a great deal of fresh
water, as well from springs as from lakes and rivers
discharging themselves into the sea, breed abundance
of eels, which may be always taken there in great
quantities by any that will fish for them. The
mercenary soldiers that served on both sides, were
wont to follow the sport together at their vacant
hours, and upon any cessation of arms; who, being
all Greeks, and having no cause of private enmity
to each other, as they would venture bravely in fight,
so in times of truce used to meet and converse
amicably together. And at this present time, while
engaged about this common business of fishing, they
fell into talk together; and some expressing their
admiration of the neighboring sea, and others telling
how much they were taken with the convenience and
commodiousness of the buildings and public works,
one of the Corinthian party took occasion to demand
of the others: "And is it possible that you who

are Grecians born, should be so forward to reduce
a city of this greatness, and enjoying so many rare
advantages, into the state of barbarism; and lend
your assistance to plant Carthaginians, that are the
worst and bloodiest of men, so much the nearer to
us? whereas you should rather wish there were many
more Sicilies to lie between them and Greece. Have
you so little sense as to believe, that they come
hither with an army, from the Pillars of Hercules
and the Atlantic Sea, to hazard themselves for the
establishment of Hicetes? who, if he had had the consideration which becomes a general, would never
have thrown out his ancestors and founders to bring
in the enemies of his country in the room of them,
when he might have enjoyed all suitable honor and
command, with consent of Timoleon and the rest of
Corinth." The Greeks that were in pay with
Hicetes, noising these discourses about their camp,
gave Mago some ground to suspect, as indeed he
had long sought for a pretence to be gone, that there
was treachery contrived against him; so that, although Hicetes entreated him to tarry, and made
it appear how much stronger they were than the
enemy, yet, conceiving they came far more short
of Timoleon in respect of courage and fortune, than
they surpassed him in number, he presently went
abroad, and set sail for Africa, letting Sicily escape
out of his hands with dishonor to himself, and for
such uncertain causes, that no human reason could
give an account of his departure.

The day after he went away, Timoleon came up
before the city, in array for a battle. But when he
and his company heard of this sudden flight, and
saw the docks all empty, they could not forbear
laughing at the cowardice of Mago, and in mockery
caused proclamation to be made through the city,

that a reward would be given to any one who could
bring them tidings whither the Carthaginian fleet
had conveyed itself from them. However, Hicetes
resolving to fight it out alone, and not quitting his
hold of the city, but sticking close to the quarters he
was in possession of, places that were well fortified
and not easy to be attacked, Timoleon divided his
forces into three parts, and fell himself upon the
side where the river Anapus ran, which was most
strong and difficult of access; and he commanded
those that were led by Isias, a Corinthian captain,
to make their assault from the post of Acradina,
while Dinarchus and Demaretus, that brought him
the last supply from Corinth, were, with a third
division, to attempt the quarter called Epipolæ. A
considerable impression being made from every side
at once, the soldiers of Hicetes were beaten off and
put to flight; and this,—that the city came to be
taken by storm, and fall suddenly into their hands,
upon the defeat and rout of the enemy,—we must in
all justice ascribe to the valor of the assailants, and
the wise conduct of their general; but that not so
much as a man of the Corinthians was either slain
or wounded in the action, this the good fortune of
Timoleon seems to challenge for her own work, as
though, in a sort of rivalry with his own personal
exertions, she made it her aim to exceed and obscure
his actions by her favors, that those who heard him
commended for his noble deeds might rather admire
the happiness, than the merit of them. For the
fame of what was done not only passed through all
Sicily, and filled Italy with wonder, but even Greece
itself, after a few days, came to ring with the greatness of his exploit; insomuch that those of Corinth,
who had as yet no certainty that their auxiliaries
were landed on the island, had tidings brought them

at the same time that they were safe and were conquerors. In so prosperous a course did affairs run, and such was the speed and celerity of execution with which fortune, as with a new ornament, set off the native lustres of the performance.

Timoleon, being master of the citadel, avoided the error which Dion had been guilty of. He spared not the place for the beauty and sumptuousness of its fabric, and, keeping clear of those suspicions which occasioned first the unpopularity and afterwards the fall of Dion, made a public crier give notice, that all the Syracusans who were willing to have a hand in the work, should bring pick-axes and mattocks, and other instruments, and help him to demolish the fortifications of the tyrants. When they all came up with one accord, looking upon that order and that day as the surest foundation of their liberty, they not only pulled down the castle, but overturned the palaces and monuments adjoining, and whatever else might preserve any memory of former tyrants. Having soon levelled and cleared the place, he there presently erected courts for administration of justice, gratifying the citizens by this means, and building popular government on the fall and ruin of tyranny. But since he had recovered a city destitute of inhabitants, some of them dead in civil wars and insurrections, and others being fled to escape tyrants, so that through solitude and want of people the great market-place of Syracuse was overgrown with such quantity of rank herbage that it became a pasture for their horses, the grooms lying along in the grass as they fed by them; while also other towns, very few excepted, were become full of stags and wild boars, so that those who had nothing else to do went frequently a hunting, and found game in the suburbs and about the walls; and not one of those who had possessed themselves of castles, or made garrisons in the country, could be persuaded to quit their present abode, or would accept an invitation to return back into the city, so much did they all dread and abhor the very name of assemblies and forms of government and public speaking, that had produced the greater part of those usurpers who had successively assumed a dominion over them,—Timoleon, therefore, with the Syracusans that remained, considering this vast desolation, and how little hope there was to have it otherwise supplied, thought good to write to the Corinthians, requesting that they would send a colony out of Greece to repeople Syracuse. For else the land about it would lie unimproved; and besides this, they expected to be involved in a greater war from Africa, having news brought them that Mago had killed himself, and that the Carthaginians, out of rage for his ill conduct in the late expedition, had caused his body to be nailed upon a cross, and that they were raising a mighty force, with design to make their descent upon Sicily the next summer.

These letters from Timoleon being delivered at Corinth, and the ambassadors of Syracuse beseeching them at the same time, that they would take upon them the care of their poor city, and once again become the founders of it, the Corinthians were not tempted by any feeling of cupidity to lay hold of the advantage. Nor did they seize and appropriate the city to themselves, but going about first to the games that are kept as sacred in Greece, and to the most numerously attended religious assemblages, they made publication by heralds, that the Corinthians, having destroyed the usurpation at Syracuse and driven out the tyrant, did thereby invite the

Syracusan exiles, and any other Siceliots, to return and inhabit the city, with full enjoyment of freedom under their own laws, the land being divided among them in just and equal proportions. And after this, sending messengers into Asia and the several islands where they understood that most of the scattered fugitives were then residing, they bade them all repair to Corinth, engaging that the Corinthians would afford them vessels and commanders, and a safe convoy, at their own charges, to Syracuse. Such generous proposals, being thus spread about, gained them the just and honorable recompense of general praise and benediction, for delivering the country from oppressors, and saving it from barbarians, and restoring it at length to the rightful owners of the place. These, when they were assembled at Corinth, and found how insufficient their company was, besought the Corinthians that they might have a supplement of other persons, as well out of their city as the rest of Greece, to go with them as joint-colonists; and so raising themselves to the number of ten thousand, they sailed together to Syracuse. By this time great multitudes, also, from Italy and Sicily, had flocked in to Timoleon, so that, as Athanis reports, their entire body amounted now to sixty thousand men. Among these he divided the whole territory, and sold the houses for a thousand talents; by which method, he both left it in the power of the old Syracusans to redeem their own, and made it a means also for raising a stock for the community, which had been so much impoverished of late, and was so unable to defray other expenses, and especially those of a war, that they exposed their very statues to sale, a regular process being observed, and sentence of auction passed upon each of them by majority of votes, as if they had been so many criminals taking their trial: in the course of which it is said that while condemnation was pronounced upon all other statues, that of the ancient usurper Gelo was exempted, out of admiration and honor and for the sake of the victory he gained over the Carthaginian forces at the river Himera.

Syracuse being thus happily revived, and replenished again by the general concourse of inhabitants from all parts, Timoleon was desirous now to rescue other cities from the like bondage, and wholly and once for all to extirpate arbitrary government out of Sicily. And for this purpose, marching into the territories of those that used it, he compelled Hicetes first to renounce the Carthaginian interest, and, demolishing the fortresses which were held by him, to live henceforth among the Leontinians as a private person. Leptines, also, the tyrant of Apollonia and divers other little towns, after some resistance made, seeing the danger he was in of being taken by force, surrendered himself; upon which Timoleon spared his life, and sent him away to Corinth, counting it a glorious thing that the mother city should expose to the view of other Greeks these Sicilian tyrants, living now in an exiled and a low condition. After this he returned to Syracuse, that he might have leisure to attend to the establishment of the new constitution, and assist Cephalus and Dionysius, who were sent from Corinth to make laws, in determining the most important points of it. In the meanwhile, desirous that his hired soldiers should not want action, but might rather enrich themselves by some plunder from the enemy, he despatched Dinarchus and Demaretus with a portion of them into the part of the island belonging to the Carthaginians, where they obliged several cities to revolt from the barbarians, and not only lived in great abundance themselves, but raised money from their spoil to carry on the war.

Meantime, the Carthaginians landed at the promontory of Lilybæum, bringing with them an army of seventy thousand men on board two hundred galleys, besides a thousand other vessels laden with engines of battery, chariots, corn, and other military stores, as if they did not intend to manage the war by piecemeal and in parts as heretofore, but to drive the Greeks altogether and at once out of all Sicily. And indeed it was a force sufficient to overpower the Siceliots, even though they had been at perfect union among themselves, and had never been enfeebled by intestine quarrels. Hearing that part of their subject territory was suffering devastation, they forthwith made toward the Corinthians with great fury, having Asdrubal and Hamilcar for their generals; the report of whose numbers and strength coming suddenly to Syracuse, the citizens were so terrified that hardly three thousand, among so many myriads of them, had the courage to take up arms and join Timoleon. The foreigners, serving for pay, were not above four thousand in all, and about a thousand of these grew faint-hearted by the way, and forsook Timoleon in his march towards the enemy, looking on him as frantic and distracted, destitute of the sense which might have been expected from his time of life, thus to venture out against an army of seventy thousand men, with no more than five thousand foot and a thousand horse; and, when he should have kept those forces to defend the city, choosing rather to remove them eight days' journey from Syracuse, so that if they were beaten from the field, they would have no retreat, nor any burial if they fell upon it. Timoleon, however, reckoned it some kind of advantage, that these had thus discovered themselves before the battle, and, encouraging the rest, led them with all speed to the river Crimesus, where it was told him the Carthaginians were drawn together.

As he was marching up an ascent, from the top of which they expected to have a view of the army and of the strength of the enemy, there met him by chance a train of mules loaded with parsley; which his soldiers conceived to be an ominous occurrence or ill-boding token, because this is the herb with which we not unfrequently adorn the sepulchres of the dead; and there is a proverb derived from the custom, used of one who is dangerously sick, that he has need of nothing but parsley. So, to ease their minds, and free them from any superstitious thoughts or forebodings of evil, Timoleon halted, and concluded an address, suitable to the occasion, by saying that a garland of triumph was here luckily brought them, and had fallen into their hands of its own accord, as an anticipation of victory: the same with which the Corinthians crown the victors in the Isthmian games, accounting chaplets of parsley the sacred wreath proper to their country; parsley being at that time still the emblem of victory at the Isthmian, as it is now at the Nemean sports; and it is not so very long ago that the pine [4] first began to be used in its place.

Timoleon, therefore, having thus bespoke his soldiers, took part of the parsley, and with it made him-

---

[4] The pine, sacred to Neptune, was the original Isthmian garland; then came parsley in its place, and then, not long before Plutarch's time, the pine was returned to again. There is a whole chapter in the Symposiaca (*V.*, *3*) devoted to a conversation on this subject. At a dinner at Corinth, given by Lucanius the priest, in the time of the games, the question is started, *why*

self a chaplet first, his captains and their companies all following the example of their leader. The soothsayers then, observing also two eagles on the wing towards them, one of which bore a snake struck through with her talons, and the other, as she flew, uttered a loud cry indicating boldness and assurance, at once showed them to the soldiers, who with one consent fell to supplicate the gods, and call them in to their assistance. It was now about the beginning of summer, and conclusion of the month called Thargelion, not far from the solstice; and the river sending up a thick mist, all the adjacent plain was at first darkened with the fog, so that for a while they could discern nothing from the enemy's camp; only a confused buzz and undistinguished mixture of voices came up to the hill from the distant motions and clamors of so vast a multitude. When the Corinthians had mounted, and stood on the top, and had laid down their bucklers to take breath and repose themselves, the sun coming round and drawing up the vapors from below, the gross foggy air that was now gathered and condensed above formed in a cloud upon the mountains; and, all the under places being clear and open, the river Crimesus appeared to them again, and they could descry the enemies passing over it, first with their formidable four horse chariots of war, and then ten thousand footmen bearing white shields, whom they guessed to be all Carthaginians, from the splendor of their arms, and the slowness and order of their march. And when now the

---

the pine is used? One of the company, a pretender to learning, shows by numerous quotations that in old times it was parsley. Lucanius, when he has finished, quietly points out by other citations that originally it was pine, and that parsley came in at a later time.

troops of various other nations, flowing in behind
them, began to throng for passage in a tumultuous
and unruly manner, Timoleon, perceiving that the
river gave them opportunity to single off whatever
number of their enemies they had a mind to engage
at once, and bidding his soldiers observe how their
forces were divided into two separate bodies by the
intervention of the stream, some being already over,
and others still to ford it, gave Demaretus command
to fall in upon the Carthaginians with his horse,
and disturb their ranks before they should be drawn
up into form of battle; and coming down into the
plain himself, forming his right and left wing of
other Sicilians, intermingling only a few strangers in
each, he placed the natives of Syracuse in the middle,
with the stoutest mercenaries he had about his own
person; and, waiting a little to observe the action
of his horse, when he saw they were not only hindered from grappling with the Carthaginians by the
armed chariots that ran to and fro before the army,
but forced continually to wheel about to escape having their ranks broken, and so to repeat their charges
anew, he took his buckler in his hand, and crying out
to the foot that they should follow him with courage
and confidence, he seemed to speak with a more than
human accent, and a voice stronger than ordinary;
whether it were that he naturally raised it so high in
the vehemence and ardor of his mind to assault the
enemy, or else, as many then thought, some god or
other spoke with him. When his soldiers quickly
gave an echo to it, and besought him to lead them on
without any further delay, he made a sign to the
horse, that they should draw off from the front
where the chariots were, and pass sidewards to attack
their enemies in the flank; then, making his vanguard firm by joining man to man and buckler to

buckler, he caused the trumpet to sound, and so bore in upon the Carthaginians.

They, for their part, stoutly received and sustained his first onset; and having their bodies armed with breastplates of iron, and helmets of brass on their heads, besides great bucklers to cover and secure them, they could easily repel the charge of the Greek spears. But when the business came to a decision by the sword, where mastery depends no less upon art than strength, all on a sudden from the mountain tops violent peals of thunder and vivid flashes of lightning broke out; following upon which the darkness, that had been hovering about the higher grounds and the crests of the hills, descending to the place of battle and bringing a tempest of rain and of wind and hail along with it, was driven upon the Greeks behind, and fell only at their backs, but discharged itself in the very faces of the barbarians, the rain beating on them, and the lightning dazzling them without cessation; annoyances that in many ways distressed at any rate the inexperienced, who had not been used to such hardships, and, in particular, the claps of thunder, and the noise of the rain and hail beating on their arms, kept them from hearing the commands of their officers. Besides which, the very mud also was a great hinderance to the Carthaginians, who were not lightly equipped, but, as I said before, loaded with heavy armor; and then their shirts underneath getting drenched, the foldings about the bosom filled with water, grew unwieldy and cumbersome to them as they fought, and made it easy for the Greeks to throw them down, and, when they were once down, impossible for them, under that weight, to disengage themselves and rise again with weapons in their hand. The river Crimesus, too, swollen partly by the rain, and partly by

the stoppage of its course with the numbers that
were passing through, overflowed its banks; and the
level ground by the side of it, being so situated as
to have a number of small ravines and hollows of
the hill-side descending upon it, was now filled with
rivulets and currents that had no certain channel, in
which the Carthaginians stumbled and rolled about,
and found themselves in great difficulty. So that, in
fine, the storm bearing still upon them, and the
Greeks having cut in pieces four hundred men of
their first ranks, the whole body of their army began
to fly. Great numbers were overtaken in the plain,
and put to the sword there; and many of them, as
they were making their way back through the river,
falling foul upon others that were yet coming over,
were borne away and overwhelmed by the waters;
but the major part, attempting to get up the hills
and so make their escape, were intercepted and
destroyed by the light-armed troops. It is said,
that of ten thousand who lay dead after the fight,
three thousand, at least, were Carthaginian citizens;
a heavy loss and great grief to their countrymen;
those that fell being men inferior to none among
them as to birth, wealth, or reputation. Nor do their
records mention that so many native Carthaginians
were ever cut off before in any one battle; as they
usually employed Africans, Spaniards, and Numidians in their wars, so that if they chanced to be defeated, it was still at the cost and damage of other
nations.

The Greeks easily discovered of what condition
and account the slain were, by the richness of their
spoils; for when they came to collect the booty, there
was little reckoning made either of brass or iron, so
abundant were better metals, and so common were
silver and gold. Passing over the river, they be-

came masters of their camp and carriages. As for captives, a great many of them were stolen away, and sold privately by the soldiers, but about five thousand were brought in and delivered up for the benefit of the public; two hundred of their chariots of war were also taken. The tent of Timoleon then presented a most glorious and magnificent appearance, being heaped up and hung round with every variety of spoils and military ornaments, among which there were a thousand breastplates of rare workmanship and beauty, and bucklers to the number of ten thousand. The victors being but few to strip so many that were vanquished, and having such valuable booty to occupy them, it was the third day after the fight before they could erect and finish the trophy of their conquest. Timoleon sent tidings of his victory to Corinth, with the best and goodliest arms he had taken as a proof of it; that he thus might render his country an object of emulation to the whole world when, of all the cities of Greece, men should there alone behold the chief temples adorned, not with Grecian spoils, nor offerings obtained by the bloodshed and plunder of their own countrymen and kindred, and attended, therefore, with sad and unhappy remembrances, but with such as had been stripped from barbarians and enemies to their nation, with the noblest titles inscribed upon them, titles telling of the justice as well as fortitude of the conquerors; namely, that the people of Corinth, and Timoleon their general, having redeemed the Greeks of Sicily from Carthaginian bondage, made oblation of these to the gods, in grateful acknowledgment of their favor.

Having done this, he left his hired soldiers in the enemy's country, to drive and carry away all they could throughout the subject-territory of Carthage, and so marched with the rest of his army to Syracuse, where he issued an edict for banishing the thousand mercenaries who had basely deserted him before the battle, and obliged them to quit the city before sunset. They, sailing into Italy, lost their lives there by the hands of the Bruttians, in spite of a public assurance of safety previously given them; thus receiving, from the divine power, a just reward of their own treachery. Mamercus, however, the tyrant of Catana, and Hicetes, after all, either envying Timoleon the glory of his exploits, or fearing him as one that would keep no agreement, nor have any peace with tyrants, made a league with the Carthaginians, and pressed them much to send a new army and commander into Sicily, unless they would be content to hazard all, and to be wholly ejected out of that island. And in consequence of this, Gisco was despatched with a navy of seventy sail. He took numerous Greek mercenaries also into pay, that being the first time they had ever been enlisted for the Carthaginian service; but then it seems the Carthaginians began to admire them, as the most irresistible soldiers of all mankind. Uniting their forces in the territory of Messena, they cut off four hundred of Timoleon's paid soldiers, and within the dependencies of Carthage, at a place called Hieræ, destroyed, by an ambuscade, the whole body of mercenaries that served under Euthymus the Leucadian; which accidents, however, made the good fortune of Timoleon accounted all the more remarkable, as these were the men that, with Philomelus of Phocis and Onomarchus, had forcibly broken into the temple of Apollo at Delphi, and were partakers with them in the sacrilege; so that, being hated and shunned by all, as persons under a curse, they were constrained to wander about in

Peloponnesus; when, for want of others, Timoleon was glad to take them into service in his expedition for Sicily, where they were successful in whatever enterprise they attempted under his conduct. But now, when all the important dangers were past, on his sending them out for the relief and defence of his party in several places, they perished and were destroyed at a distance from him, not all together, but in small parties; and the vengeance which was destined for them, so accommodating itself to the good fortune which guarded Timoleon as not to allow any harm or prejudice for good men to arise from the punishment of the wicked, the benevolence and kindness which the gods had for Timoleon was thus as distinctly recognized in his disasters as in his successes.

What most annoyed the Syracusans was their being insulted and mocked by the tyrants; as, for example, by Mamercus, who valued himself much upon his gift for writing poems and tragedies, and took occasion, when coming to present the gods with the bucklers of the hired soldiers whom he had killed, to make a boast of his victory in an insulting elegiac inscription:

> These shields, with purple, gold, and ivory wrought,
> Were won by us that but with poor ones fought.

After this, while Timoleon marched to Calauria, Hicetes made an inroad into the borders of Syracuse, where he met with considerable booty, and having done much mischief and havoc, returned back by Calauria itself, in contempt of Timoleon, and the slender force he had then with him. He, suffering Hicetes to pass forward, pursued him with his horsemen and light infantry, which Hicetes perceiving, crossed the river Damyrias, and then stood in a posture to receive him; the difficulty of the passage, and the height and steepness of the bank on each side, giving advantage enough to make him confident. A strange contention and dispute, meantime, among the officers of Timoleon, a little retarded the conflict; no one of them was willing to let another pass over before him to engage the enemy; each man claiming it as a right, to venture first and begin the onset; so that their fording was likely to be tumultuous and without order, a mere general struggle which should be the foremost. Timoleon, therefore, desiring to decide the quarrel by lot, took a ring from each of the pretenders, which he cast into his own cloak, and, after he had shaken all together, the first he drew out had, by good fortune, the figure of a trophy engraved as a seal upon it; at the sight of which the young captains all shouted for joy, and, without waiting any longer to see how chance would determine it for the rest, took every man his way through the river with all the speed they could make, and fell to blows with the enemies, who were not able to bear up against the violence of their attack, but fled in haste and left their arms behind them all alike, and a thousand dead upon the place.

Not long after, Timoleon, marching up to the city of the Leontines, took Hicetes alive, and his son Eupolemus, and Euthymus, the commander of his horse, who were bound and brought to him by their own soldiers. Hicetes and the stripling his son were then executed as tyrants and traitors; and Euthymus, though a brave man, and one of singular courage, could obtain no mercy, because he was charged with contemptuous language in disparagement of the Corinthians when they first sent their forces into Sicily: it is said that he told the Leontini

TIMOLEON

in a speech, that the news did not sound terrible, nor was any great danger to be feared because of

Corinthian women coming out of doors.[5]

So true is it that men are usually more stung and galled by reproachful words than hostile actions; and they bear an affront with less patience than an injury: to do harm and mischief by deeds is counted pardonable from enemies, as nothing less can be expected in a state of war; whereas virulent and contumelious words appear to be the expression of needless hatred, and to proceed from an excess of rancor.

When Timoleon came back to Syracuse, the citizens brought the wives and daughters of Hicetes and his son to a public trial, and condemned and put them to death. This seems to be the least pleasing action of Timoleon's life; since if he had interposed, the unhappy women would have been spared. He would appear to have disregarded the thing, and to have given them up to the citizens, who were eager to take vengeance for the wrongs done to Dion, who expelled Dionysius; since it was this very Hicetes, who took Arete the wife, and Aristomache the sister of Dion, with a son that had not yet passed his childhood, and threw them all together into the sea alive, as related in the life of Dion.

After this, he moved towards Catana against Mamercus, who gave him battle near the river Abolus,[6] and was overthrown and put to flight, los-

---

[5] "*Corinthian women, coming out of doors,*
  Blame not, if thus ye see me,"
are the words with which Medea first enters the stage and addresses the chorus in Euripides's tragedy.

[6] Or Alabus.

ing above two thousand men, a considerable part of whom were the Phœnician troops sent by Gisco to his assistance. After this defeat, the Carthaginians sued for peace; which was granted on the conditions that they should confine themselves to the country within the river Lycus,[7] that those of the inhabitants who wished to remove to the Syracusan territories should be allowed to depart with their whole families and fortunes, and, lastly, that Carthage should renounce all engagements to the tyrants. Mamercus, now forsaken and despairing of success, took ship for Italy with the design of bringing in the Lucanians against Timoleon and the people of Syracuse; but the men in his galleys turning back and landing again and delivering up Catana to Timoleon, thus obliged him to fly for his own safety to Messena, where Hippo was tyrant. Timoleon, however, coming up against them, and besieging the city both by sea and land, Hippo, fearful of the event, endeavored to slip away in a vessel; which the people of Messena surprised as it was putting off, and seizing on his person, and bringing all their children from school into the theatre, to witness the glorious spectacle of a tyrant punished, they first publicly scourged and then put him to death. Mamercus made surrender of himself to Timoleon, with the proviso, that he should be tried at Syracuse, and Timoleon should take no part in his accusation. Thither he was brought accordingly, and presenting himself to plead before the people, he essayed to pronounce an oration he had long before composed in his own defence; but finding himself interrupted by noise and clamors, and observing from their aspect and demeanor that the assembly was inexorable, he threw off his upper garment, and running across the theatre as hard as he could,

[7] Or Halycus.

dashed his head against one of the stones under the seats with intention to have killed himself; but he had not the fortune to perish, as he designed, but was taken up alive, and suffered the death of a robber.

Thus did Timoleon cut the nerves of tyranny, and put a period to their wars; and, whereas, at his first entering upon Sicily, the island was as it were become wild again, and was hateful to the very natives on account of the evils and miseries they suffered there, he so civilized and restored it, and rendered it so desirable to all men, that even strangers now came by sea to inhabit those towns and places which their own citizens had formerly forsaken and left desolate. Agrigentum and Gela, two famous cities that had been ruined and laid waste by the Carthaginians after the Attic war, were then peopled again, the one by Megellus and Pheristus from Elea, the other by Gorgus, from the island of Ceos, partly with new settlers, partly with the old inhabitants whom they collected again from various parts; to all of whom Timoleon not only afforded a secure and peaceable abode after so obstinate a war, but was further so zealous in assisting and providing for them that he was honored among them as their founder. Similar feelings also possessed to such a degree all the rest of the Sicilians, that there was no proposal for peace, nor reformation of laws, nor assignation of land, nor reconstitution of government, which they could think well of, unless he lent his aid as a chief architect, to finish and adorn the work, and superadd some touches from his own hand, which might render it pleasing both to God and man.

Although Greece had in his time produced several persons of extraordinary worth, and much renowned for their achievements, such as Timotheus and Agesilaus and Pelopidas and (Timoleon's chief model) Epaminondas, yet the lustre of their best actions was obscured by a degree of violence and labor, insomuch that some of them were matter of blame and of repentance; whereas there is not any one act of Timoleon's, setting aside the necessity he was placed under in reference to his brother, to which, as Timæus observes, we may not fitly apply that exclamation of Sophocles:—

> O gods! what Venus, or what grace divine,
> Did here with human workmanship combine? [8]

For as the poetry of Antimachus, and the painting of Dionysius, the artists of Colophon, though full of force and vigor, yet appeared to be strained and elaborate in comparison with the pictures of Nicomachus and the verses of Homer, which, besides their general strength and beauty, have the peculiar charm of seeming to have been executed with perfect ease and readiness; so the expeditions and acts of Epaminondas or Agesilaus, that were full of toil and effort, when compared with the easy and natural as well as noble and glorious achievements of Timoleon, compel our fair and unbiassed judgment to pronounce the latter not indeed the effect of fortune, but the success of fortunate merit. Though he himself indeed ascribed that success to the sole favor of fortune; and both in the letters which he wrote to his friends at Corinth, and in the speeches he made to the people of Syracuse, he would say, that he was thankful unto God, who, designing to save Sicily, was pleased to honor him with the name

[8] The lines from Sophocles are a fragment of a lost play. (*Dindorf*, 710.)

TIMOLEON

and title of the deliverance he vouchsafed it. And having built a chapel in his house, he there sacrificed to Good Hap,⁹ as a deity that had favored him, and devoted the house itself to the Sacred Genius; it being a house which the Syracusans had selected for him, as a special reward and monument of his brave exploits, granting him together with it the most agreeable and beautiful piece of land in the whole country, where he kept his residence for the most part, and enjoyed a private life with his wife and children, who came to him from Corinth. For he returned thither no more, unwilling to be concerned in the broils and tumults of Greece, or to expose himself to public envy (the fatal mischief which great commanders continually run into, from the insatiable appetite for honors and authority); but wisely chose to spend the remainder of his days in Sicily, and there partake of the blessings he himself had procured, the greatest of which was, to behold so many cities flourish, and so many thousands of people live happy through his means.

As, however, not only, as Simonides says, " On every lark must grow a crest," ¹⁰ but also in every democracy there must spring up a false accuser, so was it at Syracuse: two of their popular spokesmen, Laphystius and Demænetus by name, fell to slander Timoleon. The former of whom

---

⁹ *Automatia* in Greek; almost equivalent to Spontaneousness; his successes had come as it were of themselves. The Sacred Genius, or *Dæmon*, like the genius or *dæmon* of Socrates. His instinctive, and apparently unreasoning decisions, had been attended with such happy results as to make him unavoidably refer them to something out of himself, to some preternatural guidance.

¹⁰ Literally, " On every Corydallus." This is itself the distinctive name of the crested, or tufted lark.

requiring him to put in sureties that he would answer to an indictment that would be brought against him, Timoleon would not suffer the citizens, who were incensed at this demand, to oppose it or hinder the proceeding, since he of his own accord had been, he said, at all that trouble, and run so many dangerous risks for this very end and purpose, that every one who wished to try matters by law should freely have recourse to it. And when Demænetus, in a full audience of the people, laid several things to his charge which had been done while he was general, he made no other reply to him, but only said he was much indebted to the gods for granting the request he had so often made them, namely, that he might live to see the Syracusans enjoy that liberty of speech which they now seemed to be masters of.

Timoleon, therefore, having by confession of all done the greatest and the noblest things of any Greek of his age, and alone distinguished himself in those actions to which their orators and philosophers, in their harangues and panegyrics at their solemn national assemblies, used to exhort and incite the Greeks, and being withdrawn beforehand by happy fortune, unspotted and without blood, from the calamities of civil war, in which ancient Greece was soon after involved; having also given full proof, as of his sage conduct and manly courage to the barbarians and tyrants, so of his justice and gentleness to the Greeks, and his friends in general; having raised, too, the greater part of those trophies he won in battle, without any tears shed or any mourning worn by the citizens either of Syracuse or Corinth, and within less than eight years' space delivered Sicily from its inveterate grievances and intestine distempers, and given it up free to the native inhabitants, began, as he was now growing old, to find his eyes fail, and awhile after became perfectly blind. Not that he had done any thing himself which might occasion this defect, or was deprived of his sight by any outrage of fortune; it seems rather to have been some inbred and hereditary weakness that was founded in natural causes, which by length of time came to discover itself. For it is said, that several of his kindred and family were subject to the like gradual decay, and lost all use of their eyes, as he did, in their declining years. Athanis the historian tells us, that even during the war against Hippo and Mamercus, while he was in his camp at Mylæ, there appeared a white speck within his eye, from whence all could foresee the deprivation that was coming on him; this, however, did not hinder him then from continuing the siege, and prosecuting the war, till he got both the tyrants into his power; but upon his coming back to Syracuse, he presently resigned the authority of sole commander, and besought the citizens to excuse him from any further service, since things were already brought to so fair an issue. Nor is it so much to be wondered, that he himself should bear the misfortune without any marks of trouble; but the respect and gratitude which the Syracusans showed him when he was entirely blind, may justly deserve our admiration. They used to go themselves to visit him in troops, and brought all the strangers that travelled through their country to his house and manor, that they also might have the pleasure to see their noble benefactor; making it the great matter of their joy and exultation, that when, after so many brave and happy exploits, he might have returned with triumph into Greece, he should disregard all the glorious preparations that were there made to receive him, and choose rather to stay here and end his days among them. Of the various things decreed and done in honor of Timoleon, I consider one most signal testimony to have been the vote which they passed, that, whenever they should be at war with any foreign nation, they should make use of none but a Corinthian general. The method, also, of their proceeding in council, was a noble demonstration of the same deference for his person. For, determining matters of less consequence themselves, they always called him to advise in the more difficult cases, and such as were of greater moment. He was, on these occasions, carried through the market-place in a litter, and brought in, sitting, into the theatre, where the people with one voice saluted him by his name; and then, after returning the courtesy, and pausing for a time, till the noise of their gratulations and blessings began to cease, he heard the business in debate, and delivered his opinion. This being confirmed by a general suffrage, his servants went back with the litter through the midst of the assembly, the people waiting on him out with acclamations and applauses, and then returning to consider other public matters, which they could despatch in his absence. Being thus cherished in his old age, with all the respect and tenderness due to a common father, he was seized with a very slight indisposition, which however was sufficient, with the aid of time, to put a period to his life. There was an allotment then of certain days given, within the space of which the Syracusans were to provide whatever should be necessary for his burial, and all the neighboring country people and strangers were to make their appearance in a body; so that the funeral pomp was set out with great splendor and magnificence in all other respects, and the bier, decked with ornaments and trophies, was borne by a select body of young men over that ground where the palace and castle of Dionysius stood, before they were demolished by Timoleon. There attended on the solemnity several thousands of men and women, all crowned with flowers, and arrayed in fresh and clean attire, which made it look like the procession of a public festival; while the language of all, and their tears mingling with their praise and benediction of the dead Timoleon, manifestly showed that it was not any superficial honor, or commanded homage, which they paid him, but the testimony of a just sorrow for his death, and the expression of true affection. The bier at length being placed upon the pile of wood that was kindled to consume his corpse, Demetrius, one of their loudest criers, proceeded to read a proclamation to the following purpose: "The people of Syracuse has made a special decree to inter Timoleon, the son of Timodemus, the Corinthian, at the common expense of two hundred minas, and to honor his memory forever, by the establishment of annual prizes to be competed for in music, and horseraces, and all sorts of bodily exercise; and this, because he suppressed the tyrants, overthrew the barbarians, replenished the principal cities, that were desolate, with new inhabitants, and then restored the Sicilian Greeks to the privilege of living by their own laws." Besides this, they made a tomb for him in the market-place, which they afterwards built round with colonnades, and attached to it places of exercise for the young men, and gave it the name of the Timoleonteum. And keeping to that form and order of civil policy and observing those laws and constitutions which he left them, they lived themselves a long time in great prosperity.

ÆMILIUS PAULUS[1]

TRANSLATED BY MR. JOSEPH ARROWSMITH, LATE FELLOW OF TRINITY COLLEGE, CAMBRIDGE

ALMOST all historians agree that the Æmilii were one of the ancient and patrician houses in Rome; and those authors who affirm that king Numa was pupil to Pythagoras, tell us that the first who gave the name to his posterity was Mamercus, the son of Pythagoras, who, for his grace and address in speaking, was called Æmilius. Most of this race that have risen through their merit to reputation, also enjoyed good fortune; and even the misfortune of Lucius Paulus at the battle of Cannæ, gave testimony to his wisdom and valor. For, not being able to persuade his colleague not to hazard the battle, he, though against his judgment, joined with him in the contest, but was no companion in his flight: on the contrary, when he that was so resolute to engage deserted him in the midst of danger, he kept the field, and died fighting. This Æmilius had a daughter named Æmilia, who was married to Scipio the Great, and a son Paulus, who is the subject of my present history.

In his early manhood, which fell at a time when Rome was flourishing with illustrious characters, he was distinguished for not attaching himself to the studies usual with the young men of mark of that

[1] Born about 230 or 229 B.C., since at the time of his second consulship in 168 he was upwards of sixty years of age. He was one of the best specimens of the Roman nobles. Throughout his life of conquest and triumph he maintained a pure and unspotted character.—DR. WILLIAM SMITH.

age, nor treading the same paths to fame. For he did not practise oratory with a view to pleading causes, nor would he stoop to salute, embrace, and entertain the vulgar, which were the usual insinuating arts by which many grew popular. Not that he was incapable of either, but he chose to purchase a much more lasting glory by his valor, justice, and integrity, and in these virtues he soon outstripped all his equals.

The first honorable office he aspired to was that of ædile, which he carried against twelve competitors of such merit, that all of them in process of time were consuls. Being afterwards chosen into the number of priests called augurs, appointed amongst the Romans to observe and register divinations made by the flight of birds or prodigies in the air, he so carefully studied the ancient customs of his country, and so thoroughly understood the religion of his ancestors, that this office, which was before only esteemed a title of honor and merely upon that account sought after, by his means rose to the rank of one of the highest arts, and gave a confirmation to the correctness of the definition which some philosophers have given of religion, that it is the science of worshipping the gods. When he performed any part of his duty, he did it with great skill and utmost care, making it, when he was engaged in it, his only business, not omitting any one ceremony, or adding the least circumstance, but always insisting, with his companions of the same order, even on points that might seem inconsiderable, and urging upon them, that though they might think the deity was easily pacified, and ready to forgive faults of inadvertency, yet any such laxity was a very dangerous thing for a commonwealth to allow: because no man ever began the disturbance of his country's peace by a notorious breach of its laws; and those who are careless in trifles, give a precedent for remissness in important duties. Nor was he less severe, in requiring and observing the ancient Roman discipline in military affairs; not endeavoring, when he had the command, to ingratiate himself with his soldiers by popular flattery, though this custom prevailed at that time amongst many, who, by favor and gentleness to those that were under them in their first employment, sought to be promoted to a second; but, by instructing them in the laws of military discipline with the same care and exactness a priest would use in teaching ceremonies and dreadful mysteries, and by severity to such as transgressed and contemned those laws, he maintained his country in its former greatness, esteeming victory over enemies itself but as an accessory to the proper training and disciplining of the citizens.

Whilst the Romans were engaged in war with Antiochus the Great, against whom their most experienced commanders were employed, there arose another war in the west, and they were all up in arms in Spain. Thither they sent Æmilius, in the quality of prætor, not with six axes, which number other prætors were accustomed to have carried before them, but with twelve; so that in his prætorship he was honored with the dignity of a consul. He twice overcame the barbarians in battle, thirty thousand of whom were slain: successes chiefly to be ascribed to the wisdom and conduct of the commander, who by his great skill in choosing the advantage of the ground, and making the onset at the passage of a river, gave his soldiers an easy victory. Having made himself master of two hundred and fifty cities, whose inhabitants voluntarily yielded, and bound themselves by oath to fidelity, he left the province in peace, and returned to Rome, not enriching himself a drachma by the war. And, indeed, in general, he was but remiss in making money; though he always lived freely and generously on what he had, which was so far from being excessive, that after his death there was but barely enough left to answer his wife's dowry.

His first wife was Papiria, the daughter of Maso, who had formerly been consul. With her he lived a considerable time in wedlock, and then divorced her, though she had made him the father of noble children; being mother of the renowned Scipio, and Fabius Maximus. The reason of this separation has not come to our knowledge; but there seems to be a truth conveyed in the account of another Roman's being divorced from his wife, which may be applicable here. This person being highly blamed by his friends, who demanded, Was she not chaste? was she not fair? was she not fruitful? holding out his shoe, asked them, Whether it was not new? and well made? Yet, added he, none of you can tell where it pinches me. Certain it is, that great and open faults have often led to no separation; while mere petty repeated annoyances, arising from unpleasantness or incongruity of character, have been the occasion of such estrangement as to make it impossible for man and wife to live together with any content.

Æmilius, having thus put away Papiria, married a second wife, by whom he had two sons, whom he brought up in his own house, transferring the two former into the greatest and most noble families of Rome. The elder was adopted into the house of Fabius Maximus, who was five times consul; the younger, by the son of Scipio Africanus, his cousin-german, and was by him named Scipio.

Of the daughters of Æmilius, one was married to the son of Cato, the other to Ælius Tubero, a most worthy man, and the one Roman who best succeeded in combining liberal habits with poverty. For there were sixteen near relations, all of them of the family of the Ælii, possessed of but one farm, which sufficed them all, whilst one small house, or rather cottage, contained them, their numerous offspring, and their wives; amongst whom was the daughter of our Æmilius, who, although her father had been twice consul, and had twice triumphed, was not ashamed of her husband's poverty, but proud of his virtue that kept him poor. Far otherwise it is with the brothers and relations of this age, who, unless whole tracts of land, or at least walls and rivers, part their inheritances, and keep them at a distance, never cease from mutual quarrels. History suggests a variety of good counsel of this sort, by the way, to those who desire to learn and improve.

To proceed: Æmilius, being chosen consul, waged war with the Ligurians, or Ligustines, a people near the Alps. They were a bold and warlike nation, and their neighborhood to the Romans had begun to give them skill in the arts of war. They occupy the further parts of Italy ending under the Alps, and those parts of the Alps themselves which are washed by the Tuscan sea and face towards Africa, mingled there with Gauls and Iberians of the coast. Besides, at that time they had turned their thoughts to the sea, and sailing as far as the Pillars of Hercules in light vessels fitted for that purpose, robbed and destroyed all that trafficked in those parts. They, with an army of forty thousand, waited the coming of Æmilius, who brought with him not above eight thousand, so that the enemy was five to one when they engaged; yet he vanquished and put them to flight, forcing them to retire into their walled towns, and in this condition offered them fair conditions of accommodation; it being the policy of the Romans not utterly to destroy the Ligurians, because they were a sort of guard and bulwark against frequent attempts of the Gauls to overrun Italy. Trusting wholly therefore to Æmilius, they delivered up their towns and shipping into his hands. He, at the utmost, razed only the fortifications, and delivered their towns to them again, but took away all their shipping with him, leaving them no vessels bigger than those of three oars, and set at liberty great numbers of prisoners they had taken both by sea and land, strangers as well as Romans. These were the acts most worthy of remark in his first consulship.

Afterwards he frequently intimated his desire of being a second time consul, and was once candidate; but, meeting with a repulse and being passed by, he gave up all thought of it, and devoted himself to his duties as augur, and to the education of his children, whom he not only brought up, as he himself had been, in the Roman and ancient discipline, but also with unusual zeal in that of Greece. To this purpose he not only procured masters to teach them grammar, logic, and rhetoric, but had for them also preceptors in modelling and drawing, managers of horses and dogs, and instructors in field sports, all from Greece. And, if he was not hindered by public affairs, he himself would be with them at their studies, and see them perform their exercises, being the most affectionate father in Rome.

This was the time, in public matters, when the Romans were engaged in war with Perseus, king of the Macedonians, and great complaints were made of their commanders, who, either through their want of skill or courage, were conducting matters so shamefully, that they did less hurt to the enemy than they received from him. They that not long before had forced Antiochus the Great to quit the rest of Asia, to retire beyond Mount Taurus, and confine himself to Syria, glad to buy his peace with fifteen thousand talents; they that not long since had vanquished king Philip in Thessaly, and freed the Greeks from the Macedonian yoke; nay, had overcome Hannibal himself, who far surpassed all kings in daring and power,—thought it scorn that Perseus should think himself an enemy fit to match the Romans, and to be able to wage war with them so long on equal terms, with the remainder only of his father's routed forces; not being aware that Philip after his defeat had greatly improved both the strength and discipline of the Macedonian army. To make which appear, I shall briefly recount the story from the beginning.

Antigonus, the most powerful amongst the captains and successors of Alexander, having obtained for himself and his posterity the title of king, had a son named Demetrius, father to Antigonus, called Gonatas, and he had a son Demetrius, who, reigning some short time, died and left a young son called Philip. The chief men of Macedon, fearing great confusion might arise in his minority, called in Antigonus, cousin-german to the late king, and married him to the widow, the mother of Philip. At first they only styled him regent and general, but, when they found by experience that he governed the kingdom with moderation and to general advantage, gave him the title of king. This was he that was surnamed Doson,[2] as if he was a great promiser,

[2] Going-to-give.

and a bad performer. To him succeeded Philip, who in his youth gave great hopes of equalling the best of kings, and that he one day would restore Macedon to its former state and dignity, and prove himself the one man able to check the power of the Romans, now rising and extending over the whole world. But, being vanquished in a pitched battle by Titus Flamininus near Scotussa, his resolution failed, and he yielded himself and all that he had to the mercy of the Romans, well contented that he could escape with paying a small tribute. Yet afterwards, recollecting himself, he bore it with great impatience, and thought he lived rather like a slave that was pleased with ease, than a man of sense and courage, whilst he held his kingdom at the pleasure of his conquerors; which made him turn his whole mind to war, and prepare himself with as much cunning and privacy as possible. To this end, he left his cities on the high roads and sea-coast ungarrisoned, and almost desolate, that they might seem inconsiderable; in the meantime, collecting large forces up the country, and furnishing his inland posts, strong holds, and towns, with arms, money, and men fit for service, he thus provided himself for war, and yet kept his preparations close. He had in his armory arms for thirty thousand men; in granaries in places of strength, eight millions of bushels of corn, and as much ready money as would defray the charge of maintaining ten thousand mercenary soldiers for ten years in defence of the country. But before he could put these things into motion, and carry his designs into effect, he died for grief and anguish of mind, being sensible he had put his innocent son Demetrius to death, upon the calumnies of one that was far more guilty. Perseus, his son that survived, inherited his hatred to the Romans as well as his kingdom, but was incompetent to carry out his designs, through want of courage, and the viciousness of a character in which, among faults and diseases of various sorts, covetousness bore the chief place. There is a statement also of his not being true born; that the wife of king Philip took him from his mother Gnathænion (a woman of Argos, that earned her living as a seamstress), as soon as he was born, and passed him upon her husband as her own. And this might be the chief cause of his contriving the death of Demetrius; as he might well fear, that so long as there was a lawful successor in the family, there was no security that his spurious birth might not be revealed.

Notwithstanding all this, and though his spirit was so mean, and temper so sordid, yet, trusting to the strength of his resources, he engaged in a war with the Romans, and for a long time maintained it; repulsing and even vanquishing some generals of consular dignity, and some great armies and fleets. He routed Publius Licinius, who was the first that invaded Macedonia, in a cavalry battle, slew twenty-five hundred practised soldiers, and took six hundred prisoners; and, surprising their fleet as they rode at anchor before Oreus, he took twenty ships of burden with all their lading, sunk the rest that were freighted with corn, and, besides this, made himself master of four galleys with five banks of oars. He fought a second battle with Hostilius, a consular officer, as he was making his way into the country at Elimiæ, and forced him to retreat; and, when he afterwards by stealth designed an invasion through Thessaly, challenged him to fight, which the other feared to accept. Nay more, to show his contempt of the Romans, and that he wanted employment, as a war by the by, he made an expedition against the Dardanians, in which he slew ten thousand of those barbarian people, and brought a great spoil away. He privately, moreover, solicited the Gauls (also called Basternæ), a warlike nation, and famous for horsemen, dwelling near the Danube; and incited the Illyrians, by the means of Genthius their king, to join with him in the war. It was also reported, that the barbarians, allured by promise of rewards, were to make an irruption into Italy, through the lower Gaul by the shore of the Adriatic Sea.

The Romans, being advertised of these things, thought it necessary no longer to choose their commanders by favor or solicitation, but of their own motion to select a general of wisdom and capacity for the management of great affairs. And such was Paulus Æmilius, advanced in years, being nearly threescore, yet vigorous in his own person, and rich in valiant sons and sons-in-law, besides a great number of influential relations and friends, all of whom joined in urging him to yield to the desires of the people, who called him to the consulship. He at first manifested some shyness of the people, and withdrew himself from their importunity, professing reluctance to hold office; but, when they daily came to his doors, urging him to come forth to the place of election, and pressing him with noise and clamor, he acceded to their request. When he appeared amongst the candidates, it did not look as if it were to sue for the consulship, but to bring victory and success, that he came down into the Campus; they all received him there with such hopes and such gladness, unanimously choosing him a second time consul; nor would they suffer the lots to be cast, as was usual, to determine which province should fall to his share, but immediately decreed him the command of the Macedonian war. It is told, that when he had been proclaimed general against Perseus, and was honorably accompanied home by great numbers of people, he found his daughter Tertia, a very little girl, weeping, and taking her to him asked her why she was crying. She, catching him about the neck and kissing him, said, "O father, do you not know that Perseus is dead?" meaning a little dog of that name that was brought up in the house with her; to which Æmilius replied, "Good fortune, my daughter; I embrace the omen." This Cicero, the orator, relates in his book on divination.

It was the custom for such as were chosen consuls, from a stage designed for such purposes, to address the people, and return them thanks for their favor. Æmilius, therefore, having gathered an assembly, spoke and said, that he sued for the first consulship, because he himself stood in need of such honor; but for the second, because they wanted a general; upon which account he thought there was no thanks due: if they judged they could manage the war by any other to more advantage, he would willingly yield up his charge; but, if they confided in him, they were not to make themselves his colleagues in his office, or raise reports, and criticise his actions, but, without talking, supply him with means and assistance necessary to the carrying on of the war; for, if they proposed to command their own commander, they would render this expedition more ridiculous than the former. By this speech he inspired great reverence for him amongst the citizens, and great expectations of future success; all were well pleased, that they had passed by such as sought to be preferred by flattery, and fixed upon a commander endued with wisdom and courage to tell them the truth. So entirely did the people of Rome, that they might rule, and become masters of the world, yield obedience and service to reason and superior virtue.

That Æmilius, setting forward to the war, by a prosperous voyage and successful journey, arrived with speed and safety at his camp, I attribute to good fortune; but, when I see how the war under his command was brought to a happy issue, partly by his own daring boldness, partly by his good counsel, partly by the ready administration of his friends, partly by his presence of mind and skill to embrace the most proper advice in the extremity of danger, I cannot ascribe any of his remarkable and famous actions (as I can those of other commanders) to his so much celebrated good fortune; unless you will say that the covetousness of Perseus was the good fortune of Æmilius. The truth is, Perseus' fear of spending his money was the destruction and utter ruin of all those splendid and great preparations with which the Macedonians were in high hopes to carry on the war with success. For there came at his request ten thousand horsemen of the Basternæ, and as many foot, who were to keep pace with them, and supply their places in case of failure; all of them professed soldiers, men skilled neither in tilling of land, nor in navigation of ships, nor able to get their livings by grazing, but whose only business and single art and trade it was to fight and conquer all that resisted them. When these came into the district of Mædica, and encamped and mixed with the king's soldiers, being men of great stature, admirable at their exercises, great boasters, and loud in their threats against their enemies, they gave new courage to the Macedonians, who were ready to think the Romans would not be able to confront them, but would be struck with terror at their looks and motions, they were so strange and so formidable to behold. When Perseus had thus encouraged his men, and elevated them with these great hopes, as soon as a thousand gold pieces were demanded for each captain, he was so amazed and beside himself at the vastness of the amount, that out of mere stinginess he drew back and let himself lose their assistance, as if he had been some steward, not the enemy of the Romans, and would have to give an exact account of the expenses of the war, to those with whom he waged it. Nay, when he had his foes as tutors, to instruct him what he had to do, who, besides their other preparations, had a hundred thousand men drawn together and in readiness for their service; yet he that was to engage against so considerable a force, and in a war that was maintaining such numbers as this, nevertheless doled out his money, and put seals on his bags, and was as fearful of touching it, as if it had belonged to some one else. And all this was done by one, not descended from Lydians or Phœnicians, but who could pretend to some share of the virtues of Alexander and Philip, whom he was allied to by birth; men who conquered the world by judging that empire was to be purchased by money, not money by empire. Certainly it became a proverb, that not Philip, but his gold took the cities of Greece. And Alexander, when he undertook his expedition against the Indians, and found his Macedonians encumbered, and appear to march heavily with their Persian spoils, first set fire to his own carriages, and thence persuaded the rest to imitate his example, that thus freed they might proceed to the war without hindrance. Whereas Perseus, abounding in wealth, would not preserve himself, his children, and his kingdom, at the expense of a small part of his treasure; but chose rather to be carried away with numbers of his subjects with the name of the wealthy captive and show the Romans what great riches he had husbanded and preserved for them. For he not only played false with the Gauls, and sent them away, but also, after alluring Genthius, king of the Illyrians, by the hopes of three hundred talents, to assist him in the war, he caused the money to be counted out in the presence of his messengers, and to be sealed up. Upon which Genthius, thinking himself possessed of what he desired, committed a wicked and shameful act: he seized and imprisoned the ambassadors sent to him from the Romans. Whence Perseus, concluding that there was now no need of money to make Genthius an enemy to the Romans, but that he had given a lasting earnest of his enmity, and by his flagrant injustice sufficiently involved himself in the war, defrauded the unfortunate king of his three hundred talents, and without any concern beheld him, his wife, and children, in a short time after, carried out of their kingdom, as from their nest, by Lucius Anicius, who was sent against him with an army.

Æmilius, coming against such an adversary, made light indeed of him, but admired his preparation and power. For he had four thousand horse, and not much fewer than forty thousand full-armed foot of the phalanx; and planting himself along the seaside, at the foot of Mount Olympus, in ground with no access on any side, and on all sides fortified with fences and bulwarks of wood, remained in great security, thinking by delay and expense to weary out Æmilius. But he, in the mean time, busy in thought, weighed all counsels and all means of attack, and perceiving his soldiers, from their former want of discipline, to be impatient of delay, and ready on all occasions to teach their general his duty, rebuked them, and bade them not meddle with what was not their concern, but only take care that they and their arms were in readiness, and to use their swords like Romans when their commander should think fit to employ them. Further he ordered, that the sentinels by night should watch without javelins, that thus they might be more careful and surer to resist sleep, having no arms to defend themselves against any attacks of an enemy.

What most annoyed the army was the want of water; for only a little, and that foul, flowed out, or rather came by drops from a spring adjoining the sea; but Æmilius, considering that he was at the foot of the high and woody mountain Olympus, and conjecturing by the flourishing growth of the trees that there were springs that had their course under ground, dug a great many holes and wells along the foot of the mountain, which were presently filled with pure water escaping from its confinement into the vacuum they afforded. Although there are some, indeed, who deny that there are reservoirs of water lying ready provided out of sight, in the places from whence springs flow, and that when they appear, they merely issue and run out; on the contrary, they say, they are then formed and come into existence for the first time, by the liquefaction of the surrounding matter; and that this change is caused by density and cold, when the moist vapor, by being closely pressed together, becomes fluid. As women's breasts are not like vessels full of milk always prepared and ready to flow from them; but their nourishment being changed in their breasts, is there made milk, and from thence is pressed out. In like manner, places of the earth that are cold and full of springs, do not contain any hidden waters or receptacles which are capable, as from a source

ÆMILIUS PAULUS

always ready and furnished, of supplying all the brooks and deep rivers; but by compressing and condensing the vapors and air, they turn them into that substance. And thus places that are dug open flow by that pressure, and afford the more water (as the breasts of women do milk by their being sucked), the vapor thus moistening and becoming fluid; whereas ground that remains idle and undug is not capable of producing any water, whilst it wants that motion which is the cause of liquefaction. But those that assert this opinion, give occasion to the doubtful to argue, that on the same ground there should be no blood in living creatures, but that it must be formed by the wound, some sort of spirit or flesh being changed into a liquid and flowing matter. Moreover, they are refuted by the fact that men who dig mines, either in sieges or for metals, meet with rivers, which are not collected by little and little (as must necessarily be, if they had their being at the very instant the earth was opened), but break out at once with violence; and upon the cutting through a rock, there often gush out great quantities of water, which then as suddenly cease. But of this enough.

Æmilius lay still for some days, and it is said, that there were never two great armies so nigh, that enjoyed so much quiet. When he had tried and considered all things, he was informed that there was yet one passage left unguarded, through Perrhæbia by the temple of Apollo and the Rock.[3] Gathering, therefore, more hope from the place being left defenceless than fear from the roughness and difficulty of the passage, he proposed it for consultation. Amongst those that were present at the council, Scipio, surnamed Nasica, son-in-law

[3] Pythium and Petra, if the words be taken as proper names.

to Scipio Africanus, who afterwards was so powerful in the senate-house, was the first that offered himself to command those that should be sent to encompass the enemy. Next to him, Fabius Maximus, eldest son of Æmilius, although yet very young, offered himself with great zeal. Æmilius, rejoicing, gave them, not so many as Polybius states, but, as Nasica himself tells us in a brief letter which he wrote to one of the kings with an account of the expedition, three thousand Italians that were not Romans, and his left wing consisting of five thousand. Taking with him, besides these, one hundred and twenty horsemen, and two hundred Thracians and Cretans intermixed that Harpalus had sent, he began his journey towards the sea, and encamped near the temple of Hercules, as if he designed to embark, and so to sail round and environ the enemy. But when the soldiers had supped and it was dark, he made the captains acquainted with his real intentions, and marching all night in the opposite direction, away from the sea, till he came under the temple of Apollo, there rested his army. At this place Mount Olympus rises in height more than ten furlongs,[4] as appears by the epigram made by the man that measured it:

> The summit of Olympus, at the site
> Where stands Apollo's temple, has a height
> Of full ten furlongs by the line, and more,
> Ten furlongs, and one hundred feet, less four.
> Eumelus' son, Xenagoras, reached the place.
> Adieu, O king, and do thy pilgrim grace.

It is allowed, say the geometricians, that no mountain in height or sea in depth exceeds ten fur-

---

[4] The Greek furlong, or stadium, containing 600 Greek feet, or 606¾ English; about nine to the English mile.

longs, and yet it seems probable that Xenagoras did not take his admeasurement carelessly, but according to the rules of art, and with instruments for the purpose. Here it was that Nasica passed the night.

A Cretan deserter, who fled to the enemy during the march, discovered to Perseus the design which the Romans had to encompass him: for he, seeing that Æmilius lay still, had not suspected any such attempt. He was startled at the news, yet did not put his army in motion, but sent ten thousand mercenary soldiers and two thousand Macedonians, under command of Milo, with order to hasten and possess themselves of the passes. Polybius relates that the Romans found these men asleep when they attacked them; but Nasica says there was a sharp and severe conflict on the top of the mountain, that he himself encountered a mercenary Thracian, pierced him through with his javelin, and slew him; and that the enemy being forced to retreat, Milo stripped to his coat and fled shamefully without his armor, while he followed without danger, and conveyed the whole army down into the country.

After this event, Perseus, now grown fearful, and fallen from his hopes, removed his camp in all haste; he was under the necessity either to stop before Pydna, and there run the hazard of a battle, or disperse his army into cities, and there expect the event of the war, which, having once made its way into his country, could not be driven out without great slaughter and bloodshed. But Perseus, being told by his friends that he was much superior in number, and that men fighting in the defence of their wives and children must needs feel all the more courage, especially when all was done in the sight of their king, who himself was engaged in equal danger, was thus again encouraged; and, pitching his camp, prepared himself to fight, viewed the country, and gave out the commands, as if he designed to set upon the Romans as soon as they approached. The place was a field fit for the action of a phalanx, which requires smooth standing and even ground, and also had divers little hills, one joining another, fit for the motions whether in retreat or advance of light troops and skirmishers. Through the middle ran the rivers Æson and Leucus, which, though not very deep, it being the latter end of summer, yet were likely enough to give the Romans some trouble.

As soon as Æmilius had rejoined Nasica, he advanced in battle array against the enemy; but when he found how they were drawn up, and the number of their forces, he regarded them with admiration and surprise, and halted, considering within himself. The young commanders, eager to fight, riding along by his side, pressed him not to delay, and most of all Nasica, flushed with his late success on Olympus. To whom Æmilius answered with a smile: "So would I do, were I of your age; but many victories have taught me the ways in which men are defeated, and forbid me to engage soldiers weary with a long march, against an army drawn up and prepared for battle."

Then he gave command that the front of his army, and such as were in sight of the enemy, should form as if ready to engage, and those in the rear should cast up the trenches and fortify the camp; so that the hindmost in succession wheeling off by degrees and withdrawing, their whole order was insensibly broken up, and the army encamped without noise or trouble.

When it was night, and, supper being over, all were turning to sleep and rest, on a sudden the moon, which was then at full and high in the heavens, grew dark, and by degrees losing her light, passed through various colors, and at length was totally eclipsed. The Romans, according to their custom, clattering brass pans and lifting up firebrands and torches into the air, invoked the return of her light; the Macedonians behaved far otherwise: terror and amazement seized their whole army, and a rumor crept by degrees into their camp that this eclipse portended even that of their king. Æmilius was no novice in these things, nor was ignorant of the nature of the seeming irregularities of eclipses,—that in a certain revolution of time, the moon in her course enters the shadow of the earth and is there obscured, till, passing the region of darkness, she is again enlightened by the sun. Yet being a devout man, a religious observer of sacrifices and the art of divination, as soon as he perceived the moon beginning to regain her former lustre, he offered up to her eleven heifers. At the break of day he sacrificed as many as twenty in succession to Hercules, without any token that his offering was accepted; but at the one and twentieth, the signs promised victory to defenders. He then vowed a hecatomb and solemn sports to Hercules, and commanded his captains to make ready for battle, staying only till the sun should decline and come round to the west, lest, being in their faces in the morning, it should dazzle the eyes of his soldiers. Thus he whiled away the time in his tent, which was open towards the plain where his enemies were encamped.

When it grew towards evening, some tell us, Æmilius himself used a stratagem to induce the

enemy to begin the fight; that he turned loose a
horse without a bridle, and sent some of the
Romans to catch him, upon whose following the
beast, the battle began. Others relate that the
Thracians, under the command of one Alexander,
set upon the Roman beasts of burden that were
bringing forage to the camp; that to oppose these,
a party of seven hundred Ligurians were immediately detached, and that, relief coming still from
both armies, the main bodies at last engaged.
Æmilius, like a wise pilot, foreseeing by the present
waves and motion of the armies, the greatness of the
following storm, came out of his tent, went through
the legions, and encouraged his soldiers. Nasica,
in the mean time, who had ridden out to the skirmishers, saw the whole force of the enemy on the
point of engaging. First marched the Thracians,
who, he himself tells us, inspired him with most
terror; they were of great stature, with bright and
glittering shields and black frocks under them, their
legs armed with greaves, and they brandished, as
they moved, straight and heavily-ironed spears over
their right shoulders. Next the Thracians marched
the mercenary soldiers, armed after different fash-
ions; with these the Pæonians were mingled. These
were succeeded by a third division, of picked men,
native Macedonians, the choicest for courage and
strength, in the prime of life, gleaming with gilt
armor and scarlet coats. As these were taking
their places they were followed from the camp by
the troops in phalanx called the Brazen Shields, so
that the whole plain seemed alive with the flashing
of steel and the glistening of brass; and the hills
also with their shouts, as they cheered each other
on. In this order they marched, and with such
boldness and speed, that those that were first slain

NAVAL FIGHT DURING THE FIRST PUNIC WAR

died at but two furlongs distance from the Roman camp.

The battle being begun, Æmilius came in and found that the foremost of the Macedonians had already fixed the ends of their spears into the shields of his Romans, so that it was impossible to come near them with their swords. When he saw this, and observed that the rest of the Macedonians took the targets that hung on their left shoulders, and brought them round before them, and all at once stooped their pikes against their enemies' shields, and considered the great strength of this wall of shields, and the formidable appearance of a front thus bristling with arms, he was seized with amazement and alarm: nothing he had ever seen before had been equal to it; and in after times he frequently used to speak both of the sight and of his own sensations. These, however, he dissembled, and rode through his army without either breastplate or helmet, with a serene and cheerful countenance.

On the contrary, as Polybius relates, no sooner was the battle begun, but the Macedonian king basely withdrew to the city Pydna, under a pretence of sacrificing to Hercules: a God that is not wont to regard the faint offerings of cowards, or to fulfil unsanctioned vows. For truly it can hardly be a thing that heaven would sanction, that he that never shoots should carry away the prize; he triumph that slinks from the battle; he that takes no pains meet with success, or the wicked man prosper. But to Æmilius's petitions the god listened; he prayed for victory with his sword in his hand and fought while entreating divine assistance.

A certain Posidonius who has at some length

written a history of Perseus, and professes to have lived at the time, and to have been himself engaged in these events, denies that Perseus left the field either through fear or pretence of sacrificing, but that, the very day before the fight, he received a kick from a horse on his thigh; that though very much disabled, and dissuaded by all his friends, he commanded one of his riding-horses to be brought, and entered the field unarmed; that amongst an infinite number of darts that flew about on all sides, one of iron lighted on him, and though not with the point, yet by a glance struck him with such force on his left side, that it tore his clothes and so bruised his flesh that the mark remained a long time after. This is what Posidonius says in defence of Perseus.

The Romans not being able to make a breach in the phalanx, one Salius, a commander of the Pelignians, snatched the ensign of his company and threw it amongst the enemies; on seeing which, the Pelignians (as amongst the Italians it is always thought the greatest breach of honor to abandon a standard) rushed with great violence towards the place, where the conflict grew very fierce, and the slaughter terrible on both sides. For these endeavored to cut the spears asunder with their swords, or to beat them back with their shields, or put them by with their hands; and, on the other side, the Macedonians held their long sarissas in both hands, and pierced those that came in their way quite through their armor, no shield or corslet being able to resist the force of that weapon. The Pelignians and Marrucinians were thrown headlong to the ground, having without consideration, with mere animal fury, rushed upon a certain death. Their first ranks being slain those that were behind were forced to give back; it cannot be said they fled, but they retreated towards Mount Olocrus. When Æmilius saw this, Posidonius relates, he rent his clothes, some of his men being ready to fly, and the rest not willing to engage with a phalanx into which they could not hope to make any entrance,— a sort of palisade, as it were, impregnable and unapproachable, with its close array of long spears everywhere meeting the assailant. Nevertheless, the unequalness of the ground would not permit a widely extended front to be so exactly drawn up as to have their shields everywhere joined; and Æmilius perceived that there were a great many interstices and breaches in the Macedonian phalanx; as it usually happens in all great armies, according to the different efforts of the combatants, who in one part press forward with eagerness, and in another are forced to fall back. Taking, therefore, this occasion, with all speed he broke up his men into their cohorts, and gave them order to fall into the intervals and openings of the enemy's body, and not to make one general attack upon them all, but to engage, as they were divided, in several partial battles. These commands Æmilius gave to his captains, and they to their soldiers; and no sooner had they entered the spaces and separated their enemies, but they charged them, some on their sides where they were naked and exposed, and others, making a circuit, behind; and thus destroyed the force of the phalanx, which consisted in common action and close union. And now, come to fight man to man, or in small parties, the Macedonians smote in vain upon firm and long shields with their little swords, whilst their slight bucklers were not able to sustain the weight and force of the Roman swords, which pierced through all their armor to their bodies; they turned, in fine, and fled.

The conflict was obstinate. And here Marcus, the son of Cato, and son-in-law of Æmilius, whilst he showed all possible courage, let fall his sword. Being a young man, carefully brought up and disciplined, and, as son of so renowned a father, bound to give proof of more than ordinary virtue, he thought his life but a burden, should he live and permit his enemies to enjoy this spoil. He hurried hither and thither, and wherever he espied a friend or companion, declared his misfortune, and begged their assistance; a considerable number of brave men being thus collected, with one accord they made their way through their fellows after their leader, and fell upon the enemy; whom, after a sharp conflict, many wounds, and much slaughter, they repulsed, possessed the place that was now deserted and free, and set themselves to search for the sword, which at last they found covered with a great heap of arms and dead bodies. Overjoyed with this success, they raised the song of triumph, and with more eagerness than ever, charged the foes that yet remained firm and unbroken. In the end, three thousand of the chosen men, who kept their ground and fought valiantly to the last, were all cut in pieces, while the slaughter of such as fled was also very great. The plain and the lower part of the hills were filled with dead bodies, and the water of the river Leucus, which the Romans did not pass till the next day after the battle, was then mingled with blood. For it is said there fell more than twenty-five thousand of the enemy; of the Romans, as Posidonius relates, a hundred; as Nasica, only fourscore. This battle, though so great, was very quickly decided, it being three in the afternoon when they first engaged, and not four when the enemy was vanquished; the rest of the day was spent in the pursuit of the fugitives, whom they followed about thirteen or fourteen miles, so that it was far in the night when they returned.

All the others were met by their servants with torches, and brought back with joy and great triumph to their tents, which were set out with lights, and decked with wreaths of ivy and laurel. But the general himself was in great grief. Of the two sons that served under him in the war, the youngest was missing, whom he held most dear, and whose courage and good qualities he perceived much to excel those of his brothers. Bold and eager for distinction, and still a mere child in age, he concluded that he had perished, whilst for want of experience he had engaged himself too far amongst his enemies. His sorrow and fears became known to the army; the soldiers, quitting their suppers, ran about with lights, some to Æmilius's tent, some out of the trenches, to seek him amongst such as were slain in the first onset. There was nothing but grief in the camp, and the plain was filled with the cries of men calling out for Scipio; for, from his very youth, he was an object of admiration; endowed above any of his equals with the good qualities requisite either for command or counsel. At length, when it was late, and they almost despaired, he returned from the pursuit with only two or three of his companions, all covered with the fresh blood of his enemies, having been, like some dog of noble breed, carried away by the pleasure, greater than he could control, of his first victory. This was that Scipio that afterwards destroyed Carthage and Numantia, and was, without dispute, the first of the Romans in merit, and had the greatest authority amongst them. Thus Fortune, deferring her displeasure and jealousy of such great success to some other time, let Æmilius at present enjoy this victory, without any detraction or diminution.

As for Perseus, from Pydna he fled to Pella with his cavalry, which was as yet almost entire. But when the foot came up with them, and, upbraiding them as cowards and traitors, tried to pull them off their horses, and fell to blows, Perseus, fearing the tumult, forsook the common road, and, lest he should be known, pulled off his purple, and carried it before him, and took his crown in his hand, and, that he might the better converse with his friends, alighted from his horse and led him. Of those that were about him, one stopped, pretending to tie his shoe that was loose, another to water his horse, a third to drink himself; and thus lagging behind, by degrees left him, they having not so much reason to fear their enemies, as his cruelty; for he, disordered by his misfortune, sought to clear himself by laying the cause of the overthrow upon everybody else. He arrived at Pella in the night, where Euctus and Eudæus, two of his treasurers, came to him, and, what with their reflecting on his former faults, and their free and ill-timed admonitions and counsels, so exasperated him, that he killed them both, stabbing them with his own dagger. After this, nobody stuck to him but Evander the Cretan, Archedemus the Ætolian, and Neon the Bœotian. Of the common soldiers there followed him only those from Crete, not out of any good-will, but because they were as constant to his riches as the bees to their hive. For he carried a great treasure with him, out of which he had suffered them to take cups, bowls, and other vessels of silver and gold, to the value of fifty talents. But when he was come to Amphipolis, and afterwards to Galepsus, and his fears were a little abated, he relapsed into his old and constitutional disease of covetousness, and lamented to his friends that he had, through inadvertency, allowed some gold plate which had belonged to Alexander the Great to go into the hands of the Cretans, and besought those that had it, with tears in his eyes, to exchange with him again for money. Those that understood him thoroughly knew very well he only played the Cretan with the Cretans, but those that believed him, and restored what they had, were cheated; as he not only did not pay the money, but by craft got thirty talents more of his friends into his hands (which in a short time after fell to the enemy), and with them sailed to Samothrace, and there fled to the temple of Castor and Pollux for refuge.

The Macedonians were always accounted great lovers of their kings, but now, as if their chief prop was broken, they all gave way together, and submitted to Æmilius, and in two days made him master of their whole country. This seems to confirm the opinion which ascribes whatever he did to good fortune. The omen, also, that happened at Amphipolis, has a supernatural character. When he was sacrificing there, and the holy rites were just begun, on a sudden, lightning fell upon the altar, set the wood on fire, and completed the immolation of the sacrifice. The most signal manifestation, however, of preternatural agency appears in the story of the rumor of his success. For on the fourth day after Perseus was vanquished at Pydna, whilst the people at Rome were seeing the horse-races, a report suddenly arose at the entrance of the theatre that Æmilius had defeated Perseus in a great battle, and was reducing all Macedonia under his power; and from thence it spread amongst the people, and created general joy, with shoutings and acclamations for that whole day through the city. But when no certain author was found of the news, and every one alike had taken it at random, it was abandoned for the present, and thought no more of, until, a few days after, certain intelligence came, and then the first was looked upon as no less than a miracle, having, under an appearance of fiction, contained what was real and true. It is reported, also, that the news of the battle fought in Italy,[5] near the river Sagra, was conveyed into Peloponnesus the same day, and of that at Mycale against the Medes, to Platæa. When the Romans had defeated the Tarquins, who were combined with the Latins, a little after, there were seen at Rome two tall and comely men, who professed to bring the news from the camp. They were conjectured to be Castor and Pollux. The first man that spoke to them in the forum, near the fountain where they were cooling their horses, which were all of a foam, expressed surprise at the report of the victory, when, it is said, they smiled, and gently touched his beard with their hands, the hair of which from being black was, on the spot, changed to yellow. This gave credit to what they said, and fixed the name of Ahenobarbus, or Brazen-beard, on the man. And a thing which happened in our own time will make all these

[5] *The battle fought in Italy* (rather, *by the Italian Greeks*), *near the river Sagra*, or Sagras, is that mentioned by Justin (XX., 3), Cicero (*de Natura Deorum, II., 2*), and Strabo (*VI., 10*), in which the Locrians gave a great defeat to the Crotoniats; it took place in early history, some time before the Persian wars.

credible. For when Antonius rebelled against Domitian, and Rome was in consternation, expecting great wars from the quarter of Germany, all on a sudden, and nobody knows upon what account, the people spontaneously gave out a rumor of victory, and the news ran current through the city, that Antonius himself was slain, his whole army destroyed, and not so much as a part of it escaped; nay, this belief was so strong and positive, that many of the magistrates offered up sacrifice. But when, at length, the author was sought for, and none was to be found, it vanished by degrees, every one shifting it off from himself to another, and, at last, was lost in the numberless crowd, as in a vast ocean, and, having no solid ground to support its credit, was, in a short time, not so much as named in the city. Nevertheless, when Domitian marched out with his forces to the war, he met with messengers and letters that gave him a relation of the victory; and the rumor, it was found, had come the very day it was gained, though the distance between the places was more than twenty-five hundred miles. The truth of this no man of our time is ignorant of.

But to proceed. Cnæus Octavius, who was joined in command with Æmilius, came to an anchor with his fleet under Samothrace, where, out of respect to the gods, he permitted Perseus to enjoy the benefit of refuge, but took care that he should not escape by sea, Notwithstanding, Perseus secretly persuaded Oroandes of Crete, master of a small vessel, to convey him and his treasure away. He, however, playing the true Cretan, took in the treasure, and bade him come, in the night, with his children and most necessary attendants, to the port by the temple of Ceres; but, as soon as it was

evening, set sail without him. It had been sad
enough for Perseus to be forced to let down himself, his wife and children, through a narrow window by a wall,—people altogether unaccustomed
to hardship and flying; but that which drew a far
sadder sigh from his heart was, when he was told by
a man, as he wandered on the shore, that he had
seen Oroandes under sail in the main sea; it being
now about daybreak. So, there being no hopes left
of escaping, he fled back again to the wall, which
he and his wife recovered, though they were seen
by the Romans, before they could reach them. His
children he himself had delivered into the hands
of Ion, one that had been his favorite, but now
proved his betrayer, and was the chief cause that
forced him (beasts themselves will do so when their
young ones are taken) to come and yield himself
up to those that had them in their power. His
greatest confidence was in Nasica, and it was for
him he called, but he not being there, he bewailed
his misfortune, and, seeing there was no possible
remedy, surrendered himself to Octavius. And
here, in particular, he made it manifest that he was
possessed with a vice more sordid than covetousness itself, namely the fondness of life; by which
he deprived himself even of pity, the only thing that
fortune never takes away from the most wretched.
He desired to be brought to Æmilius, who arose
from his seat, and accompanied with his friends
went to receive him, with tears in his eyes, as a
great man fallen by the anger of the gods and his
own ill fortune; when Perseus—the most shameful
of sights—threw himself at his feet, embraced his
knees, and uttered unmanly cries and petitions, such
as Æmilius was not able to bear, nor would vouchsafe to hear: but looking on him with a sad and

angry countenance he said, "Why, unhappy man, do you thus take pains to exonerate fortune of your heaviest charge against her, by conduct that will make it seem that you are not unjustly in calamity, and that it is not your present condition, but your former happiness, that was more than your deserts? And why depreciate also my victory, and make my conquests insignificant, by proving yourself a coward, and a foe beneath a Roman? Distressed valor challenges great respect, even from enemies; but cowardice, though never so successful, from the Romans has always met with scorn." Yet for all this he took him up, gave him his hand, and delivered him into the custody of Tubero. Meantime, he himself carried his sons, his sons-in-law, and others of chief rank, especially of the younger sort, back with him into his tent, where for a long time he sat down without speaking one word, insomuch that they all wondered at him. At last, he began to discourse of fortune and human affairs. "Is it meet," said he, "for him that knows he is but man, in his greatest prosperity to pride himself, and be exalted at the conquest of a city, nation, or kingdom, and not rather well to weigh this change of fortune, in which all warriors may see an example of their common frailty, and learn a lesson that there is nothing durable or constant? For what time can men select to think themselves secure, when that of victory itself forces us more than any to dread our own fortune? and a very little consideration on the law of things, and how all are hurried round, and each man's station changed, will introduce sadness in the midst of the greatest joy. Or can you, when you see before your eyes the succession of Alexander himself, who arrived at the height of power and ruled the greatest empire, in the short space of an hour trodden under foot,—when you behold a king, that was but even now surrounded with so numerous an army, receiving nourishment to support his life from the hands of his conquerors,—can you, I say, believe there is any certainty in what we now possess, whilst there is such a thing as chance? No, young men, cast off that vain pride and empty boast of victory; sit down with humility, looking always for what is yet to come, and the possible future reverses which the divine displeasure may eventually make the end of our present happiness." It is said that Æmilius, having spoken much more to the same purpose, dismissed the young men properly humbled, and with their vain-glory and insolence thoroughly chastened and curbed by his address.

When this was done, he put his army into garrisons, to refresh themselves, and went himself to visit Greece, and to spend a short time in relaxations equally honorable and humane. For, as he passed, he eased the people's grievances, reformed their governments, and bestowed gifts upon them; to some, corn,—to others, oil out of the king's storehouses, in which, they report, there were such vast quantities laid up, that receivers and petitioners were lacking before they could be exhausted. In Delphi he found a great square pillar of white marble, designed for the pedestal of king Perseus' golden statue, on which he commanded his own to be placed, alleging that it was but just that the conquered should give place to the conquerors. In Olympia he is said to have uttered the saying everybody has heard, that Phidias had carved Homer's Jupiter. When the ten commissioners arrived from Rome, he delivered up again to the Macedonians their cities and country, granting them to live at liberty, and according to their own laws, only paying the Romans the tribute of a hundred talents, double which sum they had been wont to pay to their kings. Then he celebrated all manner of shows and games, and sacrifices to the gods, and made great entertainments and feasts; the charge of all which he liberally defrayed out of the king's treasury; and showed that he understood the ordering and placing of his guests, and how every man should be received, answerably to their rank and quality, with such nice exactness, that the Greeks were full of wonder, finding the care of these matters of pleasure did not escape him, and that though involved in such important business, he could observe correctness in these trifles. Nor was it least gratifying to him, that, amidst all the magnificent and splendid preparations, he himself was always the most grateful sight, and greatest pleasure to those he entertained. And he told those that seemed to wonder at his diligence, that there was the same spirit shown in marshalling a banquet as an army; in rendering the one formidable to the enemy, the other acceptable to the guests. Nor did men less praise his liberality, and the greatness of his soul, than his other virtues; for he would not so much as see those great quantities of silver and gold, which were heaped together out of the king's palaces, but delivered them to the quæstors, to be put into the public treasury. He only permitted his own sons, who were great lovers of learning, to take the king's books; and when he distributed rewards due to extraordinary valor, he gave his son-in-law, Ælius Tubero, a bowl that weighed five pounds. This is that Tubero we have already mentioned, who was one of sixteen relations that lived together, and were all maintained out of one little farm; and it is said, that this was the first plate that ever entered the house of the Ælii, brought thither as an honor and reward of virtue; before this time, neither they nor their wives ever made use either of silver or gold.

Having thus settled every thing well, taking his leave of the Greeks, and exhorting the Macedonians, that, mindful of the liberty they had received from the Romans, they should endeavor to maintain it by their obedience to the laws, and concord amongst themselves, he departed for Epirus, having orders from the senate, to give the soldiers that followed him in the war against Perseus the pillage of the cities of that country. That he might set upon them all at once by surprise and unawares, he summoned ten of the principal men out of each, whom he commanded, on such an appointed day, to bring all the gold and silver they had either in their private houses or temples; and, with every one of these, as if it were for this very purpose, and under a pretence of searching for and receiving the gold, he sent a centurion and a guard of soldiers; who, the set day being come, rose all at once, and at the very self-same time fell upon them, and proceeded to ransack the cities; so that in one hour a hundred and fifty thousand persons were made slaves, and threescore and ten cities sacked. Yet what was given to each soldier, out of so vast a destruction and utter ruin, amounted to no more than eleven drachmas; so that men could only shudder at the issue of a war, where the wealth of a whole nation, thus divided, turned to so little advantage and profit to each particular man.

When Æmilius had done this,—an action perfectly contrary to his gentle and mild nature,—he went down to Oricus, where he embarked his

army for Italy. He sailed up the river Tiber in
the king's galley, that had sixteen banks of oars,
and was richly adorned with captured arms and
with cloths of purple and scarlet; so that, the vessel
rowing slowly against the stream, the Romans that
crowded on the shore to meet him had a foretaste of
his following triumph. But the soldiers, who had
cast a covetous eye on the treasures of Perseus,
when they did not obtain as much as they thought
they deserved were secretly enraged and angry with
Æmilius for this, but openly complained that
he had been a severe and tyrannical commander
over them; nor were they ready to show their desire
of his triumph. When Servius Galba, who was
Æmilius's enemy, though he commanded as tribune
under him, understood this, he had the boldness
plainly to affirm that a triumph was not to be
allowed him; and sowed various calumnies amongst
the soldiers, which yet further increased their ill-
will. Nay more, he desired the tribunes of the
people, because the four hours that were remaining
of the day could not suffice for the accusation, to
let him put it off till another. But when the
tribunes commanded him to speak then, if he had
any thing to say, he began a long oration, filled
with all manner of reproaches, in which he spent
the remaining part of the time, and the tribunes,
when it was dark, dismissed the assembly. The
soldiers, growing more vehement on this, thronged
all to Galba, and entering into a conspiracy, early
in the morning beset the capitol, where the tribunes
had appointed the following assembly to be held.

As soon as it was day, it was put to the vote,
and the first tribe was proceeding to refuse the
triumph; and the news spread amongst the people
and to the senate. The people were indeed much

grieved that Æmilius should meet with such ignominy; but this was only in words, which had no effect. The chief of the senate exclaimed against it as a base action, and excited one another to repress the boldness and insolence of the soldiers, which would erelong become altogether ungovernable and violent, were they now permitted to deprive Æmilius of his triumph. Forcing a passage through the crowd, they came up in great numbers, and desired the tribunes to defer polling, till they had spoken what they had to say to the people. All things thus suspended, and silence being made, Marcus Servilius stood up, a man of consular dignity, and who had killed twenty-three of his enemies that had challenged him in single combat. "It is now more than ever," said he, "clear to my mind how great a commander our Æmilius Paulus is, when I see he was able to perform such famous and great exploits with an army so full of sedition and baseness; nor can I sufficiently wonder, that a people that seemed to glory in the triumphs over Illyrians and Ligurians, should now through envy refuse to see the Macedonian king led alive, and all the glory of Philip and Alexander in captivity to the Roman power. For is it not a strange thing for you, who, upon a slight rumor of victory that came by chance into the city, did offer sacrifices and put up your requests unto the gods that you might see the report verified, now when the general is returned with an undoubted conquest to defraud the gods of honor, and yourselves of joy, as if you feared to behold the greatness of his war-like deed, or were resolved to spare your enemy? and of the two, much better were it to put a stop to the triumph, out of pity to him, than out of envy to your general; yet to such a height of power is malice arrived amongst you, that a man without one scar to show on his skin, that is smooth and sleek with ease and home-keeping habits, will undertake to define the office and duties of a general before us, who with our own wounds have been taught how to judge the valor or the cowardice of commanders." And, at the same time, putting aside his garment, he showed an infinite number of scars upon his breast, and, turning about, he exposed some parts of his person which it is usual to conceal; and, addressing Galba, said: "You deride me for these, in which I glory before my fellow-citizens, for it is in their service, in which I have ridden night and day, that I received them; but go collect the votes, whilst I follow after, and note the base and ungrateful, and such as choose rather to be flattered and courted than commanded by their general." It is said, this speech so stopped the soldiers' mouths, and altered their minds, that all the tribes decreed a triumph for Æmilius; which was performed after this manner.

The people erected scaffolds in the Forum, in the circuses, as they call their buildings for horse-races, and in all other parts of the city where they could best behold the show. The spectators were clad in white garments; all the temples were open, and full of garlands and perfumes; the ways were cleared and kept open by numerous officers, who drove back all who crowded into or ran across the main avenue. This triumph lasted three days. On the first, which was scarcely long enough for the sight, were to be seen the statues, pictures, and colossal images, which were taken from the enemy, drawn upon two hundred and fifty chariots. On the second, was carried in a great many wagons the finest and richest armor of the Macedonians, both of brass and steel, all newly polished and glittering; the pieces of which were piled up and arranged purposely with the greatest art, so as to seem to be tumbled in heaps carelessly and by chance; helmets were thrown upon shields, coats of mail upon greaves; Cretan targets, and Thracian bucklers and quivers of arrows lay huddled amongst horses' bits, and through these there appeared the points of naked swords, intermixed with long Macedonian sarissas. All these arms were fastened together with just so much looseness that they struck against one another as they were drawn along, and made a harsh and alarming noise, so that, even as spoils of a conquered enemy, they could not be beheld without dread. After these wagons loaded with armor, there followed three thousand men who carried the silver that was coined, in seven hundred and fifty vessels, each of which weighed three talents, and was carried by four men. Others brought silver bowls and goblets and cups, all disposed in such order as to make the best show, and all curious as well for their size as the solidity of their embossed work.

On the third day, early in the morning, first came the trumpeters, who did not sound as they were wont in a procession or solemn entry, but such a charge as the Romans use when they encourage the soldiers to fight. Next followed young men wearing frocks with ornamented borders, who led to the sacrifice a hundred and twenty stalled oxen, with their horns gilded, and their heads adorned with ribbons and garlands; and with these were boys that carried basins for libation, of silver and gold. After this was brought the gold coin, which was divided into vessels that weighed three talents, like those that contained the silver; they were in number seventy-seven. These were followed by those that brought the consecrated bowl which Æmilius had caused to be made, that weighed ten talents, and was set with precious stones. Then were exposed to view the cups of Antigonus and Seleucus, and those of the Thericlean [6] make, and all the gold plate that was used at Perseus' table. Next to these came Perseus' chariot, in which his armor was placed, and on that his diadem. And, after a little intermission, the king's children were led captives, and with them a train of their attendants, masters, and teachers, all shedding tears, and stretching out hands to the spectators, and making the children themselves also beg and entreat their compassion. There were two sons and a daughter, whose tender age made them but little sensible of the greatness of their misery, which very insensibility of their condition rendered it the more deplorable; insomuch that Perseus himself was scarcely regarded as he went along, whilst pity fixed the eyes of the Romans upon the infants; and many of them could not forbear tears, and all beheld the sight with a mixture of sorrow and pleasure, until the children were passed.

After his children and their attendants came Perseus himself, clad all in black, and wearing the boots of his country; and looking like one altogether stunned and deprived of reason, through the greatness of his misfortunes. Next followed a great company of his friends and familiars, whose countenances were disfigured with grief, and who let the spectators see, by their tears and their continual

[6] Thericles, according to the more probable supposition, was a Corinthian potter; the first maker of a particular kind of cup, which long continued to bear his name.

looking upon Perseus, that it was his fortune they so much lamented, and that they were regardless of their own. Perseus sent to Æmilius to entreat that he might not be led in pomp, but be left out of the triumph; who, deriding, as was but just, his cowardice and fondness of life, sent him this answer, that as for that, it had been before, and was now, in his own power; giving him to understand that the disgrace could be avoided by death; which the faint-hearted man not having the spirit for, and made effeminate by I know not what hopes, allowed himself to appear as a part of his own spoils. After these were carried four hundred crowns, all made of gold, sent from the cities by their respective deputations to Æmilius, in honor of his victory. Then he himself came, seated on a chariot magnificently adorned (a man well worthy to be looked at, even without these ensigns of power), dressed in a robe of purple, interwoven with gold, and holding a laurel branch in his right hand. All the army, in like manner, with boughs of laurel in their hands, divided into their bands and companies, followed the chariot of their commander; some singing verses, according to the usual custom, mingled with raillery; others, songs of triumph, and the praise of Æmilius's deeds; who, indeed, was admired and accounted happy by all men, and unenvied by every one that was good; except so far as it seems the province of some god to lessen that happiness which is too great and inordinate, and so to mingle the affairs of human life that no one should be entirely free and exempt from calamities; but, as we read in Homer,[7] that those should think themselves truly

[7] "Grief is useless; cease to lament," says Achilles to Priam, his suppliant for the body of Hector. "For thus have the gods appointed for mortal men; that they should live in vexation,

blessed to whom fortune has given an equal share of good and evil.

Æmilius had four sons, of whom Scipio and Fabius, as is already related, were adopted into other families; the other two, whom he had by a second wife, and who were yet but young, he brought up in his own house. One of these died at fourteen years of age, five days before his father's triumph; the other at twelve, three days after: so that there was no Roman without a deep sense of his suffering, and who did not shudder at the cruelty of fortune, that had not scrupled to bring so much sorrow into a house replenished with happiness, rejoicing, and sacrifices, and to intermingle tears and laments with songs of victory and triumph.

Æmilius, however, reasoning justly that courage and resolution was not merely to resist armor and spears, but all the shocks of ill fortune, so met and so adapted himself to these mingled and contrasting circumstances, as to outbalance the evil with the good, and his private concerns with those of the public; and thus did not allow any thing either to take away from the grandeur, or sully the dignity of his victory. For as soon as he had buried the first of his sons, (as we have already said,) he triumphed; and the second dying almost as soon as his triumph was over, he gathered together an assembly of the people, and made an oration to them, not like a man that stood in need of comfort

---

while they themselves are untroubled. Two vessels are set upon the threshold of Zeus, of the gifts that he dispenses; one of evil things, the other of good; he who receives from both at the hand of thundering Zeus, he meets at one time with evil, and at another with good; he who receives from only one, is a miserable wretch."

from others, but one that undertook to support his fellow-citizens in their grief for the sufferings he himself underwent.

"I," he said, "who never yet feared any thing that was human, have, amongst such as were divine, always had a dread of fortune as faithless and inconstant; and, for the very reason that in this war, she had been as a favorable gale in all my affairs, I still expected some change and reflux of things. In one day I passed the Ionian sea, and reached Corcyra from Brundisium; thence in five more I sacrificed at Delphi, and in other five days came to my forces in Macedonia, where, after I had finished the usual sacrifices for the purifying of the army, I entered on my duties, and, in the space of fifteen days, put an honorable period to the war. Still retaining a jealousy of fortune, even from the smooth current of my affairs, and seeing myself secure and free from the danger of any enemy, I chiefly dreaded the change of the goddess at sea, whilst conveying home my victorious army, vast spoils, and a captive king. Nay, indeed, after I was returned to you safe, and saw the city full of joy, congratulating, and sacrifices, yet still I distrusted, well knowing that fortune never conferred any great benefits that were unmixed and unattended with probabilities of reverse. Nor could my mind, that was still as it were in labor, and always foreseeing something to befall this city, free itself from this fear, until this great misfortune befell me in my own family, and till, in the midst of those days set apart for triumph, I carried two of the best of sons, my only destined successors, one after another to their funerals. Now, therefore, I am myself safe from danger, at least as to what was my greatest care; and I trust and am verily persuaded, that for the time to come Fortune will prove constant and harmless unto you; since she has sufficiently wreaked her jealousy at our great successes on me and mine, and has made the conqueror as marked an example of human instability as the captive whom he led in triumph, with this only difference, that Perseus, though conquered, does yet enjoy his children, while the conqueror, Æmilius, is deprived of his." This was the generous and magnanimous oration Æmilius is said to have spoken to the people, from a heart truly sincere and free from all artifice.

Although he very much pitied the condition of Perseus, and studied to befriend him in what he was able, yet he could procure no other favor, than his removal from the common prison, the *Carcer,* into a more cleanly and humane place of security, where, whilst he was guarded, it is said, he starved himself to death. Others state his death to have been of the strangest and most unusual character: that the soldiers who were his guard, having conceived a spite and hatred against him for some reason, and finding no other way to grieve and afflict him, kept him from sleep, took pains to disturb him when he was disposed to rest, and found out contrivances to keep him continually awake, by which means at length he was utterly worn out, and expired. Two of his children, also, died soon after him; the third, who was named Alexander, they say proved an exquisite artist in turning and graving small figures, and learned so perfectly to speak and write the Roman language, that he became clerk to the magistrates, and behaved himself in his office with great skill and conduct.

They ascribe to Æmilius's conquest of Macedonia, this most acceptable benefit to the people, that he brought so vast a quantity of money into the public treasury, that they never paid any taxes, until Hirtius and Pansa were consuls, which was in the first war between Antony and Cæsar. This also was peculiar and remarkable in Æmilius, that though he was extremely beloved and honored by the people, yet he always sided with the nobles; nor would he either say or do any thing to ingratiate himself with the multitude, but constantly adhered to the nobility, in all political matters, which in after-times was cast in Scipio Africanus's teeth by Appius; these two being in their time the most considerable men in the city, and standing in competition for the office of censor. The one had on his side the nobles and the senate, to which party the Appii were always attached; the other, although his own interest was great, yet made use of the favor and love of the people. When, therefore, Appius saw Scipio come to the market-place, surrounded with men of mean rank, and such as were but newly made free, yet were very fit to manage a debate, to gather together the rabble, and to carry whatsoever they designed by importunity and noise, crying out with a loud voice: "Groan now," said he, "O Æmilius Paulus, if you have knowledge in your grave of what is done above, that your son aspires to be censor, by the help of Æmilius, the common crier, and Licinius Philonicus." Scipio always had the good-will of the people, because he was constantly heaping favors on them; but Æmilius, although he still took part with the nobles, yet was as much the people's favorite as those who most sought popularity and used every art to obtain it. This they made manifest, when, amongst other dignities, they thought him worthy of the office of censor, a trust accounted most sacred and of great authority, as well in other things, as in the strict examination into men's lives. For the censors had power to expel a senator, and enrol whom they judged most fit in his room, and to disgrace such young men as lived licentiously, by taking away their horses. Besides this, they were to value and assess each man's estate, and register the number of the people. There were numbered by Æmilius, 337,452 men. He declared Marcus Æmilius Lepidus first senator, who had already four times held that honor, and he removed from their office three of the senators of the least note. The same moderation he and his fellow censor, Marcius Philippus, used at the muster of the knights.

Whilst he was thus busy about many and weighty affairs, he fell sick of a disease, which at first seemed hazardous; and although after awhile it proved without danger, yet was troublesome and difficult to be cured: so that by the advice of his physicians he sailed to Velia, in South Italy, and there dwelt a long time near the sea, where he enjoyed all possible quietness. The Romans, in the mean while, longed for his return, and oftentimes by their expressions in the theatres, gave public testimony of their great desire and impatience to see him. When, therefore, the time drew nigh that a solemn sacrifice was of necessity to be offered, and he found, as he thought, his body strong enough, he came back again to Rome, and there performed the holy rites with the rest of the priests, the people in the mean time crowding about him, and congratulating his return. The next day he sacrificed again to the gods for his recovery; and, having finished the sacrifice, returned to his house and sat down to dinner, when, all on a sudden and when no change was expected, he fell into a fit of delirium, and, being quite deprived of his senses, the third day after ended a life, in which he had wanted no manner of thing which is thought to conduce to happiness. Nay, his very funeral pomp had something in it remarkable and to be admired, and his virtue was graced with the most solemn and happy rites at his burial; consisting, not in gold and ivory, or in the usual sumptuousness and splendor of such preparations, but in the good-will, honor, and love, not only of his fellow-citizens, but of his enemies themselves. For as many Spaniards, Ligurians, and Macedonians, as happened to be present at the solemnity, that were young and of vigorous bodies, took up the bier and carried it; whilst the more aged followed, calling Æmilius the benefactor and preserver of their countries. For not only at the time of his conquest had he acted to all with kindness and clemency, but, through the whole course of his life, he continued to do them good and look after their concerns, as if they had been his familiars and relations. They report, that the whole of his estate scarce amounted to three hundred and seventy thousand drachmas; to which he left his two sons coheirs; but Scipio, who was the youngest, being adopted into the more wealthy family of Africanus, gave it all to his brother. Such are said to have been the life and manners of Æmilius.

COMPARISON OF TIMOLEON WITH ÆMILIUS PAULUS

Such being the story of these two great men's lives, without doubt in the comparison very little difference will be found between them. They made war with two powerful enemies; the one against the Macedonians, and the other with the Carthaginians; and the success was in both cases glorious. One conquered Macedon from the seventh succeeding heir of Antigonus; the other freed Sicily from usurping tyrants, and restored the island to its former liberty. Unless, indeed, it be made a point on Æmilius's side, that he engaged with Perseus when his forces were entire, and composed of men that had often successfully fought with the Romans; whereas, Timoleon found Dionysius in a despairing condition, his affairs being reduced to the last extremity: or, on the contrary, it be urged in favor of Timoleon, that he vanquished several tyrants, and a powerful Carthaginian army, with an inconsiderable number of men gathered together from all parts, not with such an army as Æmilius had, of well disciplined soldiers, experienced in war, and accustomed to obey; but with such as through the hopes of gain resorted to him, unskilled in fighting and ungovernable. And when actions are equally glorious, and the means to compass them unequal, the greatest esteem is certainly due to that general who conquers with the smaller power.

Both have the reputation of having behaved themselves with an uncorrupted integrity, in all the affairs they managed: but Æmilius had the advantage of being, from his infancy, by the laws and customs of his country, brought up to the proper management of public affairs, which Timoleon brought himself to by his own efforts. And this is plain; for at that time all the Romans were uniformly orderly and obedient, respectful to the laws and to their fellow-citizens: whereas it is remarkable, that not one of the Greek generals commanding in Sicily, could keep himself uncorrupted, except Dion, and of him many entertain a jealousy that he would establish a monarchy there, after the Lacedæmonian manner. Timæus writes, that the Syracusans sent even Gylippus home dishonorably, and with a reputation lost by the unsatiable covetousness he displayed when he commanded the army. And numerous historians tell us of the wicked and perfidious acts committed by Pharax the Spartan, and Callippus the Athenian, with the view of making themselves kings of Sicily. Yet what were these men, and what strength had they, to entertain such a thought? The first of them was a follower of Dionysius, when he was expelled from Syracuse, and the other a hired captain of foot under Dion, and came into Sicily with him. But Timoleon at the request and prayers of the Syracusans, was sent to be their general, and had no need to seek for power, but had a perfect title, founded on their own offers, to hold it; and yet no sooner had he freed Sicily from her oppressors, but he willingly surrendered it.

It is truly worthy our admiration in Æmilius, that, though he conquered so great and so rich a realm as that of Macedon, yet he would not touch, nor see any of the money, nor did he advantage himself one farthing by it, though he was very generous of his own to others. I would not intend any reflection on Timoleon, for accepting of a house and handsome estate in the country, which the Syracusans presented him with; there is no dishonor in accepting; but yet there is greater glory in a refusal, and the supremest virtue is shown in not wanting what it might fairly take. And as that body is, without doubt, the most strong and healthful, which can the easiest support extreme cold and excessive heat in the change of seasons, and that the most firm and collected mind which is not puffed up with prosperity, nor dejected with adversity; so the virtue of Æmilius was eminently seen in his countenance and behavior continuing as noble and lofty upon the loss of two dear sons, as when he achieved his greatest victories and triumphs. But Timoleon, after he had justly punished his brother, a truly heroic action, let his reason yield to a causeless sorrow, and, humiliated with grief and remorse, forbore for twenty years to appear in any public place, or meddle with any affairs of the commonwealth. It is truly very commendable to abhor and shun the doing any base action; but to stand in fear of every kind of censure or disrepute, may argue a gentle and open-hearted, but not an heroic temper.

PELOPIDAS[1]

TRANSLATED BY THOMAS CREECH, OF
WADHAM COLLEGE, OXFORD

CATO Major, hearing some commend one that was rash, and inconsiderately daring in a battle, said, "There is a difference between a man's prizing valor at a great rate, and valuing life at little;" a very just remark. Antigonus, we know, at least, had a soldier, a venturous fellow, but of wretched health and constitution; the reason of whose ill looks he took the trouble to inquire into; and, on understanding from him that it was a disease, commanded his physicians to employ their utmost skill, and if possible recover him; which brave hero, when once cured, never afterwards sought danger or showed himself venturous in battle; and, when Antigonus wondered and upbraided him with his change, made no secret of the reason, and said, "Sir, you are the cause of my cowardice, by freeing me from those miseries which made me care little for life." With the same feeling, the Sybarite seems to have said of the Spartans, that it was no commendable thing in them to be so ready to die in the wars, since by that they were freed from such hard labor, and miserable living. In truth, the Sybarites, a soft and dissolute people, might very well imagine they hated life, because in their eager pursuit of virtue

---

[1] Pelopidas, the Theban general and statesman, was descended from a noble family. He took a leading part in expelling the Spartans from Thebes in 379 B.C., and from this time until his death, as related by Plutarch, there was not a year in which he was not entrusted with some important command.—DR. WILLIAM SMITH.

and glory, they were not afraid to die: but, in fact, the Lacedæmonians found their virtue secure them happiness alike in living or in dying; as we see in the epitaph that says:—

> They died, but not as lavish of their blood,
> Or thinking death itself was simply good;
> Their wishes neither were to live nor die,
> But to do both alike commendably.

An endeavor to avoid death is not blamable, if we do not basely desire to live; nor a willingness to die good and virtuous, if it proceeds from a contempt of life. And therefore Homer always takes care to bring his bravest and most daring heroes well armed into battle; and the Greek lawgivers punished those that threw away their shields, but not him that lost his sword or spear; intimating that self-defence is more a man's business than offence. This is especially true of a governor of a city, or a general; for if, as Iphicrates divides it out, the light-armed are the hands; the horse the feet; the infantry the breast; and the general the head; he, when he puts himself upon danger, not only ventures his own person, but all those whose safety depends on his; and so on the contrary. Callicratidas, therefore, though otherwise a great man, was wrong in his answer to the augur who advised him, the sacrifice being unlucky, to be careful of his life; "Sparta," said he, "will not miss one man." It was true, Callicratidas, when simply serving in any engagement either at sea or land, was but a single person, but as general, he united in his life the lives of all, and could hardly be called one, when his death involved the ruin of so many. The saying of old Antigonus was better, who, when he was to fight at Andros, and one told him, "The enemy's ships are more than ours;" replied, "For how many then wilt thou reckon me?" intimating that a brave and experienced commander is to be highly valued, one of the first duties of whose office indeed it is to save him on whose safety depends that of others. And therefore I applaud Timotheus, who, when Chares showed the wounds he had received, and his shield pierced by a dart, told him, "Yet how ashamed I was, at the siege of Samos, when a dart fell near me, for exposing myself, more like a boy than like a general in command of a large army." Indeed, where the general's hazarding himself will go far to decide the result, there he must fight and venture his person, and not mind their maxims, who would have a general die, if not *of*, at least *in* old age; but when the advantage will be but small if he gets the better, and the loss considerable if he falls, who then would desire, at the risk of the commander's life, a piece of success which a common soldier might obtain? This I thought fit to premise before the lives of Pelopidas and Marcellus, who were both great men, but who both fell by their own rashness. For, being gallant men, and having gained their respective countries great glory and reputation by their conduct in war against terrible enemies, the one, as history relates, overthrowing Hannibal, who was till then invincible; the other, in a set battle beating the Lacedæmonians, then supreme both at sea and land; they ventured at last too far, and were heedlessly prodigal of their lives, when there was the greatest need of men and commanders such as they. And this agreement in their characters and their deaths, is the reason why I compare their lives.

Pelopidas, the son of Hippoclus, was descended,

as likewise Epaminondas was, from an honorable family in Thebes; and, being brought up to opulence, and having a fair estate left him whilst he was young, he made it his business to relieve the good and deserving amongst the poor, that he might show himself lord and not slave of his estate. For amongst men, as Aristotle observes, some are too narrow-minded to use their wealth, and some are loose and abuse it; and these live perpetual slaves to their pleasures, as the others to their gain. Others permitted themselves to be obliged by Pelopidas, and thankfully made use of his liberality and kindness; but amongst all his friends, he could never persuade Epaminondas to be a sharer in his wealth. He, however, stepped down into his poverty, and took pleasure in the same poor attire, spare diet, unwearied endurance of hardships, and unshrinking boldness in war: like Capaneus in Euripides, who had

> Abundant wealth and in that wealth no pride;[2]

he was ashamed any one should think that he spent more upon his person than the meanest Theban. Epaminondas made his familiar and hereditary poverty more light and easy, by his philosophy and single life; but Pelopidas married a woman of good family, and had children; yet still thinking little of his private interests, and devoting all his time to the public, he ruined his estate: and, when his friends admonished and told him how necessary that money which he neglected was; "Yes," he replied, "necessary to Nicodemus," pointing to a blind cripple.

[2] The verse is from the Suppliants of Euripides (861), where Adrastus describes to Theseus the chiefs who fell at Thebes.

Both seemed equally fitted by nature for all sorts of excellence; but bodily exercises chiefly delighted Pelopidas, learning Epaminondas; and the one spent his spare hours in hunting, and the Palæstra, the other in hearing lectures or philosophizing. And, amongst a thousand points for praise in both, the judicious esteem nothing equal to that constant benevolence and friendship, which they inviolably preserved in all their expeditions, public actions, and administration of the commonwealth. For if any one looks on the administrations of Aristides and Themistocles, of Cimon and Pericles, of Nicias and Alcibiades, what confusion, what envy, what mutual jealousy appears? And if he then casts his eye on the kindness and reverence that Pelopidas showed Epaminondas, he must needs confess, that these are more truly and more justly styled colleagues in government and command than the others, who strove rather to overcome one another, than their enemies. The true cause of this was their virtue; whence it came that they did not make their actions aim at wealth and glory, an endeavor sure to lead to bitter and contentious jealousy; but both from the beginning being inflamed with a divine desire of seeing their country glorious by their exertions, they used to that end one another's excellences as their own. Many, indeed, think this strict and entire affection is to be dated from the battle at Mantinea,[3] where they both fought, being part of the succors that were sent from Thebes to the Lacedæmonians, their then

---

[3] *The battle at Mantinea* is the first and less famous battle, fought in the period of the Peloponnesian War by the Argives and their allies against the Lacedæmonians, and described by Thucydides in his 5th book.

friends and allies. For, being placed together amongst the infantry, and engaging the Arcadians, when the Lacedæmonian wing, in which they fought, gave ground, and many fled, they closed their shields together and resisted the assailants. Pelopidas, having received seven wounds in the forepart of his body, fell upon an heap of slain friends and enemies; but Epaminondas, though he thought him past recovery, advanced to defend his arms and body, and singly fought a multitude, resolving rather to die than forsake his helpless Pelopidas. And now, he being much distressed, being wounded in the breast by a spear, and in the arm by a sword, Agesipolis, the king of the Spartans, came to his succor from the other wing, and beyond hope delivered both.

After this the Lacedæmonians pretended to be friends to Thebes, but in truth looked with jealous suspicions on the designs and power of the city, and chiefly hated the party of Ismenias and Androclides, in which Pelopidas also was an associate, as tending to liberty, and the advancement of the commonalty. Therefore Archias, Leontidas, and Philip, all rich men, and of oligarchical principles, and immoderately ambitious, urged Phœbidas the Spartan, as he was on his way past the city with a considerable force, to surprise the Cadmea, and, banishing the contrary faction, to establish an oligarchy, and by that means subject the city to the supremacy of the Spartans. He, accepting the proposal, at the festival of Ceres unexpectedly fell on the Thebans, and made himself master of the citadel. Ismenias was taken, carried to Sparta, and in a short time murdered; but Pelopidas, Pherenicus, Androclides,[4] and

[4] *Androclides*, and *Damoclides* further on, might be more correctly written *Androclidas* or *Androcleidas*, and *Damoclidas*

many more that fled were publicly proclaimed outlaws. Epaminondas stayed at home, being not much looked after, as one whom philosophy had made inactive, and poverty incapable.

The Lacedæmonians cashiered Phœbidas, and fined him one hundred thousand drachmas, yet still kept a garrison in the Cadmea; which made all Greece wonder at their inconsistency, since they punished the doer, but approved the deed. And though the Thebans, having lost their polity, and being enslaved by Archias and Leontidas, had no hopes to get free from this tyranny, which they saw guarded by the whole military power of the Spartans, and had no means to break the yoke, unless these could be deposed from their command of sea and land; yet Leontidas and his associates, understanding that the exiles lived at Athens in favor with the people, and with honor from all the good and virtuous, formed secret designs against their lives, and, suborning some unknown fellows, despatched Androclides, but were not successful on the rest. Letters, besides, were sent from Sparta to the Athenians, warning them neither to receive nor countenance the exiles, but

or *Damocleidas,* like *Meneclidas* or *Menecleidas,* in page 247. The whole of the narrative that follows, of the way in which the plot was carried out, is ingeniously expanded so as to form the framework of Plutarch's philosophic piece ON THE GENIUS (or *daimonion*) OF SOCRATES. Caphisias, brother of Epaminondas, being at Athens shortly after as an envoy, relates it to his philosophic friends there; the interest of course being in the events, but the greater amount of space being given to the conversation that had passed on the philosophic subject, this in its turn serving to show the composure and equanimity of the noble Thebans at the time.

expel them as declared common enemies of the confederacy. But the Athenians, from their natural hereditary inclination to be kind, and also to make a grateful return to the Thebans, who had very much assisted them in restoring their democracy, and had publicly enacted, that if any Athenian would march armed through Bœotia against the tyrants, that no Bœotian should either see or hear it, did the Thebans no harm.

Pelopidas, though one of the youngest, was active in privately exciting each single exile; and often told them at their meetings, that it was both dishonorable and impious to neglect their enslaved and engarrisoned country, and, lazily contented with their own lives and safety, depend on the decrees of the Athenians, and through fear fawn on every smooth-tongued orator that was able to work upon the people: no, they must venture for this great prize, taking Thrasybulus' bold courage for example, and as he advanced from Thebes and broke the power of the Athenian tyrants, so they should march from Athens and free Thebes. When by this method he had persuaded them, they privately despatched some persons to those friends they had left at Thebes, and acquainted them with their designs. Their plans being approved, Charon, a man of the greatest distinction, offered his house for their reception; Phillidas contrived to get himself made secretary to Archias and Philip, who then held the office of polemarch or chief captain; and Epaminondas had already inflamed the youth. For, in their exercises, he had encouraged them to challenge and wrestle with the Spartans, and again, when he saw them puffed up with victory and success, sharply told them, it was the greater shame to be such cowards as to serve those whom in strength they so much excelled.

The day for action being fixed, it was agreed upon by the exiles, that Pherenicus with the rest should stay in the Thriasian plain, while some few of the younger men tried the first danger, by endeavoring to get into the city; and, if they were surprised by their enemies, the others should take care to provide for their children and parents. Pelopidas first offered to undertake the business; then Melon, Damoclides, and Theopompus, men of noble families, who, in other things loving and faithful to one another, were constant rivals only in glory and courageous exploits. They were twelve in all, and having taken leave of those that stayed behind, and sent a messenger to Charon, they went forward, clad in short coats, and carrying hounds and hunting poles with them, that they might be taken for hunters beating over the fields, and prevent all suspicion in those that met them on the way. When the messenger came to Charon, and told him they were approaching, he did not change his resolution at the sight of danger, but, being a man of his word, offered them his house. But one Hipposthenidas, a man of no ill principles, a lover of his country, and a friend to the exiles, but not of as much resolution as the shortness of time and the character of the action required, being as it were dizzied at the greatness of the approaching enterprise; and beginning now for the first time to comprehend that, relying on that weak assistance which could be expected from the exiles, they were undertaking no less a task than to shake the government, and overthrow the whole power of Sparta; went privately to his house, and sent a friend to Melon and Pelopidas, desiring them to forbear for the present, to return to Athens and expect a better opportunity. The messenger's name was Chlidon, who, going home in haste and bringing out his horse, asked for the bridle; but, his wife not knowing where it was, and, when it could not be found, telling him she had lent it to a friend, first they began to chide, then to curse one another, and his wife wished the journey might prove ill to him, and those that sent him; insomuch that Chlidon's passion made him waste a great part of the day in this quarrelling, and then, looking on this chance as an omen, he laid aside all thoughts of his journey, and went away to some other business. So nearly had these great and glorious designs, even in their very birth, lost their opportunity.

But Pelopidas and his companions, dressing themselves like countrymen, divided, and, whilst it was yet day, entered at different quarters of the city. It was, besides, a windy day, and it now just began to snow, which contributed much to their concealment, because most people were gone in doors to avoid the weather. Those, however, that were concerned in the design, received them as they came, and conducted them to Charon's house, where the exiles and the others made up forty-eight in number. The tyrants' affairs stood thus: the secretary, Phillidas, as I have already observed, was an accomplice in, and privy to all the contrivance of the exiles, and he a while before had invited Archias, with others, to an entertainment on that day, to drink freely, and meet some women of the town, on purpose that when they were drunk, and given up to their pleasures, he might deliver them over to the conspirators. But before Archias was thoroughly heated, notice was given him that the exiles were privately in the town; a true report indeed, but obscure, and not well confirmed: nevertheless, though Phillidas endeavored to divert the discourse, Archias sent one of his guard to Charon, and commanded him to attend immediately. It was evening, and Pelopidas and his friends with him in the house, were putting themselves into a fit posture for action, having their breastplates on already, and their swords girt: but at the sudden knocking at the door, one stepping forth to inquire the matter, and learning from the officer that Charon was sent for by the polemarchs, returned in great confusion and acquainted those within; and all immediately conjectured that the whole plot was discovered, and they should be cut in pieces, before so much as achieving any action to do credit to their bravery; yet all agreed that Charon should obey, and attend the polemarchs, to prevent suspicion. Charon was, indeed, a man of courage and resolution in all dangers, yet in this case he was extremely concerned, lest any should suspect that he was the traitor, and the death of so many brave citizens be laid on him. And, therefore, when he was ready to depart, he brought his son out of the women's apartment, a little boy as yet, but one of the best looking and strongest of all those of his age, and delivered him to Pelopidas with these words: " If you find me a traitor, treat this boy as an enemy without any mercy." The concern which Charon showed, drew tears from many; but all protested vehemently against his supposing any one of them so mean-spirited and base, at the appearance of approaching danger, as to suspect or blame him; and therefore, desired him not to involve his son, but to set him out of harm's way; that so he, perhaps, escaping the tyrant's power, might live to revenge the city and his friends. Charon, however, refused to remove him, and asked, "What life, what safety could be more honorable, than to die bravely with his father, and such generous companions?" Thus, imploring the protection of the gods, and saluting and encouraging them all, he departed, considering with himself, and composing his voice and countenance, that he might look as little like as possible to what in fact he really was.

When he was come to the door, Archias with Phillidas [5] came out to him, and said, " I have heard, Charon, that there are some men just come, and lurking in the town, and that some of the citizens are resorting to them." Charon was at first disturbed, but asking, "Who are they? and who conceals them?" and finding Archias did not thoroughly understand the matter, he concluded that none of those privy to the design had given this information, and replied, "Do not disturb yourselves for an empty rumor: I will look into it, however, for no report in such a case is to be neglected." Phillidas, who stood by, commended him, and leading back Archias, got him deep in drink, still prolonging the entertainment with the hopes of the women's company at last. But when Charon returned, and found the men prepared, not as if they hoped for safety and success, but to die bravely and with the slaughter of their enemies, he told Pelopidas and his friends the truth, but pretended to others in the house that Archias talked to him about something else, inventing a story for the occasion. This storm was just blowing over, when fortune brought another; for a messenger came with

---

[5] *Archias with Phillidas* should be, as appears by the parallel passage in the dialogue De Genio Socratis, *Archias with Philippus* or *Philip*.

a letter from one Archias, the Hierophant at Athens, to his namesake Archias, who was his friend and guest. This did not merely contain a vague conjectural suspicion, but, as appeared afterwards, disclosed every particular of the design. The messenger being brought in to Archias, who was now pretty well drunk, and delivering the letter, said to him, "The writer of this desired it might be read at once; it is on urgent business." Archias, with a smile, replied, "Urgent business to-morrow," and so receiving the letter, he put it under his pillow, and returned to what he had been speaking of with Phillidas; and these words of his are a proverb to this day amongst the Greeks.

Now when the opportunity seemed convenient for action, they set out in two companies; Pelopidas and Damoclides with their party went against Leontidas and Hypates, that lived near together; Charon and Melon against Archias and Philip, having put on women's apparel over their breastplates, and thick garlands of fir and pine to shade their faces; and so, as soon as they came to the door, the guests clapped and gave an huzza, supposing them to be the women they expected. But when the conspirators had looked about the room, and carefully marked all that were at the entertainment, they drew their swords, and making at Archias and Philip amongst the tables, disclosed who they were. Phillidas persuaded some few of his guests to sit still, and those that got up and endeavored to assist the polemarchs, being drunk, were easily despatched. But Pelopidas and his party met with a harder task; as they attempted Leontidas, a sober and formidable man, and when they came to his house found his doors shut, he being already gone to bed. They knocked a long time before any one would answer, but, at last, a servant that heard them, coming out and unbarring the door, as soon as the gate gave way, they rushed in, and, overturning the man, made all haste to Leontidas's chamber. But Leontidas, guessing at the matter by the noise and running, leaped from his bed and drew his dagger, but forgot to put out the lights, and by that means make them fall foul on one another in the dark. As it was, being easily seen by reason of the light, he received them at his chamber door, and stabbed Cephisodorus, the first man that entered: on his falling, the next that he engaged was Pelopidas; and the passage being narrow and Cephisodorus's body lying in the way, there was a fierce and dangerous conflict. At last Pelopidas prevailed, and having killed Leontidas, he and his companions went in pursuit of Hypates, and after the same manner broke into his house. He perceived the design, and fled to his neighbors; but they closely followed, and caught and killed him.

This done they joined Melon, and sent to hasten the exiles they had left in Attica: and called upon the citizens to maintain their liberty, and taking down the spoils from the porches, and breaking open all the armorers' shops that were near, equipped those that came to their assistance. Epaminondas and Gorgidas came in already armed, with a gallant train of young men, and the best of the old. Now the city was in a great excitement and confusion, a great noise and hurry, lights set up in every house, men running here and there; however, the people did not as yet gather into a body, but, amazed at the proceedings, and not clearly understanding the matter waited for the day. And, therefore, the Spartan officers were thought to have been in fault for not falling on at once, since their garrison consisted of about fifteen hundred men, and many of the citizens ran to them; but, alarmed with the noise, the fires, and the confused running of the people, they kept quietly within the Cadmea. As soon as day appeared, the exiles from Attica came in armed, and there was a general assembly of the people. Epaminondas and Gorgidas brought forth Pelopidas and his party, encompassed by the priests, who held out garlands, and exhorted the people to fight for their country and their gods. The assembly, at their appearance, rose up in a body, and with shouts and acclamations received the men as their deliverers and benefactors.

Then Pelopidas, being chosen chief captain [6] of Bœotia, together with Melon and Charon, proceeded at once to blockade the citadel, and stormed it on all sides, being extremely desirous to expel the Lacedæmonians, and free the Cadmea, before an army could come from Sparta to their relief. And he just so narrowly succeeded, that they, having surrendered on terms and departed, on their way home met Cleombrotus at Megara marching towards Thebes with a considerable force. The Spartans condemned and executed Herippidas and Arcissus, two of their governors [7] at Thebes, and Lysanoridas the third being severely fined, fled Peloponnesus. This action so closely resembling that of Thrasybulus, in the courage of the actors, the danger, the encounters, and equally crowned with success, was called the sister of it by the Greeks. For we can scarcely find any other examples where so small and weak a party of men by bold courage overcame such numerous and powerful enemies, or brought greater blessings to their coun-

[6] Bœotarch.   [7] Harmostæ.

try by so doing. But the subsequent change of affairs made this action the more famous; for the war which forever ruined the pretensions of Sparta to command, and put an end to the supremacy she then exercised alike by sea and by land, proceeded from that night, in which Pelopidas not surprising any fort, or castle, or citadel, but coming, the twelfth man, to a private house, loosed and broke, if we may speak truth in metaphor, the chains of the Spartan sway, which before seemed of adamant and indissoluble.

But now the Lacedæmonians invading Bœotia with a great army, the Athenians, affrighted at the danger, declared themselves no allies to Thebes, and prosecuting those that stood for the Bœotian interest, executed some, and banished and fined others: and the cause of Thebes, destitute of allies, seemed in a desperate condition. But Pelopidas and Gorgidas, holding the office of captains of Bœotia, designing to breed a quarrel between the Lacedæmonians and Athenians, made this contrivance. One Sphodrias, a Spartan, a man famous indeed for courage in battle, but of no sound judgment, full of ungrounded hopes and foolish ambition, was left with an army at Thespiæ, to receive and succor the Theban renegades. To him Pelopidas and his colleagues privately sent a merchant, one of their friends, with money, and, what proved more efficient, advice,—that it more became a man of his worth to set upon some great enterprise, and that he should, making a sudden incursion on the unprotected Athenians, surprise the Piræus; since nothing could be so grateful to Sparta, as to take Athens; and the Thebans, of course, would not stir to the assistance of men whom they now hated and looked upon as traitors. Sphodrias, being at last wrought upon, marched into Attica by night with his army, and advanced as far as Eleusis; but there his soldiers' hearts failing, after exposing his project and involving the Spartans in a dangerous war, he retreated to Thespiæ. After this, the Athenians zealously sent supplies to Thebes, and putting to sea, sailed to many places, and offered support and protection to all those of the Greeks who were willing to revolt.

The Thebans, meantime, singly, having many skirmishes with the Spartans in Bœotia, and fighting some battles, not great indeed, but important as training and instructing them, thus had their minds raised, and their bodies inured to labor, and gained both experience and courage by these frequent encounters; insomuch that we have it related that Antalcidas, the Spartan, said to Agesilaus, returning wounded from Bœotia, "Indeed, the Thebans have paid you handsomely for instructing them in the art of war, against their wills." In real truth, however, Agesilaus was not their master in this, but those that prudently and opportunely, as men do young dogs, set them on their enemies, and brought them safely off after they had tasted the sweets of victory and resolution. Of all those leaders, Pelopidas deserves the most honor: as after they had once chosen him general, he was every year in command as long as he lived; either captain of the sacred band, or, what was most frequent, chief captain [8] of Bœotia. About Platæa and Thespiæ the Spartans were routed and put to flight, and Phœbidas, that surprised the Cadmea, slain; and at Tanagra a considerable force was worsted, and the leader [9] Panthoides killed. But these encounters, though they raised the victor's spirits,

[8] Bœotarch. [9] Harmost.

did not thoroughly dishearten the unsuccessful; for
there was no set battle, or regular fighting, but
mere incursions on advantage, in which, according to
occasion, they charged, retired again, or pursued.
But the battle at Tegyræ, which seemed a prelude
to Leuctra, won Pelopidas a great reputation; for
none of the other commanders could claim any
hand in the design, nor the enemies any show of
victory. The city of the Orchomenians siding with
the Spartans, and having received two companies [10]
for its guard, he kept a constant eye upon it, and
watched his opportunity. Hearing that the garrison had moved into Locris, and hoping to find
Orchomenus defenceless, he marched with his sacred
band, and some few horsemen. But when he approached the city, and found that a reinforcement
of the garrison was on its march from Sparta, he
made a circuit round the foot of the mountains, and
retreated with his little army through Tegyræ, that
being the only way he could pass. For the river
Melas, almost as soon as it rises, spreads itself
into marshes and navigable pools, and makes all
the plain between impassable. A little below the
marshes stands the temple and oracle of Apollo
Tegyræus, forsaken not long before that time, having flourished till the Median wars, Echecrates
then being priest. Here they profess that the god
was born; the neighboring mountain is called Delos,
and there the river Melas comes again into a channel; behind the temple rise two springs, admirable
for the sweetness, abundance, and coolness of the
streams; one they call Phœnix, the other Elæa, even
to the present time, as if Lucina had not been
delivered between two trees, but fountains. A place
hard by, called Ptoum, is shown, where they say

[10] Mŏras.

she was affrighted by the appearance of a boar; and the stories of the Python and Tityus are in like manner appropriated by these localities. I omit many of the points that are used as arguments. For our tradition does not rank this god amongst those that were born, and then made immortal, as Hercules and Bacchus, whom their virtue raised above a mortal and passible condition; but Apollo is one of the eternal unbegotten deities, if we may collect any certainty concerning these things, from the statements of the oldest and wisest in such subjects.

As the Thebans were retreating from Orchomenus towards Tegyræ, the Spartans, at the same time marching from Locris, met them. As soon as they came in view, advancing through the straits, one told Pelopidas, "We are fallen into our enemy's hands;" he replied, "And why not they into ours?" and immediately commanded his horse to come up from the rear and charge, while he himself drew his infantry, being three hundred in number, into a close body, hoping by that means, at whatsoever point he made the attack, to break his way through his more numerous enemies. The Spartans had two companies, (the company consisting, as Ephorus states, of five hundred; Callisthenes says seven hundred; others, as Polybius, nine hundred;) and their leaders, Gorgoleon and Theopompus, confident of success, advanced upon the Thebans. The charge being made with much fury, chiefly where the commanders were posted, the Spartan captains that engaged Pelopidas were first killed; and those immediately around them suffering severely, the whole army was thus disheartened, and opened a lane for the Thebans, as if they desired to pass through and escape. But when Pelopidas entered, and turning against those that stood their ground, still went on with a bloody slaughter, an open flight ensued amongst the Spartans. The pursuit was carried but a little way, because they feared the neighboring Orchomenians, and the reinforcement from Lacedæmon; they had succeeded, however, in fighting a way through their enemies, and overpowering their whole force; and, therefore, erecting a trophy, and spoiling the slain, they returned home extremely encouraged with their achievements. For in all the great wars there had ever been against Greeks or barbarians, the Spartans were never before beaten by a smaller company than their own; nor, indeed, in a set battle, when their number was equal. Hence their courage was thought irresistible, and their high repute before the battle made a conquest already of enemies, who thought themselves no match for the men of Sparta even on equal terms. But this battle first taught the other Greeks, that not only Eurotas, or the country between Babyce and Cnacion, breeds men of courage and resolution; but that where the youth are ashamed of baseness, and ready to venture in a good cause, where they fly disgrace more than danger, there, wherever it be, are found the bravest and most formidable opponents.

Gorgidas, according to some, first formed the Sacred Band of three hundred chosen men, to whom, as being a guard for the citadel, the State allowed provision, and all things necessary for exercise: and hence they were called the city band, as citadels of old were usually called cities. Others say that it was composed of young men attached to each other by personal affection, and a pleasant saying of Pammenes is current, that Homer's Nestor was not well skilled in ordering an army, when he advised the Greeks to rank tribe and tribe, and family and family together, that

> So tribe might tribe, and kinsmen kinsmen aid,[11]

but that he should have joined lovers and their beloved. For men of the same tribe or family little value one another when dangers press; but a band cemented by friendship grounded upon love, is never to be broken, and invincible; since the lovers, ashamed to be base in sight of their beloved, and the beloved before their lovers, willingly rush into danger for the relief of one another. Nor can that be wondered at; since they have more regard for their absent lovers than for others present; as in the instance of the man, who, when his enemy was going to kill him, earnestly requested him to run him through the breast, that his lover might not blush to see him wounded in the back. It is a tradition likewise, that Iolaüs, who assisted Hercules in his labors and fought at his side, was beloved of him; and Aristotle observes, that even in his time, lovers plighted their faith at Iolaus's tomb. It is likely, therefore, that this band was called sacred on this account; as Plato calls a lover a divine friend. It is stated that it was never beaten till the battle at Chæronea: and when Philip, after the fight, took a view of the slain, and came to the place where the three hundred that fought his phalanx lay dead together, he wondered, and understanding that it was the band of lovers, he shed tears and said, "Perish any man who suspects that these men either did or suffered any thing that was base."

---

[11] The line is from Nestor's speech, Iliad II., 363.

It was not the disaster of Laius,[12] as the poets imagine, that first gave rise to this form of attachment amongst the Thebans, but their law-givers, designing to soften, whilst they were young, their natural fierceness, brought, for example, the pipe into great esteem, both in serious and sportive occasions, and gave great encouragement to these friendships in the Palæstra, to temper the manners and characters of the youth. With a view to this they did well, again, to make Harmony, the daughter of Mars and Venus, their tutelar deity; since, where force and courage is joined with gracefulness and winning behavior, a harmony ensues that combines all the elements of society in perfect consonance and order.—Gorgidas distributed this Sacred Band all through the front ranks of the infantry and thus made their gallantry less conspicuous; not being united in one body, but mingled with so many others of inferior resolution, they had no fair opportunity of showing what they could do. But Pelopidas, having sufficiently tried their bravery at Tegyræ, where they had fought alone, and around his own person, never afterward divided them, but keeping them entire, and as one man, gave them the first duty in the greatest battles. For as horses run brisker in a chariot than singly, not that their joint force divides the air with greater ease, but because being matched one against the other, emulation kindles and inflames their courage; thus he thought, brave men, provoking one another to noble actions, would prove most serviceable and most resolute, where all were united together.

[12] *The disaster of Laius,* or, more correctly, *what befell Laius,* alludes to the tale of his carrying away Chrysippus, the son of Pelops by the nymph Danais, an obscure story, which is, however, mentioned elsewhere by Plutarch.

Now when the Lacedæmonians had made peace with the other Greeks, and united all their strength against the Thebans only, and their king, Cleombrotus, had passed the frontier with ten thousand foot and one thousand horse, and not only subjection, as heretofore, but total dispersion and annihilation threatened, and Bœotia was in a greater fear than ever,—Pelopidas, leaving his house, when his wife followed him on his way, and with tears begged him to be careful of his life, made answer, "Private men, my wife, should be advised to look to themselves, generals to save others." And when he came to the camp, and found the chief captains [13] disagreeing, he, first, joined the side of Epaminondas, who advised to fight the enemy; though Pelopidas himself was not then in office as chief captain of Bœotia, but in command of the Sacred Band, and trusted as it was fit a man should be, who had given his country such proofs of his zeal for its freedom. And so, when a battle was agreed on, and they encamped in front of the Spartans at Leuctra, Pelopidas saw a vision, which much discomposed him. In that plain lie the bodies of the daughters of one Scedasus,[14] called from the place Leuctridæ, having been buried there, after having been ravished by some Spartan strangers. When this base and lawless deed was done, and their father could get no satisfaction at Lacedæmon, with

---

[13] Bœotarchs.

[14] Scedasus was a man who lived at Leuctra, and had daughters named Hippo and Molpia. These were violated by men of Lacedæmon, Parathemidas, Phrudarchidas, and Parthenius. The young women hung themselves, and the father, after going in vain to Sparta to seek redress, came home to Leuctra and killed himself.

bitter imprecations on the Spartans, he killed himself at his daughters' tombs: and, from that time, the prophecies and oracles still warned them to have a great care of the divine vengeance at Leuctra. Many, however, did not understand the meaning, being uncertain about the place, because there was a little maritime town of Laconia called Leuctron, and near Megalopolis in Arcadia a place of the same name; and the villany was committed long before this battle.

Now Pelopidas, being asleep in the camp, thought he saw the maidens weeping about their tombs, and cursing the Spartans, and Scedasus commanding, if they desired the victory, to sacrifice a virgin with chestnut hair to his daughters. Pelopidas looked on this as an harsh and impious injunction, but rose and told it to the prophets and commanders of the army, some of whom contended, that it was fit to obey, and adduced as examples from the ancients, Menœceus, son of Creon; Macaria, daughter of Hercules; and from later times, Pherecydes the philosopher, slain by the Lacedæmonians, and his skin, as the oracles advised, still kept by their kings. Leonidas, again, warned by the oracle, did as it were sacrifice himself for the good of Greece; Themistocles offered human victims to Bacchus Omestes, before the engagement at Salamis; and success showed their actions to be good. On the contrary, Agesilaus going from the same place, and against the same enemies that Agamemnon did, and, being commanded in a dream at Aulis to sacrifice his daughter, was so weak as to disobey; the consequence of which was, that his expedition was unsuccessful and inglorious. But some on the other side urged that such a barbarous and impious oblation could not be pleasing to any

Superior Beings: that typhons and giants did not preside over the world, but the general father of gods and men; that it was absurd to imagine any divinities or powers delighted in slaughter and sacrifices of men; or, if there were any such, they were to be neglected, as weak and unable to assist; such unreasonable and cruel desires could only proceed from, and live in weak and depraved minds.

The commanders thus disputing, and Pelopidas being in a great perplexity, a mare colt, breaking from the herd, ran through the camp, and when she came to the place where they were, stood still; and whilst some admired her bright chestnut color, others her mettle, or the strength and fury of her neighing, Theocritus, the augur, took thought, and cried out to Pelopidas, "O good friend! look, the sacrifice is come; expect no other virgin, but use that which the gods have sent thee." With that they took the colt, and, leading her to the maidens' sepulchres, with the usual solemnity and prayers, offered her with joy, and spread through the whole army the account of Pelopidas's dream, and how they had given the required sacrifice.

In the battle, Epaminondas, bending his phalanx to the left, that, as much as possible, he might divide the right wing, composed of Spartans, from the other Greeks, and distress Cleombrotus, by a fierce charge in column on that wing, the enemies perceived the design, and began to change their order, to open and extend their right wing, and, as they far exceeded him in number, to encompass Epaminondas. But Pelopidas with the three hundred came rapidly up, before Cleombrotus could extend his line, and close up his divisions, and so fell upon the Spartans while in disorder; though the Lacedæmonians, the expertest and most practised soldiers of all mankind, used to train and accustom themselves to nothing so much as to keep themselves from confusion upon any change of position, and to follow any leader, or right hand man, and form in order, and fight on what part soever dangers press. In this battle, however, Epaminondas with his phalanx, neglecting the other Greeks, and charging them alone, and Pelopidas coming up with such incredible speed and fury, so broke their courage, and baffled their art, that there began such a flight and slaughter amongst the Spartans, as was never before known. And so Pelopidas, though in no high office, but only captain of a small band, got as much reputation by the victory, as Epaminondas, who was general and chief captain of Bœotia.

Into Peloponnesus, however, they both advanced together as colleagues in supreme command, and gained the greater part of the nations there from the Spartan confederacy; Elis, Argos, all Arcadia, and much of Laconia itself. It was the dead of winter, and but few of the last days of the month remained, and, in the beginning of the next, new officers were to succeed, and whoever failed to deliver up his charge, forfeited his head. Therefore, the other chief captains fearing the law, and to avoid the sharpness of the winter, advised a retreat. But Pelopidas joined with Epaminondas, and, encouraging his countrymen, led them against Sparta, and, passing the Eurotas, took many of the towns, and wasted the country as far as the sea. This army consisted of seventy thousand Greeks, of which number the Thebans could not make the twelfth part; but the reputation of the men made all their allies contented to follow them as leaders, though no articles to that effect had been made. For, indeed, it seems the first and paramount law, that he that wants a defender, is naturally a subject to him that is able to defend: as mariners, though in a calm or in the port they grow insolent, and brave the pilot, yet when a storm comes, and danger is at hand, they all attend, and put their hopes in him. So the Argives, Eleans, and Arcadians, in their congresses, would contend with the Thebans for superiority in command, yet in a battle, or any hazardous undertaking, of their own will followed their Theban captains. In this expedition, they united all Arcadia into one body, and, expelling the Spartans that inhabited Messenia, they called back the old Messenians, and established them in Ithome in one body;—and, returning through Cenchreæ, they dispersed the Athenians, who designed to set upon them in the straits, and hinder their march.

For these exploits, all the other Greeks loved their courage, and admired their success; but among their own citizens, envy, still increasing with their glory, prepared them no pleasing nor agreeable reception. Both were tried for their lives, because they did not deliver up their command in the first month, Bucatius, as the law required, but kept it four months longer, in which time they did these memorable actions in Messenia, Arcadia, and Laconia. Pelopidas was first tried, and therefore in greatest danger, but both were acquitted. Epaminondas bore the accusation and trial very patiently, esteeming it a great and essential part of courage and generosity, not to resent injuries in political life. But Pelopidas, being a man of a fiercer temper, and stirred on by his friends to revenge the affront, took the following occasion. Meneclidas, the orator, was one of those that had met with Melon and Pelopidas at Charon's house; but

not receiving equal honor, and being powerful in
his speech, but loose in his manners, and ill natured,
he abused his natural endowments, even after this
trial, to accuse and calumniate his betters. He
excluded Epaminondas from the chief captaincy,
and for a long time kept the upper hand of him;
but he was not powerful enough to bring Pelopidas
out of the people's favor, and therefore endeavored
to raise a quarrel between him and Charon. And
since it is some comfort to the envious, to make
those men, whom themselves cannot excel, appear
worse than others, he studiously enlarged upon
Charon's actions in his speeches to the people, and
made panegyrics on his expeditions and victories;
and, of the victory which the horsemen won at
Platæa, before the battle at Leuctra, under
Charon's command, he endeavored to make the
following sacred memorial. Androcydes, the Cyzi-
cenian, had undertaken to paint a previous battle
for the city, and was at work in Thebes; and when
the revolt began, and the war came on, the Thebans
kept the picture that was then almost finished.
This picture Meneclidas persuaded them to dedicate, inscribed with Charon's name, designing by
that means to obscure the glory of Epaminondas
and Pelopidas. This was a ludicrous piece of pretension; to set a single victory, where only one
Gerandas, an obscure Spartan, and forty more
were slain, above such numerous and important
battles. This motion Pelopidas opposed, as contrary to law, alleging that it was not the custom of
the Thebans to honor any single man, but to
attribute the victory to their country; yet in all
the contest, he extremely commended Charon, and
confined himself to showing Meneclidas to be a
troublesome and envious fellow, asking the Thebans,

if they had done nothing that was excellent,[15].... insomuch that Meneclidas was severely fined; and he, being unable to pay, endeavored afterwards to disturb the government. These things give us some light into Pelopidas's life.

Now when Alexander, the tyrant of Pheræ, made open war against some of the Thessalians, and had designs against all, the cities sent an embassy to Thebes, to desire succors and a general; and Pelopidas, knowing that Epaminondas was detained by the Peloponnesian affairs, offered himself to lead the Thessalians, being unwilling to let his courage and skill lie idle, and thinking it unfit that Epaminondas should be withdrawn from his present duties. When he came into Thessaly with his army, he presently took Larissa, and endeavored to reclaim Alexander, who submitted, and bring him, from being a tyrant, to govern gently, and according to law; but finding him untractable and brutish, and hearing great complaints of his lust and cruelty, Pelopidas began to be severe, and used him roughly, insomuch that the tyrant stole away privately with his guard. But Pelopidas, leaving the Thessalians fearless of the tyrant, and friends amongst themselves, marched into Macedonia, where Ptolemy was then at war with Alexander, the king of Macedon; both parties having sent for him to hear and determine their differences, and assist the one that appeared injured. When he came, he reconciled them, called back the exiles, and, receiving for hostages Philip the king's brother, and thirty children of the nobles, he brought them to Thebes; showing the other Greeks how wide a reputation the Thebans had gained for honesty and courage. This was that Philip who afterward endeavored to

[15] Some words are probably lost here.

enslave the Greeks: then he was a boy, and lived with Pammenes in Thebes; and hence some conjecture, that he took Epaminondas's actions for the rule of his own; and perhaps, indeed, he did take example from his activity and skill in war, which, however, was but a small portion of his virtues; of his temperance, justice, generosity, and mildness, in which he was truly great, Philip enjoyed no share, either by nature or imitation.

After this, upon a second complaint of the Thessalians against Alexander of Pheræ, as a disturber of the cities, Pelopidas was joined with Ismenias, in an embassy to him; but led no forces from Thebes, not expecting any war, and therefore was necessitated to make use of the Thessalians upon the emergency. At the same time, also, Macedon was in confusion again, as Ptolemy had murdered the king, and seized the government: but the king's friends sent for Pelopidas, and he, being willing to interpose in the matter, but having no soldiers of his own, enlisted some mercenaries in the country, and with them marched against Ptolemy. When they faced one another, Ptolemy corrupted these mercenaries with a sum of money, and persuaded them to revolt to him; but yet, fearing the very name and reputation of Pelopidas, he came to him as his superior, submitted, begged his pardon, and protested that he kept the government only for the brothers of the dead king, and would prove a friend to the friends, and an enemy to the enemies of Thebes; and, to confirm this, he gave his son, Philoxenus, and fifty of his companions, for hostages. These Pelopidas sent to Thebes; but he himself, being vexed at the treachery of the mercenaries, and understanding that most of their goods, their wives and children, lay at Pharsalus, so that if he could take them, the injury would be sufficiently revenged, got together some of the Thessalians, and marched to Pharsalus. When he had just entered the city, Alexander, the tyrant, appeared before it with an army; but Pelopidas and his friends, thinking that he came to clear himself from those crimes that were laid to his charge, went to him; and though they knew very well that he was profligate and cruel, yet they imagined that the authority of Thebes, and their own dignity and reputation, would secure them from violence. But the tyrant, seeing them come unarmed and alone, seized them, and made himself master of Pharsalus. Upon this his subjects were much intimidated, thinking that after so great and so bold an iniquity, he would spare none, but behave himself toward all, and in all matters, as one despairing of his life.

The Thebans, when they heard of this, were very much enraged, and despatched an army, Epaminondas being then in disgrace, under the command of other leaders. When the tyrant brought Pelopidas to Pheræ, at first he permitted those that desired it to speak with him, imagining that this disaster would break his spirit, and make him appear contemptible. But when Pelopidas advised the complaining Pheræans to be comforted, as if the tyrant was now certain in a short time to smart for his injuries, and sent to tell him, "That it was absurd daily to torment and murder his wretched innocent subjects, and yet spare him, who, he well knew, if ever he got his liberty, would be bitterly revenged;" the tyrant, wondering at his boldness and freedom of speech, replied, "And why is Pelopidas in haste to die?" He, hearing of it, rejoined, "That you may be the sooner ruined, being then more hated by the gods than now." From that time he forbade any to converse with him; but Thebe, the daughter of Jason and wife to Alexander, hearing from the keepers of the bravery and noble behavior of Pelopidas, had a great desire to see and speak with him. Now when she came into the prison, and, as a woman, could not at once discern his greatness in his calamity, only, judging by the meanness of his attire and general appearance, that he was used basely and not befitting a man of his reputation, she wept. Pelopidas, at first not knowing who she was, stood amazed; but when he understood, saluted her by her father's name— Jason and he having been friends and familiars— and she saying, " I pity your wife, Sir," he replied, " And I you, that though not in chains, can endure Alexander." This touched the woman, who already hated Alexander for his cruelty and injustice, for his general debaucheries, and for his abuse of her youngest brother. She, therefore, often went to Pelopidas, and, speaking freely of the indignities she suffered, grew more enraged, and more exasperated against Alexander.

The Theban generals that were sent into Thessaly did nothing, but, being either unskilful or unfortunate, made a dishonorable retreat, for which the city fined each of them ten thousand drachmas, and sent Epaminondas with their forces. The Thessalians, inspirited by the fame of this general, at once began to stir, and the tyrant's affairs were at the verge of destruction; so great was the fear that possessed his captains and his friends, and so eager the desire of his subjects to revolt, in hope of his speedy punishment. But Epaminondas, more solicitous for the safety of Pelopidas than his own glory, and fearing that if things came to extremity,

Alexander would grow desperate, and, like a wild beast, turn and worry him, did not prosecute the war to the utmost; but, hovering still over him with his army, he so handled the tyrant as not to leave him any confidence, and yet not to drive him to despair and fury. He was aware of his savageness, and the little value he had for right and justice, insomuch that sometimes he buried men alive, and sometimes dressed them in bear's and boar's skins, and then baited them with dogs, or shot at them for his divertisement. At Melibœa and Scotussa, two cities, his allies, he called all the inhabitants to an assembly, and then surrounded them and cut them to pieces with his guards. He consecrated the spear with which he killed his uncle Polyphron, and, crowning it with garlands, sacrificed to it as a god, and called it Tychon. And once seeing a tragedian act Euripides's Troades, he left the theatre; but sending for the actor, bade him not to be concerned at his departure, but act as he had been used to do, as it was not in contempt of him that he departed, but because he was ashamed that his citizens should see him, who never pitied any man that he murdered, weep at the sufferings of Hecuba and Andromache. This tyrant, however, alarmed at the very name, report, and appearance of an expedition under the conduct of Epaminondas, presently

>Dropped like a craven cock his conquered wing,

and sent an embassy to entreat and offer satisfaction. Epaminondas refused to admit such a man as an ally to the Thebans, but granted him a truce of thirty days, and, Pelopidas and Ismenias being delivered up, returned home.

Now the Thebans, understanding that the Spartans and Athenians had sent an embassy to the Persians for assistance, themselves, likewise, sent Pelopidas; an excellent design to increase his glory, no man having ever before passed through the dominions of the king with greater fame and reputation. For the glory that he won against the Spartans, did not creep slowly or obscurely; but, after the fame of the first battle at Leuctra was gone abroad, the report of new victories continually following, exceedingly increased, and spread his celebrity far and near. Whatever satraps or generals or commanders he met, he was the object of their wonder and discourse; "This is the man," they said, "who hath beaten the Lacedæmonians from sea and land, and confined that Sparta within Taÿgetus and Eurotas, which, but a little before, under the conduct of Agesilaus, was entering upon a war with the great king about Susa and Ecbatana." This pleased Artaxerxes, and he was the more inclined to show Pelopidas attention and honor, being desirous to seem reverenced, and attended by the greatest. But when he saw him and heard his discourse, more solid than the Athenians, and not so haughty as the Spartans, his regard was heightened, and, truly acting like a king, he openly showed the respect that he felt for him; and this the other ambassadors perceived. Of all other Greeks he had been thought to have done Antalcidas, the Spartan, the greatest honor, by sending him that garland dipped in an unguent, which he himself had worn at an entertainment. Indeed, he did not deal so delicately with Pelopidas, but, according to the custom, gave him the most splendid and considerable presents, and granted him his desires,—that the Grecians should be free, Messenia inhabited, and the Thebans accounted the king's hereditary friends. With these answers, but not accepting one of the presents, except what was a pledge of kindness and good-will, he returned. This behavior of Pelopidas ruined the other ambassadors: the Athenians condemned and executed their Timagoras, and, indeed, if they did it for receiving so many presents from the king, their sentence was just and good; as he not only took gold and silver, but a rich bed, and slaves to make it, as if the Greeks were unskilful in that art; besides eighty cows and herdsmen, professing he needed cow's milk for some distemper; and, lastly, he was carried in a litter to the seaside, with a present of four talents for his attendants. But the Athenians, perhaps, were not so much irritated at his greediness for the presents. For Epicrates [16] the baggage-carrier not only confessed to the people that he had received gifts from the king, but made a motion, that instead of nine archons, they should yearly choose nine poor citizens to be sent ambassadors to the king, and enriched by his presents, and the people only laughed at the joke. But they were vexed that the Thebans obtained their desires, never considering that Pelopidas's fame was more powerful than all their rhetorical discourse, with a man who still inclined to the victorious in arms. This embassy, having obtained

---

[16] *One Epicrates, a baggage carrier,* as it is in some editions, should at any rate be *Epicrates the baggage carrier (skeuophoros)*; perhaps *Epicrates, the shield carrier (sakesphoros,* a name which he has in the Comic writers (*Aristophanes, Ecclesiasuzæ,* 71, and *Plato, Legati, fragm.* 3), because of his immense shield-like beard. Epicrates was long prominent as a public speaker; he took part in the expulsion of the thirty tyrants and in all the subsequent political proceedings, and is the subject of one of the extant orations of Lysias.

the restitution of Messenia, and the freedom of the other Greeks, got Pelopidas a great deal of goodwill at his return.

At this time, Alexander the Pheræan falling back to his old nature, and having seized many of the Thessalian cities, and put garrisons upon the Achæans of Phthiotis, and the Magnesians, the cities, hearing that Pelopidas was returned, sent an embassy to Thebes, requesting succors, and him for their leader. The Thebans willingly granted their desire; and now when all things were prepared, and the general beginning to march, the sun was eclipsed, and darkness spread over the city at noonday. Now when Pelopidas saw them startled at the prodigy, he did not think it fit to force on men who were afraid and out of heart, nor to hazard seven thousand of his citizens; and therefore with only three hundred horse volunteers,[17] set forward himself to Thessaly, much against the will of the augurs and his fellow-citizens in general, who all imagined this marked portent to have reference to this great man. But he was heated against Alexander for the injuries he had received, and hoped likewise, from the discourse which formerly he had with Thebe, that his family by this time was divided and in disorder. But the glory of the expedition chiefly excited him; for he was extremely desirous at this time, when the Lacedæmonians were sending out military officers to assist Dionysius the Sicilian tyrant, and the Athenians took Alexander's pay, and honored him with a brazen statue as a benefactor, that the Thebans should be seen, alone, of

---

[17] In the line, after *three hundred horse volunteers*, should be added *and mercenary soldiers;* but the text appears to be uncertain.

all the Greeks, undertaking the cause of those who were oppressed by tyrants, and destroying the violent and illegal forms of government in Greece.

When Pelopidas was come to Pharsalus, he formed an army, and presently marched against Alexander; and Alexander understanding that Pelopidas had few Thebans with him, and that his own infantry was double the number of the Thessalians, faced him at Thetidium. Some one told Pelopidas, "The tyrant meets us with a great army;" "So much the better," he replied, "for then we shall overcome the more." Between the two armies lay some steep high hills about Cynoscephalæ, which both parties endeavored to take by their foot. Pelopidas commanded his horse, which were good and many, to charge that of the enemies; they routed and pursued them through the plain. But Alexander, meantime, took the hills, and charging the Thessalian foot that came up later, and strove to climb the steep and craggy ascent, killed the foremost, and the others, much distressed, could do the enemies no harm. Pelopidas, observing this, sounded a retreat to his horse, and gave orders that they should charge the enemies that kept their ground; and he himself, taking his shield, quickly joined those that fought about the hills, and, advancing to the front, filled his men with such courage and alacrity, that the enemies imagined they came with other spirits and other bodies to the onset. They stood two or three charges, but finding these come on stoutly, and the horse, also, returning from the pursuit, gave ground, and retreated in order. Pelopidas now perceiving, from the rising ground, that the enemy's army was, though not yet routed, full of disorder and confusion, stood and looked about for Alexander; and when he saw him in the right wing, encouraging and ordering his mercenaries, he could not moderate his anger, but inflamed at the sight, and blindly following his passion, regardless alike of his own life and his command, advanced far before his soldiers, crying out and challenging the tyrant who did not dare to receive him, but retreating, hid himself amongst his guard. The foremost of the mercenaries that came hand to hand were driven back by Pelopidas, and some killed; but many at a distance shot through his armor and wounded him, till the Thessalians, in anxiety for the result, ran down from the hill to his relief, but found him already slain. The horse came up, also, and routed the phalanx, and, following the pursuit a great way, filled the whole country with the slain, which were above three thousand.

No one can wonder that the Thebans then present, should show great grief at the death of Pelopidas, calling him their father, deliverer, and instructor in all that was good and commendable. But the Thessalians and the allies, out-doing in their public edicts all the just honors that could be paid to human courage, gave, in their display of feeling, yet stronger demonstrations of the kindness they had for him. It is stated, that none of the soldiers, when they heard of his death, would put off their armor, unbridle their horses, or dress their wounds, but, still hot and with their arms on, ran to the corpse, and, as if he had been yet alive and could see what they did, heaped up spoils about his body. They cut off their horses' manes and their own hair, many kindled no fire in their tents, took no supper, and silence and sadness was spread over all the army; as if they had not gained the greatest and most glorious victory, but were overcome by the tyrant, and enslaved. As soon as it was known in the cities, the magistrates, youths, children, and priests, came out to meet the body, and brought trophies, crowns, and suits of golden armor; and, when he was to be interred, the elders of the Thessalians came and begged the Thebans, that they might give the funeral; and one of them said, "Friends, we ask a favor of you, that will prove both an honor and comfort to us in this our great misfortune. The Thessalians shall never again wait on the living Pelopidas, never give honors, of which he can be sensible, but if we may have his body, adorn his funeral, and inter him, we shall hope to show, that we esteem his death a greater loss to the Thessalians than to the Thebans. You have lost only a good general, we both a general and our liberty. For how shall we dare to desire from you another captain, since we cannot restore Pelopidas?"

The Thebans granted their request, and there was never a more splendid funeral in the opinion of those, who do not think the glory of such solemnities consists only in gold, ivory, and purple; as Philistus did, who extravagantly celebrates the funeral of Dionysius, in which his tyranny concluded like the pompous exit of some great tragedy. Alexander the Great, at the death of Hephæstion, not only cut off the manes of his horses and his mules, but took down the battlements from the city walls, that even the towns might seem mourners, and, instead of their former beauteous appearance, look bald at his funeral. But such honors, being commanded and forced from the mourners, attended with feelings of jealousy towards those who received them, and of hatred towards those who exacted them, were no testimonies of love and respect, but of the barbaric pride, luxury, and insolence of those who lavished their wealth in these vain and undesirable displays. But that a man of common rank, dying in a strange country, neither his wife, children, nor kinsmen present, none either asking or compelling it, should be attended, buried, and crowned by so many cities that strove to exceed one another in the demonstrations of their love, seems to be the sum and completion of happy fortune. For the death of happy men is not, as Æsop observes, most grievous, but most blessed, since it secures their felicity, and puts it out of fortune's power. And that Spartan advised well, who, embracing Diagoras, that had himself been crowned in the Olympic Games, and saw his sons and grandchildren victors, said, "Die, Diagoras, for thou canst not be a god." And yet who would compare all the victories in the Pythian and Olympian games put together, with one of those enterprises of Pelopidas, of which he successfully performed so many? Having spent his life in brave and glorious actions, he died at last in the chief command, for the thirteenth time, of the Bœotians, fighting bravely and in the act of slaying a tyrant, in defence of the liberty of the Thessalians.

His death, as it brought grief, so likewise it produced advantage to the allies; for the Thebans, as soon as they heard of his fall, delayed not their revenge, but presently sent seven thousand foot and seven hundred horse, under the command of Malcitas and Diogiton. And they, finding Alexander weak and without forces, compelled him to restore the cities he had taken, to withdraw his garrisons from the Magnesians and Achæans of Phthiotis, and swear to assist the Thebans against whatsoever enemies they should require. This contented the Thebans, but punishment overtook the tyrant for his wickedness, and the death of Pelopidas was revenged by Heaven in the following manner. Pelopidas, as I have already mentioned, had taught his wife Thebe not to fear the outward splendor and show of the tyrant's defences, since she was admitted within them. She, of herself, too, dreaded his inconstancy, and hated his cruelty; and, therefore, conspiring with her three brothers, Tisiphonus, Pytholaus, and Lycophron, made the following attempt upon him. All the other apartments were full of the tyrant's night guards, but their bed-chamber was an upper room, and before the door lay a chained dog to guard it, which would fly at all but the tyrant and his wife and one servant that fed him. When Thebe, therefore, designed to kill her husband, she hid her brothers all day in a room hard by, and she, going in alone, according to her usual custom, to Alexander who was asleep already, in a little time came out again, and commanded the servant to lead away the dog, for Alexander wished to rest quietly. She covered the stairs with wool, that the young men might make no noise as they came up; and then, bringing up her brothers with their weapons, and leaving them at the chamber door, she went in, and brought away the tyrant's sword that hung over his head, and showed it them for a confirmation that he was fast asleep. The young men appearing fearful, and unwilling to do the murder, she chid them, and angrily vowed she would wake Alexander, and discover the conspiracy; and so, with a lamp in her hand, she conducted them in, they being both ashamed and afraid, and brought them to the bed; when one of them caught him by the feet, the other pulled him backward by the hair, and the third ran him through. The death was more speedy, perhaps, than was fit; but, in that he was the first tyrant that was killed by the contrivance of his wife, and as his corpse was abused, thrown out, and trodden under foot by the Pheræans, he seems to have suffered what his villanies deserved.

MARCELLUS[1]

TRANSLATED BY WALTER CHARLTON, M.D., FELLOW OF THE ROYAL COLLEGE OF PHYSICIANS, LONDON

THEY say that Marcus Claudius, who was five times consul of the Romans, was the son of Marcus; and that he was the first of his family called Marcellus; that is, *martial,* as Posidonius affirms. He was, indeed, by long experience skilful in the art of war, of a strong body, valiant of hand, and by natural inclination addicted to war. This high temper and heat he showed conspicuously in battle; in other respects he was modest and obliging, and so far studious of Greek learning and discipline, as to honor and admire those that excelled in it, though he did not himself attain a proficiency in them equal to his desire, by reason of his employments. For if ever there were any men, whom, as Homer says, Heaven—

> From their first youth unto their utmost age
> Appointed the laborious wars to wage,[2]

certainly they were the chief Romans of that time; who in their youth had war with the Carthaginians in Sicily, in their middle age with the Gauls in the

---

[1] His first consulship was in 222 B.C.; his fifth and last consulship in 208 B.C. Marcellus appears to have been harsh, unyielding, and cruel; but he was a brave and experienced officer, and to him as much as to any other single commander was due the successful resistance which the Romans made to Hannibal after Cannæ.—DR. WILLIAM SMITH.

[2] The verses are from the fourteenth Iliad, 86.

MARCELLUS

defence of Italy itself; and, at last, when now grown old, struggled again with Hannibal and the Carthaginians, and wanted in their latest years what is granted to most men, exemption from military toils; their rank and their great qualities still making them be called upon to undertake the command.

Marcellus, ignorant or unskilful of no kind of fighting, in single combat surpassed himself; he never declined a challenge, and never accepted without killing his challenger. In Sicily, he protected and saved his brother Otacilius when surrounded in battle, and slew the enemies that pressed upon him; for which act he was by the generals, while he was yet but young, presented with crowns and other honorable rewards; and, his good qualities more and more displaying themselves, he was created Curule Ædile by the people, and by the high-priests Augur; which is that priesthood to which chiefly the law assigns the observation of auguries. In his ædileship, a certain mischance brought him to the necessity of bringing an impeachment into the senate. He had a son named Marcus, of great beauty, in the flower of his age, and no less admired for the goodness of his character. This youth, Capitolinus, a bold and ill-mannered man, Marcellus's colleague, sought to abuse. The boy at first himself repelled him; but when the other again persecuted him, told his father. Marcellus, highly indignant, accused the man in the senate: where he, having appealed to the tribunes of the people, endeavored by various shifts and exceptions to elude the impeachment; and, when the tribunes refused their protection, by flat denial rejected the charge. As there was no witness of the fact, the senate thought fit to call the youth himself before them: on witnessing whose blushes and tears, and shame mixed with the highest indignation, seeking no further evidence of the crime, they condemned Capitolinus, and set a fine upon him; of the money of which, Marcellus caused silver vessels for libation to be made, which he dedicated to the gods.

After the end of the first Punic war, which lasted one and twenty years, the seeds of Gallic tumults sprang up, and began again to trouble Rome. The Insubrians, a people inhabiting the subalpine region of Italy, strong in their own forces, raised from among the other Gauls aids of mercenary soldiers, called Gæsatæ. And it was a sort of miracle, and special good fortune for Rome, that the Gallic war was not coincident with the Punic, but that the Gauls had with fidelity stood quiet as spectators, while the Punic war continued, as though they had been under engagements to await and attack the victors, and now only were at liberty to come forward. Still the position itself, and the ancient renown of the Gauls, struck no little fear into the minds of the Romans, who were about to undertake a war so near home and upon their own borders; and regarded the Gauls, because they had once taken their city, with more apprehension than any people, as is apparent from the enactment which from that time forth provided, that the high-priests should enjoy an exemption from all military duty, except only in Gallic insurrections.

The great preparations, also, made by the Romans, for war, (for it is not reported that the people of Rome ever had at one time so many legions in arms, either before or since,) and their extraordinary sacrifices, were plain arguments of their fear. For though they were most averse to barbarous and cruel rites, and entertained more than any nation

THE MACEDONIAN PHALANX IN THE DEFILES OF THRACIA

the same pious and reverent sentiments of the gods with the Greeks; yet, when this war was coming upon them, they then, from some prophecies in the Sibyls' books, put alive under ground a pair of Greeks, one male, the other female; and likewise two Gauls, one of each sex, in the market called the beast-market:[3] continuing even to this day to offer to these Greeks and Gauls certain secret ceremonial observances in the month of November.

In the beginning of this war, in which the Romans sometimes obtained remarkable victories, sometimes were shamefully beaten, nothing was done toward the determination of the contest, until Flaminius and Furius, being consuls, led large forces against the Insubrians. At the time of their departure, the river that runs through the country of Picenum was seen flowing with blood; there was a report, that three moons had been seen at once at Ariminum; and, in the consular assembly, the augurs declared, that the consuls had been unduly and inauspiciously created. The senate, therefore, immediately sent letters to the camp, recalling the consuls to Rome with all possible speed, and commanding them to forbear from acting against the enemies, and to abdicate the consulship on the first opportunity. These letters being brought to Flaminius, he deferred to open them till, having defeated and put to flight the enemy's forces, he wasted and ravaged their borders. The people, therefore, did not go forth to meet him when he returned with huge spoils; nay, because he had not instantly obeyed the command in the letters, by which he was recalled, but slighted and contemned them, they were very near denying him the honor of a triumph. Nor was the triumph sooner passed than they deposed

[3] The Forum Boarium.

him, with his colleague, from the magistracy, and reduced them to the state of private citizens. So much were all things at Rome made to depend upon religion; they would not allow any contempt of the omens and the ancient rites, even though attended with the highest success; thinking it to be of more importance to the public safety, that the magistrates should reverence the gods, than that they should overcome their enemies. Thus Tiberius Sempronius, whom for his probity and virtue the citizens highly esteemed, created Scipio Nasica and Caius Marcius, consuls to succeed him: and when they were gone into their provinces, lit upon books concerning the religious observances, where he found something he had not known before; which was this. When the consul took his auspices, he sat without the city in a house, or tent, hired for that occasion; but, if it happened that he, for any urgent cause, returned into the city, without having yet seen any certain signs, he was obliged to leave that first building, or tent, and to seek another to repeat the survey from. Tiberius, it appears, in ignorance of this, had twice used the same building before announcing the new consuls. Now, understanding his error, he referred the matter to the senate: nor did the senate neglect this minute fault, but soon wrote expressly of it to Scipio Nasica and Caius Marcius; who, leaving their provinces and without delay returning to Rome, laid down their magistracy. This happened at a later period. About the same time, too, the priesthood was taken away from two men of very great honor, Cornelius Cethegus and Quintus Sulpicius: from the former, because he had not rightly held out the entrails of a beast slain for sacrifice; from the latter, because, while he was immolating, the tufted cap which the Flamens wear had fallen from his head. Minucius, the dictator, who had already named Caius Flaminius master of the horse, they deposed from his command, because the squeak of a mouse was heard, and put others into their places. And yet, notwithstanding, by observing so anxiously these little niceties they did not run into any superstition, because they never varied from nor exceeded the observances of their ancestors.

So soon as Flaminius with his colleague had resigned the consulate, Marcellus was declared consul by the presiding officers called Interreges; and, entering into the magistracy, chose Cnæus Cornelius his colleague. There was a report that, the Gauls proposing a pacification, and the senate also inclining to peace, Marcellus inflamed the people to war; but a peace appears to have been agreed upon, which the Gæsatæ broke; who, passing the Alps, stirred up the Insubrians, (they being thirty thousand in number, and the Insubrians more numerous by far;) and, proud of their strength, marched directly to Acerræ, a city seated on the north of the river Po. From thence Britomartus,[4] king of the Gæsatæ, taking with him ten thousand soldiers, harassed the country round about. News of which being brought to Marcellus, leaving his colleague at Acerræ with the foot and all the heavy arms and a third part of the horse, and carrying with him the rest of the horse and six hundred light armed foot, marching night and day without remission, he staid not till he came up to these ten thousand near a Gaulish village called Clastidium, which not long before had been reduced under the Roman juris-

---

[4] Britomartus, or Britomatus, is the Greek form of the name, given in Latin as Viridomarus.

diction. Nor had he time to refresh his soldiers, or to give them rest. For the barbarians, that were then present, immediately observed his approach, and contemned him, because he had very few foot with him. The Gauls were singularly skilful in horsemanship, and thought to excel in it; and as at present they also exceeded Marcellus in number, they made no account of him. They, therefore, with their king at their head, instantly charged upon him, as if they would trample him under their horses' feet, threatening all kind of cruelties. Marcellus, because his men were few, that they might not be encompassed and charged on all sides by the enemy, extended his wings of horse, and, riding about, drew out his wings of foot in length, till he came near to the enemy. Just as he was in the act of turning round to face the enemy, it so happened that his horse, startled with their fierce look and their cries, gave back, and carried him forcibly aside. Fearing lest this accident, if converted into an omen, might discourage his soldiers, he quickly brought his horse round to confront the enemy, and made a gesture of adoration to the sun, as if he had wheeled about not by chance, but for a purpose of devotion. For it was customary to the Romans, when they offered worship to the gods, to turn round; and in this moment of meeting the enemy, he is said to have vowed the best of the arms to Jupiter Feretrius.

The king of the Gauls beholding Marcellus, and from the badges of his authority conjecturing him to be the general, advanced some way before his embattled army, and with a loud voice challenged him, and, brandishing his lance, fiercely ran in full career at him; exceeding the rest of the Gauls in stature, and with his armor, that was adorned with gold and silver and various colors, shining like lightning. These arms seeming to Marcellus, while he viewed the enemy's army drawn up in battalia, to be the best and fairest, and thinking them to be those he had vowed to Jupiter, he instantly ran upon the king, and pierced through his breastplate with his lance; then pressing upon him with the weight of his horse, threw him to the ground, and with two or three strokes more, slew him. Immediately he leapt from his horse, laid his hand upon the dead king's arms, and, looking up toward Heaven, thus spoke: "O Jupiter Feretrius, arbiter of the exploits of captains, and of the acts of commanders in war and battles, be thou witness that I, a general, have slain a general; I, a consul, have slain a king with my own hand, third of all the Romans; and that to thee I consecrate these first and most excellent of the spoils. Grant to us to despatch the relics of the war, with the same course of fortune." Then the Roman horse joining battle not only with the enemy's horse, but also with the foot who attacked them, obtained a singular and unheard of victory. For never before or since have so few horse defeated such numerous forces of horse and foot together. The enemies being to a great number slain, and the spoils collected, he returned to his colleague, who was conducting the war, with ill success, against the enemies near the greatest and most populous of the Gallic cities, Milan. This was their capital, and, therefore, fighting valiantly in defence of it, they were not so much besieged by Cornelius, as they besieged him. But Marcellus having returned, and the Gæsatæ retiring as soon as they were certified of the death of the king and the defeat of his army, Milan was taken. The rest of their towns, and all they had, the Gauls delivered up of their own accord to the Romans, and had peace upon equitable conditions granted to them.

Marcellus alone, by a decree of the senate, triumphed. The triumph was in magnificence, opulence, spoils, and the gigantic bodies of the captives, most remarkable. But the most grateful and most rare spectacle of all was the general himself, carrying the arms of the barbarian king to the god to whom he had vowed them. He had taken a tall and straight stock of an oak, and had lopped and formed it to a trophy. Upon this he fastened and hung round about the arms of the king, arranging all the pieces in their suitable places. The procession advancing solemnly, he, carrying this trophy, ascended the chariot; and thus, himself the fairest and most glorious triumphant image, was conveyed into the city. The army adorned with shining armor followed in order, and with verses composed for the occasion and with songs of victory celebrated the praises of Jupiter and of their general. Then entering the temple of Jupiter Feretrius, he dedicated his gift; the third, and to our memory the last, that ever did so. The first was Romulus, after having slain Acron, king of the Cæninenses: the second, Cornelius Cossus, who slew Tolumnius the Etruscan: after them Marcellus, having killed Britomartus, king of the Gauls; after Marcellus, no man. The god to whom these spoils were consecrated is called Jupiter *Feretrius,* from the trophy carried on the *feretrum,* one of the Greek words which at that time still existed in great numbers in Latin: or, as others say, it is the surname of the Thundering Jupiter, derived from *ferire,* to strike. Others there are who would have the name to be deduced from the *strokes* that are given in fight;

since even now in battles, when they press upon their enemies, they constantly call out to each other, *strike,* in Latin, *feri.* Spoils in general they call Spolia, and these in particular Opima; though, indeed, they say that Numa Pompilius in his commentaries, makes mention of first, second, and third Spolia Opima; and that he prescribes that the first taken be consecrated to Jupiter Feretrius, the second to Mars, the third to Quirinus; as also that the reward of the first be three hundred *asses;* of the second, two hundred; of the third, one hundred. The general account, however, prevails, that those spoils only are Opima, which the general first takes in set battle, and takes from the enemy's chief captain whom he has slain with his own hand. But of this enough. The victory and the ending of the war was so welcome to the people of Rome, that they sent to Apollo of Delphi, in testimony of their gratitude, a present of a golden cup of an hundred pound weight,[5] and gave a great part of the spoil to their associate cities, and took care that many presents should be sent also to Hiero, king of the Syracusans, their friend and ally.

When Hannibal invaded Italy, Marcellus was despatched with a fleet to Sicily. And when the army had been defeated at Cannæ, and many thousands of them perished, and few had saved themselves by flying to Canusium, and all feared lest

---

[5] *A golden cup of a hundred pounds weight* is quite uncertain; there is no number given in the present text of Plutarch; Amyot, who translates "du poids de cent marcs," may have had the number before him in a manuscript now lost; but *litrōn,* pounds, which is all there is in the Greek, is changed by some critics into *lutrōn,* spoils,—*a golden cup from the produce of the spoils.*

Hannibal, who had destroyed the strength of the Roman army, should advance at once with his victorious troops to Rome, Marcellus first sent for the protection of the city fifteen hundred soldiers, from the fleet. Then, by decree of the senate, going to Canusium, having heard that many of the soldiers had come together in that place, he led them out of the fortifications to prevent the enemy from ravaging the country. The chief Roman commanders had most of them fallen in battles; and the citizens complained, that the extreme caution of Fabius Maximus, whose integrity and wisdom gave him the highest authority, verged upon timidity and inaction. They confided in him to keep them out of danger, but could not expect that he would enable them to retaliate. Fixing, therefore, their thoughts upon Marcellus, and hoping to combine his boldness, confidence, and promptitude with Fabius's caution and prudence, and to temper the one by the other, they sent, sometimes both with consular command, sometimes one as consul, the other as proconsul, against the enemy. Posidonius writes, that Fabius was called the buckler, Marcellus the sword of Rome. Certainly, Hannibal himself confessed that he feared Fabius as a schoolmaster, Marcellus as an adversary: the former, lest he should be hindered from doing mischief; the latter, lest he should receive harm himself.

And first, when among Hannibal's soldiers, proud of their victory, carelessness and boldness had grown to a great height, Marcellus, attacking all their stragglers and plundering parties, cut them off, and by little and little diminished their forces. Then carrying aid to the Neapolitans and Nolans, he confirmed the minds of the former, who, indeed, were of their own accord faithful enough to the

Romans; but in Nola he found a state of discord, the senate not being able to rule and keep in the common people, who were generally favorers of Hannibal. There was in the town one Bantius, a man renowned for his high birth and courage. This man, after he had fought most fiercely at Cannæ, and had killed many of the enemies, at last was found lying in a heap of dead bodies, covered with darts, and was brought to Hannibal, who so honored him, that he not only dismissed him without ransom, but also contracted friendship with him, and made him his guest. In gratitude for this great favor, he became one of the strongest of the partisans of Hannibal, and urged the people to revolt. Marcellus could not be induced to put to death a man of such eminence, and who had endured such dangers in fighting on the Roman side; but, knowing himself able, by the general kindliness of his disposition and in particular by the attractiveness of his address, to gain over a character whose passion was for honor, one day when Bantius saluted him, he asked him who he was; not that he knew him not before, but seeking an occasion of further conference. When Bantius had told who he was, Marcellus, seeming surprised with joy and wonder, replied: "Are you that Bantius, whom the Romans commend above the rest that fought at Cannæ, and praise as the one man that not only did not forsake the consul Paulus Æmilius, but received in his own body many darts thrown at him?" Bantius owning himself to be that very man, and showing his scars: "Why then," said Marcellus, "did not you, having such proofs to show of your affection to us, come to me at my first arrival here? Do you think that we are unwilling to requite with favor those who have well deserved, and who are honored even by our enemies?" He followed up his courtesies by a present of a war-horse, and five hundred drachmas in money. From that time Bantius became the most faithful assistant and ally of Marcellus, and a most keen discoverer of those that attempted innovation and sedition.

These were many, and had entered into a conspiracy to plunder the baggage of the Romans, when they should make an irruption against the enemy. Marcellus, therefore, having marshalled his army within the city, placed the baggage near to the gates, and, by an edict, forbade the Nolans to go to the walls. Thus, outside the city, no arms could be seen; by which prudent device he allured Hannibal to move his army in some disorder to the city, thinking that things were in a tumult there. Then Marcellus, the nearest gate being, as he had commanded, thrown open, issuing forth with the flower of his horse in front, charged the enemy. By and by the foot, sallying out of another gate, with a loud shout joined in the battle. And while Hannibal opposes part of his forces to these, the third gate also is opened, out of which the rest break forth, and on all quarters fall upon the enemies, who were dismayed at this unexpected encounter, and did but feebly resist those with whom they had been first engaged, because of their attack by these others that sallied out later. Here Hannibal's soldiers, with much bloodshed and many wounds, were beaten back to their camp, and for the first time turned their backs to the Romans. There fell in this action, as it is related, more than five thousand of them; of the Romans, not above five hundred. Livy does not affirm, that either the victory, or the slaughter of the enemy was so great; but certain it is, that the adventure brought great glory to Marcellus, and to the Romans, after their calamities, a great revival of confidence, as they began now to entertain a hope, that the enemy with whom they contended was not invincible, but liable like themselves to defeats.

Therefore, the other consul being deceased, the people recalled Marcellus, that they might put him into his place; and, in spite of the magistrates, succeeded in postponing the election till his arrival, when he was by all the suffrages created consul. But because it happened to thunder, the augurs accounting that he was not legitimately created, and yet not daring, for fear of the people, to declare their sentence openly, Marcellus voluntarily resigned the consulate, retaining however his command. Being created proconsul, and returning to the camp at Nola, he proceeded to harass those that followed the party of the Carthaginian; on whose coming with speed to succor them, Marcellus declined a challenge to a set battle, but when Hannibal had sent out a party to plunder, and now expected no fight, he broke out upon him with his army. He had distributed to the foot long lances, such as are commonly used in naval fights; and instructed them to throw them with great force at convenient distance against the enemies who were inexperienced in that way of darting, and used to fight with short darts hand to hand. This seems to have been the cause of the total rout and open flight of all the Carthaginians who were then engaged: there fell of them five thousand; four elephants were killed, and two taken; but, what was of greatest moment, on the third day after, more than three hundred [6] horse,

[6] *Three hundred* should probably be *thirteen hundred*. Livy, whom Plutarch appears to be following in the narrative, says 1272.

Spaniards and Numidians mixed, deserted to him, a disaster that had never to that day happened to Hannibal, who had long kept together in harmony an army of barbarians, collected out of many various and discordant nations. Marcellus and his successors in all this war made good use of the faithful service of these horsemen.

He now was a third time created consul, and sailed over into Sicily. For the success of Hannibal had excited the Carthaginians to lay claim to that whole island; chiefly because after the murder of the tyrant Hieronymus, all things had been in tumult and confusion at Syracuse. For which reason the Romans also had sent before to that city a force under the conduct of Appius, as prætor. While Marcellus was receiving that army, a number of Roman soldiers cast themselves at his feet, upon occasion of the following calamity. Of those that survived the battle at Cannæ, some had escaped by flight, and some were taken alive by the enemy; so great a multitude, that it was thought there were not remaining Romans enough to defend the walls of the city. And yet the magnanimity and constancy of the city was such, that it would not redeem the captives from Hannibal, though it might have done so for a small ransom; a decree of the senate forbade it, and chose rather to leave them to be killed by the enemy, or sold out of Italy; and commanded that all who had saved themselves by flight should be transported into Sicily, and not permitted to return into Italy, until the war with Hannibal should be ended. These, therefore, when Marcellus was arrived in Sicily, addressed themselves to him in great numbers; and casting themselves at his feet, with much lamentation and tears humbly besought him to admit them to honorable service; and promised to make it appear by their future fidelity and exertions, that that defeat had been received rather by misfortune than by cowardice. Marcellus, pitying them, petitioned the senate by letters, that he might have leave at all times to recruit his legions out of them. After much debate about the thing, the senate decreed they were of opinion that the commonwealth did not require the service of cowardly soldiers; if Marcellus perhaps thought otherwise, he might make use of them, provided no one of them be honored on any occasion with a crown or military gift, as a reward of his virtue or courage. This decree stung Marcellus; and on his return to Rome, after the Sicilian war was ended, he upbraided the senate, that they had denied to him, who had so highly deserved of the republic, liberty to relieve so great a number of citizens in great calamity.

At this time Marcellus, first incensed by injuries done him by Hippocrates, commander of the Syracusans, (who, to give proof of his good affection to the Carthaginians, and to acquire the tyranny to himself, had killed a number of Romans at Leontini,) besieged and took by force the city of Leontini; yet violated none of the townsmen; only deserters, as many as he took, he subjected to the punishment of the rods and axe. But Hippocrates, sending a report to Syracuse, that Marcellus had put all the adult population to the sword, and then coming upon the Syracusans, who had risen in tumult upon that false report, made himself master of the city. Upon this Marcellus moved with his whole army to Syracuse, and, encamping near the wall, sent ambassadors into the city to relate to the Syracusans the truth of what had been done in Leontini. When these could not prevail by treaty, the whole power being now in the hands of Hippocrates, he proceeded to attack the city both by land and by sea. The land forces were conducted by Appius: Marcellus, with sixty galleys, each with five rows of oars, furnished with all sorts of arms and missiles, and a huge bridge of planks laid upon eight ships chained together, upon which was carried the engine to cast stones and darts, assaulted the walls, relying on the abundance and magnificence of his preparations, and on his own previous glory; all which, however, were, it would seem, but trifles for Archimedes and his machines.

These machines he had designed and contrived, not as matters of any importance, but as mere amusements in geometry; in compliance with king Hiero's desire and request, some little time before, that he should reduce to practice some part of his admirable speculations in science, and by accommodating the theoretic truth to sensation and ordinary use, bring it more within the appreciation of people in general. Eudoxus and Archytas had been the first originators of this far-famed and highly prized art of mechanics, which they employed as an elegant illustration of geometrical truths, and as a means of sustaining experimentally, to the satisfaction of the senses, conclusions too intricate for proof by words and diagrams. As, for example, to solve the problem, so often required in constructing geometrical figures, given the two extreme, to find the two mean lines of a proportion, both these mathematicians had recourse to the aid of instruments, adapting to their purpose certain curves and sections of lines.[7] But what with Plato's indignation at it, and his invectives against it as the mere

[7] The *mesolabes* or *mesolabium*, was the name by which this instrument was commonly known.

corruption and annihilation of the one good of geometry,—which was thus shamefully turning its back upon the unembodied objects of pure intelligence to recur to sensation, and to ask help (not to be obtained without base subservience and depravation) from matter; so it was that mechanics came to be separated from geometry, and, repudiated and neglected by philosophers, took its place as a military art. Archimedes, however, in writing to king Hiero, whose friend and near relation he was, had stated, that given the force, any given weight might be moved, and even boasted, we are told, relying on the strength of demonstration, that if there were another earth, by going into it he could remove this. Hiero being struck with amazement at this, and entreating him to make good this problem by actual experiment, and show some great weight moved by a small engine, he fixed accordingly upon a ship of burden out of the king's arsenal, which could not be drawn out of the dock without great labor and many men; and loading her with many passengers and a full freight, sitting himself the while far off, with no great endeavor, but only holding the head of the pulley in his hand and drawing the cord by degrees, he drew the ship in a straight line, as smoothly and evenly, as if she had been in the sea. The king, astonished at this, and convinced of the power of the art, prevailed upon Archimedes to make him engines accommodated to all the purposes, offensive and defensive, of a siege. These the king himself never made use of, because he spent almost all his life in a profound quiet, and the highest affluence. But the apparatus was, in a most opportune time, ready at hand for the Syracusans, and with it also the engineer himself.

When, therefore, the Romans assaulted the walls

in two places at once, fear and consternation stupefied the Syracusans, believing that nothing was able to resist that violence and those forces. But when Archimedes began to ply his engines, he at once shot against the land forces all sorts of missile weapons, and immense masses of stone that came down with incredible noise and violence, against which no man could stand; for they knocked down those upon whom they fell, in heaps, breaking all their ranks and files. In the mean time huge poles thrust out from the walls over the ships, sunk some by the great weights which they let down from on high upon them; others they lifted up into the air by an iron hand or beak like a crane's beak, and, when they had drawn them up by the prow, and set them on end upon the poop, they plunged them to the bottom of the sea; or else the ships, drawn by engines within, and whirled about, were dashed against steep rocks that stood jutting out under the walls, with great destruction of the soldiers that were aboard them. A ship was frequently lifted up to a great height in the air (a dreadful thing to behold), and was rolled to and fro, and kept swinging, until the mariners were all thrown out, when at length it was dashed against the rocks, or let fall. At the engine that Marcellus brought upon the bridge of ships, which was called *Sambuca* from some resemblance it had to an instrument of music, while it was as yet approaching the wall, there was discharged a piece of a rock of ten talents' weight, then a second and a third, which, striking upon it with immense force and with a noise like thunder, broke all its foundation to pieces, shook out all its fastenings, and completely dislodged it from the bridge. So Marcellus, doubtful what counsel to pursue, drew off his ships to a safer distance, and sounded a retreat to his forces on land. They then took a resolution of coming up under the walls, if it were possible, in the night; thinking that as Archimedes used ropes stretched at length in playing his engines, the soldiers would now be under the shot, and the darts would, for want of sufficient distance to throw them, fly over their heads without effect. But he, it appeared, had long before framed for such occasion engines accommodated to any distance, and shorter weapons; and had made numerous small openings in the walls, through which, with engines of a shorter range, unexpected blows were inflicted on the assailants. Thus, when they who thought to deceive the defenders came close up to the walls, instantly a shower of darts and other missile weapons was again cast upon them. And when stones came tumbling down perpendicularly upon their heads, and, as it were, the whole wall shot out arrows at them, they retired. And now, again, as they were going off, arrows and darts of a longer range inflicted a great slaughter among them, and their ships were driven one against another; while they themselves were not able to retaliate in any way. For Archimedes had provided and fixed most of his engines immediately under the wall; whence the Romans, seeing that infinite mischiefs overwhelmed them from no visible means, began to think they were fighting with the gods.

Yet Marcellus escaped unhurt, and, deriding his own artificers and engineers, "What," said he, "must we give up fighting with this geometrical Briareus, who plays pitch and toss with our ships, and, with the multitude of darts which he showers at a single moment upon us, really outdoes the hundred-handed giants of mythology?" And, doubtless, the rest of the Syracusans were but the body of Archimedes' designs, one soul moving and governing all; for, laying aside all other arms, with his alone they infested the Romans, and protected themselves. In fine, when such terror had seized upon the Romans, that, if they did but see a little rope or a piece of wood from the wall, instantly crying out, that there it was again, Archimedes was about to let fly some engine at them, they turned their backs and fled, Marcellus desisted from conflicts and assaults, putting all his hope in a long siege. Yet Archimedes possessed so high a spirit, so profound a soul, and such treasures of scientific knowledge, that though these inventions had now obtained him the renown of more than human sagacity, he yet would not deign to leave behind him any commentary or writing on such subjects; but, repudiating, as sordid and ignoble the whole trade of engineering, and every sort of art that lends itself to mere use and profit, he placed his whole affection and ambition in those purer speculations where there can be no reference to the vulgar needs of life; studies, the superiority of which to all others is unquestioned, and in which the only doubt can be, whether the beauty and grandeur of the subjects examined, or the precision and cogency of the methods and means of proof, most deserve our admiration. It is not possible to find in all geometry more difficult and intricate questions, or more simple and lucid explanations. Some ascribe this to his natural genius; while others think that incredible effort and toil produced these, to all appearance, easy and unlabored results. No amount of investigation of yours would succeed in attaining the proof, and yet once seen, you immediately believe you would have discovered it; by so smooth and so rapid a path he leads you to the conclusion required. And thus it ceases to be incredible that (as is commonly told of him), the charm of his familiar and domestic Siren made him forget his food and neglect his person, to that degree that when he was occasionally carried by absolute violence to bathe, or have his body anointed, he used to trace geometrical figures in the ashes of the fire, and diagrams in the oil on his body, being in a state of entire preoccupation, and, in the truest sense, divine possession with his love and delight in science. His discoveries were numerous and admirable; but he is said to have requested his friends and relations that when he was dead, they would place over his tomb a sphere containing a cylinder, inscribing it with the ratio which the containing solid bears to the contained.[8]

Such was Archimedes, who now showed himself, and, so far as lay in him, the city also, invincible. While the siege continued, Marcellus took Megara, one of the earliest founded of the Greek cities in Sicily, and capturing also the camp of Hippocrates at Acilæ, killed above eight thousand men, having attacked them whilst they were engaged in forming their fortifications. He overran a great part of Sicily; gained over many towns from the Carthaginians, and overcame all that dared to encounter him. As the siege went on, one Damippus, a Lacedæmonian, putting to sea in a ship from Syracuse, was taken. When the Syracusans much desired to redeem this man, and there were many

---

[8] The solid content of a sphere is exactly two-thirds of that of the circumscribing cylinder. Among the works still extant of Archimedes, there are two books on the sphere and cylinder. The tomb, as thus described, was found, covered with weeds, by Cicero, when serving as quæstor in Sicily.

meetings and treaties about the matter betwixt them and Marcellus, he had opportunity to notice a tower into which a body of men might be secretly introduced, as the wall near to it was not difficult to surmount, and it was itself carelessly guarded. Coming often thither, and entertaining conferences about the release of Damippus, he had pretty well calculated the height of the tower, and got ladders prepared. The Syracusans celebrated a feast to Diana; this juncture of time, when they were given up entirely to wine and sport, Marcellus laid hold of, and, before the citizens perceived it, not only possessed himself of the tower, but, before the break of day, filled the wall around with soldiers, and made his way into the Hexapylum. The Syracusans now beginning to stir, and to be alarmed at the tumult, he ordered the trumpets everywhere to sound, and thus frightened them all into flight, as if all parts of the city were already won, though the most fortified, and the fairest, and most ample quarter was still ungained. It is called Acradina, and was divided by a wall from the outer city, one part of which they call Neapolis, the other Tycha. Possessing himself of these, Marcellus, about break of day, entered through the Hexapylum, all his officers congratulating him. But looking down from the higher places upon the beautiful and spacious city below, he is said to have wept much, commiserating the calamity that hung over it, when his thoughts represented to him, how dismal and foul the face of the city would in a few hours be, when plundered and sacked by the soldiers. For among the officers of his army there was not one man that durst deny the plunder of the city to the soldiers' demands; nay, many were instant that it should be set on fire and laid level to the ground: but this

Marcellus would not listen to. Yet he granted, but with great unwillingness and reluctance, that the money and slaves should be made prey; giving orders, at the same time, that none should violate any free person, nor kill, misuse, or make a slave of any of the Syracusans. Though he had used this moderation, he still esteemed the condition of that city to be pitiable, and, even amidst the congratulations and joy, showed his strong feelings of sympathy and commiseration at seeing all the riches accumulated during a long felicity, now dissipated in an hour. For it is related, that no less prey and plunder was taken here, than afterward in Carthage. For not long after, they obtained also the plunder of the other parts of the city, which were taken by treachery; leaving nothing untouched but the king's money, which was brought into the public treasury. But nothing afflicted Marcellus so much as the death of Archimedes; who was then, as fate would have it, intent upon working out some problem by a diagram, and having fixed his mind alike and his eyes upon the subject of his speculation, he never noticed the incursion of the Romans, nor that the city was taken. In this transport of study and contemplation, a soldier, unexpectedly coming up to him, commanded him to follow to Marcellus; which he declining to do before he had worked out his problem to a demonstration, the soldier, enraged, drew his sword and ran him through. Others write, that a Roman soldier, running upon him with a drawn sword, offered to kill him; and that Archimedes, looking back, earnestly besought him to hold his hand a little while, that he might not leave what he was then at work upon inconclusive and imperfect; but the soldier, nothing moved by his entreaty, instantly killed him. Others again relate, that as Archimedes was carrying to Marcellus mathematical instruments, dials, spheres, and angles, by which the magnitude of the sun might be measured to the sight, some soldiers seeing him, and thinking that he carried gold in a vessel, slew him. Certain it is, that his death was very afflicting to Marcellus; and that Marcellus ever after regarded him that killed him as a murderer; and that he sought for his kindred and honored them with signal favors.

Indeed, foreign nations had held the Romans to be excellent soldiers and formidable in battle; but they had hitherto given no memorable example of gentleness, or humanity, or civil virtue; and Marcellus seems first to have shown to the Greeks, that his countrymen were most illustrious for their justice. For such was his moderation to all with whom he had any thing to do, and such his benignity also to many cities and private men, that, if any thing hard or severe was decreed concerning the people of Enna, Megara, or Syracuse, the blame was thought to belong rather to those upon whom the storm fell, than to those who brought it upon them. One example of many I will commemorate. In Sicily there is a town called Engyium, not indeed great, but very ancient and ennobled by the presence of the goddesses, called the Mothers. The temple, they say, was built by the Cretans; and they show some spears and brazen helmets, inscribed with the names of Meriones, and (with the same spelling as in Latin) of Ulysses,[9] who consecrated them to the goddesses. This city highly favoring the party of the Carthaginians, Nicias, the most eminent of the citizens, counselled them to go

[9] *Oulixes* or *Ulixes*, the original Latin form, not as in proper Greek *Odysseus*.

over to the Romans; to that end acting freely and openly in harangues to their assemblies, arguing the imprudence and madness of the opposite course. They, fearing his power and authority, resolved to deliver him in bonds to the Carthaginians. Nicias, detecting the design, and seeing that his person was secretly kept in watch, proceeded to speak irreligiously to the vulgar of the Mothers, and showed many signs of disrespect, as if he denied and contemned the received opinion of the presence of those goddesses; his enemies the while rejoicing that he, of his own accord, sought the destruction hanging over his head. When they were just now about to lay hands upon him, an assembly was held, and here Nicias, making a speech to the people concerning some affair then under deliberation, in the midst of his address, cast himself upon the ground; and soon after, while amazement (as usually happens on such surprising occasions) held the assembly immovable, raising and turning his head round, he began in a trembling and deep tone, but by degrees raised and sharpened his voice. When he saw the whole theatre struck with horror and silence, throwing off his mantle and rending his tunic, he leaps up half naked, and runs towards the door, crying out aloud that he was driven by the wrath of the Mothers. When no man durst, out of religious fear, lay hands upon him or stop him, but all gave way before him, he ran out of the gate, not omitting any shriek or gesture of men possessed and mad. His wife, conscious of his counterfeiting, and privy to his design, taking her children with her, first cast herself as a suppliant before the temple of the goddesses; then, pretending to seek her wandering husband, no man hindering her, went out of the town in safety; and by this means they all escaped to Marcellus at Syracuse. After many other such affronts offered him by the men of Engyium, Marcellus, having taken them all prisoners and cast them into bonds, was preparing to inflict upon them the last punishment; when Nicias, with tears in his eyes, addressed himself to him. In fine, casting himself at Marcellus's feet, and deprecating for his citizens, he begged most earnestly their lives, chiefly those of his enemies. Marcellus, relenting, set them all at liberty, and rewarded Nicias with ample lands and rich presents. This history is recorded by Posidonius the philosopher.

Marcellus, at length recalled by the people of Rome to the immediate war at home, to illustrate his triumph, and adorn the city, carried away with him a great number of the most beautiful ornaments of Syracuse. For, before that, Rome neither had, nor had seen, any of those fine and exquisite rarities; nor was any pleasure taken in graceful and elegant pieces of workmanship. Stuffed with barbarous arms and spoils stained with blood, and everywhere crowned with triumphal memorials and trophies, she was no pleasant or delightful spectacle for the eyes of peaceful or refined spectators: but, as Epaminondas named the fields of Bœotia the stage of Mars; and Xenophon called Ephesus the workhouse of war;[10] so, in my judgment, may you call Rome, at that time, (to use the words of Pindar,) " the precinct of the peaceless Mars." Whence

[10] Ephesus was *the workhouse of war* when Agesilaus made it his head-quarters in his Asiatic campaigns. The quotation from Pindar is from the beginning of the 2nd Pythian ode. *Rude, unrefined, only for great things good,* is the description of Hercules in fragment No. 1 of the Licymnius. The words are quoted elsewhere by Plutarch as applying to Cimon; see Vol. III., p. 202.

Marcellus was more popular with the people in general, because he had adorned the city with beautiful objects that had all the charms of Grecian grace and symmetry; but Fabius Maximus, who neither touched nor brought away any thing of this kind from Tarentum, when he had taken it, was more approved of by the elder men. He carried off the money and valuables, but forbade the statues to be moved; adding, as it is commonly related, "Let us leave to the Tarentines these offended gods." They blamed Marcellus, first, for placing the city in an invidious position, as it seemed now to celebrate victories and lead processions of triumph, not only over men, but also over the gods as captives; then, that he had diverted to idleness, and vain talk about curious arts and artificers, the common people, which, bred up in wars and agriculture, had never tasted of luxury and sloth, and, as Euripides said of Hercules, had been

> Rude, unrefined, only for great things good,

so that now they misspent much of their time in examining and criticizing trifles. And yet, notwithstanding this reprimand, Marcellus made it his glory to the Greeks themselves, that he had taught his ignorant countrymen to esteem and admire the elegant and wonderful productions of Greece.

But when the envious opposed his being brought triumphant into the city, because there were some relics of the war in Sicily, and a third triumph would be looked upon with jealousy, he gave way. He triumphed upon the Alban mount, and thence entered the city in *ovation,* as it is called in Latin, in Greek *eua;* but in this ovation he was neither carried in a chariot, nor crowned with laurel, nor ushered by trumpets sounding; but went afoot with shoes on, many flutes or pipes sounding in concert, while he passed along, wearing a garland of myrtle, in a peaceable aspect, exciting rather love and respect than fear. Whence I am, by conjecture, led to think that, originally, the difference observed betwixt ovation and triumph, did not depend upon the greatness of the achievements, but the manner of performing them. For they who, having fought a set battle, and slain the enemy, returned victors, led that martial, terrible triumph, and, as the ordinary custom then was, in lustrating the army, adorned the arms and the soldiers with a great deal of laurel. But they who, without force, by colloquy, persuasion, and reasoning, had done the business, to these captains custom gave the honor of the unmilitary and festive ovation. For the pipe is the badge of peace, and myrtle the plant of Venus, who more than the rest of the gods and goddesses abhors force and war. It is called ovation, not, as most think, from the Greek *euasmus,* because they act it with shouting and cries of *Eua*: for so do they also the proper triumphs. The Greeks have wrested the word to their own language, thinking that this honor, also, must have some connection with Bacchus, who in Greek has the titles of Euius and Thriambus.[11] But the thing is otherwise. For it was the custom for commanders, in their triumph, to immolate an ox, but in their ovation, a sheep: hence they named it *Ovation,* from the Latin *ovis.* It is worth observing, how exactly opposite the sacrifices appointed by the Spartan legislator are, to those of the Romans. For at Lacedæmon, a captain, who

[11] The old Greek word *thriambus* was accordingly employed as an equivalent to the Latin *triumphus,* which, though a little different in sense, is always rendered by it.

had performed the work he undertook by cunning, or courteous treaty, on laying down his command immolated an ox; he that did the business by battle, offered a cock; the Lacedæmonians, though most warlike, thinking an exploit performed by reason and wisdom, to be more excellent and more congruous to man, than one effected by mere force and courage. Which of the two is to be preferred, I leave to the determination of others.

Marcellus being the fourth time consul, his enemies suborned the Syracusans to come to Rome to accuse him, and to complain that they had suffered indignities and wrongs, contrary to the conditions granted them. It happened that Marcellus was in the capitol offering sacrifice when the Syracusans petitioned the senate, yet sitting, that they might have leave to accuse him and present their grievances. Marcellus's colleague, eager to protect him in his absence, put them out of the court. But Marcellus himself came as soon as he heard of it. And first, in his curule chair as consul, he referred to the senate the cognizance of other matters; but when these were transacted, rising from his seat, he passed as a private man into the place where the accused were wont to make their defence, and gave free liberty to the Syracusans to impeach him. But they, struck with consternation by his majesty and confidence, stood astonished, and the power of his presence now, in his robe of state, appeared far more terrible and severe than it had done when he was arrayed in armor. Yet reanimated at length by Marcellus's rivals, they began their impeachment, and made an oration in which pleas of justice mingled with lamentation and complaint; the sum of which was, that being allies and friends of the people of Rome, they had, notwithstanding, suffered things which other commanders had abstained from inflicting upon enemies. To this Marcellus answered; that they had committed many acts of hostility against the people of Rome, and had suffered nothing but what enemies conquered and captured in war, cannot possibly be protected from suffering: that it was their own fault they had been made captives, because they refused to give ear to his frequent attempts to persuade them by gentle means: neither were they forced into war by the power of tyrants, but had rather chosen the tyrants themselves for the express object that they might make war. The orations ended, and the Syracusans, according to the custom, having retired, Marcellus left his colleague to ask the sentences, and withdrawing with the Syracusans, staid expecting at the doors of the senate-house; not in the least discomposed in spirit, either with alarm at the accusation, or by anger against the Syracusans; but with perfect calmness and serenity attending the issue of the cause. The sentences at length being all asked, and a decree of the senate made in vindication of Marcellus, the Syracusans, with tears flowing from their eyes, cast themselves at his knees, beseeching him to forgive themselves there present, and to be moved by the misery of the rest of their city, which would ever be mindful of, and grateful for, his benefits. Thus Marcellus, softened by their tears and distress, was not only reconciled to the deputies, but ever afterwards continued to find opportunity of doing kindness to the Syracusans. The liberty which he had restored to them, and their rights, laws, and goods that were left, the senate confirmed. Upon which account the Syracusans, besides other signal honors, made a law, that if Marcellus should at any time come into

Sicily, or any of his posterity, the Syracusans should wear garlands and offer public sacrifice to the gods.

After this he moved against Hannibal. And whereas the other consuls and commanders, since the defeat received at Cannæ, had all made use of the same policy against Hannibal, namely, to decline coming to a battle with him; and none had had the courage to encounter him in the field, and put themselves to the decision by the sword; Marcellus entered upon the opposite course, thinking that Italy would be destroyed by the very delay by which they looked to wear out Hannibal; and that Fabius, who, adhering to his cautious policy, waited to see the war extinguished, while Rome itself meantime wasted away, (like timid physicians, who, dreading to administer remedies, stay waiting, and believe that what is the decay of the patient's strength is the decline of the disease,) was not taking a right course to heal the sickness of his country. And first, the great cities of the Samnites, which had revolted, came into his power; in which he found a large quantity of corn and money, and three thousand of Hannibal's soldiers, that were left for the defence. After this, the proconsul Cnæus Fulvius with eleven tribunes of the soldiers being slain in Apulia, and the greatest part of the army also at the same time cut off, he despatched letters to Rome, and bade the people be of good courage, for that he was now upon the march against Hannibal, to turn his triumph into sadness. On these letters being read, Livy writes, that the people were not only not encouraged, but more discouraged than before. For the danger, they thought, was but the greater in proportion as Marcellus was of more value than Fulvius. He, as he had written, advancing into the territories of the Lucanians, came up to him at Numistro, and, the enemy keeping himself upon the hills, pitched his camp in a level plain, and the next day drew forth his army in order for fight. Nor did Hannibal refuse the challenge. They fought long and obstinately on both sides, victory yet seeming undecided, when, after three hours conflict, night hardly parted them. The next day, as soon as the sun was risen, Marcellus again brought forth his troops, and ranged them among the dead bodies of the slain, challenging Hannibal to solve the question by another trial. When he dislodged and drew off, Marcellus, gathering up the spoils of the enemies, and burying the bodies of his slain soldiers, closely followed him. And though Hannibal often used stratagems, and laid ambushes to entrap Marcellus, yet he could never circumvent him. By skirmishes, meantime, in all of which he was superior, Marcellus gained himself such high repute, that, when the time of the Comitia at Rome was near at hand, the senate thought fit rather to recall the other consul from Sicily, than to withdraw Marcellus from his conflict with Hannibal; and on his arrival they bid him name Quintus Fulvius dictator. For the dictator is created neither by the people, nor by the senate; but the consul or the prætor, before the popular assembly, pronounces him to be dictator, whom he himself chooses. Hence he is called dictator, *dicere* meaning to name. Others say, that he is named dictator, because his word is a *law,* and he orders what he pleases, without submitting it to the vote. For the Romans call the orders of magistrates, *Edicts.*

And now because Marcellus's colleague, who was recalled from Sicily, had a mind to name another man dictator, and would not be forced to change his opinion, he sailed away by night back to Sicily. So the common people made an order, that Quintus Fulvius should be chosen dictator: and the senate, by an express, commanded Marcellus to nominate him. He obeying proclaimed him dictator according to the order of the people; but the office of proconsul was continued to himself for a year. And having arranged with Fabius Maximus, that while he besieged Tarentum, he himself would, by following Hannibal and drawing him up and down, detain him from coming to the relief of the Tarentines, he overtook him at Canusium: and as Hannibal often shifted his camp, and still declined the combat, he everywhere sought to engage him. At last pressing upon him while encamping, by light skirmishes he provoked him to a battle; but night again divided them in the very heat of the conflict. The next day Marcellus again showed himself in arms, and brought up his forces in array. Hannibal, in extreme grief, called his Carthaginians together to an harangue; and vehemently prayed them, to fight to-day worthily of all their former successes; "For you see," said he, "how, after such great victories, we have not liberty to respire, nor to repose ourselves, though victors; unless we drive this man back." Then the two armies joining battle, fought fiercely; when the event of an untimely movement showed Marcellus to have been guilty of an error. The right wing being hard pressed upon, he commanded one of the legions to be brought up to the front. This change disturbing the array and posture of the legions, gave the victory to the enemies; and there fell two thousand seven hundred Romans. Marcellus, after he had retreated into his camp, called his soldiers together; "I see," said he, "many

Roman arms and bodies, but I see not so much as one Roman." To their entreaties for his pardon, he returned a refusal while they remained beaten, but promised to give it so soon as they should overcome; and he resolved to bring them into the field again the next day, that the fame of their victory might arrive at Rome before that of their flight. Dismissing the assembly, he commanded barley instead of wheat to be given to those companies that had turned their backs. These rebukes were so bitter to the soldiers, that though a great number of them were grievously wounded, yet they relate there was not one to whom the general's oration was not more painful and smarting than his wounds.

The day breaking, a scarlet toga, the sign of instant battle, was displayed. The companies marked with ignominy, begged they might be posted in the foremost place, and obtained their request. Then the tribunes bring forth the rest of the forces, and draw them up. On news of which, "O strange!" said Hannibal, "what will you do with this man, who can bear neither good nor bad fortune? He is the only man who neither suffers us to rest when he is victor, nor rests himself when he is overcome. We shall have, it seems, perpetually to fight with him; as in good success his confidence, and in ill success his shame, still urges him to some further enterprise?" Then the armies engaged. When the fight was doubtful, Hannibal commanded the elephants to be brought into the first battalion, and to be driven upon the van of the Romans. When the beasts, trampling upon many, soon caused disorder, Flavius, a tribune of soldiers, snatching an ensign, meets them, and wounding the first elephant with the spike at the bottom of the ensign staff, puts him to flight. The beast turned round upon the next, and drove back both him and the rest that followed. Marcellus, seeing this, pours in his horse with great force upon the elephants, and upon the enemy disordered by their flight. The horse, making a fierce impression, pursued the Carthaginians home to their camp, while the elephants, wounded, and running upon their own party, caused a considerable slaughter. It is said, more than eight thousand were slain; of the Roman army three thousand, and almost all wounded. This gave Hannibal opportunity to retire in the silence of the night, and to remove to greater distance from Marcellus; who was kept from pursuing by the number of his wounded men, and removed, by gentle marches, into Campania, and spent the summer at Sinuessa, engaged in restoring them.

But as Hannibal, having disentangled himself from Marcellus, ranged with his army round about the country, and wasted Italy free from all fear, at Rome Marcellus was evil spoken of. His detractors induced Publicius Bibulus, tribune of the people, an eloquent and violent man, to undertake his accusation. He, by assiduous harangues, prevailed upon the people to withdraw from Marcellus the command of the army; "Seeing that Marcellus," said he, "after brief exercise in the war, has withdrawn as it might be from the wrestling ground to the warm baths to refresh himself." Marcellus, on hearing this, appointed lieutenants over his camp, and hasted to Rome to refute the charges against him: and there found ready drawn up an impeachment consisting of these calumnies. At the day prefixed, in the Flaminian circus, into which place the people had assembled themselves, Bibulus rose and accused him. Marcellus himself answered, briefly and simply: but the first and most approved men of the city spoke largely and in high terms, very freely advising the people not to show themselves worse judges than the enemy, condemning Marcellus of timidity, from whom alone of all their captains the enemy fled, and as perpetually endeavored to avoid fighting with him, as to fight with others. When they made an end of speaking, the accuser's hope to obtain judgment so far deceived him, that Marcellus was not only absolved, but the fifth time created consul.

No sooner had he entered upon this consulate, but he suppressed a great commotion in Etruria, that had proceeded near to revolt, and visited and quieted the cities. Then, when the dedication of the temple, which he had vowed out of his Sicilian spoils to Honor and Virtue, was objected to by the priests, because they denied that one temple could be lawfully dedicated to two gods, he began to adjoin another to it, resenting the priests' opposition, and almost converting the thing into an omen. And, truly, many other prodigies also affrighted him; some temples had been struck with lightning, and in Jupiter's temple mice had gnawed the gold; it was reported also, that an ox had spoke, and that a boy had been born with a head like an elephant's. All which prodigies had indeed been attended to, but due reconciliation had not been obtained from the gods. The aruspices therefore detained him at Rome, glowing and burning with desire to return to the war. For no man was ever inflamed with so great desire of any thing, as was he to fight a battle with Hannibal. It was the subject of his dreams in the night, the topic of all his consultations with his friends and familiars, nor did he present to the gods any other wish, but that he might meet Hannibal in the field. And I think, that he would most gladly have set upon him, with both armies environed within a single camp. Had he not been even loaded with honors, and had he not given proofs in many ways of his maturity of judgment and of prudence equal to that of any commander, you might have said, that he was agitated by a youthful ambition, above what became a man of that age: for he had passed the sixtieth year of his life when he began his fifth consulship.

The sacrifices having been offered, and all that belonged to the propitiation of the gods performed, according to the prescription of the diviners, he at last with his colleague went forth to carry on the war. He tried all possible means to provoke Hannibal, who at that time had a standing camp betwixt Bantia and Venusia. Hannibal declined an engagement, but having obtained intelligence that some troops were on their way to the town of Locri Epizephyrii, placing an ambush under the little hill of Petelia, he slew two thousand five hundred soldiers. This incensed Marcellus to revenge; and he therefore moved nearer Hannibal. Betwixt the two camps was a little hill, a tolerably secure post, covered with wood; it had steep descents on either side, and there were springs of water seen trickling down. This place was so fit and advantageous, that the Romans wondered that Hannibal, who had come thither before them, had not seized upon it, but had left it to the enemies. But to him the place had seemed commodious indeed for a camp, but yet more commodious for an ambuscade; and to that use he chose to put it. So in the wood and the hollows he hid a number of archers and spearmen, confident that the commodiousness of the place would allure the Romans. Nor was he deceived in his expectation. For presently in the Roman camp they talked and disputed, as if they had all been captains, how the place ought to be seized, and what great advantage they should thereby gain upon the enemies, chiefly if they transferred their camp thither, at any rate, if they strengthened the place with a fort. Marcellus resolved to go, with a few horse, to view it. Having called a diviner he proceeded to sacrifice. In the first victim the aruspex showed him the liver without a head, in the second the head appeared of unusual size, and all the other indications highly promising. When these seemed sufficient to free them from the dread of the former, the diviners declared, that they were all the more terrified by the latter: because entrails too fair and promising, when they appear after others that are maimed and monstrous, render the change doubtful and suspicious. But

> Nor fire nor brazen wall can keep out fate;[12]

as Pindar observes. Marcellus, therefore, taking with him his colleague Crispinus, and his son, a tribune of soldiers, with two hundred and twenty horse at most, (among whom there was not one Roman, but all were Etruscans, except forty Fregellans, of whose courage and fidelity he had on all occasions received full proof,) goes to view the place. The hill was covered with woods all over; on the top of it sat a scout concealed from the sight of the enemy, but having the Roman camp exposed to his view. Upon signs received from him, the men that were placed in ambush, stirred not till Marcellus came near; and then all starting

[12] The fragment from Pindar is No. 256, in Boeckh; nothing more is known of it.

up in an instant, and encompassing him from all sides, attacked him with darts, struck about and wounded the backs of those that fled, and pressed upon those who resisted. These were the forty Fregellans. For though the Etruscans fled in the very beginning of the fight, the Fregellans formed themselves into a ring, bravely defending the consuls, till Crispinus, struck with two darts, turned his horse to fly away; and Marcellus's side was run through with a lance with a broad head. Then the Fregellans, also, the few that remained alive, leaving the fallen consul, and rescuing young Marcellus, who also was wounded, got into the camp by flight. There were slain not much above forty; five lictors and eighteen horsemen came alive into the enemy's hands. Crispinus also died of his wounds a few days after. Such a disaster as the loss of both consuls in a single engagement, was one that had never before befallen the Romans.

Hannibal, little valuing the other events, so soon as he was told of Marcellus's death, immediately hasted to the hill. Viewing the body, and continuing for some time to observe its strength and shape, he allowed not a word to fall from him expressive of the least pride or arrogancy, nor did he show in his countenance any sign of gladness, as another perhaps would have done, when his fierce and troublesome enemy had been taken away; but amazed by so sudden and unexpected an end, taking off nothing but his ring, gave order to have the body properly clad and adorned, and honorably burned. The relics, put into a silver urn, with a crown of gold to cover it, he sent back to his son. But some of the Numidians setting upon those that were carrying the urn, took it from them by force, and cast away the bones; which being told to Hannibal, "It is impossible, it seems then," he said, "to do any thing against the will of God!" He punished the Numidians; but took no further care of sending or re-collecting the bones; conceiving that Marcellus so fell, and so lay unburied, by a certain fate. So Cornelius Nepos and Valerius Maximus have left upon record: but Livy and Augustus Cæsar affirm, that the urn was brought to his son, and honored with a magnificent funeral. Besides the monuments raised for him at Rome, there was dedicated to his memory at Catana in Sicily, an ample wrestling place called after him; statues and pictures, out of those he took from Syracuse, were set up in Samothrace, in the temple of the gods, named Cabiri, and in that of Minerva at Lindus, where also there was a statue of him, says Posidonius, with the following inscription:—

> This was, O stranger, once Rome's star divine,
> Claudius Marcellus of an ancient line;
> To fight her wars seven times her consul made,
> Low in the dust her enemies he laid.

The writer of the inscription has added to Marcellus's five consulates, his two proconsulates. His progeny continued in high honor even down to Marcellus, son of Octavia, sister of Augustus, whom she bore to her husband Caius Marcellus; and who died, a bridegroom, in the year of his ædileship, having not long before married Cæsar's daughter. His mother, Octavia, dedicated the library to his honor and memory, and Cæsar, the theatre which bears his name.

COMPARISON OF PELOPIDAS WITH MARCELLUS

THESE are the memorable things I have found in historians, concerning Marcellus and Pelopidas. Betwixt which two great men, though in natural character and manners they nearly resembled each other, because both were valiant and diligent, daring and high-spirited, there was yet some diversity in the one point, that Marcellus in many cities which he reduced under his power, committed great slaughter; but Epaminondas and Pelopidas never after any victory put men to death, or reduced citizens to slavery. And we are told, too, that the Thebans would not, had these been present, have taken the measures they did, against the Orchomenians. Marcellus's exploits against the Gauls are admirable and ample; when, accompanied by a few horse, he defeated and put to flight a vast number of horse and foot together, (an action you cannot easily in historians find to have been done by any other captain,) and took their king prisoner. To which honor Pelopidas aspired, but did not attain; he was killed by the tyrant in the attempt. But to these you may perhaps oppose those two most glorious battles at Leuctra and Tegyræ; and we have no statement of any achievement of Marcellus, by stealth or ambuscade, such as were those of Pelopidas, when he returned from exile, and killed the tyrants at Thebes; which, indeed, may claim to be called the first in rank of all achievements ever performed by secresy and cunning. Hannibal was, indeed, a most formidable enemy for the Romans; but so for that matter were the Lacedæmonians for the Thebans. And that these were, in the fights of Leuctra and Tegyræ, beaten and put to flight by Pelopidas, is confessed; whereas, Polybius writes, that Hannibal was never so much as once vanquished by Marcellus, but remained invincible in all encounters, till Scipio came. I myself, indeed, have followed rather Livy, Cæsar, Cornelius Nepos, and, among the Greeks, king Juba, in stating that the troops of Hannibal were in some encounters routed and put to flight by Marcellus; but certainly these defeats conduced little to the sum of the war. It would seem as if they had been merely feints of some sort on the part of the Carthaginian. What was indeed truly and really admirable was, that the Romans, after the defeat of so many armies, the slaughter of so many captains, and, in fine, the confusion of almost the whole Roman empire, still showed a courage equal to their losses, and were as willing as their enemies to engage in new battles. And Marcellus was the one man who overcame the great and inveterate fear and dread, and revived, raised, and confirmed the spirits of the soldiers to that degree of emulation and bravery, that would not let them easily yield the victory, but made them contend for it to the last. For the same men, whom continual defeats had accustomed to think themselves happy, if they could but save themselves by running from Hannibal, were by him taught to esteem it base and ignominious to return safe but unsuccessful; to be ashamed to confess that they had yielded one step in the terrors of the fight; and to grieve to extremity if they were not victorious.

In short, as Pelopidas was never overcome in any battle, where himself was present and commanded in chief, and as Marcellus gained more victories than any of his contemporaries, truly he that

PELOPIDAS AND MARCELLUS

could not be easily overcome, considering his many successes, may fairly be compared with him who was undefeated. Marcellus took Syracuse; whereas Pelopidas was frustrated of his hope of capturing Sparta. But in my judgment, it was more difficult to advance his standards even to the walls of Sparta, and to be the first of mortals that ever passed the river Eurotas in arms, than it was to reduce Sicily; unless, indeed, we say that that adventure is with more of right to be attributed to Epaminondas, as was also the Leuctrian battle; whereas Marcellus's renown, and the glory of his brave actions came entire and undiminished to him alone. For he alone took Syracuse; and without his colleague's help defeated the Gauls, and, when all others declined, alone, without one companion, ventured to engage with Hannibal; and changing the aspect of the war first showed the example of daring to attack him.

I cannot commend the death of either of these great men; the suddenness and strangeness of their ends gives me a feeling rather of pain and distress. Hannibal has my admiration, who, in so many severe conflicts, more than can be reckoned in one day, never received so much as one wound. I honor Chrysantes also, (in Xenophon's Cyropædia,) [1] who, having raised his sword in the act of striking his enemy, so soon as a retreat was sounded, left him, and retired sedately and modestly. Yet the

---

[1] The passage referred to in the Cyropædia is the 1st chapter of the 4th book. It is not certain how much of the sentiment contained, a little below, in the two verses of the translation, belongs to what Euripides said. Plutarch, who gives it in an unmetrical form here, quotes elsewhere two lines identical with the latter part. *But if it be lawful to die, then it is noble to*

anger which provoked Pelopidas to pursue revenge in the heat of fight, may excuse him.

> The first thing for a captain is to gain
> Safe victory; the next to be with honor slain,

as Euripides says. For then he cannot be said to *suffer* death; it is rather to be called an action. The very object, too, of Pelopidas's victory, which consisted in the slaughter of the tyrant, presenting itself to his eyes, did not wholly carry him away unadvisedly: he could not easily expect again to have another equally glorious occasion for the exercise of his courage, in a noble and honorable cause. But Marcellus, when it made little to his advantage, and when no such violent ardor as present danger naturally calls out transported him to passion, throwing himself into danger, fell into an unexplored ambush; he, namely, who had borne five consulates, led three triumphs, won the spoils and glories of kings and victories, to act the part of a mere scout or sentinel, and to expose all his achievements to be trod under foot by the mercenary Spaniards and Numidians, who sold themselves and their lives to the Carthaginians; so that even they themselves felt unworthy, and almost grudged themselves the unhoped for success of having cut off, among a few Fregellan scouts, the most valiant,

die, making virtue (or *honor*) *the term of our life.* Grotius gives, as a translation of the whole:—

> Vincere vivereque optima res est;
> Si moriendum est, ita dulce mori
> Vitam ut virtus sorbeat in se.

See Matthiæ's Euripides, (*Fragment, incert.,* 110).

the most potent, and most renowned of the Romans. Let no man think that we have thus spoken out of a design to accuse these noble men; it is merely an expression of frank indignation in their own behalf, at seeing them thus wasting all their other virtues upon that of bravery, and throwing away their lives, as if the loss would be only felt by themselves, and not by their country, allies, and friends.

After Pelopidas's death, his friends, for whom he died, made a funeral for him; the enemies, by whom he had been killed, made one for Marcellus. A noble and happy lot indeed the former; yet there is something higher and greater in the admiration rendered by enemies to the virtue that had been their own obstacle, than in the grateful acknowledgments of friends. Since, in the one case, it is virtue alone that challenges itself the honor; while, in the other, it may be rather men's personal profit and advantage that is the real origin of what they do.

ARISTIDES[1]

TRANSLATED BY JOHN COOPER, FELLOW OF
TRINITY COLLEGE, CAMBRIDGE

ARISTIDES, the son of Lysimachus, was of the tribe Antiochis, and township of Alopece. As to his wealth, statements differ; some say he passed his life in extreme poverty, and left behind him two daughters whose indigence long kept them unmarried: but Demetrius, the Phalerian, in opposition to this general report, professes in his Socrates, to know a farm at Phalerum going by Aristides's name, where he was interred; and, as marks of his opulence, adduces first, the office of archon eponymus, which he obtained by the lot of the bean; which was confined to the highest assessed families, called the Pentacosiomedimni; second, the ostracism, which was not usually inflicted on the poorer citizens, but on those of great houses, whose station exposed them to envy; third and last, that he left certain tripods in the temple of Bacchus, offerings for his victory in conducting the representation of dramatic performances, which were even in our age still to be seen, retaining this inscription upon them, " The tribe Antiochis obtained the victory: Aristides defrayed the charges: Archestratus's play was acted." But this argument, though in appearance the strongest, is of the least moment of any. For Epaminondas, who all the world knows was edu-

[1] Aristides, surnamed the "Just," born of an ancient and noble family, fought as the commander of his tribe at Marathon, 490 B.C., and next year 489 was archon. He died after 471, probably in 468, so poor that he did not leave enough to pay for his funeral.—DR. WILLIAM SMITH.

cated, and lived his whole life, in much poverty, and also Plato, the philosopher, exhibited magnificent shows, the one an entertainment of flute-players, the other of dithyrambic singers; Dion, the Syracusan, supplying the expenses of the latter, and Pelopidas those of Epaminondas. For good men do not allow themselves in any inveterate and irreconcilable hostility to receiving presents from their friends, but while looking upon those that are accepted to be hoarded up and with avaricious intentions, as sordid and mean, they do not refuse such as, apart from all profit, gratify the pure love of honor and magnificence. Panætius, again, shows that Demetrius was deceived concerning the tripod by an identity of name. For, from the Persian war to the end of the Peloponnesian, there are upon record only two of the name of Aristides, who defrayed the expense of representing plays and gained the prize, neither of which was the same with the son of Lysimachus; but the father of the one was Xenophilus, and the other lived at a much later time, as the way of writing, which is that in use since the time of Euclides,[2] and the addition of the name of Archestratus prove, a name which, in the time of the Persian war, no writer mentions, but which several, during the Peloponnesian war, record as that of a dramatic poet. The argument of Panætius re-

[2] *The way of writing in use since the time of Euclides* differed from the previous usage more particularly in the introduction of the Ionic letters *eta* and *omega*, the long *e* and *o*, which up to that date had never appeared in public inscriptions or documents. The year of the archonship of Euclides is 403 B.C., the first after the end of the Peloponnesian War; in the course of which the thirty tyrants were expelled, the amnesty decreed, and the democracy reëstablished.

quires to be more closely considered. But as for the ostracism, every one was liable to it, whom his reputation, birth, or eloquence raised above the common level; insomuch that even Damon, preceptor to Pericles, was thus banished, because he seemed a man of more than ordinary sense. And, moreover, Idomeneus says, that Aristides was not made archon by the lot of the bean, but the free election of the people. And if he held the office after the battle of Platæa, as Demetrius himself has written, it is very probable that his great reputation and success in the war, made him be preferred for his virtue to an office which others received in consideration of their wealth. But Demetrius manifestly is eager not only to exempt Aristides, but Socrates likewise, from poverty, as from a great evil; telling us that the latter had not only a house of his own, but also seventy minæ put out at interest with Crito.

Aristides being the friend and supporter of that Clisthenes, who settled the government after the expulsion of the tyrants, and emulating and admiring Lycurgus the Lacedæmonian above all politicians, adhered to the aristocratical principles of government; and had Themistocles, son to Neocles, his adversary on the side of the populace. Some say that, being boys and bred up together from their infancy, they were always at variance with each other in all their words and actions as well serious as playful, and that in this their early contention they soon made proof of their natural inclinations; the one being ready, adventurous, and subtle, engaging readily and eagerly in every thing; the other of a staid and settled temper, intent on the exercise of justice, not admitting any degree of falsity, indecorum, or trickery, no, not so much as at his play.

Ariston of Chios[3] says the first origin of the enmity which rose to so great a height, was a love affair; they were rivals for the affection of the beautiful Stesilaus of Ceos, and were passionate beyond all moderation, and did not lay aside their animosity when the beauty that had excited it passed away; but, as if it had only exercised them in it, immediately carried their heats and differences into public business.

Themistocles, therefore, joining an association of partisans, fortified himself with considerable strength; insomuch that when some one told him that were he impartial, he would make a good magistrate; "I wish," replied he, "I may never sit on that tribunal where my friends shall not plead a greater privilege than strangers." But Aristides walked, so to say, alone on his own path in politics, being unwilling, in the first place, to go along with his associates in ill doing, or to cause them vexation by not gratifying their wishes; and, secondly, observing that many were encouraged by the support they had in their friends to act injuriously, he was cautious; being of opinion that the integrity of his words and actions was the only right security for a good citizen.

However, Themistocles making many dangerous alterations, and withstanding and interrupting him in the whole series of his actions, Aristides also was necessitated to set himself against all Themistocles did, partly in self-defence, and partly to impede his power from still increasing by the favor of the multitude; esteeming it better to let slip some public conveniences, rather than that he by prevailing

---

[3] More correctly perhaps, both here and elsewhere, Ariston of Ceos. There were two philosophical writers of the name, Ariston of Chios, a Stoic, and Ariston of Ceos, a Peripatetic.

should become powerful in all things. In fine, when he once had opposed Themistocles in some measures that were expedient, and had got the better of him, he could not refrain from saying, when he left the assembly, that unless they sent Themistocles and himself to the barathrum,[4] there could be no safety for Athens. Another time, when urging some proposal upon the people, though there were much opposition and stirring against it, he yet was gaining the day; but just as the president of the assembly was about to put it to the vote, perceiving by what had been said in debate the inexpediency of his advice, he let it fall. Also he often brought in his bills by other persons, lest Themistocles, through party spirit against him, should be any hindrance to the good of the public.

In all the vicissitudes of public affairs, the constancy he showed was admirable, not being elated with honors, and demeaning himself tranquilly and sedately in adversity; holding the opinion that he ought to offer himself to the service of his country without mercenary views and irrespectively of any reward, not only of riches, but even of glory itself. Hence it came, probably, that at the recital of these verses of Æschylus in the theatre, relating to Amphiaraus,

> For not at seeming just, but being so
> He aims; and from his depth of soil below,
> Harvests of wise and prudent counsels grow,[5]

[4] A pit into which the dead bodies of malefactors, or perhaps living malefactors themselves were thrown. "The gallows" perhaps is the English term most nearly corresponding to the barathrum, as commonly spoken of in the Athenian popular language.

[5] The verses from Æschylus relating to Amphiaraus are

the eyes of all the spectators turned on Aristides, as if this virtue, in an especial manner, belonged to him.

He was a most determined champion for justice, not only against feelings of friendship and favor, but wrath and malice. Thus it is reported of him that when prosecuting the law against one who was his enemy, on the judges after accusation refusing to hear the criminal, and proceeding immediately to pass sentence upon him, he rose in haste from his seat and joined in petition with him for a hearing, and that he might enjoy the privilege of the law. Another time, when judging between two private persons, on the one declaring his adversary had very much injured Aristides; "Tell me rather, good friend," he said, "what wrong he has done you; for it is your cause, not my own, which I now sit judge of." Being chosen to the charge of the public revenue, he made it appear, that not only those of his time, but the preceding officers, had alienated much treasure, and especially Themistocles:—

> Well known he was an able man to be,
> But with his fingers apt to be too free.

Therefore, Themistocles associating several persons against Aristides, and impeaching him when he gave in his accounts, caused him to be condemned of robbing the public; so Idomeneus states; but the best and chiefest men of the city much resenting it, he was not only exempted from the fine imposed upon him, but likewise again called to the same employment. Pretending now to repent him of his former practice, and carrying himself with more

from the Seven against Thebes, lines 574 to 576. *Well known he was, &c.*, is ascribed to Euripides.

remissness, he became acceptable to such as pillaged the treasury, by not detecting or calling them to an exact account. So that those who had their fill of the public money began highly to applaud Aristides, and sued to the people, making interest to have him once more chosen treasurer. But when they were upon the point of election, he reproved the Athenians. "When I discharged my office well and faithfully," said he, "I was insulted and abused; but now that I have allowed the public thieves in a variety of malpractices, I am considered an admirable patriot. I am more ashamed, therefore, of this present honor than of the former sentence; and I commiserate your condition, with whom it is more praiseworthy to oblige ill men than to conserve the revenue of the public." Saying thus, and proceeding to expose the thefts that had been committed, he stopped the mouths of those who cried him up and vouched for him, but gained real and true commendation from the best men.

When Datis, being sent by Darius under pretence of punishing the Athenians for their burning of Sardis, but in reality to reduce the Greeks under his dominion, landed at Marathon and laid waste the country, among the ten commanders appointed by the Athenians for the war, Miltiades was of the greatest name; but the second place, both for reputation and power, was possessed by Aristides: and when his opinion to join battle was added to that of Miltiades, it did much to incline the balance. Every leader by his day having the command in chief, when it came to Aristides's turn, he delivered it into the hands of Miltiades, showing his fellow officers, that it is not dishonorable to obey and follow wise and able men, but, on the contrary, noble and prudent. So appeasing their

rivalry, and bringing them to acquiesce in one and
the best advice, he confirmed Miltiades in the
strength of an undivided and unmolested authority.
For now every one, yielding his day of command,
looked for orders only to him. During the fight
the main body of the Athenians being the hardest
put to it, the barbarians, for a long time, making
opposition there against the tribes Leontis and
Antiochis, Themistocles and Aristides being ranged
together, fought valiantly; the one being of the
tribe Leontis, the other of the Antiochis. But
after they had beaten the barbarians back to their
ships, and perceived that they sailed not for the
isles, but were driven in by the force of sea and
wind towards the country of Attica; fearing lest
they should take the city, unprovided of defence,
they hurried away thither with nine tribes, and
reached it the same day. Aristides, being left with
his tribe at Marathon to guard the plunder and
prisoners, did not disappoint the opinion they had
of him. Amidst the profusion of gold and silver, all
sorts of apparel, and other property, more than can
be mentioned, that were in the tents and the vessels
which they had taken, he neither felt the desire
to meddle with any thing himself, nor suffered
others to do it; unless it might be some who took
away any thing unknown to him; as Callias, the
torch-bearer,[6] did. One of the barbarians, it seems,
prostrated himself before this man, supposing him
to be a king by his hair and fillet; and, when he
had so done, taking him by the hand, showed him
a great quantity of gold hid in a ditch. But Callias,
most cruel and impious of men, took away the
treasure, but slew the man, lest he should tell of

[6] In the festivals of Eleusinian Ceres; an office hereditary
in the family of Callias.

him. Hence, they say, the comic poets gave his family the name of *Laccopluti,* or enrichèd by the ditch, alluding to the place where Callias found the gold. Aristides, immediately after this, was archon; although Demetrius, the Phalerian, says he held the office a little before he died, after the battle of Platæa. But in the records of the successors of Xanthippides, in whose year Mardonius was overthrown at Platæa, amongst very many there mentioned, there is not so much as one of the same name as Aristides: while immediately after Phænippus, during whose term of office they obtained the victory of Marathon, Aristides is registered.

Of all his virtues, the common people were most affected with his justice, because of its continual and common use; and thus, although of mean fortune and ordinary birth, he possessed himself of the most kingly and divine appellation of Just; which kings, however, and tyrants have never sought after; but have taken delight to be surnamed besiegers of cities, thunderers, conquerors, or eagles again, and hawks;[7] affecting, it seems, the reputation which proceeds from power and violence, rather than that of virtue. Although the divinity, to whom they desire to compare and assimilate themselves, excels, it is supposed, in three things, immortality, power, and virtue; of which three, the noblest and divinest is virtue. For the elements and vacuum have an everlasting existence; earthquakes, thunders, storms, and torrents have great power; but in justice and equity nothing partici-

---

[7] Demetrius Poliorcetes, or the besieger, Ptolemy Ceraunus, or Thunder, and Demetrius Nicator, the conqueror, are the probable examples alluded to; with Pyrrhus who had the name of Aetus, the eagle, and Antiochus surnamed Hierax, the hawk.

pates except by means of reason and the knowledge of that which is divine. And thus, taking the three varieties of feeling commonly entertained towards the deity, the sense of his happiness, fear, and honor of him, people would seem to think him blest and happy for his exemption from death and corruption, to fear and dread him for his power and dominion, but to love, honor, and adore him for his justice. Yet though thus disposed, they covet that immortality which our nature is not capable of, and that power the greatest part of which is at the disposal of fortune; but give virtue, the only divine good really in our reach, the last place, most unwisely; since justice makes the life of such as are in prosperity, power, and authority the life of a god, and injustice turns it to that of a beast.

Aristides, therefore, had at first the fortune to be beloved for his surname, but at length envied. Especially when Themistocles spread a rumor amongst the people, that, by determining and judging all matters privately, he had destroyed the courts of judicature, and was secretly making way for a monarchy in his own person, without the assistance of guards. Moreover, the spirit of the people, now grown high, and confident with their late victory, naturally entertained feelings of dislike to all of more than common fame and reputation. Coming together, therefore, from all parts into the city, they banished Aristides by the ostracism, giving their jealousy of his reputation the name of fear of tyranny. For ostracism was not the punishment of any criminal act, but was speciously said to be the mere depression and humiliation of excessive greatness and power; and was in fact a gentle relief and mitigation of envious feeling, which was thus allowed to vent itself in inflicting no intolerable injury, only a ten years' banishment. But after it came to be exercised upon base and villanous fellows, they desisted from it; Hyperbolus, being the last whom they banished by the ostracism.

The cause of Hyperbolus's banishment is said to have been this. Alcibiades and Nicias, men that bore the greatest sway in the city, were of different factions. As the people, therefore, were about to vote the ostracism, and obviously to decree it against one of them, consulting together and uniting their parties, they contrived the banishment of Hyperbolus. Upon which the people, being offended, as if some contempt or affront was put upon the thing, left off and quite abolished it. It was performed, to be short, in this manner. Every one taking an *ostracon,* a sherd, that is, or piece of earthenware, wrote upon it the citizen's name he would have banished, and carried it to a certain part of the market-place surrounded with wooden rails. First, the magistrates numbered all the sherds in gross (for if there was less than six thousand, the ostracism was imperfect); then, laying every name by itself, they pronounced him whose name was written by the larger number, banished for ten years, with the enjoyment of his estate. As, therefore, they were writing the names on the sherds, it is reported that an illiterate clownish fellow, giving Aristides his sherd, supposing him a common citizen, begged him to write *Aristides* upon it; and he being surprised and asking if Aristides had ever done him any injury, "None at all," said he, "neither know I the man; but I am tired of hearing him everywhere called the Just." Aristides, hearing this, is said to have made no reply, but returned the sherd with his own name inscribed. At his departure from the city, lifting up his hands to heaven, he made a prayer, (the reverse, it would seem, of that of Achilles,) that the Athenians might never have any occasion which should constrain them to remember Aristides.

Nevertheless, three years after, when Xerxes marched through Thessaly and Bœotia into the country of Attica, repealing the law, they decreed the return of the banished: chiefly fearing Aristides, lest, joining himself to the enemy, he should corrupt and bring over many of his fellow-citizens to the party of the barbarians; much mistaking the man, who, already before the decree, was exerting himself to excite and encourage the Greeks to the defence of their liberty. And afterwards, when Themistocles was general with absolute power, he assisted him in all ways both in action and counsel; rendering, in consideration of the common security, the greatest enemy he had the most glorious of men. For when Eurybiades was deliberating to desert the isle of Salamis, and the gallies of the barbarians putting out by night to sea surrounded and beset the narrow passage and islands, and nobody was aware how they were environed, Aristides, with great hazard, sailed from Ægina through the enemy's fleet; and coming by night to Themistocles's tent, and calling him out by himself; "If we have any discretion," said he, "Themistocles, laying aside at this time our vain and childish contention, let us enter upon a safe and honorable dispute, vying with each other for the preservation of Greece; you in the ruling and commanding, I in the subservient and advising part; even, indeed, as I now understand you to be alone adhering to the best advice, in counselling without any delay to engage in the straits. And in this, though our own party oppose, the enemy seems to assist you. For the sea behind, and all around us, is covered with their fleet; so that we are under a necessity of approving ourselves men of courage, and fighting, whether we will or no; for there is no room left us for flight." To which Themistocles answered, "I would not willingly, Aristides, be overcome by you on this occasion; and shall endeavor, in emulation of this good beginning, to outdo it in my actions." Also relating to him the stratagem he had framed against the barbarians, he entreated him to persuade Eurybiades and show him, how it was impossible they should save themselves without an engagement; as he was the more likely to be believed. Whence, in the council of war, Cleocritus, the Corinthian, telling Themistocles that Aristides did not like his advice, as he was present and said nothing, Aristides answered, That he should not have held his peace, if Themistocles had not been giving the best advice; and that he was now silent not out of any good-will to the person, but in approbation of his counsel.

Thus the Greek captains were employed. But Aristides perceiving Psyttalea, a small island that lies within the straits over against Salamis, to be filled by a body of the enemy, put aboard his small boats the most forward and courageous of his countrymen, and went ashore upon it; and, joining battle with the barbarians, slew them all, except such more remarkable persons as were taken alive. Amongst these were three children of Sandauce, the king's sister, whom he immediately sent away to Themistocles, and it is stated that in accordance with a certain oracle, they were, by the command of Euphrantides, the seer, sacrificed to Bacchus, called Omestes, or the devourer. But Aristides, placing armed men all around the island, lay in wait for such as were cast upon it, to the intent that none of his friends should perish, nor any of his enemies escape. For the closest engagement of the ships, and the main fury of the whole battle, seems to have been about this place; for which reason a trophy was erected in Psyttalea.

After the fight, Themistocles, to sound Aristides, told him they had performed a good piece of service, but there was a better yet to be done, the keeping Asia in Europe, by sailing forthwith to the Hellespont, and cutting in sunder the bridge. But Aristides, with an exclamation, bid him think no more of it, but deliberate and find out means for removing the Mede, as quickly as possible, out of Greece; lest being enclosed, through want of means to escape, necessity should compel him to force his way with so great an army. So Themistocles once more despatched Arnaces, the eunuch, his prisoner, giving him in command privately to advertise the king that he had diverted the Greeks from their intention of setting sail for the bridges, out of the desire he felt to preserve him.

Xerxes, being much terrified with this, immediately hasted to the Hellespont. But Mardonius was left with the most serviceable part of the army, about three hundred thousand men, and was a formidable enemy, confident in his infantry, and writing messages of defiance to the Greeks: "You have overcome by sea men accustomed to fight on land, and unskilled at the oar; but there lies now the open country of Thessaly; and the plains of Bœotia offer a broad and worthy field for brave men, either horse or foot, to contend in." But he sent privately to the Athenians, both by letter and word of mouth from the king, promising to rebuild their city, to give them a vast sum of money, and constitute them lords of all Greece on condition they were not engaged in the war. The Lacedæmonians, receiving news of this, and fearing, despatched an embassy to the Athenians, entreating that they would send their wives and children to Sparta, and receive support from them for their superannuated. For, being despoiled both of their city and country, the people were suffering extreme distress. Having given audience to the ambassadors, they returned an answer, upon the motion of Aristides, worthy of the highest admiration; declaring, that they forgave their enemies if they thought all things purchasable by wealth, than which they knew nothing of greater value; but that they felt offended at the Lacedæmonians, for looking only to their present poverty and exigence, without any remembrance of their valor and magnanimity, offering them their victuals, to fight in the cause of Greece. Aristides, making this proposal and bringing back the ambassadors into the assembly, charged them to tell the Lacedæmonians, that all the treasure on the earth or under it, was of less value with the people of Athens, than the liberty of Greece. And, showing the sun to those who came from Mardonius, " as long as that retains the same course, so long," said he, " shall the citizens of Athens wage war with the Persians for the country which has been wasted, and the temples that have been profaned and burnt by them." Moreover, he proposed a decree, that the priests should anathematize him who sent any herald to the Medes, or deserted the alliance of Greece.

When Mardonius made a second incursion into the country of Attica, the people passed over again into the isle of Salamis. Aristides, being sent to Lacedæmon, reproved them for their delay and neglect in abandoning Athens once more to the barbarians; and demanded their assistance for that part of Greece, which was not yet lost. The Ephori, hearing this, made show of sporting all day, and of carelessly keeping holy day, (for they were then celebrating the Hyacinthian festival,) but in the night, selecting five thousand Spartans, each of whom was attended by seven Helots, they sent them forth unknown to those from Athens. And when Aristides again reprehended them, they told him in derision that he either doted or dreamed, for the army was already at Oresteum, in their march towards the *strangers;* as they called the Persians. Aristides answered, that they jested unseasonably, deluding their friends, instead of their enemies. Thus says Idomeneus. But in the decree of Aristides, not himself, but Cimon, Xanthippus, and Myronides are appointed ambassadors.

Being chosen general for the war, he repaired to Platæa, with eight thousand Athenians, where Pausanias, generalissimo of all Greece, joined him with the Spartans; and the forces of the other Greeks came in to them. The whole encampment of the barbarians extended all along the bank of the river Asopus, their numbers being so great, there was no enclosing them all, but their baggage and most valuable things were surrounded with a square bulwark, each side of which was the length of ten furlongs.

Tisamenus, the Elean, had prophesied to Pausanias and all the Greeks, and foretold them victory if they made no attempt upon the enemy, but stood on their defence. But Aristides sending to Delphi, the god answered, that the Athenians should overcome their enemies, in case they made supplication to Jupiter and Juno of Cithæron, Pan, and the nymphs Sphragitides, and sacrificed to the heroes Androcrates, Leucon, Pisander, Damocrates, Hypsion, Actæon, and Polyidus; and if they fought within their own territories in the plain of Ceres Eleusinia and Proserpine. Aristides was perplexed upon the tidings of this oracle: since the heroes to whom it commanded him to sacrifice had been chieftains of the Platæans, and the cave of the nymphs Sphragitides was on the top of Mount Cithæron, on the side facing the setting sun of summer time; in which place, as the story goes, there was formerly an oracle, and many that lived in the district were inspired with it, whom they called *Nympholepti,* possessed with the nymphs. But the plain of Ceres Eleusinia, and the offer of victory to the Athenians, if they fought in their own territories, recalled them again, and transferred the war into the country of Attica. In this juncture, Arimnestus, who commanded the Platæans, dreamed that Jupiter, the Saviour, asked him what the Greeks had resolved upon; and that he answered, " To-morrow, my Lord, we march our army to Eleusis, and there give the barbarians battle according to the directions of the oracle of Apollo." And that the god replied, they were utterly mistaken, for that the places spoken of by the oracle were within the bounds of Platæa, and if they sought there they should find them. This manifest vision having appeared to Arimnestus, when he awoke he sent for the most aged and experienced of his countrymen, with whom communicating and examining the matter, he found that near Hysiæ, at the foot of Mount Cithæron, there was a very ancient temple called the temple of Ceres Eleusinia and Proserpine. He therefore forthwith took Aristides to the place, which was very convenient for drawing up an army of foot, because the slopes at the bottom of the mountain Cithæron rendered the plain, where it comes up to the temple, unfit for the movements of cavalry. Also, in the same place, there was the fane of Androcrates, environed with a thick shady grove. And that the oracle might be accomplished in all particulars for the hope of victory, Arimnestus proposed, and the Platæans decreed, that the frontiers of their country towards Attica should be removed, and the land given to the Athenians, that they might fight in defence of Greece in their own proper territory. This zeal and liberality of the Platæans became so famous, that Alexander, many years after, when he had obtained the dominion of all Asia, upon erecting the walls of Platæa, caused proclamation to be made by the herald at the Olympic games, that the king did the Platæans this favor in consideration of their nobleness and magnanimity, because, in the war with the Medes, they freely gave up their land and zealously fought with the Greeks.

The Tegeatans, contesting the post of honor with the Athenians, demanded, that, according to custom, the Lacedæmonians being ranged on the right wing of the battle, they might have the left, alleging several matters in commendation of their ancestors. The Athenians being indignant at the claim, Aristides came forward; "To contend with the Tegeatans," said he, "for noble descent and valor, the present time permits not: but this we say to you, O you Spartans, and you the rest of the Greeks, that place neither takes away nor contributes courage: we shall endeavor by crediting and maintaining the post you assign us, to reflect no dishonor on our former performances. For we are come, not to differ with our friends, but to fight our enemies; not to extol our ancestors, but ourselves to behave as valiant men. This battle will manifest how much each city, captain, and private soldier is worth to Greece." The council of war, upon this address, decided for the Athenians, and gave them the other wing of the battle.

All Greece being in suspense, and especially the affairs of the Athenians unsettled, certain persons of great families and possessions having been impoverished by the war, and seeing all their authority and reputation in the city vanished with their wealth, and others in possession of their honors and places, convened privately at a house in Platæa, and conspired for the dissolution of the democratic government; and, if the plot should not succeed, to ruin the cause and betray all to the barbarians. These matters being in agitation in the camp, and many persons already corrupted, Aristides, perceiving the design, and dreading the present juncture of time, determined neither to let the business pass unanimadverted upon, nor yet altogether to expose it; not knowing how many the accusation might reach, and willing to set bounds to his justice with a view to the public convenience. Therefore, of many that were concerned, he apprehended eight only, two of whom, who were first proceeded against and most guilty, Æschines of Lampra, and Agesias of Acharnæ, made their escape out of the camp. The rest he dismissed; giving opportunity to such as thought themselves concealed, to take courage and repent; intimating that they had in the war a great tribunal, where they might clear their guilt by manifesting their sincere and good intentions towards their country.

After this, Mardonius made trial of the Grecian courage, by sending his whole number of horse, in which he thought himself much the stronger, against them, while they were all pitched at the foot of Mount Cithæron, in strong and rocky places, except the Megarians. They, being three thousand in number, were encamped on the plain, where they were damaged by the horse charging and making inroads upon them on all hands. They sent, therefore, in haste to Pausanias, demanding relief, as not being able alone to sustain the great numbers of the barbarians. Pausanias, hearing this, and perceiving the tents of the Megarians already hid by the multitude of darts and arrows, and themselves driven together into a narrow space, was at a loss himself how to aid them with his battalion of heavy-armed Lacedæmonians. He proposed it, therefore, as a point of emulation in valor and love of distinction, to the commanders and captains who were around him, if any would voluntarily take upon them the defence and succor of the Megarians. The rest being backward, Aristides undertook the enterprise for the Athenians, and sent Olympiodorus, the most valiant of his inferior officers, with three hundred chosen men and some archers under his command. These being soon in readiness, and running upon the enemy, as soon as Masistius, who commanded the barbarians' horse, a man of wonderful courage and of extraordinary bulk and comeliness of person, perceived it, turning his steed he made towards them. And they sustaining the shock and joining battle with him, there was a sharp conflict, as though by this encounter they were to try the success of the whole war. But after Masistius's horse received a wound, and flung him, and he falling could hardly raise himself through the weight of his armor, the Athenians, pressing upon him with blows, could not easily get at his person, armed as he was, his breast, his head, and his limbs all over, with gold and brass and iron; but one of them at last, running him in at the visor of his helmet, slew him; and the rest of the Persians, leaving the body, fled. The greatness of the Greek success was known, not by the multitude of the slain, (for an inconsiderable number were killed,) but by the sorrow the barbarians expressed. For they shaved themselves, their horses, and mules for the death of Masistius, and filled the plain with howling and lamentation; having lost a person, who, next to Mardonius himself, was by many degrees the chief among them, both for valor and authority.

After this skirmish of the horse, they kept from fighting a long time; for the soothsayers, by the sacrifices, foretold the victory both to Greeks and Persians, if they stood upon the defensive part only, but if they became aggressors, the contrary. At length Mardonius, when he had but a few days' provision, and the Greek forces increased continually by some or other that came in to them, impatient of delay, determined to lie still no longer, but, passing Asopus by daybreak, to fall unexpectedly upon the Greeks; and signified the same over night to the captains of his host. But about midnight, a certain horseman stole into the Greek camp, and coming to the watch, desired them to call Aristides, the Athenian, to him. He coming speedily; "I am," said the stranger, "Alexander, king of the Macedonians, and am arrived here through the greatest danger in the world for the good-will I bear you, lest a sudden onset should dismay you, so as to behave in the fight worse than usual. For to-morrow Mardonius will give you battle, urged, not by any hope of success or courage, but by want of victuals, since, indeed, the prophets prohibit him the battle, the sacrifices and oracles being unfavorable; and the army is in despondency and consternation; but necessity forces him to try his fortune, or sit still and endure the last extremity of want." Alexander, thus saying, entreated Aristides to take notice and remember him, but not to tell any other. But he told him, it was not convenient to conceal the matter from Pausanias (because he was general); as for any other, he would keep it secret from them till the battle was fought; but if the Greeks obtained the victory, that then no one should be ignorant of Alexander's good-will and kindness towards them. After this, the king of the Macedonians rode back again, and Aristides went to Pausanias's tent and told him; and they sent for the rest of the captains and gave orders that the army should be in battle array.

Here, according to Herodotus, Pausanias spoke to Aristides, desiring him to transfer the Athenians to the right wing of the army opposite to the Persians, (as they would do better service against them, having been experienced in their way of combat, and emboldened with former victories,) and to give him the left, where the Medizing Greeks were to make their assault. The rest of the Athenian captains regarded this as an arrogant and interfering act on the part of Pausanias; because, while permitting the rest of the army to keep their stations, he removed them only from place to place, like so many Helots, opposing them to the greatest strength of the enemy. But Aristides said, they were altogether in the wrong. If so short a time ago they contested the left wing with the Tegeatans, and gloried in being preferred before them, now, when the Lacedæmonians give them place in the right, and yield them in a manner the leading of the army, how is it they are discontented with the honor that is done them, and do not look upon it as an advantage to have to fight, not against their countrymen and kindred, but barbarians, and such as were by nature their enemies? After this, the Athenians very readily changed places with the Lacedæmonians, and there went words amongst them as they were encouraging each other, that the enemy approached with no better arms or stouter hearts than those who fought the battle of Marathon; but had the same bows and arrows, and the same embroidered coats and gold, and the same delicate bodies and effeminate minds within; "while we have the same weapons and bodies, and our courage augmented by our victories; and fight not like others in defence of our country only, but for the trophies of Salamis and Marathon; that they may not be looked upon as due to Miltiades or fortune, but to the people of Athens." Thus, therefore, were they making haste to change the order of their battle. But the Thebans, understanding it by some deserters, forthwith acquainted Mardonius; and he, either for fear of the Athenians, or a desire to engage the Lacedæmonians, marched over his Persians to the other wing, and commanded the Greeks of his party to be posted opposite to the Athenians. But this change was observed on the other side, and Pausanias, wheeling about again, ranged himself on the right, and Mardonius, also, as at first, took the left wing over against the Lacedæmonians. So the day passed without action.

After this, the Greeks determined in council to remove their camp some distance, to possess themselves of a place convenient for watering; because the springs near them were polluted and destroyed by the barbarian cavalry. But night being come, and the captains setting out towards the place designed for their encamping, the soldiers were not very ready to follow, and keep in a body, but, as soon as they had quitted their first entrenchments, made towards the city of Platæa; and there was much tumult and disorder as they dispersed to various quarters and proceeded to pitch their tents. The Lacedæmonians, against their will, had the fortune to be left by the rest. For Amompharetus, a brave and daring man, who had long been burning with desire of the fight, and resented their many lingerings and delays, calling the removal of the camp a mere running away and flight, protested he would not desert his post, but would there remain with his company, and sustain the charge of Mardonius. And when Pausanias came to him and told him he did these things by the common vote and determination of the Greeks, Amompharetus taking up a great stone and flinging it at Pausanias's feet, and "by this token," said he, "do I give my suffrage for the battle, nor have I any concern with the cowardly consultations and decrees of other men." Pausanias, not knowing what to do in the present juncture, sent to the Athenians, who were drawing off, to stay to accompany him; and so he himself set off with the rest of the army for Platæa, hoping thus to make Amompharetus move.

Meantime, day came upon them; and Mardonius (for he was not ignorant of their deserting their camp) having his army in array, fell upon the Lacedæmonians with great shouting and noise of barbarous people, as if they were not about to join battle, but crush the Greeks in their flight. Which within a very little came to pass. For Pausanias, perceiving what was done, made a halt, and commanded every one to put themselves in order for the battle; but either through his anger with Amompharetus, or the disturbance he was in by reason of the sudden approach of the enemy, he forgot to give the signal to the Greeks in general. Whence it was, that they did not come in immediately, or in a body, to their assistance, but by small companies and straggling, when the fight was already begun. Pausanias, offering sacrifice, could not procure favorable omens, and so commanded the Lacedæmonians, setting down their shields at their feet to abide quietly and attend his directions, making no resistance to any of their enemies. And, he sacrificing again a second time, the horse charged, and some of the Lacedæmonians were wounded. At this time, also, Callicrates, who, we are told, was the most comely man in the army, being shot with an arrow and upon the point of expiring, said, that he lamented not his death (for he came from home to lay down his life in the defence of Greece) but that he died without action. The case was indeed hard, and the forbearance of the men wonderful; for they let the enemy charge without repelling them; and, expecting their proper opportunity from the gods and their general, suffered themselves to be wounded and slain in their ranks. And some say, that while Pausanias was at sacrifice and prayers, some space out of the battle-array, certain Lydians, falling suddenly upon him, plundered and scattered the sacrifice: and that Pausanias and his company, having no arms, beat them with staves and whips; and that in imitation of this attack, the whipping the boys about the altar, and after it the Lydian procession, are to this day practised in Sparta.

Pausanias, therefore, being troubled at these things, while the priest went on offering one sacrifice

after another, turns himself towards the temple
with tears in his eyes, and, lifting up his hands to
heaven, besought Juno of Cithæron, and the other
tutelar gods of the Platæans, if it were not in the
fates for the Greeks to obtain the victory, that they
might not perish, without performing some remarkable thing, and by their actions demonstrating to their
enemies, that they waged war with men of courage,
and soldiers. While Pausanias was thus in the act
of supplication, the sacrifices appeared propitious,
and the soothsayers foretold victory. The word
being given, the Lacedæmonian battalion of foot
seemed, on the sudden, like some one fierce animal,
setting up his bristles, and betaking himself to the
combat; and the barbarians perceived that they
encountered with men who would fight it to the
death. Therefore, holding their wicker-shields before them, they shot their arrows amongst the
Lacedæmonians. But they, keeping together in the
order of a phalanx, and falling upon the enemies,
forced their shields out of their hands, and, striking
with their pikes at the breasts and faces of the Persians, overthrew many of them; who, however, fell not
either unrevenged or without courage. For taking
hold of the spears with their bare hands, they broke
many of them, and betook themselves not without
effect to the sword; and making use of their falchions and scimitars, and wresting the Lacedæmonians' shields from them, and grappling with them,
it was a long time that they made resistance.

Meanwhile, for some time, the Athenians stood
still, waiting for the Lacedæmonians to come up.
But when they heard much noise as of men engaged
in fight, and a messenger, they say, came from
Pausanias, to advertise them of what was going on,
they soon hasted to their assistance. And as they

passed through the plain to the place where the noise was, the Greeks, who took part with the enemy, came upon them. Aristides, as soon as he saw them, going a considerable space before the rest, cried out to them, conjuring them by the guardian gods of Greece to forbear the fight, and be no impediment or stop to those, who were going to succor the defenders of Greece. But when he perceived they gave no attention to him, and had prepared themselves for the battle, then turning from the present relief of the Lacedæmonians, he engaged them, being five thousand in number. But the greatest part soon gave way and retreated, as the barbarians also were put to flight. The sharpest conflict is said to have been against the Thebans, the chiefest and most powerful persons among them at that time siding zealously with the Medes, and leading the multitude not according to their own inclinations, but as being subjects of an oligarchy.

The battle being thus divided, the Lacedæmonians first beat off the Persians; and a Spartan, named Arimnestus, slew Mardonius by a blow on the head with a stone, as the oracle in the temple of Amphiaraus had foretold to him. For Mardonius sent a Lydian thither, and another person, a Carian, to the cave of Trophonius. This latter, the priest of the oracle answered in his own language. But the Lydian sleeping in the temple of Amphiaraus, it seemed to him that a minister of the divinity stood before him and commanded him to be gone; and on his refusing to do it, flung a great stone at his head, so that he thought himself slain with the blow. Such is the story.—They drove the fliers within their walls of wood; and, a little time after, the Athenians put the Thebans to flight, killing three hundred of the chiefest and of greatest note among them in the actual fight itself. For when they began to fly, news came that the army of the barbarians was besieged within their palisade: and so giving the Greeks opportunity to save themselves, they marched to assist at the fortifications; and coming in to the Lacedæmonians, who were altogether unhandy and unexperienced in storming, they took the camp with great slaughter of the enemy. For of the three hundred thousand, forty thousand only are said to have escaped with Artabazus; while on the Greeks' side there perished in all thirteen hundred and sixty: of which fifty-two were Athenians, all of the tribe Æantis, that fought, says Clidemus, with the greatest courage of any; and for this reason the men of this tribe used to offer sacrifice for the victory, as enjoined by the oracle, to the nymphs Sphragitides at the expense of the public: ninety-one were Lacedæmonians, and sixteen Tegeatans. It is strange, therefore, upon what grounds Herodotus can say, that they only, and none other, encountered the enemy; for the number of the slain and their monuments testify that the victory was obtained by all in general; and if the rest had been standing still, while the inhabitants of three cities only had been engaged in the fight, they would not have set on the altar the inscription:—

> The Greeks, when by their courage and their might,
> They had repelled the Persian in the fight,
> The common altar of freed Greece to be,
> Reared this to Jupiter who guards the free.[8]

They fought this battle on the fourth day of the month Boëdromion, according to the Athenians, but according to the Bœotians, on the twenty-seventh of

[8] The inscription is by Simonides. Plutarch's text omits one line, which is found elsewhere in one of his minor works.

Panemus;—on which day there is still a convention of the Greeks at Platæa, and the Platæans still offer sacrifice for the victory to Jupiter of freedom. As for the difference of days, it is not to be wondered at, since even at the present time, when there is a far more accurate knowledge of astronomy, some begin the month at one time, and some at another.

After this, the Athenians not yielding the honor of the day to the Lacedæmonians, nor consenting they should erect a trophy, things were not far from being ruined by dissension amongst the armed Greeks; had not Aristides, by much soothing and counselling the commanders, especially Leocrates and Myronides, pacified and persuaded them to leave the thing to the decision of the Greeks. And on their proceeding to discuss the matter, Theogiton, the Megarian, declared the honor of the victory was to be given some other city, if they would prevent a civil war; after him Cleocritus of Corinth rising up, made people think he would ask the palm for the Corinthians, (for next to Sparta and Athens, Corinth was in greatest estimation); but he delivered his opinion, to the general admiration, in favor of the Platæans; and counselled to take away all contention by giving them the reward and glory of the victory, whose being honored could be distasteful to neither party. This being said, first Aristides gave consent in the name of the Athenians, and Pausanias, then, for the Lacedæmonians. So, being reconciled, they set apart eighty talents for the Platæans, with which they built the temple and dedicated the image to Minerva, and adorned the temple with pictures, which even to this very day retain their lustre. But the Lacedæmonians and Athenians, each erected a trophy apart by themselves. On their consulting the oracle about offering sacrifice, Apollo answered, that they should dedicate an altar to Jupiter of freedom, but should not sacrifice till they had extinguished the fires throughout the country, as having been defiled by the barbarians, and had kindled unpolluted fire at the common altar at Delphi. The magistrates of Greece, therefore, went forthwith and compelled such as had fire to put it out; and Euchidas, a Platæan, promising to fetch fire, with all possible speed, from the altar of the god, went to Delphi, and having sprinkled and purified his body, crowned himself with laurel; and taking the fire from the altar ran back to Platæa, and got back there before sunset, performing in one day a journey of a thousand furlongs; and saluting his fellow-citizens and delivering them the fire, he immediately fell down, and in a short time after expired. But the Platæans, taking him up, interred him in the temple of Diana Euclia, setting this inscription over him: " Euchidas ran to Delphi and back again in one day." Most people believe that Euclia is Diana, and call her by that name. But some say she was the daughter of Hercules, by Myrto, the daughter of Menœtius, and sister of Patroclus, and, dying a virgin, was worshipped by the Bœotians and Locrians. Her altar and image are set up in all their market-places, and those of both sexes that are about marrying, sacrifice to her before the nuptials.

A general assembly of all the Greeks being called, Aristides proposed a decree, that the deputies and religious representatives of the Greek states should assemble annually at Platæa, and every fifth year celebrate the Eleutheria, or games of freedom. And that there should be a levy upon all Greece, for the war against the barbarians, of ten thousand spearmen, one thousand horse, and a hundred sail of ships; but the Platæans to be exempt, and sacred to the service of the gods, offering sacrifice for the welfare of Greece. These things being ratified, the Platæans undertook the performance of annual sacrifice to such as were slain and buried in that place; which they still perform in the following manner. On the sixteenth day of Mæmacterion (which with the Bœotians is Alalcomenus) they make their procession, which, beginning by break of day, is led by a trumpeter sounding for onset; then follow certain chariots loaded with myrrh and garlands; and then a black bull; then come the young men of free birth carrying libations of wine and milk in large two-handed vessels, and jars of oil and precious ointments, none of servile condition being permitted to have any hand in this ministration, because the men died in defence of freedom; after all comes the chief magistrate of Platæa, (for whom it is unlawful at other times either to touch iron, or wear any other colored garment but white,) at that time apparelled in a purple robe; and, taking a water-pot out of the city record-office, he proceeds, bearing a sword in his hand, through the middle of the town to the sepulchres. Then drawing water out of a spring, he washes and anoints the monuments, and sacrificing the bull upon a pile of wood, and making supplication to Jupiter and Mercury of the earth, invites those valiant men who perished in the defence of Greece, to the banquet and the libations of blood. After this, mixing a bowl of wine, and pouring out for himself, he says, " I drink to those who lost their lives for the liberty of Greece." These solemnities the Platæans observe to this day.

Aristides perceived that the Athenians, after

their return into the city, were eager for a democracy; and deeming the people to deserve consideration on account of their valiant behavior, as also that it was a matter of difficulty, they being well armed, powerful, and full of spirit with their victories, to oppose them by force, he brought forward a decree, that the archons be chosen out of the whole body of the Athenians. And on Themistocles telling the people in assembly that he had some advice for them, which could not be given in public, but was most important for the advantage and security of the city, they appointed Aristides alone to hear and consider it with him. And on his acquainting Aristides that his intent was to set fire to the arsenal of the Greeks, for by that means should the Athenians become supreme masters of all Greece, Aristides, returning to the assembly, told them, that nothing was more advantageous than what Themistocles designed, and nothing more unjust. The Athenians, hearing this, gave Themistocles order to desist; such was the love of justice felt by the people, and such the credit and confidence they reposed in Aristides.

Being sent in joint commission with Cimon to the war, he took notice that Pausanias and the other Spartan captains made themselves offensive by imperiousness and harshness to the confederates; and by being himself gentle and considerate with them and by the courtesy and disinterested temper which Cimon, after his example, manifested in the expeditions, he stole away the chief command from the Lacedæmonians, neither by weapons, ships, or horses, but by equity and wise policy. For the Athenians being endeared to the Greeks by the justice of Aristides and by Cimon's moderation, the tyranny and selfishness of Pausanias rendered them yet more desirable. He on all occasions treated the commanders of the confederates haughtily and roughly; and the common soldiers he punished with stripes, or standing under the iron anchor for a whole day together; neither was it permitted for any to provide straw for themselves to lie on, or forage for their horses, or to come near the springs to water before the Spartans were furnished, but servants with whips drove away such as approached. And when Aristides once was about to complain and expostulate with Pausanias, he told him, with an angry look, that he was not at leisure, and gave no attention to him. The consequence was that the sea captains and generals of the Greeks, in particular, the Chians, Samians, and Lesbians, came to Aristides and requested him to be their general, and to receive the confederates into his command, who had long desired to relinquish the Spartans and come over to the Athenians. But he answered, that he saw both equity and necessity in what they said, but their fidelity required the test of some action, the commission of which would make it impossible for the multitude to change their minds again. Upon which Uliades, the Samian, and Antagoras of Chios, conspiring together, ran in near Byzantium on Pausanias's galley, getting her between them as she was sailing before the rest. But when Pausanias, beholding them, rose up and furiously threatened soon to make them know that they had been endangering not his galley, but their own countries, they bid him go his way, and thank Fortune that fought for him at Platæa; for hitherto, in reverence to that, the Greeks had forborne from inflicting on him the punishment he deserved. In fine, they all went off and joined the Athenians. And here the magnanimity of the Lacedæmonians was wonderful. For when they perceived that their generals were becoming corrupted by the greatness of their authority, they voluntarily laid down the chief command, and left off sending any more of them to the wars, choosing rather to have citizens of moderation and consistent in the observance of their customs, than to possess the dominion of all Greece.

Even during the command of the Lacedæmonians, the Greeks paid a certain contribution towards the maintenance of the war; and being desirous to be rated city by city in their due proportion, they desired Aristides of the Athenians, and gave him command, surveying the country and revenue, to assess every one according to their ability and what they were worth. But he, being so largely empowered, Greece as it were submitting all her affairs to his sole management, went out poor, and returned poorer; laying the tax not only without corruption and injustice, but to the satisfaction and convenience of all. For as the ancients celebrated the age of Saturn, so did the confederates of Athens Aristides's taxation, terming it the happy time of Greece; and that more especially, as the sum was in a short time doubled, and afterwards trebled. For the assessment which Aristides made, was four hundred and sixty talents. But to this Pericles added very near one third part more; for Thucydides says, that in the beginning of the Peloponnesian war, the Athenians had coming in from their confederates six hundred talents. But after Pericles's death, the demagogues, increasing by little and little, raised it to the sum of thirteen hundred talents; not so much through the war's being so expensive and chargeable either by its length or ill success, as by their alluring the people to spend upon largesses and play-house allowances, and in erecting statues and temples. Aristides, therefore, having acquired a wonderful and great reputation by this levy of the tribute, Themistocles is said to have derided him, as if this had been not the commendation of a man, but a money-bag; a retaliation, though not in the same kind, for some free words which Aristides had used. For he, when Themistocles once was saying that he thought the highest virtue of a general was to understand and foreknow the measures the enemy would take, replied, "This, indeed, Themistocles, is simply necessary, but the excellent thing in a general is to keep his hands from taking money."

Aristides, moreover, made all the people of Greece swear to keep the league, and himself took the oath in the name of the Athenians, flinging wedges of redhot iron into the sea, after curses against such as should make breach of their vow. But afterwards, it would seem, when things were in such a state as constrained them to govern with a stronger hand, he bade the Athenians to throw the perjury upon him, and manage affairs as convenience required. And, in general, Theophrastus tells us, that Aristides was, in his own private affairs, and those of his fellow-citizens, rigorously just, but that in public matters he acted often in accordance with his country's policy, which demanded, sometimes, not a little injustice. It is reported of him that he said in a debate, upon the motion of the Samians for removing the treasure from Delos to Athens, contrary to the league, that the thing indeed was not just, but was expedient.

In fine, having established the dominion of his city over so many people, he himself remained indigent; and always delighted as much in the glory of being poor, as in that of his trophies; as is

evident from the following story. Callias, the
torchbearer, was related to him: and was prosecuted
by his enemies in a capital cause, in which, after
they had slightly argued the matters on which they
indicted him, they proceeded, beside the point, to
address the judges: "You know," said they, "Aristides, the son of Lysimachus, who is the admiration
of all Greece. In what a condition do you think
his family is in at his house, when you see him
appear in public in such a threadbare cloak? Is it
not probable that one who, out of doors, goes thus
exposed to the cold, must want food and other
necessaries at home? Callias, the wealthiest of the
Athenians, does nothing to relieve either him or his
wife and children in their poverty, though he is
his own cousin, and has made use of him in many
cases, and often reaped advantage by his interest
with you." But Callias, perceiving the judges were
moved more particularly by this, and were exasperated against him, called in Aristides, requiring him
to testify that when he frequently offered him
divers presents, and entreated him to accept them,
he had refused, answering, that it became him better to be proud of his poverty than Callias of his
wealth: since there are many to be seen that make
a good, or a bad use of riches, but it is difficult,
comparatively, to meet with one who supports
poverty in a noble spirit; those only should be
ashamed of it who incurred it against their wills.
On Aristides deposing these facts in favor of
Callias, there was none who heard them, that went
not away desirous rather to be poor like Aristides,
than rich as Callias. Thus Æschines, the scholar of
Socrates, writes. But Plato declares,[9] that of all
the great and renowned men in the city of Athens,

[9] What Plato declares is found in the Gorgias.

he was the only one worthy of consideration; for Themistocles, Cimon, and Pericles filled the city with porticoes, treasure, and many other vain things, but Aristides guided his public life by the rule of justice. He showed his moderation very plainly in his conduct towards Themistocles himself. For though Themistocles had been his adversary in all his undertakings, and was the cause of his banishment, yet when he afforded a similar opportunity of revenge, being accused to the city, Aristides bore him no malice; but while Alcmæon, Cimon, and many others, were prosecuting and impeaching him, Aristides alone, neither did, nor said any ill against him, and no more triumphed over his enemy in his adversity, than he had envied him his prosperity.

Some say Aristides died in Pontus, during a voyage upon the affairs of the public. Others that he died of old age at Athens, being in great honor and veneration amongst his fellow-citizens. But Craterus, the Macedonian, relates his death as follows. After the banishment of Themistocles, he says, the people growing insolent, there sprung up a number of false and frivolous accusers, impeaching the best and most influential men and exposing them to the envy of the multitude, whom their good fortune and power had filled with self-conceit. Amongst these, Aristides was condemned of bribery, upon the accusation of Diophantus of Amphitrope, for taking money from the Ionians when he was collector of the tribute; and being unable to pay the fine, which was fifty minæ, sailed to Ionia, and died there. But of this Craterus brings no written proof, neither the sentence of his condemnation, nor the decree of the people; though in general it is tolerably usual with him to set down such things and to cite his authors. Almost all others who have

spoken of the misdeeds of the people towards their
generals, collect them all together, and tell us of
the banishment of Themistocles, Miltiades's bonds,
Pericles's fine, and the death of Paches [10] in the
judgment hall, who, upon receiving sentence, killed
himself on the hustings, with many things of the
like nature. They add the banishment of Aristides;
but of this his condemnation, they make no mention.

Moreover, his monument is to be seen at Phalerum, which they say was built him by the city,
he not having left enough even to defray funeral
charges. And it is stated, that his two daughters
were publicly married out of the prytaneum, or
state-house, by the city, which decreed each of them
three thousand drachmas for her portion; and that
upon his son Lysimachus, the people bestowed a
hundred minas of money, and as many acres of
planted land, and ordered him besides, upon the
motion of Alcibiades, four drachmas a day.
Furthermore, Lysimachus leaving a daughter,
named Polycrite, as Callisthenes says, the people
voted her, also, the same allowance for food with
those that obtained the victory in the Olympic
Games. But Demetrius the Phalerian, Hieronymus the Rhodian, Aristoxenus the musician, and
Aristotle, (if the Treatise of Nobility is to be
reckoned among the genuine pieces of Aristotle,)
say that Myrto, Aristides's granddaughter, lived
with Socrates the philosopher, who indeed had an-

---

[10] The death of Paches *in the judgment-hall* is an incorrect
expression. Paches, after his suppression of the revolt of Lesbos,
was brought to trial, on his return home, and *killed himself in
the presence of the people assembled to try him, as he stood
on the speaker's stand* (the *hustings*). Compare the account
in the beginning of the life of Nicias, Vol. III., p. 296.

other wife, but took her into his house, being a widow, by reason of her indigence, and want of the necessaries of life. But Panætius sufficiently confutes this in his books concerning Socrates. Demetrius the Phalerian, in his Socrates, says, he knew one Lysimachus, son to the daughter of Aristides, extremely poor, who used to sit near what is called the Iaccheum, and sustained himself by a table for interpreting dreams; and that, upon his proposal and representations, a decree was passed by the people, to give the mother and aunt of this man half a drachma a day. The same Demetrius, when he was legislating himself, decreed each of these women a drachma *per diem*. And it is not to be wondered at, that the people of Athens should take such care of people living in the city, since hearing the granddaughter of Aristogiton was in a low condition in the isle of Lemnos, and so poor nobody would marry her, they brought her back to Athens, and, marrying her to a man of good birth, gave a farm at Potamus as her marriage-portion; and of similar humanity and bounty the city of Athens, even in our age, has given numerous proofs, and is justly admired and respected in consequence.

MARCUS CATO[1]

TRANSLATED BY SIR JOHN LITCOTT, LATE
FELLOW OF KING'S COLLEGE, CAMBRIDGE

MARCUS CATO, we are told, was born at Tusculum, though (till he betook himself to civil and military affairs) he lived and was bred up in the country of the Sabines, where his father's estate lay. His ancestors seeming almost entirely unknown, he himself praises his father Marcus, as a worthy man and a brave soldier, and Cato, his great grandfather too, as one who had often obtained military prizes, and who, having lost five horses under him, received, on the account of his valor, the worth of them out of the public exchequer. Now it being the custom among the Romans to call those who, having no repute by birth, made themselves eminent by their own exertions, new men or upstarts, they called even Cato himself so, and so he confessed himself to be as to any public distinction or employment, but yet asserted that in the exploits and virtues of his ancestors he was very ancient. His third name originally was not Cato, but Priscus, though afterwards he had the surname of Cato, by reason of his abilities; for the Romans call a skilful or experienced man, *Catus*. He was of a ruddy complexion, and grey-eyed; as the writer, who, with no

---

[1] Cato entered upon his brilliant and highly successful military career in 217 B.C. at the age of 17. In later life was distinguished in civil affairs, as a statesman, orator, the first prose writer of any value among the Romans, and composed the first Roman history in the Latin tongue. He died in 149 B.C., at the age of 85.—DR. WILLIAM SMITH.

good-will, made the following epigram upon him, lets us see:—

> Porcius, who snarls at all in every place,
> With his grey eyes, and with his fiery face,
> Even after death will scarce admitted be
> Into the infernal realms by Hecate.

He gained, in early life, a good habit of body by working with his own hands, and living temperately, and serving in war; and seemed to have an equal proportion both of health and strength. And he exerted and practised his eloquence through all the neighborhood and little villages; thinking it as requisite as a second body, and an all but necessary organ to one who looks forward to something above a mere humble and inactive life. He would never refuse to be counsel for those who needed him, and was, indeed, early reckoned a good lawyer, and, ere long, a capable orator.

Hence his solidity and depth of character showed itself gradually, more and more to those with whom he was concerned, and claimed, as it were, employment in great affairs, and places of public command. Nor did he merely abstain from taking fees for his counsel and pleading, but did not even seem to put any high price on the honor which proceeded from such kind of combats, seeming much more desirous to signalize himself in the camp and in real fights; and while yet but a youth, had his breast covered with scars he had received from the enemy; being (as he himself says) but seventeen years old, when he made his first campaign; in the time when Hannibal, in the height of his success, was burning and pillaging all Italy. In engagements he would strike boldly, without flinching, stand firm to his ground, fix a bold countenance upon his enemies, and with a harsh threatening voice accost them, justly thinking himself and telling others, that such a rugged kind of behavior sometimes terrifies the enemy more than the sword itself. In his marches, he bore his own arms on foot, whilst one servant only followed, to carry the provisions for his table, with whom he is said never to have been angry or hasty, whilst he made ready his dinner or supper, but would, for the most part, when he was free from military duty, assist and help him himself to dress it. When he was with the army, he used to drink only water; unless, perhaps, when extremely thirsty, he might mingle it with a little vinegar; or if he found his strength fail him, take a little wine.

The little country house of Manius Curius, who had been thrice carried in triumph, happened to be near his farm; so that often going thither, and contemplating the small compass of the place, and plainness of the dwelling, he formed an idea of the mind of the person, who, being one of the greatest of the Romans, and having subdued the most warlike nations, nay, had driven Pyrrhus out of Italy, now, after three triumphs, was contented to dig in so small a piece of ground, and live in such a cottage. Here it was that the ambassadors of the Samnites, finding him boiling turnips in the chimney corner, offered him a present of gold; but he sent them away with this saying; that he, who was content with such a supper, had no need of gold; and that he thought it more honorable to conquer those who possessed the gold, than to possess the gold itself. Cato, after reflecting upon these things, used to return, and reviewing his own farm, his servants, and housekeeping, increase his labor, and retrench all superfluous expenses.

When Fabius Maximus took Tarentum, Cato,

being then but a youth, was a soldier under him; and being lodged with one Nearchus, a Pythagorean, desired to understand some of his doctrine, and hearing from him the language, which Plato also uses,—that pleasure is evil's chief bait; the body the principal calamity of the soul; and that those thoughts which most separate and take it off from the affections of the body, most enfranchise and purify it; he fell in love the more with frugality and temperance. With this exception, he is said not to have studied Greek until when he was pretty old; and in rhetoric, to have then profited a little by Thucydides, but more by Demosthenes: his writings, however, are considerably embellished with Greek sayings and stories; nay, many of these, translated word for word, are placed with his own apophthegms and sentences.

There was a man of the highest rank, and very influential among the Romans, called Valerius Flaccus, who was singularly skilful in discerning excellence yet in the bud, and, also, much disposed to nourish and advance it. He, it seems, had lands bordering upon Cato's; nor could he but admire, when he understood from his servants the manner of his living, how he labored with his own hands, went on foot betimes in the morning to the courts to assist those who wanted his counsel; how, returning home again, when it was winter, he would throw a loose frock[2] over his shoulders, and in the sum-

---

[2] Plutarch's Greek word is *exomis,* a woollen shirt with the right side open to leave the right arm and shoulder free.— *Without any thing, nudus,* sometimes means, with only the tunic, or ordinary woollen shirt or under-frock, but here it seems to be almost literal, with only a cloth about the loins, or apron on, a *campestre.*

mer time would work without any thing on among
his domestics, sit down with them, eat of the same
bread, and drink of the same wine. When they
spoke, also, of other good qualities, his fair dealing
and moderation, mentioning also some of his wise
sayings, he ordered, that he should be invited to
supper; and thus becoming personally assured of
his fine temper and his superior character which,
like a plant, seemed only to require culture and a
better situation, he urged and persuaded him to
apply himself to state affairs at Rome. Thither,
therefore, he went, and by his pleading soon gained
many friends and admirers; but, Valerius chiefly
assisting his promotion, he first of all got appointed
tribune in the army, and afterwards was made
quæstor, or treasurer. And now becoming eminent
and noted, he passed, with Valerius himself, through
the greatest commands, being first his colleague
as consul, and then censor. But among all the
ancient senators, he most attached himself to Fabius
Maximus; not so much for the honor of his person,
and greatness of his power, as that he might have
before him his habit and manner of life, as the best
examples to follow: and so he did not hesitate to
oppose Scipio the Great,[3] who, being then but a
young man, seemed to set himself against the
power of Fabius, and to be envied by him. For
being sent together with him as treasurer, when
he saw him, according to his natural custom, make
great expenses, and distribute among the soldiers
without sparing, he freely told him that the expense
in itself was not the greatest thing to be considered,

---

[3] *Scipio the great* did not *seem to envy,* but, on the contrary, as the right translation would stand, *to be envied by Fabius.* See the account at the end of the life of Fabius Maximus, Vol. I.

but that he was corrupting the ancient frugality of the soldiers, by giving them the means to abandon themselves to unnecessary pleasures and luxuries. Scipio answered, that he had no need for so accurate a treasurer, (bearing on as he was, so to say, full sail to the war,) and that he owed the people an account of his actions, and not of the money he spent. Hereupon Cato returned from Sicily, and, together with Fabius, made loud complaints in the open senate of Scipio's lavishing unspeakable sums, and childishly loitering away his time in wrestling matches and comedies, as if he were not to make war, but holiday; and thus succeeded in getting some of the tribunes of the people sent to call him back to Rome, in case the accusations should prove true. But Scipio demonstrating, as it were, to them, by his preparations, the coming victory, and, being found merely to be living pleasantly with his friends, when there was nothing else to do, but in no respect because of that easiness and liberality at all the more negligent in things of consequence and moment, without impediment, set sail towards the war.

Cato grew more and more powerful by his eloquence, so that he was commonly called the Roman Demosthenes, but his manner of life was yet more famous and talked of. For oratorical skill was, as an accomplishment, commonly studied and sought after by all young men; but he was very rare who would cultivate the old habits of bodily labor, or prefer a light supper, and a breakfast which never saw the fire; or be in love with poor clothes and a homely lodging, or could set his ambition rather on doing without luxuries than on possessing them. For now the state, unable to keep its purity by reason of its greatness, and having so many affairs, and people from all parts under its government, was fain to admit many mixed customs, and new examples of living. With reason, therefore, everybody admired Cato, when they saw others sink under labors, and grow effeminate by pleasures; and yet beheld him unconquered by either, and that not only when he was young and desirous of honor, but also when old and greyheaded, after a consulship and triumph; like some famous victor in the games, persevering in his exercise and maintaining his character to the very last. He himself says, that he never wore a suit of clothes which cost more than a hundred drachmas; and that, when he was general and consul, he drank the same wine which his workmen did; and that the meat or fish which was bought in the market for his dinner, did not cost above thirty *asses*. All which was for the sake of the commonwealth, that so his body might be the hardier for the war. Having a piece of embroidered Babylonian tapestry left him, he sold it; because none of his farm-houses were so much as plastered. Nor did he ever buy a slave for above fifteen hundred drachmas; as he did not seek for effeminate and handsome ones, but able, sturdy workmen, horse-keepers and cowherds: and these he thought ought to be sold again, when they grew old, and no useless servants fed in a house. In short, he reckoned nothing a good bargain, which was superfluous; but whatever it was, though sold for a farthing, he would think it a great price, if you had no need of it; and was for the purchase of lands for sowing and feeding, rather than grounds for sweeping and watering.

Some imputed these things to petty avarice, but others approved of him, as if he had only the more strictly denied himself for the rectifying and amending of others. Yet certainly, in my judgment, it marks an over-rigid temper, for a man to take the work out of his servants as out of brute beasts, turning them off and selling them in their old age, and thinking there ought to be no further commerce between man and man, than whilst there arises some profit by it. We see that kindness or humanity has a larger field than bare justice to exercise itself in; law and justice we cannot, in the nature of things, employ on others than men; but we may extend our goodness and charity even to irrational creatures; and such acts flow from a gentle nature, as water from an abundant spring. It is doubtless the part of a kind-natured man to keep even worn-out horses and dogs, and not only take care of them when they are foals and whelps, but also when they are grown old. The Athenians, when they built their Hecatompedon,[4] turned those mules loose to feed freely, which they had observed to have done the hardest labor. One of these (they say) came once of itself to offer its service, and ran along with, nay, and went before, the teams which drew the waggons up to the acropolis, as if it would incite and encourage them to draw more stoutly; upon which there passed a vote, that the creature should be kept at the public charge even till it died. The graves of Cimon's horses, which thrice won the Olympian races, are yet to be seen close by his own monument. Old Xanthippus,[5] too, (amongst many others who buried the dogs they had bred up,) entombed his which swam after his galley to Salamis, when the people fled from Athens, on the

[4] The Parthenon; built on the site of an older temple which had borne the name of Hecatompedon, or "a hundred feet long." The name was retained for the new building.

[5] The father of Pericles.

top of a cliff, which they call the dog's tomb to this day. Nor are we to use living creatures like old shoes or dishes, and throw them away when they are worn out or broken with service; but if it were for nothing else, but by way of study and practice in humanity, a man ought always to prehabituate himself in these things to be of a kind and sweet disposition. As to myself, I would not so much as sell my draught ox on the account of his age, much less for a small piece of money sell a poor old man, and so chase him, as it were, from his own country, by turning him not only out of the place where he has lived a long while, but also out of the manner of living he has been accustomed to, and that more especially when he would be as useless to the buyer as to the seller. Yet Cato for all this glories that he left that very horse in Spain, which he used in the wars when he was consul, only because he would not put the public to the charge of his freight. Whether these acts are to be ascribed to the greatness or pettiness of his spirit, let every one argue as they please.

For his general temperance, however, and self-control, he really deserves the highest admiration. For when he commanded the army, he never took for himself, and those that belonged to him, above three bushels of wheat for a month, and somewhat less than a bushel and a half a day of barley for his baggage-cattle. And when he entered upon the government of Sardinia, where his predecessors had been used to require tents, bedding, and clothes upon the public account, and to charge the state heavily with the cost of provisions and entertainments for a great train of servants and friends, the difference he showed in his economy was something incredible. There was nothing of any sort for which he put the public to expense; he would walk without a carriage to visit the cities, with one only of the common town officers, who carried his dress, and a cup to offer libation with. Yet, though he seemed thus easy and sparing to all who were under his power, he, on the other hand, showed most inflexible severity and strictness, in what related to public justice, and was rigorous, and precise in what concerned the ordinances of the commonwealth; so that the Roman government, never seemed more terrible, nor yet more mild, than under his administration.

His very manner of speaking seemed to have such a kind of idea with it; for it was courteous, and yet forcible; pleasant, yet overwhelming; facetious, yet austere; sententious, and yet vehement: like Socrates, in the description of Plato,[6] who seemed outwardly to those about him to be but a simple, talkative, blunt fellow; whilst at the bottom he was full of such gravity and matter, as would even move tears, and touch the very hearts of his auditors. And, therefore, I know not what has persuaded some to say, that Cato's style was chiefly like that of Lysias. However, let us leave those to judge of these things, who profess most to distinguish between the several kinds of oratorical style in Latin; whilst we write down some of his memorable sayings; being of the opinion that a man's character appears much more by his words, than, as some think it does, by his looks.

Being once desirous to dissuade the common

[6] For *Socrates in the description of Plato*, see the Symposium, (National Library Edition, Vol. III., p. 347), a famous portraiture, placed in the mouth of Alcibiades. Cato is compared, rather at random, to Lysias, in Cicero's Brutus, chapter 16.

people of Rome, from their unseasonable and impetuous clamor for largesses and distributions of corn, he began thus to harangue them: "It is a difficult task, O citizens, to make speeches to the belly, which has no ears." Reproving, also, their sumptuous habits, he said, it was hard to preserve a city, where a fish sold for more than an ox. He had a saying, also, that the Roman people were like sheep; for they, when single, do not obey, but when altogether in a flock, they follow their leaders: "So you," said he, "when you have got together in a body, let yourselves be guided by those whom singly you would never think of being advised by." Discoursing of the power of women: "Men," said he, "usually command women; but we command all men, and the women command us." But this, indeed, is borrowed from the sayings of Themistocles, who, when his son was making many demands of him by means of the mother, said, "O woman, the Athenians govern the Greeks; I govern the Athenians, but you govern me, and your son governs you; so let him use his power sparingly, since, simple as he is, he can do more than all the Greeks together." Another saying of Cato's was, that the Roman people did not only fix the value of such and such purple dyes, but also of such and such habits of life: "For," said he, "as dyers most of all dye such colors as they see to be most agreeable, so the young men learn, and zealously affect what is most popular with you." He also exhorted them, that if they were grown great by their virtue and temperance, they should not change for the worse; but if intemperance and vice had made them great, they should change for the better; for by that means they were grown indeed quite great enough. He would say, likewise, of men who wanted to be continually in office, that apparently they did not know their road; since they could not do without beadles to guide them on it. He also reproved the citizens for choosing still the same men as their magistrates: "For you will seem," said he, "either not to esteem government worth much, or to think few worthy to hold it." Speaking, too, of a certain enemy of his, who lived a very base and discreditable life: "It is considered," he said, "rather as a curse than a blessing on him, that this fellow's mother prays that she may leave him behind her." Pointing at one who had sold the land which his father had left him, and which lay near the sea-side, he pretended to express his wonder at his being stronger even than the sea itself; for what it washed away with a great deal of labor, he with a great deal of ease drank away. When the senate, with a great deal of splendor, received king Eumenes on his visit to Rome, and the chief citizens strove who should be most about him, Cato appeared to regard him with suspicion and apprehension; and when one that stood by, too, took occasion to say, that he was a very good prince, and a great lover of the Romans: "It may be so," said Cato, "but by nature this same animal of a king, is a kind of man-eater;" nor, indeed, were there ever kings who deserved to be compared with Epaminondas, Pericles, Themistocles, Manius Curius, or Hamilcar, surnamed Barcas. He used to say, too, that his enemies envied him; because he had to get up every day before light, and neglect his own business to follow that of the public. He would also tell you, that he had rather be deprived of the reward for doing well, than not to suffer the punishment for doing ill; and that he could pardon all offenders but himself.

MARCUS CATO

The Romans having sent three ambassadors to Bithynia, of whom one was gouty, another had his scull trepanned, and the other seemed little better than a fool; Cato, laughing, gave out, that the Romans had sent an embassy, which had neither feet, head, nor heart.[7] His interest being entreated by Scipio, on account of Polybius, for the Achæan exiles, and there happening to be a great discussion in the senate about it, some being for, and some against their return; Cato, standing up, thus delivered himself: "Here do we sit all day long, as if we had nothing to do, but beat our brains whether these old Greeks should be carried to their graves by the bearers here, or by those in Achæa." The senate voting their return, it seems that a few days after Polybius's friends further wished that it should be moved in the senate, that the said banished persons should receive again the honors which they first had in Achæa; and, to this purpose, they sounded Cato for his opinion; but he, smiling, answered, that Polybius, Ulysses like, having escaped out of the Cyclops' den, wanted, it would seem, to go back again because he had left his cap and belt behind him.[8] He used to assert, also, that wise men profited more by fools, than fools by wise men; for that wise men avoided the faults of fools, but that fools would not imitate the good examples of wise men. He

---

[7] Both the Romans and the Greeks conceived of the region of the heart, the chest, as the seat not of emotion, nor of will and courage merely, but more especially of judgment, deliberation, and practical sense. Thus the Greeks derived their word for moral wisdom from *phrēn*, the diaphragm, and the Romans by *egregie cordatus homo* meant a wise statesman.

[8] Polybius having once succeeded in pushing his request through the senate, was acting as unwisely in venturing his case

would profess, too, that he was more taken with
young men that blushed, than with those who looked
pale; and that he never desired to have a soldier
that moved his hands too much in marching, and his
feet too much in fighting; or snored louder than he
shouted. Ridiculing a fat overgrown man: "What
use," said he, "can the state turn a man's body to,
when all between the throat and groin is taken up
by the belly?" When one who was much given to
pleasures desired his acquaintance, begging his pardon, he said, he could not live with a man whose
palate was of a quicker sense than his heart. He
would likewise say, that the soul of a lover lived in
the body of another: and that in his whole life he
most repented of three things; one was, that he had
trusted a secret to a woman; another, that he went
by water when he might have gone by land; the
third, that he had remained one whole day without
doing any business of moment.[9] Applying himself
to an old man who was committing some vice:
"Friend," said he, "old age has of itself blemishes
enough; do not you add to it the deformity of vice."
Speaking to a tribune, who was reputed a poisoner,
and was very violent for the bringing in of a bill,
in order to make a certain law: "Young man," cried
he, "I know not which would be better, to drink
what you mix, or confirm what you would put up
for a law." Being reviled by a fellow who lived

there again, as Ulysses would have done, had he, after once
getting out of the cave of Cyclops, gone back into it to fetch
his cap and belt. The cap and belt, the ensigns of the traveller,
would be familiar to every one from the representations of
Ulysses.

[9] Or, according to another translation, "without making his
will."

a profligate and wicked life: "A contest," replied he, "is unequal between you and me; for you can hear ill words easily, and can as easily give them; but it is unpleasant to me to give such, and unusual to hear them." Such was his manner of expressing himself in his memorable sayings.

Being chosen consul, with his friend and familiar Valerius Flaccus, the government of that part of Spain which the Romans call the Hither Spain, fell to his lot. Here, as he was engaged in reducing some of the tribes by force, and bringing over others by good words, a large army of barbarians fell upon him, so that there was danger of being disgracefully forced out again. He therefore called upon his neighbors, the Celtiberians, for help; and on their demanding two hundred talents for their assistance, everybody else thought it intolerable, that ever the Romans should promise barbarians a reward for their aid; but Cato said, there was no discredit or harm in it; for if they overcame, they would pay them out of the enemy's purse, and not out of their own; but if they were overcome, there would be nobody left either to demand the reward or to pay it. However, he won that battle completely, and after that, all his other affairs succeeded splendidly. Polybius says, that by his command the walls of all the cities, on this side the river Bætis, were in one day's time demolished, and yet there were a great many of them full of brave and warlike men. Cato himself says, that he took more cities than he stayed days in Spain. Neither is this a mere rhodomontade, if it be true, that the number was four hundred. And though the soldiers themselves had got much in the fights, yet he distributed a pound of silver to every man of them, saying, it was better, that many of the

Romans should return home with silver, rather than a few with gold. For himself he affirms, that of all the things that were taken, nothing came to him beyond what he ate and drank. " Neither do I find fault," continued he, " with those that seek to profit by these spoils, but I had rather compete in valor with the best, than in wealth with the richest, or with the most covetous in love of money." Nor did he merely keep himself clear from taking any thing, but even all those who more immediately belonged to him. He had five servants with him in the army; one of whom called Paccus, bought three boys, out of those who were taken captive; which Cato coming to understand, the man rather than venture into his presence, hanged himself. Cato sold the boys, and carried the price he got for them into the public exchequer.

Scipio the Great, being his enemy, and desiring, whilst he was carrying all things so successfully, to obstruct him, and take the affairs of Spain into his own hands, succeeded in getting himself appointed his successor in the government, and, making all possible haste, put a term to Cato's authority. But he, taking with him a convoy of five cohorts of foot, and five hundred horse to attend him home, overthrew by the way the Lacetanians, and taking from them six hundred deserters, caused them all to be beheaded; upon which Scipio seemed to be in indignation, but Cato, in mock disparagement of himself, said, " Rome would become great indeed, if the most honorable and great men would not yield up the the first place of valor to those who were more obscure, and when they who were of the commonalty (as he himself was) would contend in valor with those who were most eminent in birth and honor." The senate having voted to change nothing of what had been established by Cato, the government passed away under Scipio to no manner of purpose, in idleness and doing nothing; and so diminished his credit much more than Cato's. Nor did Cato, who now received a triumph, remit after this and slacken the reins of virtue, as many do, who strive not so much for virtue's sake, as for vainglory, and having attained the highest honors, as the consulship and triumphs, pass the rest of their life in pleasure and idleness, and quit all public affairs. But he, like those who are just entered upon public life for the first time, and thirst after gaining honor and glory in some new office, strained himself, as if he were but just setting out; and offering still publicly his service to his friends and citizens, would give up neither his pleadings nor his soldiery.

He accompanied and assisted Tiberius Sempronius, as his lieutenant, when he went into Thrace and to the Danube; and, in the quality of tribune, went with Manius Acilius into Greece, against Antiochus the Great, who, after Hannibal, more than any one struck terror into the Romans. For having reduced once more under a single command almost the whole of Asia, all, namely, that Seleucus Nicator had possessed, and having brought into obedience many warlike nations of the barbarians, he longed to fall upon the Romans, as if they only were now worthy to fight with him. So across he came with his forces, pretending, as a specious cause of the war, that it was to free the Greeks, who had indeed no need of it, they having been but newly delivered from the power of king Philip and the Macedonians, and made independent, with the free use of their own laws, by the goodness of the Romans themselves; so that all Greece was in commotion and excitement, having been corrupted by the hopes of royal aid which the popular leaders in their cities put them into. Manius, therefore, sent ambassadors to the different cities; and Titus Flamininus (as is written in the account of him) suppressed and quieted most of the attempts of the innovators, without any trouble. Cato brought over the Corinthians, those of Patræ and of Ægium, and spent a good deal of time at Athens. There is also an oration of his said to be extant, which he spoke in Greek to the people; in which he expressed his admiration of the virtue of the ancient Athenians, and signified that he came with a great deal of pleasure to be a spectator of the beauty and greatness of their city. But this is a fiction; for he spoke to the Athenians by an interpreter, though he was able to have spoken himself; but he wished to observe the usage of his own country, and laughed at those who admired nothing but what was in Greek. Jesting upon Postumius Albinus, who had written an historical work in Greek, and requested that allowances might be made for his attempt, he said, that allowance indeed might be made, if he had done it under the express compulsion of an Amphictyonic decree. The Athenians, he says, admired the quickness and vehemence of his speech; for an interpreter would be very long in repeating what he expressed with a great deal of brevity; but on the whole he professed to believe, that the words of the Greeks came only from their lips, whilst those of the Romans came from their hearts.

Now Antiochus, having occupied with his army the narrow passages about Thermopylæ, and added palisades and walls to the natural fortifications of the place, sat down there, thinking he had done

enough to divert the war; and the Romans, indeed,
seemed wholly to despair of forcing the passage;
but Cato, calling to mind the compass and circuit
which the Persians had formerly made to come at
this place, went forth in the night, taking along
with him part of the army. Whilst they were
climbing up, the guide, who was a prisoner, missed
the way, and wandering up and down by impracticable and precipitous paths, filled the soldiers with
fear and despondency. Cato, perceiving the danger,
commanded all the rest to halt, and stay where they
were, whilst he himself, taking along with him one
Lucius Manlius, a most expert man at climbing
mountains, went forward with a great deal of labor
and danger, in the dark night, and without the least
moonshine, among the wild olive trees, and steep
craggy rocks, there being nothing but precipices
and darkness before their eyes, till they struck into
a little pass which they thought might lead down
into the enemy's camp. There they put up marks
upon some conspicuous peaks which surmount the
hill called Callidromon, and returning again, they
led the army along with them to the said marks,
till they got into their little path again, and there
once made a halt; but when they began to go
further, the path deserted them at a precipice, where
they were in another strait and fear; nor did they
perceive that they were all this while near the
enemy. And now the day began to give some
light, when they seemed to hear a noise, and
presently after to see the Greek trenches and the
guard at the foot of the rock. Here, therefore,
Cato halted his forces, and commanded the troops
from Firmum only, without the rest, to stick by
him, as he had always found them faithful and
ready. And when they came up and formed around

him in close order, he thus spoke to them. "I desire," he said, "to take one of the enemy alive, that so I may understand what men these are who guard the passage; their number; and with what discipline, order, and preparation they expect us; but this feat," continued he, "must be an act of a great deal of quickness and boldness, such as that of lions, when they dart upon some timorous animal." Cato had no sooner thus expressed himself, but the Firmans forthwith rushed down the mountain, just as they were, upon the guard, and, falling unexpectedly upon them, affrighted and dispersed them all. One armed man they took, and brought to Cato, who quickly learned from him, that the rest of the forces lay in the narrow passage about the king; that those who kept the tops of the rocks were six hundred choice Ætolians. Cato, therefore, despising the smallness of their number and carelessness, forthwith drawing his sword, fell upon them with a great noise of trumpets and shouting. The enemy, perceiving them thus tumbling, as it were, upon them from the precipices, flew to the main body, and put all things into disorder there.

In the mean time, whilst Manius was forcing the works below, and pouring the thickest of his forces into the narrow passages, Antiochus was hit in the mouth with a stone, so that his teeth being beaten out by it, he felt such excessive pain, that he was fain to turn away with his horse; nor did any part of his army stand the shock of the Romans. Yet, though there seemed no reasonable hope of flight, where all paths were so difficult, and where there were deep marshes and steep rocks, which looked as if they were ready to receive those who should stumble, the fugitives, nevertheless, crowding and pressing together in the narrow passages, destroyed even one another in their terror of the swords and blows of the enemy. Cato (as it plainly appears) was never oversparing of his own praises, and seldom shunned boasting of any exploit; which quality, indeed, he seems to have thought the natural accompaniment of great actions; and with these particular exploits he was highly puffed up; he says, that those who saw him that day pursuing and slaying the enemies, were ready to assert, that Cato owed not so much to the public, as the public did to Cato; nay, he adds, that Manius the consul, coming hot from the fight, embraced him for a great while, when both were all in a sweat; and then cried out with joy, that neither he himself, no, nor all the people together, could make him a recompense equal to his actions. After the fight he was sent to Rome, that he himself might be the messenger of it; and so, with a favorable wind, he sailed to Brundusium, and in one day got from thence to Tarentum; and having travelled four days more, upon the fifth, counting from the time of his landing, he arrived at Rome, and so brought the first news of the victory himself; and filled the whole city with joy and sacrifices, and the people with the belief, that they were able to conquer every sea and every land.

These are pretty nearly all the eminent actions of Cato, relating to military affairs: in civil policy, he was of opinion, that one chief duty consisted in accusing and indicting criminals. He himself prosecuted many, and he would also assist others who prosecuted them, nay would even procure such, as he did the Petilii against Scipio; but not being able to destroy him, by reason of the nobleness of his family, and the real greatness of his mind, which enabled him to trample all calumnies underfoot,

Cato at last would meddle no more with him; yet joining with the accusers against Scipio's brother Lucius, he succeeded in obtaining a sentence against him, which condemned him to the payment of a large sum of money to the state; and being insolvent, and in danger of being thrown into jail, he was, by the interposition of the tribunes of the people, with much ado dismissed. It is also said of Cato, that when he met a certain youth, who had effected the disgrace of one of his father's enemies, walking in the market-place, he shook him by the hand, telling him, that this was what we ought to sacrifice to our dead parents—not lambs and goats, but the tears and condemnations of their adversaries. But neither did he himself escape with impunity in his management of affairs; for if he gave his enemies but the least hold, he was still in danger, and exposed to be brought to justice. He is reported to have escaped at least fifty indictments;[10] and one above the rest, which was the last, when he was eighty-six years[11] old, about which time he uttered the well-known saying, that it was hard for him who had lived with one generation of men, to plead now before another. Neither did he make this the last of his lawsuits; for, four years after, when he was fourscore and ten, he accused Servilius Galba: so that his life and actions extended, we may say, as Nestor's did, over three ordinary ages of man. For, having had many contests, as

---

[10] *He is reported to have escaped at least fifty indictments* should be, *to have defended himself in at least fifty causes.*

[11] Plutarch is evidently in error as to the date of this incident and the one related in the following sentence, since Dr. William Smith and other modern authorities state that Cato died at the age of 85.—JAMES L. PERKINS.

we have related, with Scipio the Great, about affairs of state, he continued them down even to Scipio the younger, who was the adopted grandson of the former, and the son of that Paulus, who overthrew Perseus and the Macedonians.

Ten years after his consulship, Cato stood for the office of censor, which was indeed the summit of all honor, and in a manner the highest step in civil affairs; for besides all other power, it had also that of an inquisition into every one's life and manners. For the Romans thought that no marriage, or rearing of children, nay, no feast or drinking-bout ought to be permitted according to every one's appetite or fancy, without being examined and inquired into; being indeed of opinion, that a man's character was much sooner perceived in things of this sort, than in what is done publicly and in open day. They chose, therefore, two persons, one out of the patricians, the other out of the commons, who were to watch, correct, and punish, if any one ran too much into voluptuousness, or transgressed the usual manner of life of his country; and these they called Censors. They had power to take away a horse,[12] or expel out of the senate any one who lived intemperately and out of order. It was also their business to take an estimate of what every one was worth, and to put down in registers everybody's birth and quality; besides many other prerogatives. And there-

---

[12] *Equum adimere,* to inflict on any member of the order of horsemen or *equites,* the forfeiture of the horse that was allowed him: in other words, to degrade from the equestrian dignity; to deprive of the lowest distinction of rank. The equestrian dignity depended, up to the end of the republic, on the possession of a certain amount of property, united with free birth from two generations.

fore the chief nobility opposed his pretensions to it. Jealousy prompted the patricians, who thought that it would be a stain to everybody's nobility, if men of no original honor should rise to the highest dignity and power; while others, conscious of their own evil practices, and of the violation of the laws and customs of their country, were afraid of the austerity of the man; which, in an office of such great power was likely to prove most uncompromising and severe. And so consulting among themselves, they brought forward seven candidates in opposition to him, who sedulously set themselves to court the people's favor by fair promises, as though what they wished for was indulgent and easy government. Cato, on the contrary, promising no such mildness, but plainly threatening evil livers, from the very hustings openly declared himself; and exclaiming, that the city needed a great and thorough purgation, called upon the people, if they were wise, not to choose the gentlest, but the roughest of physicians; such a one, he said, he was, and Valerius Flaccus, one of the patricians, another; together with him, he doubted not but he should do something worth the while, and that, by cutting to pieces and burning like a hydra,[13] all luxury and voluptuousness. He added, too, that he saw all the rest endeavoring after the office with ill intent, because they were afraid of those who would exercise it justly, as they ought. And so truly great and so worthy of great men to be its leaders was, it would seem, the Roman people, that they did not fear the severity and grim countenance of Cato, but rejecting those

[13] Wherever Hercules cut off one head from the Lernæan hydra, two new ones sprung up in its place; until he applied fire and cauterized the wounds.

smooth promisers who were ready to do all things to ingratiate themselves, they took him, together with Flaccus; obeying his recommendations not as though he were a candidate, but as if he had had the actual power of commanding and governing already.

Cato named as chief of the senate, his friend and colleague Lucius Valerius Flaccus, and expelled, among many others, Lucius Quintius, who had been consul seven years before, and (which was greater honor to him than the consulship) brother to that Titus Flamininus, who overthrew king Philip. The reason he had for his expulsion, was this. Lucius, it seems, took along with him in all his commands, a youth, whom he had kept as his companion from the flower of his age, and to whom he gave as much power and respect as to the chiefest of his friends and relations.

Now it happened that Lucius being consular governor of one of the provinces, the youth setting himself down by him, as he used to do, among other flatteries with which he played upon him, when he was in his cups, told him he loved him so dearly that, "though there was a show of gladiators to be seen at Rome, and I," he said, "had never beheld one in my life; and though I, as it were, longed to see a man killed, yet I made all possible haste to come to you." Upon this Lucius, returning his fondness, replied, "Do not be melancholy on that account; I can remedy that." Ordering therefore, forthwith, one of those condemned to die to be brought to the feast, together with the headsman and axe, he asked the youth if he wished to see him executed. The boy answering that he did, Lucius commanded the executioner to cut off his neck; and this several historians mention; and

Cicero, indeed, in his dialogue *de Senectute,* introduces Cato relating it himself. But Livy says, that he that was killed was a Gaulish deserter, and that Lucius did not execute him by the stroke of the executioner, but with his own hand; and that it is so stated in Cato's speech.

Lucius being thus expelled out of the senate by Cato, his brother took it very ill, and appealing to the people, desired that Cato should declare his reasons; and when he began to relate this transaction of the feast, Lucius endeavored to deny it; but Cato challenging him to a formal investigation,[14] he fell off and refused it, so that he was then acknowledged to suffer deservedly. Afterwards, however, when there was some show at the theatre, he passed by the seats where those who had been consuls used to be placed, and taking his seat a great way off, excited the compassion of the common people, who presently with a great noise made him go forward, and as much as they could, tried to set right and salve over what had happened. Manilius, also, who, according to the public expectation, would have been next consul, he threw out of the senate, because, in the presence of his daughter, and in open day, he had kissed his wife. He said, that as for himself, his wife never came into his arms except when there was great thunder; so that it was a jest with him, that it was a pleasure for him, when Jupiter thundered.

His treatment of Lucius, likewise, the brother of Scipio, and one who had been honored with a triumph, occasioned some odium against Cato; for

---

[14] A *sponsio,* or wager, in which a sum of money was deposited on each side, and forfeited by the party against whom judgment went.

he took his horse from him, and was thought to do it with a design of putting an affront on Scipio Africanus, now dead. But he gave most general annoyance, by retrenching people's luxury; for though (most of the youth being thereby already corrupted) it seemed almost impossible to take it away with an open hand and directly, yet going, as it were, obliquely around, he caused all dress, carriages, women's ornaments, household furniture, whose price exceeded one thousand five hundred drachmas, to be rated at ten times as much as they were worth; intending by thus making the assessments greater, to increase the taxes paid upon them. He also ordained that upon every thousand *asses* of property of this kind, three [15] should be paid, so that people, burdened with these extra charges, and seeing others of as good estates, but more frugal and sparing, paying less into the public exchequer, might be tired out of their prodigality. And thus, on the one side, not only those were disgusted at Cato, who bore the taxes for the sake of their luxury, but those, too, who on the other side laid by their luxury for fear of the taxes. For people in general reckon, that an order not to display their riches, is equivalent to the taking away their riches; because riches are seen much more in superfluous, than in necessary, things. Indeed, this was what excited the wonder of Ariston the philosopher; that we account those who possess superfluous things more happy than those who abound with what is necessary and useful. But when one of his friends asked Scopas, the rich Thessalian, to give him some article of no great utility, saying that it was not a thing that he had any great need

[15] Whereas the usual charge was probably one *as* in a thousand.

or use for himself, "In truth," replied he, "it is just these useless and unnecessary things that make my wealth and happiness." Thus the desire of riches does not proceed from a natural passion within us, but arises rather from vulgar out-of-doors opinion of other people.

Cato, notwithstanding, being little solicitous as to those who exclaimed against him, increased his austerity. He caused the pipes, through which some persons brought the public water into their own houses and gardens, to be cut, and threw down all buildings which jutted out into the common streets. He beat down also the price in contracts for public works to the lowest, and raised it in contracts for farming the taxes to the highest sum; by which proceedings he drew a great deal of hatred on himself. Those who were of Titus Flamininus's party cancelled in the senate all the bargains and contracts made by him for the repairing and carrying on of the sacred and public buildings, as unadvantageous to the commonwealth. They incited also the boldest of the tribunes of the people to accuse him, and to fine him two talents. They likewise much opposed him in building the court or basilica, which he caused to be erected at the common charge, just by the senate-house, in the market-place, and called by his own name, the Porcian. However, the people, it seems, liked his censorship wondrously well; for, setting up a statue for him in the temple of the goddess of Health, they put an inscription under it, not recording his commands in war or his triumph, but to the effect, that this was Cato the Censor, who, by his good discipline and wise and temperate ordinances, reclaimed the Roman commonwealth when it was declining and sinking down into vice. Before this honor was done to himself, he used to laugh at those who loved such kind of things, saying, that they did not see that they were taking pride in the workmanship of brass-founders and painters; whereas the citizens bore about his best likeness in their breasts. And when any seemed to wonder, that he should have never a statue, while many ordinary persons had one; "I would," said he, "much rather be asked, why I have not one, than why I have one." In short, he would not have any honest citizen endure to be praised, except it might prove advantageous to the commonwealth. Yet still he had passed the highest commendation on himself; for he tells us that those who did any thing wrong, and were found fault with, used to say, it was not worth while to blame them; for they were not Catos. He also adds, that they who awkwardly mimicked some of his actions, were called left-handed Catos; and that the senate in perilous times would cast their eyes on him, as upon a pilot in a ship, and that often when he was not present they put off affairs of greatest consequence. These things are indeed also testified of him by others; for he had a great authority in the city, alike for his life, his eloquence, and his age.

He was also a good father, an excellent husband to his wife, and an extraordinary economist; and as he did not manage his affairs of this kind carelessly, and as things of little moment, I think I ought to record a little further whatever was commendable in him in these points. He married a wife more noble than rich; being of opinion, that the rich and the high-born are equally haughty and proud; but that those of noble blood, would be more ashamed of base things, and consequently more obedient to their husbands in all that was fit and right. A man who beat his wife or child, laid violent hands, he said, on what was most sacred; and a good husband he reckoned worthy of more praise than a great senator; and he admired the ancient Socrates for nothing so much, as for having lived a temperate and contented life with a wife who was a scold, and children who were half-witted.

As soon as he had a son born, though he had never such urgent business upon his hands, unless it were some public matter, he would be by when his wife washed it, and dressed it in its swaddling clothes. For she herself suckled it, nay, she often too gave her breast to her servants' children, to produce, by sucking the same milk, a kind of natural love in them to her son. When he began to come to years of discretion, Cato himself would teach him to read, although he had a servant, a very good grammarian, called Chilo, who taught many others; but he thought not fit, as he himself said, to have his son reprimanded by a slave, or pulled, it may be, by the ears when found tardy in his lesson: nor would he have him owe to a servant the obligation of so great a thing as his learning; he himself, therefore, (as we were saying,) taught him his grammar, law, and his gymnastic exercises. Nor did he only show him, too, how to throw a dart, to fight in armor, and to ride, but to box also and to endure both heat and cold, and to swim over the most rapid and rough rivers. He says, likewise, that he wrote histories, in large characters, with his own hand, that so his son without stirring out of the house, might learn to know about his countrymen and forefathers: nor did he less abstain from speaking any thing obscene before his son, than if it had been in the presence of the sacred virgins, called vestals. Nor would he ever go into the bath with him; which seems indeed to have been the common custom of the Romans. Sons-in-law used to avoid bathing with fathers-in-law, disliking to see one another naked: but having, in time, learned of the Greeks to strip before men, they have since taught the Greeks to do it even with the women themselves.

Thus, like an excellent work, Cato formed and fashioned his son to virtue; nor had he any occasion to find fault with his readiness and docility; but as he proved to be of too weak a constitution for hardships, he did not insist on requiring of him any very austere way of living. However, though delicate in health, he proved a stout man in the field, and behaved himself valiantly when Paulus Æmilius fought against Perseus; where when his sword was struck from him by a blow, or rather slipped out of his hand by reason of its moistness, he so keenly resented it, that he turned to some of his friends about him, and taking them along with him again, fell upon the enemy; and having by a long fight and much force cleared the place, at length found it among great heaps of arms, and the dead bodies of friends as well as enemies piled one upon another. Upon which Paulus, his general, much commended the youth; and there is a letter of Cato's to his son, which highly praises his honorable eagerness for the recovery of his sword. Afterwards he married Tertia, Æmilius Paulus's daughter, and sister to Scipio; nor was he admitted into this family less for his own worth than his father's. So that Cato's care in his son's education came to a very fitting result.

He purchased a great many slaves out of the captives taken in war, but chiefly bought up the young ones, who were capable to be, as it were, broken and taught like whelps and colts. None

of these ever entered another man's house except
sent either by Cato himself or his wife. If any
one of them were asked what Cato did, they
answered merely, that they did not know. When a
servant was at home, he was obliged either to do
some work or sleep; for indeed Cato loved those
most who used to lie down often to sleep, accounting
them more docile than those who were wakeful, and
more fit for any thing when they were refreshed
with a little slumber. Being also of opinion, that
the great cause of the laziness and misbehavior of
slaves was their running after their pleasures, he
fixed a certain price for them to pay for permission amongst themselves, but would suffer no con-
nections out of the house. At first, when he was
but a poor soldier, he would not be difficult in any
thing which related to his eating, but looked upon
it as a pitiful thing to quarrel with a servant for
the belly's sake; but afterwards when he grew
richer, and made any feasts for his friends and
colleagues in office, as soon as supper was over he
used to go with a leathern thong and scourge those
who had waited or dressed the meat carelessly. He
always contrived, too, that his servants should have
some difference one among another, always suspecting and fearing a good understanding between
them. Those who had committed any thing worthy
of death, he punished, if they were found guilty
by the verdict of their fellow-servants. But being
after all much given to the desire of gain, he looked
upon agriculture rather as a pleasure than profit;
resolving, therefore, to lay out his money in safe
and solid things, he purchased ponds, hot baths,
grounds full of fuller's earth, remunerative lands,
pastures, and woods; from all which he drew large
returns, nor could Jupiter himself, he used to say,

do him much damage. He was also given to the
form of usury, which is considered most odious, in
traffic by sea; and that thus:—he desired that those
whom he put out his money to, should have many
partners; and when the number of them and their
ships came to be fifty, he himself took one share
through Quintio his freedman, who therefore was
to sail with the adventurers, and take a part in all
their proceedings; so that thus there was no danger
of losing his whole stock, but only a little part, and
that with a prospect of great profit.[16] He likewise
lent money to those of his slaves who wished to
borrow, with which they bought also other young
ones, whom, when they had taught and bred up at
his charges, they would sell again at the year's end;
but some of them Cato would keep for himself,
giving just as much for them as another had offered.
To incline his son to be of this kind of temper, he
used to tell him, that it was not like a man, but
rather like a widow woman, to lessen an estate.
But the strongest indication of Cato's avaricious
humor was when he took the boldness to affirm,
that he was a most wonderful, nay, a godlike man,
who left more behind him than he had received.

He was now grown old, when Carneades the
Academic, and Diogenes the Stoic, came as deputies from Athens to Rome, praying for release from
a penalty of five hundred talents laid on the Athenians, in a suit, to which they did not appear, in
which the Oropians were plaintiffs, and Sicyonians judges. All the most studious youth im-

---

[16] He lent money to the company, at high interest, and took
one share himself. On this share he could not lose much, and
it gave him the advantage of sending his agent, Quintio, to see
that all was fair.

mediately waited on these philosophers, and frequently, with admiration, heard them speak. But the gracefulness of Carneades's oratory, whose ability was really greatest, and his reputation equal to it, gathered large and favorable audiences, and erelong filled, like a wind, all the city with the sound of it. So that it soon began to be told, that a Greek, famous even to admiration, winning and carrying all before him, had impressed so strange a love upon the young men, that quitting all their pleasures and pastimes, they ran mad, as it were, after philosophy; which indeed much pleased the Romans in general; nor could they but with much pleasure see the youth receive so welcomely the Greek literature, and frequent the company of learned men. But Cato, on the other side, seeing this passion for words flowing into the city, from the beginning, took it ill, fearing lest the youth should be diverted that way, and so should prefer the glory of speaking well before that of arms, and doing well. And when the fame of the philosophers increased in the city, and Caius Acilius, a person of distinction, at his own request, became their interpreter to the senate at their first audience, Cato resolved, under some specious pretence, to have all philosophers cleared out of the city; and, coming into the senate, blamed the magistrates for letting these deputies stay so long a time without being despatched, though they were persons that could easily persuade the people to what they pleased; that therefore in all haste something should be determined about their petition, that so they might go home again to their own schools, and declaim to the Greek children, and leave the Roman youth, to be obedient, as hitherto, to their own laws and governors.

Yet he did this not out of any anger, as some think, to Carneades; but because he wholly despised philosophy, and out of a kind of pride, scoffed at the Greek studies and literature; as, for example, he would say, that Socrates was a prating seditious fellow, who did his best to tyrannize over his country, to undermine the ancient customs, and to entice and withdraw the citizens to opinions contrary to the laws. Ridiculing the school of Isocrates, he would add, that his scholars grew old men before they had done learning with him, as if they were to use their art and plead causes in the court of Minos in the next world. And to frighten his son from any thing that was Greek, in a more vehement tone than became one of his age, he pronounced, as it were, with the voice of an oracle, that the Romans would certainly be destroyed when they began once to be infected with Greek literature; though time indeed has shown the vanity of this his prophecy; as, in truth, the city of Rome has risen to its highest fortune, while entertaining Grecian learning. Nor had he an aversion only against the Greek philosophers, but the physicians also; for having, it seems, heard how Hippocrates, when the king of Persia sent for him, with offers of a fee of several talents, said, that he would never assist barbarians who were enemies to the Greeks; he affirmed, that this was now become a common oath taken by all physicians, and enjoined his son to have a care and avoid them; for that he himself had written a little book of prescriptions for curing those who were sick in his family; he never enjoined fasting to any one, but ordered them either vegetables, or the meat of a duck, pigeon, or leveret; such kind of diet being of light digestion, and fit for sick folks, only it made those who ate it, dream a little too much; and by the use of this kind of physic, he said, he not only made himself and those about him well, but kept them so.

However, for this his presumption, he seemed not to have escaped unpunished; for he lost both his wife and his son; though he himself, being of a strong robust constitution, held out longer; so that he would often, even in his old days, address himself to women, and when he was past a lover's age, married a young woman, upon the following pretence. Having lost his own wife, he married his son to the daughter of Paulus Æmilius, who was sister to Scipio; so that being now a widower himself, he had a young girl who came privately to visit him; but the house being very small, and a daughter-in-law also in it, this practice was quickly discovered; for the young woman seeming once to pass through it a little too boldly, the youth, his son, though he said nothing, seemed to look somewhat indignantly upon her. The old man perceiving and understanding that what he did was disliked, without finding any fault, or saying a word, went away as his custom was, with his usual companions to the market: and among the rest, he called aloud to one Salonius, who had been a clerk under him, and asked him whether he had married his daughter? He answered, no, nor would he, till he had consulted him. Said Cato, "Then I have found out a fit son-in-law for you, if he should not displease by reason of his age; for in all other points there is no fault to be found in him; but he is indeed, as I said, extremely old." However, Salonius desired him to undertake the business, and to give the young girl to whom he pleased, she being a humble servant of his, who stood in need of his care and patronage. Upon this Cato, without any more ado, told him, he desired to have the damsel himself. These words, as may well be imagined, at first astonished the man, conceiving that Cato was as far off from marrying, as he from a likelihood of being allied to the family of one who had been consul, and had triumphed; but perceiving him in earnest, he consented willingly; and, going onwards to the forum, they quickly completed the bargain.

Whilst the marriage was in hand Cato's son, taking some of his friends along with him, went and asked his father if it were for any offence he brought in a stepmother upon him? But Cato cried out, "Far from it, my son, I have no fault to find with you nor any thing of yours; only I desire to have many children, and to leave the commonwealth more such citizens as you are." Pisistratus, the tyrant of Athens, made, they say, this answer to his sons, when they were grown men, when he married his second wife, Timonassa of Argos, by whom he had, it is said, Iophon and Thessalus. Cato had a son by this second wife, to whom from his mother, he gave the surname of Salonius.[17] In the mean time, his eldest died in his prætorship; of whom Cato often makes mention in his books, as having been a good man. He is said, however, to have borne the loss moderately, and like a philosopher, and was nothing the more remiss in attending to affairs of state; so that he did not, as Lucius Lucullus and Metellus Pius did, grow languid in his old age, as though public business were a duty once to be discharged, and then quitted; nor did he, like Scipio Africanus, because envy had struck at his glory, turn from the public, and change and pass away the rest of his life without doing any thing; but as one persuaded Dionysius,

[17] More correctly Salonianus.

that the most honorable tomb he could have, would be to die in the exercise of his dominion; so Cato thought that old age to be the most honorable, which was busied in public affairs; though he would, now and then, when he had leisure, recreate himself with husbandry and writing.

And, indeed, he composed various books and histories; and in his youth, he addicted himself to agriculture for profit's sake; for he used to say, he had but two ways of getting—agriculture and parsimony; and now, in his old age, the first of these gave him both occupation and a subject of study. He wrote one book on country matters,[18] in which he treated particularly even of making cakes, and preserving fruit; it being his ambition to be curious and singular in all things. His suppers, at his country-house, used also to be plentiful; he daily invited his friends and neighbors about him, and passed the time merrily with them; so that his company was not only agreeable to those of the same age, but even to younger men; for he had had experience in many things, and had been concerned in much, both by word and deed, that was worth hearing. He looked upon a good table, as the best place for making friends; where the commendations of brave and good citizens were usually introduced, and little said of base and unworthy ones; as Cato would not give leave in his company to have any thing, either good or ill, said about them.

Some will have the overthrow of Carthage to have been one of his last acts of state; when, indeed, Scipio the younger, did by his valor give it the last blow, but the war, chiefly by the counsel and advice of Cato, was undertaken on the following occasion. Cato was sent to the Carthaginians and

---

[18] De re rustica.

Masinissa, king of Numidia, who were at war with one another, to know the cause of their difference. He, it seems, had been a friend of the Romans from the beginning; and they, too, since they were conquered by Scipio, were of the Roman confederacy, having been shorn of their power by loss of territory, and a heavy tax. Finding Carthage, not (as the Romans thought) low and in an ill condition, but well manned, full of riches and all sorts of arms and ammunition, and perceiving the Carthaginians carry it high, he conceived that it was not a time for the Romans to adjust affairs between them and Masinissa; but rather that they themselves would fall into danger, unless they should find means to check this rapid new growth of Rome's ancient irreconcilable enemy. Therefore, returning quickly to Rome, he acquainted the senate, that the former defeats and blows given to the Carthaginians, had not so much diminished their strength, as it had abated their imprudence and folly; that they were not become weaker, but more experienced in war, and did only skirmish with the Numidians, to exercise themselves the better to cope with the Romans: that the peace and league they had made was but a kind of suspension of war which awaited a fairer opportunity to break out again.

Moreover, they say that, shaking his gown, he took occasion to let drop some African figs before the senate. And on their admiring the size and beauty of them, he presently added, that the place that bore them was but three days' sail from Rome. Nay, he never after this gave his opinion, but at the end he would be sure to come out with this sentence, "ALSO, CARTHAGE, METHINKS, OUGHT UTTERLY TO BE DESTROYED." But Publius Scipio Nasica would always declare his opinion to the contrary, in these words, "It seems requisite to me that Carthage should still stand." For seeing his countrymen to be grown wanton and insolent, and the people made, by their prosperity, obstinate and disobedient to the senate, and drawing the whole city, whither they would, after them, he would have had the fear of Carthage to serve as a bit to hold in the contumacy of the multitude; and he looked upon the Carthaginians as too weak to overcome the Romans, and too great to be despised by them. On the other side, it seemed a perilous thing to Cato, that a city which had been always great, and was now grown sober and wise, by reason of its former calamities, should still lie, as it were, in wait for the follies and dangerous excesses of the over-powerful Roman people; so that he thought it the wisest course to have all outward dangers removed, when they had so many inward ones among themselves.

Thus Cato, they say, stirred up the third and last war against the Carthaginians: but no sooner was the said war begun, than he died, prophesying of the person that should put an end to it, who was then only a young man; but, being tribune in the army, he in several fights gave proof of his courage and conduct. The news of which being brought to Cato's ears at Rome, he thus expressed himself:—

> The only wise man of them all is he,
> The others e'en as shadows flit and flee.[19]

This prophecy Scipio soon confirmed by his actions. Cato left no posterity, except one son by his

[19] The quotation is from the 10th book of the Odyssey, line 495: *Among the dead, whom Ulysses is to visit, Tiresias*, Circe tells him, *alone has retained his wisdom after death, the rest flit about as shadows.*

second wife, who was named, as we said, Cato Salonius; and a grandson by his eldest son, who died. Cato Salonius died when he was prætor, but his son Marcus was afterwards consul, and he was grandfather of Cato the philosopher, who for virtue and renown was one of the most eminent personages of his time.[20]

[20] It is uncertain whether Plutarch made a mistake in history, or wrote the sentence carelessly; probably the former: but in fact, Salonius, or Salonianus, was the grandfather of the younger Cato, the contemporary of Cicero and Cæsar.

COMPARISON OF ARISTIDES WITH MARCUS CATO

HAVING mentioned the most memorable actions of these great men, if we now compare the whole life of the one with that of the other, it will not be easy to discern the difference between them, lost as it is amongst such a number of circumstances in which they resemble each other. If, however, we examine them in detail as we might some piece of poetry, or some picture, we shall find this common to them both, that they advanced themselves to great honor and dignity in the commonwealth, by no other means than their own virtue and industry. But it seems when Aristides appeared, Athens was not at its height of grandeur and plenty, the chief magistrates and officers of his time being men only of moderate and equal fortunes among themselves. The estimate of the greatest estates then, was five hundred medimns; that of the second, or knights, three hundred; of the third and last called Zeugitæ, two hundred. But Cato, out of a petty village from a country life, leaped into the commonwealth, as it were into a vast ocean; at a time when there were no such governors as the Curii, Fabricii, and Hostilii. Poor laboring men were not then advanced from the plough and spade to be governors and magistrates; but greatness of family, riches, profuse gifts, distributions, and personal application were what the city looked to; keeping a high hand, and, in a manner, insulting over those that courted preferment. It was not as great a matter to have Themistocles for an adversary, a person of mean extraction and small fortune, (for he was not worth, it is said, more than four or five talents when he first applied himself to public affairs,) as to contest with a Scipio Africanus, a Servius Galba, and a Quintius Flamininus, having no other aid but a tongue free to assert right.

Besides, Aristides at Marathon, and again at Platæa, was but one commander out of ten; whereas Cato was chosen consul with a single colleague, having many competitors, and with a single colleague, also, was preferred before seven most noble and eminent pretenders to be censor. But Aristides was never principal in any action; for Miltiades carried the day at Marathon, at Salamis Themistocles, and at Platæa, Herodotus tells us, Pausanias got the glory of that noble victory: and men like Sophanes, and Aminias, Callimachus, and Cynægyrus, behaved themselves so well in all those engagements, as to contest it with Aristides even for the second place. But Cato not only in his consulship was esteemed the chief in courage and conduct in the Spanish war, but even whilst he was only serving as tribune at Thermopylæ, under another's command, he gained the glory of the victory, for having, as it were, opened a wide gate for the Romans to rush in upon Antiochus, and for having brought the war on his back, whilst he only minded what was before his face. For that victory, which was beyond disptue all Cato's own work, cleared Asia out of Greece, and by that means made way afterwards for Scipio into Asia. Both of them, indeed, were always victorious in war; but at home Aristides stumbled, being banished and oppressed by the faction of Themistocles; yet Cato, notwithstanding he had almost all the chief and most powerful of Rome for his adversaries, and wrestled with them even to his old age, kept still his footing. Engaging also in many public suits, sometimes plaintiff, sometimes defendant, he cast the most, and came off clear with all; thanks to his eloquence, that bulwark and powerful instrument to which more truly, than to chance or his fortune, he owed it, that he sustained himself unhurt to the last. Antipater justly gives it as a high commendation to Aristotle the philosopher, writing of him after his death, that among his other virtues, he was endowed with a faculty of persuading people which way he pleased.

Questionless, there is no perfecter endowment in man than political virtue, and of this Economics[1] is commonly esteemed not the least part; for a city, which is a collection of private households, grows into a stable commonwealth by the private means of prosperous citizens that compose it. Lycurgus by prohibiting gold and silver in Sparta, and making iron, spoiled by the fire, the only currency, did not by these measures discharge them from minding their household affairs, but cutting off luxury, the corruption and tumor of riches, he provided there should be an abundant supply of all necessary and useful things for all persons, as much as any other lawmaker ever did; being more apprehensive of a poor, needy, and indigent member of a community, than of the rich and haughty. And in this management of domestic concerns, Cato was as great as in the government of public affairs; for he increased

---

[1] Economics, in the proper Greek sense, being for the household or family, or *œcos*, what politics are for the state, or *polis*. The former word has originally no more to do with money-matters than the latter; but as earning the family's maintenance is the more obvious and prominent part of household management, Economics, in course of time, became restricted to this sense, and thence again was extended to money-matters in general.

his estate, and became a master to others in economy
and husbandry; upon which subjects he collected
in his writings many useful observations. On the
contrary Aristides, by his poverty, made justice
odious, as if it were the pest and impoverisher of a
family, and beneficial to all, rather than to those
that were endowed with it. Yet Hesiod urges us
alike to just dealing and to care of our households,
and inveighs against idleness as the origin of injustice; and Homer admirably says:—

> Work was not dear, nor household cares to me,
> Whose increase rears the thriving family;
> But well-rigged ships were always my delight,
> And wars, and darts, and arrows of the fight:[2]

as if the same characters carelessly neglected their
own estates, and lived by injustice and rapine from
others. For it is not as the physicians say of oil,
that outwardly applied, it is very wholesome, but
taken inwardly detrimental, that thus a just man
provides carefully for others, and is heedless of himself and his own affairs: but in this Aristides's
political virtues seem to be defective; since, according to most authors, he took no care to leave his
daughters a portion, or himself enough to defray
his funeral charges: whereas Cato's family produced
senators and generals to the fourth generation; his
grandchildren, and their children, came to the highest preferments. But Aristides, who was the principal man of Greece, though extreme poverty reduced some of his to get their living by juggler's
tricks, others, for want, to hold out their hands for
public alms; leaving none means to perform any
noble action, or worthy his dignity.

[2] The lines from Homer are from the Odyssey (*XIV.*, 222).

Yet why should this needs follow? since poverty is dishonorable not in itself, but when it is a proof of laziness, intemperance, luxury, and carelessness; whereas in a person that is temperate, industrious, just, and valiant, and who uses all his virtues for the public good, it shows a great and lofty mind. For he has no time for great matters, who concerns himself with petty ones; nor can he relieve many needs of others, who himself has many needs of his own. What most of all enables a man to serve the public is not wealth, but content and independence; which, requiring no superfluity at home, distracts not the mind from the common good. God alone is entirely exempt from all want: of human virtues, that which needs least, is the most absolute and most divine. For as a body bred to a good habit, requires nothing exquisite either in clothes or food, so a sound man and a sound household keep themselves up with a small matter. Riches ought to be proportioned to the use we have of them; for he that scrapes together a great deal, making use of but little, is not independent; for if he wants them not, it is folly in him to make provision for things which he does not desire; or if he does desire them, and restrains his enjoyment out of sordidness, he is miserable. I would fain know of Cato himself, if we seek riches that we may enjoy them, why is he proud of having a great deal, and being contented with little? But if it be noble, as it is, to feed on coarse bread, and drink the same wine with our hinds, and not to covet purple, and plastered houses, neither Aristides, nor Epaminondas, nor Manius Curius, nor Caius Fabricius wanted necessaries, who took no pains to get those things whose use they approved not. For it was not worth the while of a man who esteemed turnips a most delicate food,

ARISTIDES AND MARCUS CATO

and who boiled them himself, whilst his wife made bread, to brag so often of a half-penny, and write a book to show how a man may soonest grow rich; the very good of being contented with little is because it cuts off at once the desire and the anxiety for superfluities. Hence Aristides, it is told, said, on the trial of Callias, that it was for them to blush at poverty, who were poor against their wills; they who like him were willingly so, might glory in it. For it is ridiculous to think Aristides's neediness imputable to his sloth, who might fairly enough by the spoil of one barbarian, or seizing one tent, have become wealthy. But enough of this.

Cato's expeditions added no great matter to the Roman empire, which already was so great, as that in a manner it could receive no addition; but those of Aristides are the noblest, most splendid, and distinguished actions the Grecians ever did, the battles at Marathon, Salamis, and Platæa. Nor indeed is Antiochus, nor the destruction of the walls of the Spanish towns, to be compared with Xerxes, and the destruction by sea and land of so many myriads of enemies; in all of which noble exploits Aristides yielded to none, though he left the glory, and the laurels, like the wealth and money, to those who needed and thirsted more greedily after them: because he was superior to those also. I do not blame Cato for perpetually boasting and preferring himself before all others, though in one of his orations he says, that it is equally absurd to praise and dispraise one's self: yet he who does not so much as desire others' praises, seems to me more perfectly virtuous, than he who is always extolling himself. A mind free from ambition is a main help to political gentleness: ambition, on the contrary, is hardhearted, and the greatest fomenter of envy; from which Aristides was wholly exempt; Cato very subject to it. Aristides assisted Themistocles in matters of highest importance, and, as his subordinate officer, in a manner raised Athens: Cato, by opposing Scipio, almost broke and defeated his expedition against the Carthaginians, in which he overthrew Hannibal, who till then was even invincible; and, at last, by continually raising suspicions and calumnies against him, he chased him from the city, and inflicted a disgraceful sentence on his brother for robbing the state.

Finally, that temperance which Cato always highly cried up, Aristides preserved truly pure and untainted. But Cato's marriage, unbecoming his dignity and age, is a considerable disparagement, in this respect, to his character. For it was not decent for him at that age to bring home to his son and his wife a young woman, the daughter of a common paid clerk in the public service: but whether it were for his own gratification or out of anger at his son, both the fact and the pretence were unworthy. For the reason he pretended to his son was false: for if he desired to get more as worthy children, he ought to have married a well-born wife; not to have contented himself, so long as it was unnoticed, with a woman to whom he was not married; and, when it was discovered, he ought not to have chosen such a father-in-law as was easiest to be got, instead of one whose affinity might be honorable to him.

PHILOPŒMEN[1]

TRANSLATED BY THOMAS SHORT, M.D.

CLEANDER was a man of high birth and great power in the city of Mantinea, but by the chances of the time happened to be driven from thence. There being an intimate friendship betwixt him and Craugis, the father of Philopœmen, who was a person of great distinction, he settled at Megalopolis, where, while his friend lived, he had all he could desire. When Craugis died, he repaid the father's hospitable kindness in the care of the orphan son; by which means Philopœmen was educated by him, as Homer says Achilles was by Phœnix, and from his infancy moulded to lofty and noble inclinations. But Ecdemus and Demophanes had the principal tuition of him, after he was past the years of childhood. They were both Megalopolitans; they had been scholars in the academic philosophy, and friends to Arcesilaus, and had, more than any of their contemporaries, brought philosophy to bear upon action, and state affairs. They had freed their country from tyranny by the death of Aristodemus, whom they caused to be killed; they had assisted Aratus in driving out the tyrant Nicocles from Sicyon; and, at the request of the Cyreneans, whose city was in a state of extreme disorder and confusion, went thither by sea, and succeeded in establishing good government and happily settling their

[1] Philopœmen, one of the few great men that Greece produced in the decline of her political independence, who is called by Roman admirers "the last of the Greeks," was born about 252 B.C. His tragic death as related by Plutarch occurred about 183 B.C.—DR. WILLIAM SMITH.

commonwealth. And among their best actions they themselves counted the education of Philopœmen, thinking they had done a general good to Greece, by giving him the nurture of philosophy. And indeed all Greece (which looked upon him as a kind of latter birth brought forth, after so many noble leaders, in her decrepid age) loved him wonderfully; and, as his glory grew, increased his power. And one of the Romans, to praise him, calls him the last of the Greeks; as if after him Greece had produced no great man, nor who deserved the name of Greek.

His person was not, as some fancy, deformed; for his likeness is yet to be seen at Delphi. The mistake of the hostess of Megara was occasioned, it would seem, merely by his easiness of temper and his plain manners. This hostess having word brought her, that the General of the Achæans[2] was coming to her house in the absence of her husband, was all in a hurry about providing his supper. Philopœmen, in an ordinary cloak, arriving in this point of time, she took him for one of his own train who had been sent on before, and bid him lend her his hand in her household work. He forthwith threw off his cloak, and fell to cutting up the fire-wood. The husband returning, and seeing him at it, "What," says he, "may this mean, O Philopœmen?" "I am," replied he in his Doric dialect, "paying the penalty of my ugly looks." Titus Flamininus, jesting with him upon his figure, told him one day, he had well-shaped hands and feet, but no belly: and he was indeed slender in the

[2] The captain-general or president, (*strategus* in Greek, and *prætor* in Latin writers,) of the cities composing the Achæan league; a magistrate, annually elected, who commanded their armies, and presided in the meetings of their congress.

waist. But this raillery was meant to the poverty of his fortune; for he had good horse and foot, but often wanted money to entertain and pay them. These are the common anecdotes told of Philopœmen.

The love of honor and distinction was, in his character, not unalloyed with feelings of personal rivalry and resentment. He made Epaminondas his great example, and came not far behind him in activity, sagacity, and incorruptible integrity; but his hot contentious temper continually carried him out of the bounds of that gentleness, composure, and humanity which had marked Epaminondas, and this made him thought a pattern rather of military than of civil virtue. He was strongly inclined to the life of a soldier even from his childhood, and he studied and practised all that belonged to it, taking great delight in managing of horses, and handling of weapons. Because he was naturally fitted to excel in wrestling, some of his friends and tutors recommended his attention to athletic exercises. But he would first be satisfied whether it would not interfere with his becoming a good soldier. They told him, as was the truth, that the one life was directly opposite to the other; the requisite state of body, the ways of living, and the exercises all different: the professed athlete sleeping much, and feeding plentifully, punctually regular in his set times of exercise and rest, and apt to spoil all by every little excess, or breach of his usual method; whereas the soldier ought to train himself in every variety of change and irregularity, and, above all, to bring himself to endure hunger and loss of sleep without difficulty. Philopœmen, hearing this, not only laid by all thoughts of wrestling and contemned it then, but when he came to be general, discouraged it by all marks of reproach and dishonor he could imagine, as a thing which made men, otherwise excellently fit for war, to be utterly useless and unable to fight on necessary occasions.

When he left off his masters and teachers, and began to bear arms in the incursions which his citizens used to make upon the Lacedæmonians for pillage and plunder, he would always march out the first, and return the last. When there was nothing to do, he sought to harden his body, and make it strong and active by hunting, or laboring in his ground. He had a good estate about twenty furlongs from the town, and thither he would go every day after dinner and supper; and when night came, throw himself upon the first mattress in his way, and there sleep as one of the laborers. At break of day he would rise with the rest, and work either in the vineyard or at the plough; from thence return again to the town, and employ his time with his friends, or the magistrates in public business. What he got in the wars, he laid out on horses, or arms, or in ransoming captives; but endeavored to improve his own property the justest way, by tillage; and this not slightly, by way of diversion, but thinking it his strict duty, so to manage his own fortune, as to be out of the temptation of wronging others.

He spent much time on eloquence and philosophy, but selected his authors, and cared only for those by whom he might profit in virtue. In Homer's fictions his attention was given to whatever he thought apt to raise the courage. Of all other books he was most devoted to the commentaries of Evangelus on military tactics, and also took delight, at leisure hours, in the histories of Alexander;

thinking that such reading, unless undertaken for mere amusement and idle conversation, was to the purpose for action. Even in speculations on military subjects it was his habit to neglect maps and diagrams, and to put the theorems to practical proof on the ground itself. He would be exercising his thoughts, and considering, as he travelled, and arguing with those about him of the difficulties of steep or broken ground, what might happen at rivers, ditches, or mountain-passes, in marching in close or in open, in this or in that particular form of battle. The truth is, he indeed took an immoderate pleasure in military operations and in warfare, to which he devoted himself, as the special means for exercising all sorts of virtue, and utterly contemned those who were not soldiers, as drones and useless in the commonwealth.

When he was thirty years of age, Cleomenes, king of the Lacedæmonians, surprised Megalopolis by night, forced the guards, broke in, and seized the market-place. Philopœmen came out upon the alarm, and fought with desperate courage, but could not beat the enemy out again; yet he succeeded in effecting the escape of the citizens, who got away while he made head against the pursuers, and amused Cleomenes, till, after losing his horse and receiving several wounds, with much ado he came off himself, being the last man in the retreat. The Megalopolitans escaped to Messene, whither Cleomenes sent to offer them their town and goods again. Philopœmen perceiving them to be only too glad at the news, and eager to return, checked them with a speech, in which he made them sensible, that what Cleomenes called restoring the city, was, rather, possessing himself of the citizens, and through their means securing also the city for the future. The mere solitude would, of itself, erelong force him away, since there was no staying to guard empty houses and naked walls. These reasons withheld the Megalopolitans, but gave Cleomenes a pretext to pillage and destroy a great part of the city, and carry away a great booty.

Awhile after king Antigonus coming down to succor the Achæans, they marched with their united forces against Cleomenes; who, having seized the avenues, lay advantageously posted on the hills of Sellasia. Antigonus drew up close by him, with a resolution to force him in his strength. Philopœmen, with his citizens, was that day placed among the horse, next to the Illyrian foot, a numerous body of bold fighters, who completed the line of battle, forming, together with the Achæans, the reserve. Their orders were to keep their ground, and not engage till from the other wing, where the king fought in person, they should see a red coat lifted up on the point of a spear. The Achæans obeyed their order, and stood fast; but the Illyrians were led on by their commanders to the attack. Euclidas, the brother of Cleomenes, seeing the foot thus severed from the horse, detached the best of his light-armed men, commanding them to wheel about, and charge the unprotected Illyrians in the rear. This charge putting things in confusion, Philopœmen, considering those light-armed men would be easily repelled, went first to the king's officers to make them sensible what the occasion required. But they not minding what he said, but slighting him as a hare-brained fellow, (as indeed he was not yet of any repute sufficient to give credit to a proposal of such importance,) he charged with his own citizens, and at the first encounter disordered, and soon after put the troops to flight with great slaughter. Then, to encourage the king's army further, to bring them all upon the enemy while he was in confusion, he quitted his horse, and fighting with extreme difficulty in his heavy horseman's dress, in rough uneven ground, full of water-courses and hollows, had both his thighs struck through with a thonged javelin. It was thrown with great force, so that the head came out on the other side, and made a severe, though not a mortal, wound. There he stood awhile, as if he had been shackled, unable to move. The fastening which joined the thong to the javelin made it difficult to get it drawn out, nor would any about him venture to do it. But the fight being now at the hottest, and likely to be quickly decided, he was transported with the desire of partaking in it, and struggled and strained so violently, setting one leg forward, the other back, that at last he broke the shaft in two; and thus got the pieces pulled out. Being in this manner set at liberty, he caught up his sword, and running through the midst of those who were fighting in the first ranks, animated his men, and set them afire with emulation. Antigonus, after the victory, asked the Macedonians, to try them, how it happened the horse had charged without orders before the signal? They answering, that they were against their wills forced to it by a young man of Megalopolis, who had fallen in before his time: "that young man," replied Antigonus, smiling, "did like an experienced commander."

This, as was natural, brought Philopœmen into great reputation. Antigonus was earnest to have him in his service, and offered him very advantageous conditions, both as to command and pay. But Philopœmen, who knew that his nature brooked not to be under another, would not accept them; yet not enduring to live idle, and hearing of wars in Crete, for practice' sake he passed over thither. He spent some time among those very warlike, and, at the same time, sober and temperate men, improving much by experience in all sorts of service; and then returned with so much fame, that the Achæans presently chose him commander of the horse. These horsemen at that time had neither experience nor bravery, it being the custom to take any common horses, the first and cheapest they could procure, when they were to march; and on almost all occasions they did not go themselves, but hired others in their places, and staid at home. Their former commanders winked at this, because, it being an honor among the Achæans to serve on horseback, these men had great power in the commonwealth, and were able to gratify or molest whom they pleased. Philopœmen, finding them in this condition, yielded not to any such considerations, nor would pass it over as formerly; but went himself from town to town, where, speaking with the young men, one by one, he endeavored to excite a spirit of ambition and love of honor among them, using punishment also, where it was necessary. And then by public exercises, reviews, and contests in the presence of numerous spectators, in a little time he made them wonderfully strong and bold, and, which is reckoned of greatest consequence in military service, light and agile. With use and industry they grew so perfect, to such a command of their horses, such a ready exactness in wheeling round in their troops, that in any change of posture the whole body seemed to move with all the facility and promptitude, and, as it were, with the single will of one man. In the great battle, which they fought with the Ætolians and Eleans by the river Larissus, he set them an example himself. Damophantus, general of the Elean horse, singled out Philopœmen, and rode with full speed at him. Philopœmen awaited his charge, and, before receiving the stroke, with a violent blow of his spear threw him dead to the ground: upon whose fall the enemy fled immediately. And now Philopœmen was in everybody's mouth, as a man who in actual fighting with his own hand yielded not to the youngest, nor in good conduct to the oldest, and than whom there came not into the field any better soldier or commander.

Aratus, indeed, was the first who raised the Achæans, inconsiderable till then, into reputation and power, by uniting their divided cities into one commonwealth and establishing amongst them an humane and truly Grecian form of government; and hence it happened, as in running waters, where when a few little particles of matter once stop, others stick to them, and one part strengthening another, the whole becomes firm and solid; so in a general weakness, when every city relying only on itself, all Greece was giving way to an easy dissolution, the Achæans, first forming themselves into a body, then drawing in their neighbors round about, some by protection, delivering them from their tyrants, others by peaceful consent and by naturalization, designed at last to bring all Peloponnesus into one community. Yet while Aratus lived, they depended much on the Macedonians, courting first Ptolemy, then Antigonus and Philip, who all took part continually in whatever concerned the affairs of Greece. But when Philopœmen came to command, the Achæans, feeling themselves a match for the most powerful of their enemies, declined foreign support. The truth is, Aratus, as we have written in his life, was not of so warlike a temper, but did most by policy and gentleness, and friendships with foreign princes; but Philopœmen being a man both of execution and command, a great soldier, and fortunate in his first attempts, wonderfully heightened both the power and courage of the Achæans, accustomed to victory under his conduct.

But first he altered what he found amiss in their arms, and form of battle. Hitherto they had used light, thin bucklers, too narrow to cover the body, and javelins much shorter than pikes. By which means they were skilful in skirmishing at a distance, but in a close fight had much the disadvantage. Then in drawing their forces up for battle, they were never accustomed to form in regular divisions; and their line being unprotected either by the thick array of projecting spears or by their shields, as in the Macedonian phalanx, where the soldiers shoulder close and their shields touch, they were easily opened, and broken. Philopœmen reformed all this, persuading them to change the narrow target and short javelin, into a large shield and long pike; to arm their heads, bodies, thighs, and legs; and instead of loose skirmishing, fight firmly and foot to foot. After he had brought them all to wear full armor, and by that means into the confidence of thinking themselves now invincible, he turned what before had been idle profusion and luxury into an honorable expense. For being long used to vie with each other in their dress, the furniture of their houses, and service of their tables, and to glory in outdoing one another, the disease by custom was grown incurable, and there was no possibility of removing it altogether. But he diverted the passion, and brought them, instead of these superfluities, to love useful and more manly display, and, reducing their other expenses, to take delight in appearing magnificent in their equipage of war. Nothing then was to be seen in the shops but plate breaking up, or melting down, gilding of breastplates, and studding bucklers and bits with silver; nothing in the places of exercise, but horses managing, and young men exercising their arms; nothing in the hands of the women, but helmets and crests of feathers to be dyed, and military cloaks and riding-frocks to be embroidered; the very sight of all which quickening and raising their spirits, made them contemn dangers, and feel ready to venture on any honorable dangers. Other kinds of sumptuosity give us pleasure, but make us effeminate; the tickling of the sense slackening the vigor of the mind; but magnificence of this kind strengthens and heightens the courage; as Homer makes Achilles at the sight of his new arms exulting with joy, and on fire to use them. When Philopœmen had obtained of them to arm, and set themselves out in this manner, he proceeded to train them, mustering and exercising them perpetually; in which they obeyed him with great zeal and eagerness. For they were wonderfully pleased with their new form of battle, which, being so knit and cemented together, seemed almost incapable of being broken. And then their arms, which for their riches and beauty they wore with pleasure, becoming light and easy to them with constant use, they longed for nothing more than to try them with an enemy, and fight in earnest.

The Achæans at that time were at war with Machanidas, the tyrant of Lacedæmon, who, having a strong army, watched all opportunities of becoming entire master of Peloponnesus. When intelligence came that he was fallen upon the Mantineans, Philopœmen forthwith took the field, and marched towards him. They met near Mantinea, and drew up in sight of the city. Both, besides the whole strength of their several cities, had a good number of mercenaries in pay. When they came to fall on, Machanidas, with his hired soldiers, beat the spearmen and the Tarentines whom Philopœmen had placed in the front. But when he should have charged immediately into the main battle, which stood close and firm, he hotly followed the chase; and instead of attacking the Achæans, passed on beyond them, while they remained drawn up in their place. With so untoward a beginning the rest of the confederates gave themselves up for lost; but Philopœmen, professing to make it a matter of small consequence, and observing the enemy's oversight, who had thus left an opening in their main body, and exposed their own phalanx, made no sort of motion to oppose them, but let them pursue the chase freely, till they had placed themselves at a great distance from him. Then seeing the Lacedæmonians before him deserted by their horse, with their flanks quite bare, he charged suddenly, and surprised them without a commander, and not so much as expecting an encounter, as, when they saw Machanidas driving the beaten enemy before him, they thought the victory already gained. He overthrew them with great slaughter, (they report above four thousand killed in the place,) and then faced about against Machanidas, who was returning with his mercenaries from the pursuit. There happened to be a broad deep ditch between them, alongside of which both rode their horses for awhile, the one trying to get over and fly, the other to hinder him. It looked less like the contest between two generals than like the last defence of some wild beast, brought to bay by the keen huntsman Philopœmen, and forced to fight for his life. The tyrant's horse was mettled and strong; and feeling the bloody spurs in his sides, ventured to take the ditch. He had already so far reached the other side, as to have planted his fore-feet upon it, and was struggling to raise himself with these, when Simmias and Polyænus, who used to fight by the side of Philopœmen, came up on horseback to his assistance. But Philopœmen, before either of them, himself met Machanidas; and perceiving that the horse with his head high reared, covered his master's body, he turned his own a little, and holding his javelin by the middle, drove it against the tyrant with all his force, and tumbled him dead into the ditch. Such is the precise posture in which he stands at Delphi in the brazen statue which the Achæans set up of him, in admiration of his valor in this single combat, and conduct during the whole day.

We are told that at the Nemean games, a little after this victory, Philopœmen being then General the second time, and at leisure on the occasion of the solemnity, first showed the Greeks his army drawn up in full array as if they were to fight, and executed with it all the manœuvres of a battle with wonderful order, strength, and celerity. After which he went into the theatre, while the musicians were singing for the prize, followed by the young soldiers in their military cloaks and their scarlet frocks under their armor, all in the very height of bodily vigor, and much alike in age, showing a high respect to their general; yet breathing at the same time a noble confidence in themselves, raised by success in many glorious encounters. Just at their coming in, it so happened, that the musician Pylades, with a voice well suited to the lofty style of the poet, was in the act of commencing the Persians of Timotheus,

Under his conduct Greece was glorious and was free.

The whole theatre at once turned to look at Philopœmen, and clapped with delight; their hopes venturing once more to return to their country's former reputation; and their feelings almost rising to the height of their ancient spirit.

It was with the Achæans as with young horses, which go quietly with their usual riders, but grow unruly and restive under strangers. The soldiers, when any service was in hand, and Philopœmen not at their head, grew dejected and looked about for him; but if he once appeared, came presently to themselves, and recovered their confidence and courage, being sensible that this was the only one of their commanders whom the enemy could not endure to face; but, as appeared in several occasions, were frighted with his very name. Thus we find that Philip, king of Macedon, thinking to terrify the Achæans into subjection again, if he could rid his hands of Philopœmen, employed some persons privately to assassinate him. But the treachery coming to light, he became infamous, and lost his character through Greece. The Bœotians besieging Megara, and ready to carry the town by storm, upon a groundless rumor, that Philopœmen was at hand with succor, ran away, and left their scaling ladders at the wall behind them. Nabis, (who was tyrant of Lacedæmon after Machanidas,) had surprised Messene at a time when Philopœmen was out of command. He tried to persuade Lysippus, then General of the Achæans, to succor Messene: but not prevailing with him, because, he said, the enemy being now within it, the place was irrecoverably lost, he resolved to go himself, without order or commission, followed merely by his own immediate fellow-citizens who went with him as their general by commission from nature, which had made him fittest to command. Nabis, hearing of his coming, though his army quartered within the town, thought it not convenient to stay; but stealing out of the furthest gate with his men, marched away with all the speed he could, thinking himself a happy man if he could get off with safety. And he did escape; but Messene was rescued.

All hitherto makes for the praise and honor of Philopœmen. But when at the request of the Gortynians he went away into Crete to command for them, at a time when his own country was distressed by Nabis, he exposed himself to the charge of either cowardice, or unseasonable ambition of honor amongst foreigners. For the Megalopolitans were then so pressed, that, the enemy being master of the field and encamping almost at their gates, they were forced to keep themselves within their walls, and sow their very streets. And he in the mean time, across the seas, waging war and commanding in chief in a foreign nation, furnished his ill-wishers with matter enough for their reproaches. Some said he took the offer of the Gortynians, because the Achæans chose other generals, and left him but a private man. For he could not endure to sit still, but looking upon war and command in it as his great business, always coveted to be employed. And this agrees with what he once aptly said of king Ptolemy. Somebody was praising him for keeping his army and himself in an admirable state of discipline and exercise: "And what praise," replied Philopœmen, "for a king of his years, to be always preparing, and never performing?" However, the Megalopolitans, thinking themselves betrayed, took it so ill, that they were about to banish him. But the Achæans put an end to that design, by sending their General, Aristæus, to Megalopolis, who, though he were at difference with Philopœmen about affairs of the commonwealth, yet would not suffer him to be banished. Philopœmen finding himself upon this account out of favor with his citizens, induced divers neighboring places to renounce obedience to them, suggesting to them to urge that from the beginning they were not subject to their taxes, or laws, or any way under their command. In these pretences he openly took their part, and fomented seditious movements amongst the Achæans in general against Megalopolis. But these things happened a while after.

While he stayed in Crete, in the service of the Gortynians, he made war not like a Peloponnesian and Arcadian, fairly in the open field, but fought with them at their own weapon, and turning their stratagems and tricks against themselves, showed them they played craft against skill, and were but children to an experienced soldier. Having acted here with great bravery, and great reputation to himself, he returned into Peloponnesus, where he found Philip beaten by Titus Quintius, and Nabis at war both with the Romans and Achæans. He was at once chosen general against Nabis, but venturing to fight by sea, met, like Epaminondas, with a result very contrary to the general expectation, and his own former reputation. Epaminondas, however, according to some statements, was backward by design, unwilling to give his countrymen an appetite for the advantages of the sea, lest from good soldiers, they should by little and little turn, as Plato [8] says, to ill mariners. And therefore he returned from Asia and the Islands without doing any thing, on purpose. Whereas Philopœmen, thinking his skill in land-service would equally avail at sea, learned how great a part of valor experience is, and how much it imports in the management of things to be accustomed to them. For he was not only put to the worst in the fight for want of skill, but having rigged up an old ship, which had been a famous vessel forty years before, and shipped his citizens in her, she foundering, he was in danger of losing them all. But finding the enemy, as if he had been driven out of the sea, had, in contempt of him, besieged Gythium, he presently set sail again, and, taking them unexpectedly, dispersed and careless after their victory, landed in the night, burnt their camp, and killed a great number.

A few days after, as he was marching through a rough country, Nabis came suddenly upon him. The Achæans were dismayed, and in such difficult ground where the enemy had secured the advantage, despaired to get off with safety. Philopœmen made a little halt, and, viewing the ground, soon made it appear, that the one important thing in war is skill in drawing up an army. For by advancing only a few paces, and, without any confusion or trouble, altering his order according to the nature of the place, he immediately relieved himself from every difficulty, and then charging, put the enemy to flight. But when he saw they fled, not towards the city, but dispersed every man a different way

[8] The passage of Plato, about the Athenians becoming *ill mariners,* is in the fourth book of the Laws.

all over the field, which for wood and hills, brooks
and hollows was not passable by horse, he sounded
a retreat, and encamped by broad daylight. Then
foreseeing the enemy would endeavor to steal scat-
teringly into the city in the dark, he posted strong
parties of the Achæans all along the watercourses
and sloping ground near the walls. Many of
Nabis's men fell into their hands. For returning
not in a body, but as the chance of flight had disposed of every one, they were caught like birds
ere they could enter into the town.

These actions obtained him distinguished marks
of affection and honor in all the theatres of Greece,
but not without the secret ill-will of Titus Flamininus, who was naturally eager for glory, and
thought it but reasonable a consul of Rome should
be otherwise esteemed by the Achæans, than a
common Arcadian; especially as there was no comparison between what he, and what Philopœmen
had done for them, he having by one proclamation
restored all Greece, as much as had been subject to
Philip and the Macedonians, to liberty. After this,
Titus made peace with Nabis, and Nabis was cir-
cumvented and slain by the Ætolians. Things
being then in confusion at Sparta, Philopœmen laid
hold of the occasion, and coming upon them with
an army, prevailed with some by persuasion, with
others by fear, till he brought the whole city over
to the Achæans. As it was no small matter for
Sparta to become a member of Achæa, this action
gained him infinite praise from the Achæans, for
having strengthened their confederacy by the addition of so great and powerful a city, and not a little
good-will from the nobility of Sparta itself, who
hoped they had now procured an ally, who would
defend their freedom. Accordingly, having raised

a sum of one hundred and twenty silver talents by the sale of the house and goods of Nabis, they decreed him the money, and sent a deputation in the name of the city to present it. But here the honesty of Philopœmen showed itself clearly to be a real, uncounterfeited virtue. For first of all, there was not a man among them who would undertake to make him this offer of a present, but every one excusing himself, and shifting it off upon his fellow, they laid the office at last on Timolaus, with whom he had lodged at Sparta. Then Timolaus came to Megalopolis, and was entertained by Philopœmen; but struck into admiration with the dignity of his life and manners, and the simplicity of his habits, judging him to be utterly inaccessible to any such considerations, he said nothing, but pretending other business, returned without a word mentioned of the present. He was sent again, and did just as formerly. But the third time with much ado, and faltering in his words, he acquainted Philopœmen with the good-will of the city of Sparta to him. Philopœmen listened obligingly and gladly; and then went himself to Sparta, where he advised them, not to bribe good men and their friends, of whose virtue they might be sure without charge to themselves; but to buy off and silence ill citizens, who disquieted the city with their seditious speeches in the public assemblies; for it was better to bar liberty of speech in enemies, than friends. Thus it appeared how much Philopœmen was above bribery.

Diophanes being afterwards General of the Achæans, and hearing the Lacedæmonians were bent on new commotions, resolved to chastise them; they, on the other side, being set upon war, were embroiling all Peloponnesus. Philopœmen on this occasion did all he could to keep Diophanes quiet and to make him sensible that as the times went, while Antiochus and the Romans were disputing their pretensions with vast armies in the heart of Greece, it concerned a man in his position to keep a watchful eye over them, and dissembling, and putting up with any less important grievances, to preserve all quiet at home. Diophanes would not be ruled, but joined with Titus, and both together falling into Laconia, marched directly to Sparta. Philopœmen, upon this, took, in his indignation, a step which certainly was not lawful, nor in the strictest sense just, but boldly and loftily conceived. Entering into the town himself, he, a private man as he was, refused admission to both the consul of Rome, and the General of the Achæans, quieted the disorders in the city, and reunited it on the same terms as before to the Achæan confederacy.

Yet afterwards, when he was General himself, upon some new misdemeanor of the Lacedæmonians, he brought back those who had been banished, put, as Polybius writes, eighty, according to Aristocrates three hundred and fifty, Spartans to death, razed the walls, took away a good part of their territory and transferred it to the Megalopolitans, forced out of the country and carried into Achæa all who had been made citizens of Sparta by tyrants, except three thousand who would not submit to banishment. These he sold for slaves, and with the money, as if to insult over them, built a colonnade at Megalopolis. Lastly, unworthily trampling upon the Lacedæmonians in their calamities, and gratifying his hostility by a most oppressive and arbitrary action, he abolished the laws of Lycurgus, and forced them to educate their children, and live after the manner of the Achæans; as though, while they kept to the discipline of Lycurgus, there was no humbling their haughty spirits. In their present distress and adversity they allowed Philopœmen thus to cut the sinews of their common wealth asunder, and behaved themselves humbly and submissively. But afterwards in no long time, obtaining the support of the Romans, they abandoned their new Achæan citizenship; and as much as in so miserable and ruined a condition they could, reëstablished their ancient discipline.

When the war betwixt Antiochus and the Romans broke out in Greece, Philopœmen was a private man. He repined grievously, when he saw Antiochus lay idle at Chalcis, spending his time in unseasonable courtship and weddings, while his men lay dispersed in several towns, without order or commanders, and minding nothing but their pleasures. He complained much that he was not himself in office, and said he envied the Romans their victory; and that if he had had the fortune to be then in command, he would have surprised and killed the whole army in the taverns.

When Antiochus was overcome, the Romans pressed harder upon Greece, and encompassed the Achæans with their power; the popular leaders in the several cities yielded before them; and their power speedily, under the divine guidance, advanced to the consummation due to it in the revolutions of fortune. Philopœmen, in this conjuncture, carried himself like a good pilot in a high sea, sometimes shifting sail, and sometimes yielding, but still steering steady; and omitting no opportunity nor effort to keep all who were considerable, whether for eloquence or riches, fast to the defence of their common liberty.

Aristænus,[4] a Megalopolitan of great credit among the Achæans, but always a favorer of the Romans, saying one day in the senate, that the Romans should not be opposed, or displeased in any way, Philopœmen heard him with an impatient silence; but at last, not able to hold longer, said angrily to him, "And why be in such haste, wretched man, to behold the end of Greece?" Manius,[5] the Roman consul, after the defeat of Antiochus, requested the Achæans to restore the banished Lacedæmonians to their country, which motion was seconded and supported by all the interest of Titus. But Philopœmen crossed it, not from ill-will to the men, but that they might be beholden to him and the Achæans, not to Titus and the Romans. For when he came to be General himself, he restored them. So impatient was his spirit of any subjection, and so prone his nature to contest every thing with men in power.

Being now threescore and ten, and the eighth time General, he was in hope to pass in quiet, not only the year of his magistracy, but his remaining life. For as our diseases decline, as it is supposed, with our declining bodily strength, so the quarreling humor of the Greeks abated much with their failing political greatness. But fortune or some divine retributive power threw him down in the close of his life, like a successful runner who stumbles at the goal. It is reported, that being in company where one was praised for a great commander, he replied, there was no great account to be made of a man, who had suffered himself to be taken alive by his enemies.

[4] *Aristænus* (this is the more recognized form) is the same as the *Aristæus* of page *supra;* the readings vary.

[5] Manius Acilius Glabrio.

A few days after, news came that Dinocrates the Messenian, a particular enemy to Philopœmen, and for his wickedness and villanies generally hated, had induced Messene to revolt from the Achæans, and was about to seize upon a little place called Colonis. Philopœmen lay then sick of a fever at Argos. Upon the news he hasted away, and reached Megalopolis, which was distant above four hundred furlongs, in a day. From thence he immediately led out the horse, the noblest of the city, young men in the vigor of their age, and eager to proffer their service, both from attachment to Philopœmen, and zeal for the cause. As they marched towards Messene, they met with Dinocrates, near the hill of Evander,[6] charged and routed him. But five hundred fresh men, who, being left for a guard to the country, came in late, happening to appear, the flying enemy rallied again about the hills. Philopœmen, fearing to be enclosed, and solicitous for his men, retreated over ground extremely disadvantageous, bringing up the rear himself. As he often faced, and made charges upon the enemy, he drew them upon himself; though they merely made movements at a distance, and shouted about him, nobody daring to approach him. In his care to save every single man, he left his main body so often, that at last he found himself alone among the thickest of his enemies. Yet even then none durst come up to him, but being pelted at a distance, and driven to stony steep places, he had great difficulty, with much spurring, to guide his horse

[6] *The hill of Evander* is thought to be a mis-reading for the hill of *Evas* (or *Evan*, in the accusative case), mentioned by Polybius and Pausanias. Polybius, the historian, is *the general's son*, who *carried the urn*, mentioned later.

aright. His age was no hinderance to him, for with perpetual exercise it was both strong and active; but being weakened with sickness, and tired with his long journey, his horse stumbling, he fell encumbered with his arms, and faint, upon a hard and rugged piece of ground. His head received such a shock with the fall, that he lay awhile speechless, so that the enemy, thinking him dead, began to turn and strip him. But when they saw him lift up his head and open his eyes, they threw themselves all together upon him, bound his hands behind him, and carried him off, every kind of insult and contumely being lavished on him who truly had never so much as dreamed of being led in triumph by Dinocrates.

The Messenians, wonderfully elated with the news, thronged in swarms to the city gates. But when they saw Philopœmen in a posture so unsuitable to the glory of his great actions and famous victories, most of them, struck with grief and cursing the deceitful vanity of human fortune, even shed tears of compassion at the spectacle. Such tears by little and little turned to kind words, and it was almost in everybody's mouth that they ought to remember what he had done for them, and how he had preserved the common liberty, by driving away Nabis. Some few, to make their court to Dinocrates, were for torturing and then putting him to death as a dangerous and irreconcilable enemy; all the more formidable to Dinocrates, who had taken him prisoner, should he after this misfortune, regain his liberty. They put him at last into a dungeon underground, which they called the treasury, a place into which there came no air nor light from abroad; and, which, having no doors, was closed with a great stone. This they rolled into the entrance and fixed, and placing a guard about it, left him. In the mean time Philopœmen's soldiers, recovering themselves after their flight, and fearing he was dead when he appeared nowhere, made a stand, calling him with loud cries, and reproaching one another with their unworthy and shameful escape; having betrayed their general, who, to preserve their lives, had lost his own. Then returning after much inquiry and search, hearing at last that he was taken, they sent away messengers round about with the news. The Achæans resented the misfortune deeply, and decreed to send and demand him; and, in the mean time, drew their army together for his rescue.

While these things passed in Achæa, Dinocrates, fearing that any delay would save Philopœmen, and resolving to be beforehand with the Achæans, as soon as night had dispersed the multitude, sent in the executioner with poison, with orders not to stir from him till he had taken it. Philopœmen had then laid down, wrapt up in his cloak, not sleeping, but oppressed with grief and trouble; but seeing light, and a man with poison by him, struggled to sit up; and, taking the cup, asked the man if he heard any thing of the horsemen, particularly Lycortas? The fellow answering, that the most part had got off safe, he nodded, and looking cheerfully upon him, "It is well," he said "that we have not been every way unfortunate;" and without a word more, drank it off, and laid him down again. His weakness offering but little resistance to the poison, it despatched him presently.

The news of his death filled all Achæa with grief and lamentation. The youth, with some of the chief of the several cities, met at Megalopolis with a resolution to take revenge without delay.

They chose Lycortas general, and falling upon the Messenians, put all to fire and sword, till they all with one consent made their submission. Dinocrates, with as many as had voted for Philopœmen's death, anticipated their vengeance and killed themselves. Those who would have had him tortured, Lycortas put in chains and reserved for severer punishment. They burnt his body, and put the ashes into an urn, and then marched homeward, not as in an ordinary march, but with a kind of solemn pomp, half triumph, half funeral, crowns of victory on their heads, and tears in their eyes, and their captive enemies in fetters by them. Polybius, the general's son, carried the urn, so covered with garlands and ribbons as scarcely to be visible; and the noblest of the Achæans accompanied him. The soldiers followed fully armed and mounted, with looks neither altogether sad as in mourning, nor lofty as in victory. The people from all towns and villages in their way, flocked out to meet him, as at his return from conquest, and, saluting the urn, fell in with the company, and followed on to Megalopolis; where, when the old men, the women and children were mingled with the rest, the whole city was filled with sighs, complaints, and cries, the loss of Philopœmen seeming to them the loss of their own greatness, and of their rank among the Achæans. Thus he was honorably buried according to his worth, and the prisoners were stoned about his tomb.

Many statues were set up, and many honors decreed to him by the several cities. One of the Romans in the time of Greece's affliction, after the destruction of Corinth, publicly accusing Philopœmen, as if he had been still alive, of having been the enemy of Rome, proposed that these memorials should all be removed. A discussion ensued, speeches were made, and Polybius answered the sycophant at large. And neither Mummius nor the lieutenants would suffer the honorable monuments of so great a man to be defaced, though he had often crossed both Titus and Manius. They justly distinguished, and as became honest men, betwixt usefulness and virtue,—what is good in itself, and what is profitable to particular parties,—judging thanks and reward due to him who does a benefit, from him who receives it, and honor never to be denied by the good to the good. And so much concerning Philopœmen.

FLAMININUS[1]

WHAT Titus Quintius Flamininus, whom we select as a parallel to Philopœmen, was in personal appearance, those who are curious may see by the brazen statue of him, which stands in Rome near that of the great Apollo, brought from Carthage, opposite to the Circus Maximus, with a Greek inscription upon it. The temper of his mind is said to have been of the warmest both in anger and in kindness; not indeed equally so in both respects; as in punishing, he was ever moderate, never inflexible; but whatever courtesy or good turn he set about, he went through with it, and was as perpetually kind and obliging to those on whom he had poured his favors, as if they, not he, had been the benefactors: exerting himself for the security and preservation of what he seemed to consider his noblest possessions, those to whom he had done good. But being ever thirsty after honor, and passionate for glory, if any thing of a greater and more extraordinary nature were to be done, he was eager to be the doer of it himself; and took more pleasure in those that needed, than in those that were capable of conferring favors; looking on the

---

[1] The manuscripts generally write the name, incorrectly, Flaminius, and it is very possible that Plutarch, who was not by any means perfect in his knowledge of Latin, made the mistake himself. Titus was the name by which Flamininus was commonly known to the Greeks.

Flamininus, the distinguished Roman general, was consul 198 B.C., and had the conduct of the war against Philip of Macedonia, which he brought to a close in 197 by the defeat of Philip. He died about 174.—DR. WILLIAM SMITH.

former as objects for his virtue, and on the latter as competitors in glory.

Rome had then many sharp contests going on, and her youth betaking themselves early to the wars, learned betimes the art of commanding; and Flamininus, having passed through the rudiments of soldiery, received his first charge in the war against Hannibal, as tribune under Marcellus, then consul. Marcellus, indeed, falling into an ambuscade, was cut off. But Titus, receiving the appointment of governor, as well of Tarentum, then retaken, as of the country about it, grew no less famous for his administration of justice, than for his military skill. This obtained him the office of leader and founder of two colonies which were sent into the cities of Narnia and Cossa;[2] which filled him with loftier hopes, and made him aspire to step over those previous honors which it was usual first to pass through, the offices of tribune of the people, prætor and ædile, and to level his aim immediately at the consulship. Having these colonies, and all their interest ready at his service, he offered himself as candidate; but the tribunes of the people, Fulvius and Manius,[3] and their party, strongly opposed him; alleging how unbecoming a thing it was, that a man of such raw years, one who was yet, as it were, untrained, uninitiated in the first sacred rites and mysteries of government, should,

---

[2] Commissions of Three, were appointed for various purposes in all periods of the Roman Republic; and one of the commonest occasions was this of establishing a colony, and dividing land. Such a commission might consist of two, five, or even twenty members, but we most frequently read of *triumviri coloniæ deducendæ agroque dividundo.*

[3] Manius Curio is meant.

in contempt of the laws, intrude and force himself into the sovereignty.

However, the senate remitted it to the people's choice and suffrage; who elected him (though not then arrived at his thirtieth year) consul with Sextus Ælius. The war against Philip and the Macedonians fell to Titus by lot, and some kind fortune, propitious at that time to the Romans, seems to have so determined it; as neither the people nor the state of things which were now to be dealt with, were such as to require a general who would always be upon the point of force and mere blows, but rather were accessible to persuasion and gentle usage. It is true that the kingdom of Macedon furnished supplies enough to Philip for actual battle with the Romans; but to maintain a long and lingering war, he must call in aid from Greece; must thence procure his supplies; there find his means of retreat; Greece, in a word, would be his resource for all the requisites of his army. Unless, therefore, the Greeks could be withdrawn from siding with Philip, this war with him must not expect its decision from a single battle. Now Greece (which had not hitherto held much correspondence with the Romans, but first began an intercourse on this occasion) would not so soon have embraced a foreign authority, instead of the commanders she had been inured to, had not the general of these strangers been of a kind gentle nature, one who worked rather by fair means than force; of a persuasive address in all applications to others, and no less courteous, and open to all addresses of others to him; and above all bent and determined on justice. But the story of his actions will best illustrate these particulars.

Titus observed that both Sulpicius and Publius,

who had been his predecessors in that command, had
not taken the field against the Macedonians till late
in the year; and then, too, had not set their hands
properly to the war, but had kept skirmishing and
scouting here and there for passes and provisions,
and never came to close fighting with Philip. He
resolved not to trifle away a year, as they had done,
at home in ostentation of the honor, and in domestic administration, and only then to join the army,
with the pitiful hope of protracting the term of
office through a second year, acting as consul in
the first, and as general in the latter. He was,
moreover, infinitely desirous to employ his authority
with effect upon the war, which made him slight
those home-honors and prerogatives. Requesting,
therefore, of the senate, that his brother Lucius
might act with him as admiral of the navy, and
taking with him to be the edge, as it were, of the
expedition three thousand still young and vigorous
soldiers, of those who, under Scipio, had defeated
Asdrubal in Spain, and Hannibal in Africa, he got
safe into Epirus; and found Publius[4] encamped
with his army, over against Philip, who had long
made good the pass over the river Apsus, and the
straits there; Publius not having been able, for the
natural strength of the place, to effect any thing
against him. Titus therefore took upon himself
the conduct of the army, and, having dismissed
Publius, examined the ground. The place is in
strength not inferior to Tempe, though it lacks the
trees and green woods, and the pleasant meadows
and walks that adorn Tempe. The Apsus, making
its way between vast and lofty mountains which all
but meet above a single deep ravine in the midst,
is not unlike the river Peneus, in the rapidity of its

[4] Publius Villius, his predecessor in command.

current, and in its general appearance. It covers the foot of those hills, and leaves only a craggy, narrow path cut out beside the stream, not easily passable at any time for an army, but not at all when guarded by an enemy.

There were some, therefore, who would have had Titus make a circuit through Dassaretis, and take an easy and safe road by the district of Lyncus. But he, fearing that if he should engage himself too far from the sea in barren and untilled countries, and Philip should decline fighting, he might, through want of provisions, be constrained to march back again to the seaside without effecting any thing, as his predecessor had done before him, embraced the resolution of forcing his way over the mountains. But Philip, having possessed himself of them with his army, showered down his darts and arrows from all parts upon the Romans. Sharp encounters took place, and many fell wounded and slain on both sides, and there seemed but little likelihood of thus ending the war; when some of the men, who fed their cattle thereabouts, came to Titus with a discovery, that there was a roundabout way which the enemy neglected to guard; through which they undertook to conduct his army, and to bring it within three days at furthest, to the top of the hills. To gain the surer credit with him, they said that Charops, son of Machatas, a leading man in Epirus, who was friendly to the Romans, and aided them (though, for fear of Philip, secretly), was privy to the design. Titus gave their information belief, and sent a captain with four thousand foot, and three hundred horse; these herdsmen being their guides, but kept in bonds. In the daytime they lay still under the covert of the hollow and woody places, but in the night they marched by moonlight, the moon being then at the full. Titus, having detached this party, lay quiet with his main body, merely keeping up the attention of the enemy by some slight skirmishing. But when the day arrived, that those who stole round, were expected upon the top of the hill, he drew up his forces early in the morning, as well the light-armed as the heavy, and, dividing them into three parts, himself led the van, marching his men up the narrow passage along the bank, darted at by the Macedonians, and engaging, in this difficult ground, hand to hand with his assailants; whilst the other two divisions on either side of him, threw themselves with great alacrity among the rocks. Whilst they were struggling forward, the sun rose, and a thin smoke, like a mist hanging on the hills, was seen rising at a distance, unperceived by the enemy, being behind them, as they stood on the heights; and the Romans, also, as yet under suspense, in the toil and difficulty they were in, could only doubtfully construe the sight according to their desires. But as it grew thicker and thicker, blackening the air, and mounting to a greater height, they no longer doubted but it was the fire-signal of their companions; and, raising a triumphant shout, forcing their way onwards, they drove the enemy back into the roughest ground; while the other party echoed back their acclamations from the top of the mountain.

The Macedonians fled with all the speed they could make; there fell, indeed, not more than two thousand of them; for the difficulties of the place rescued them from pursuit. But the Romans pillaged their camp, seized upon their money and slaves, and, becoming absolute masters of the pass, traversed all Epirus; but with such order and discipline, with such temperance and moderation, that, though they were far from the sea, at a great distance from their vessels, and stinted of their monthly allowance of corn, and though they had much difficulty in buying, they nevertheless abstained altogether from plundering the country, which had provisions enough of all sorts in it. For intelligence being received that Philip making a flight, rather than a march, through Thessaly, forced the inhabitants from the towns to take shelter in the mountains, burnt down the towns themselves, and gave up as spoil to his soldiers all the property which it had been found impossible to remove, abandoning, as it would seem, the whole country to the Romans, Titus was, therefore, very desirous, and entreated his soldiers that they would pass through it as if it were their own, or as if a place trusted into their hands; and, indeed, they quickly perceived, by the event, what benefit they derived from this moderate and orderly conduct. For they no sooner set foot in Thessaly, but the cities opened their gates, and the Greeks, within Thermopylæ, were all eagerness and excitement to ally themselves with them. The Achæans abandoned their alliance with Philip, and voted to join with the Romans in actual arms against him; and the Opuntians, though the Ætolians, who were zealous allies of the Romans, were willing and desirous to undertake the protection of the city, would not listen to proposals from them; but, sending for Titus, intrusted and committed themselves to his charge.

It is told of Pyrrhus, that when first, from an adjacent hill or watchtower which gave him a prospect of the Roman army, he descried them drawn up in order, he observed, that he saw nothing barbarian-like in this barbarian line of battle. And all who came near Titus, could not choose but say as much of him, at their first view. For they who had been told by the Macedonians of an invader, at the head of a barbarian army, carrying everywhere slavery and destruction on his sword's point; when, in lieu of such an one, they met a man, in the flower of his age, of a gentle and humane aspect, a Greek in his voice and language, and a lover of honor, were wonderfully pleased and attracted; and when they left him they filled the cities, wherever they went, with favorable feelings for him, and with the belief that in him they might find the protector and asserter of their liberties. And when afterwards, on Philip's professing a desire for peace, Titus made a tender to him of peace and friendship, upon the condition that the Greeks be left to their own laws, and that he should withdraw his garrisons, which he refused to comply with, now after these proposals, the universal belief even of the favorers and partisans of Philip was, that the Romans came not to fight against the Greeks, but for the Greeks, against the Macedonians.

Accordingly, all the rest of Greece came to peaceable terms with him. But as he marched into Bœotia, without committing the least act of hostility, the nobility and chief men of Thebes came out of their city to meet him, devoted under the influence of Brachylles to the Macedonian alliance, but desirous at the same time to show honor and deference to Titus; as they were, they conceived, in amity with both parties. Titus received them in the most obliging and courteous manner, but kept going gently on, questioning and inquiring of them, and sometimes entertaining them with narratives of his own, till his soldiers might a little recover from the weariness of their journey. Thus passing on, he and the Thebans came together into their city not much to their satisfaction; but yet they could not well deny him entrance, as a good number of his men attended him in. Titus, however, now he was within, as if he had not had the city at his mercy, came forward and addressed them, urging them to join the Roman interest. King Attalus followed to the same effect. And he, indeed, trying to play the advocate, beyond what it seems his age could bear, was seized, in the midst of his speech, with a sudden flux or dizziness, and swooned away; and, not long after, was conveyed by ship into Asia, and died there. The Bœotians joined the Roman alliance.

But now, when Philip sent an embassy to Rome, Titus despatched away agents on his part, too, to solicit the senate, if they should continue the war, to continue him in his command, or if they determined an end to that, that he might have the honor of concluding the peace. Having a great passion for distinction, his fear was, that if another general were commissioned to carry on the war, the honor even of what was passed, would be lost to him; and his friends transacted matters so well on his behalf, that Philip was unsuccessful in his proposals, and the management of the war was confirmed in his hands. He no sooner received the senate's determination, but, big with hopes, he marches directly into Thessaly, to engage Philip; his army consisting of twenty-six thousand men, out of which the Ætolians furnished six thousand foot and four hundred horse. The forces of Philip were much about the same number. In this eagerness to encounter, they advanced against each other, till both were near Scotussa, where they resolved to hazard a battle. Nor had the approach of these two formidable armies the effect that might have been supposed, to strike into the generals a mutual terror of each other; it rather inspired them with ardor and ambition; on the Romans' part, to be the conquerors of Macedon, a name which Alexander had made famous amongst them for strength and valor; whilst the Macedonians, on the other hand, esteeming of the Romans as an enemy very different from the Persians, hoped, if victory stood on their side, to make the name of Philip more glorious than that of Alexander. Titus, therefore, called upon his soldiers to play the part of valiant men, because they were now to act their parts upon the most illustrious theatre of the world, Greece, and to contend with the bravest antagonists. And Philip, on the other side, commenced an harangue to his men, as usual before an engagement, and to be the better heard, (whether it were merely a mischance, or the result of unseasonable haste, not observing what he did,) mounted an eminence outside their camp, which proved to be a burying-place; and much disturbed by the despondency that seized his army at the unluckiness of the omen, all that day kept in his camp, and declined fighting.

But on the morrow, as day came on, after a soft and rainy night, the clouds changing into a mist filled all the plain with thick darkness; and a dense foggy air descending, by the time it was full day, from the adjacent mountains into the ground betwixt the two camps, concealed them from each other's view. The parties sent out on either side, some for ambuscade, some for discovery, falling in upon one another quickly after they were thus detached, began the fight at what are called the Cynos

Cephalæ,[5] a number of sharp tops of hills that stand close to one another, and have the name from some resemblance in their shape. Now many vicissitudes and changes happening, as may well be expected, in such an uneven field of battle, sometimes hot pursuit and sometimes as rapid a flight, the generals on both sides kept sending in succors from the main bodies, as they saw their men pressed or giving ground, till at length the heavens clearing up, let them see what was going on, upon which the whole armies engaged. Philip, who was in the right wing, from the advantage of the higher ground which he had, threw on the Romans the whole weight of his phalanx, with a force which they were unable to sustain; the dense array of spears, and the pressure of the compact mass overpowering them. But the king's left wing being broken up by the hilliness of the place, Titus observing it, and cherishing little or no hopes on that side where his own gave ground, makes in all haste to the other, and there charges in upon the Macedonians; who, in consequence of the inequality and roughness of the ground, could not keep their phalanx entire, nor line their ranks to any great depth, (which is the great point of their strength,) but were forced to fight man for man under heavy and unwieldy armor. For the Macedonian phalanx is like some single powerful animal, irresistible so long as it is embodied into one, and keeps its order, shield touching shield, all as in a piece; but if it be once broken, not only is the joint-force lost, but the individual soldiers also who composed it, lose each one his own single strength, because of the nature of their armor; and because each of them is strong, rather, as he makes a part of the whole, than in himself.

[5] The Dog-heads.

When these were routed, some gave chase to the
flyers, others charged the flanks of those Macedonians who were still fighting, so that the conquering
wing, also, was quickly disordered, took to flight,
and threw down its arms. There were then slain
no less than eight thousand, and about five thousand
were taken prisoners; and the Ætolians were blamed
as having been the main occasion that Philip himself got safe off. For whilst the Romans were
in pursuit, they fell to ravaging and plundering the camp, and did it so completely, that
when the others returned, they found no booty
in it.

This bred at first hard words, quarrels, and
misunderstandings betwixt them. But, afterwards,
they galled Titus more, by ascribing the victory to
themselves, and prepossessing the Greeks with reports
to that effect; insomuch that poets, and people in
general in the songs that were sung or written in
honor of the action, still ranked the Ætolians foremost. One of the pieces most current was the
following epigram:—

> Naked and tombless see, O passer-by,
> The thirty thousand men of Thessaly,
> Slain by the Ætolians and the Latin band,
> That came with Titus from Italia's land:
> Alas for mighty Macedon! that day,
> Swift as a roe, king Philip fled away.

This was composed by Alcæus in mockery of Philip,
exaggerating the number of the slain. However,
being everywhere repeated, and by almost everybody, Titus was more nettled at it than Philip.
The latter merely retorted upon Alcæus with some
elegiac verses of his own:—

> Naked and leafless see, O passer-by,
> The cross that shall Alcæus crucify.

But such little matters extremely fretted Titus, who was ambitious of a reputation among the Greeks; and he, therefore, acted in all after-occurrences by himself, paying but very slight regard to the Ætolians. This offended them in their turn; and when Titus listened to terms of accommodation, and admitted an embassy upon the proffers of the Macedonian king, the Ætolians made it their business to publish through all the cities of Greece, that this was the conclusion of all; that he was selling Philip a peace, at a time when it was in his hand to destroy the very roots of the war, and to overthrow the power which had first inflicted servitude upon Greece. But whilst, with these and the like rumors, the Ætolians labored to shake the Roman confederates, Philip, making overtures of submission of himself and his kingdom to the discretion of Titus and the Romans, puts an end to those jealousies, as Titus by accepting them, did to the war. For he reinstated Philip in his kingdom of Macedon, but made it a condition that he should quit Greece, and that he should pay one thousand talents; he took from him also, all his shipping, save ten vessels; and sent away Demetrius, one of his sons, hostage to Rome; improving his opportunity to the best advantage, and taking wise precautions for the future. For Hannibal the African, a professed enemy to the Roman name, an exile from his own country, and not long since arrived at king Antiochus's court, was already stimulating that prince, not to be wanting to the good fortune that had been hitherto so propitious to his affairs; the magnitude of his successes having gained him the surname of the Great. He had begun to level his aim at universal monarchy, but above all he was eager to measure himself with the Romans. Had not, therefore, Titus upon a principle of prudence and foresight, lent an ear to peace, and had Antiochus found the Romans still at war in Greece with Philip, and had these two, the most powerful and warlike princes of that age, confederated for their common interests against the Roman state, Rome might once more have run no less a risk, and been reduced to no less extremities than she had experienced under Hannibal. But now, Titus opportunely introducing this peace between the wars, despatching the present danger before the new one had arrived, at once disappointed Antiochus of his first hopes, and Philip of his last.

When the ten commissioners, delegated to Titus from the senate, advised him to restore the rest of Greece to their liberty, but that Corinth, Chalcis, and Demetrias should be kept garrisoned for security against Antiochus; the Ætolians, on this, breaking out into loud accusations, agitated all the cities, calling upon Titus to strike off the shackles of Greece, (so Philip used to term those three cities,) and asking the Greeks, whether it were not matter of much consolation to them, that, though their chains weighed heavier, yet they were now smoother and better polished than formerly, and whether Titus were not deservedly admired by them as their benefactor, who had unshackled the feet of Greece, and tied her up by the neck? Titus, vexed and angry at this, made it his request to the senate, and at last prevailed in it, that the garrisons in these cities should be dismissed, that so the Greeks might be no longer debtors to him for a partial, but for an entire, favor. It was now the time of the celebration of the Isthmian games; and the seats around the race-course were crowded with an unusual multitude of spectators; Greece, after long wars, having regained not only peace, but hopes of liberty, and being able once more to keep holiday in safety. A trumpet sounded to command silence; and the crier, stepping forth amidst the spectators, made proclamation, that the Roman senate, and Titus Quintius, the proconsular general, having vanquished king Philip and the Macedonians, restored the Corinthians, Locrians, Phocians, Eubœans, Achæans of Phthiotis, Magnetians, Thessalians, and Perrhæbians to their own lands, laws, and liberties; remitting all impositions upon them, and withdrawing all garrisons from their cities. At first, many heard not at all, and others not distinctly, what was said; but there was a confused and uncertain stir among the assembled people, some wondering, some asking, some calling out to have it proclaimed again. When, therefore, fresh silence was made, the crier raising his voice, succeeded in making himself generally heard; and recited the decree again. A shout of joy followed it, so loud that it was heard as far as the sea. The whole assembly rose and stood up; there was no further thought of the entertainment; all were only eager to leap up and salute and address their thanks to the deliverer and champion of Greece. What we often hear alleged, in proof of the force of human voices, was actually verified upon this occasion. Crows that were accidentally flying over the course, fell down dead into it. The disruption of the air must be the cause of it; for the voices being numerous, and the acclamation violent, the air breaks with it, and can no longer give support to the birds; but lets them tumble, like one that should attempt to walk upon a vacuum; unless we should rather imagine them to fall and die, shot with the noise as with a dart. It is possible, too, that there may be a circular agitation of the air, which, like marine whirlpools, may have a violent direction of this sort given to it from the excess of its fluctuation.

But for Titus; the sports being now quite at an end, so beset was he on every side, and by such multitudes, that had he not, foreseeing the probable throng and concourse of the people, timely withdrawn, he would scarce, it is thought, have ever got clear of them. When they had tired themselves with acclamations all about his pavilion, and night was now come, wherever friends or fellow-citizens met, they joyfully saluted and embraced each other, and went home to feast and carouse together. And there, no doubt, redoubling their joy, they began to recollect and talk of the state of Greece, what wars she had incurred in defence of her liberty, and yet was never perhaps mistress of a more settled or grateful one than this which other men's labors had won for her: almost without one drop of blood, or one citizen's loss to be mourned for, she had this day had put into her hands the most glorious of rewards, and best worth the contending for. Courage and wisdom are, indeed, rarities amongst men, but of all that is good, a just man it would seem is the most scarce. Such as Agesilaus, Lysander, Nicias, and Alcibiades, knew how to play the general's part, how to manage a war, how to bring off their men victorious by land and sea; but how to employ that success to generous and honest purposes, they had not known. For should a man except the achievement at Marathon, the sea-fight at Salamis, the engagements at Platæa and Thermopylæ, Cimon's exploits at Eurymedon, and on the coasts of Cyprus, Greece fought all her battles against, and to enslave, herself; she erected all her trophies to her own shame and misery, and was brought to ruin and desolation almost wholly by the guilt and ambition of her great men. A foreign people, appearing just to retain some embers, as it were, some faint remainders of a common character derived to them from their ancient sires, a nation from whom it was a mere wonder that Greece should reap any benefit by word or thought, these are they who have retrieved Greece from her severest dangers and distresses, have rescued her out of the hands of insulting lords and tyrants, and reinstated her in her former liberties.[6]

Thus they entertained their tongues and thoughts; whilst Titus by his actions made good what had been proclaimed. For he immediately despatched away Lentulus to Asia, to set the Bargylians free, Titillius to Thrace, to see the garrisons of Philip removed out of the towns and islands there, while Publius Villius set sail, in order to treat with Antiochus about the freedom of the Greeks under him. Titus himself passed on to Chalcis, and sailing thence to Magnesia, dismantled the garrisons there, and surrendered the government into the people's hands. Shortly after, he was appointed at Argos to preside in the Nemean games, and did his part in the management of that solemnity singularly well; and made a second publication there by the crier, of liberty to the Greeks; and, visiting all the cities, he exhorted them to the practice of obedience to law, of constant justice, and unity, and friendship one towards another.

[6] Many stories ascribed the origin of Rome actually to Greek settlers. But it would appear that the Greek might even, in consideration of the close connection between the heroes on both sides in the Iliad, regard a Trojan descent as a sort of relationship.

FLAMININUS

He suppressed their factions, brought home their political exiles; and, in short, his conquest over the Macedonians did not seem to give him a more lively pleasure, than to find himself prevalent in reconciling Greeks with Greeks; so that their liberty seemed now the least part of the kindness he conferred upon them.

The story goes, that when Lycurgus the orator had rescued Xenocrates the philosopher from the collectors who were hurrying him away to prison for non-payment of the alien tax,⁊ and had them punished for the license they had been guilty of, Xenocrates afterwards meeting the children of Lycurgus, " My sons," said he, " I am nobly repaying your father for his kindness; he has the praises of the whole people in return for it." But the returns which attended Titus Quintius and the Romans, for their beneficence to the Greeks, terminated not in empty praises only; for these proceedings gained them, deservedly, credit and confidence, and thereby power, among all nations, for many not only admitted the Roman commanders, but even sent and entreated to be under their protection; neither was this done by popular governments alone, or by single cities; but kings oppressed by kings, cast themselves into these protecting hands. Insomuch that in a very short time (though perchance not without divine influence in it) all the world did homage to them. Titus himself thought more highly of his liberation of Greece than of any other of his actions, as appears by the inscription with which he dedicated some silver targets, together with his own shield, to Apollo at Delphi:—

⁊ The *metœcium* paid at Athens, by all *metœci* or resident foreigners: an annual charge of twelve drachmas on each family.

> Ye Spartan Tyndarids, twin sons of Jove,
> Who in swift horsemanship have placed your love,
> Titus, of great Æneas' race, leaves this
> In honor of the liberty of Greece.

He offered also to Apollo a golden crown, with this inscription:—

> This golden crown upon thy locks divine,
> O blest Latona's son, was set to shine
> By the great captain of the Ænean name.
> O Phœbus, grant the noble Titus fame!

The same event has twice occurred to the Greeks in the city of Corinth. Titus, then, and Nero again in our days, both at Corinth, and both alike at the celebration of the Isthmian games, permitted the Greeks to enjoy their own laws and liberty. The former (as has been said) proclaimed it by the crier; but Nero did it in the public meeting place from the tribunal, in a speech which he himself made to the people. This, however, was long after.

Titus now engaged in a most gallant and just war upon Nabis, that most profligate and lawless tyrant of the Lacedæmonians, but in the end disappointed the expectations of the Greeks. For when he had an opportunity of taking him, he purposely let it slip, and struck up a peace with him, leaving Sparta to bewail an unworthy slavery; whether it were that he feared, if the war should be protracted, Rome would send a new general who might rob him of the glory of it; or that emulation and envy of Philopœmen (who had signalized himself among the Greeks upon all other occasions, but in that war especially had done wonders both for matter of courage and counsel, and whom the Achæans magnified in their theatres, and put into the same balance of glory with Titus,) touched him to the quick; and that he scorned that an ordinary Arcadian, who had but commanded in a few rencounters upon the confines of his native district, should be spoken of in terms of equality with a Roman consul, waging war as the protector of Greece in general. But, besides, Titus was not without an apology too for what he did, namely, that he put an end to the war only when he foresaw that the tyrant's destruction must have been attended with the ruin of the other Spartans.

The Achæans, by various decrees, did much to show Titus honor: none of these returns, however, seemed to come up to the height of the actions that merited them, unless it were one present they made him, which affected and pleased him beyond all the rest; which was this. The Romans, who in the war with Hannibal had the misfortune to be taken captives, were sold about here and there, and dispersed into slavery; twelve hundred in number were at that time in Greece. The reverse of their fortune always rendered them objects of compassion; but more particularly, as well might be, when they now met, some with their sons, some with their brothers, others with their acquaintance; slaves with their free, and captives with their victorious countrymen. Titus, though deeply concerned on their behalf, yet took none of them from their masters by constraint. But the Achæans, redeeming them at five pounds [8] a man, brought them altogether into one place, and made a present of them to him, as he was just going on shipboard, so that he now sailed away with the

---

[8] Greek pounds, or minas, of a hundred drachmas: five of them making a little more than twenty English pounds: or nearly one hundred dollars.

fullest satisfaction; his generous actions having procured him as generous returns, worthy a brave man and a lover of his country. This seemed the most glorious part of all his succeeding triumph; for these redeemed Romans (as it is the custom for slaves, upon their manumission, to shave their heads and wear felt-hats) followed in that habit in the procession. To add to the glory of this show, there were the Grecian helmets, the Macedonian targets and long spears, borne with the rest of the spoils in public view, besides vast sums of money; Tuditanus says, 3,713 pounds weight of massy gold, 43,270 of silver, 14,514 pieces of coined gold, called Philippics, which was all over and above the thousand talents which Philip owed, and which the Romans were afterwards prevailed upon, chiefly by the mediation of Titus, to remit to Philip, declaring him their ally and confederate, and sending him home his hostage son.

Shortly after, Antiochus entered Greece with a numerous fleet, and a powerful army, soliciting the cities there to sedition and revolt; abetted in all and seconded by the Ætolians, who for this long time had borne a grudge and secret enmity to the Romans, and now suggested to him, by way of a cause and pretext of war, that he came to bring the Greeks liberty. When, indeed, they never wanted it less, as they were free already, but, in lack of really honorable grounds, he was instructed to employ these lofty professions. The Romans, in the interim, in great apprehension of revolutions and revolt in Greece, and of his great reputation for military strength, despatched the consul Manius Acilius to take the charge of the war, and Titus, as his lieutenant, out of regard to the Greeks; some of whom he no sooner saw, but he confirmed them

in the Roman interests; others, who began to falter,
like a timely physician, by the use of the strong
remedy of their own affection for himself, he was
able to arrest in the first stage of the disease, before they had committed themselves to any great
error. Some few there were whom the Ætolians
were beforehand with, and had so wholly perverted
that he could do no good with them; yet these,
however angry and exasperated before, he saved
and protected when the engagement was over. For
Antiochus, receiving a defeat at Thermopylæ, not
only fled the field, but hoisted sail instantly for
Asia. Manius, the consul, himself invaded and besieged a part of the Ætolians, while king Philip had
permission to reduce the rest. Thus while, for instance, the Dolopes and Magnetians on the one
hand, the Athamanes and Aperantians on the other,
were ransacked by the Macedonians, and while
Manius laid Heraclea waste, and besieged Naupactus, then in the Ætolians' hands, Titus, still with a
compassionate care for Greece, sailed across from
Peloponnesus to the consul; and began first of all to
chide him, that the victory should be owing alone
to his arms, and yet he should suffer Philip to bear
away the prize and profit of the war, and sit wreaking his anger upon a single town, whilst the Macedonians overran several nations and kingdoms. But
as he happened to stand then in view of the besieged, they no sooner spied him out, but they call
to him from their wall, they stretch forth their
hands, they supplicate and entreat him. At the
time, he said not a word, but turning about with
tears in his eyes, went his way. Some little while
after, he discussed the matter so effectually with
Manius, that he won him over from his passion and
prevailed with him to give a truce and time to the

Ætolians, to send deputies to Rome to petition the senate for terms of moderation.

But the hardest task, and that which put Titus to the greatest difficulty was, to entreat with Manius for the Chalcidians, who had incensed him on account of a marriage which Antiochus had made in their city, even whilst the war was on foot; a match noways suitable in point of age, he an elderly man being enamored with a mere girl; and as little proper for the time, in the midst of a war. She was the daughter of one Cleoptolemus, and is said to have been wonderfully beautiful. The Chalcidians, in consequence, embraced the king's interests with zeal and alacrity, and let him make their city the basis of his operations during the war. Thither, therefore, he made with all speed, when he was routed, and fled; and reaching Chalcis, without making any stay, taking this young lady, and his money and friends with him, away he sails to Asia. And now Manius's indignation carrying him in all haste against the Chalcidians, Titus hurried after him, endeavoring to pacify and to entreat him; and, at length, succeeded both with him and the chief men among the Romans.

The Chalcidians, thus owing their lives to Titus, dedicated to him all the best and most magnificent of their sacred buildings, inscriptions upon which may be seen to run thus to this day: THE PEOPLE DEDICATE THIS GYMNASIUM TO TITUS AND TO HERCULES; so again: THE PEOPLE CONSECRATE THE DELPHINIUM [9] TO TITUS AND TO HERCULES; and what is yet more, even in our time, a priest of Titus was

---

[9] The Delphinium would properly be a building erected originally in honor of Apollo Delphinius, whose festival, as celebrated at Athens, is described by Plutarch in the life of Theseus.

FLAMININUS

formally elected and declared; and after sacrifice and libation, they sing a set song, much of which for the length of it we omit, but shall transcribe the closing verses:—

> The Roman Faith, whose aid of yore,
> Our vows were offered to implore,
> We worship now and evermore.
> To Rome, to Titus, and to Jove,
> O maidens, in the dances move.
> Dances and Io-Pæans too
> Unto the Roman Faith are due,
> O Savior Titus, and to you.

Other parts of Greece also heaped honors upon him suitable to his merits, and what made all those honors true and real, was the surprising good-will and affection which his moderation and equity of character had won for him. For if he were at any time at variance with anybody in matters of business, or out of emulation and rivalry, (as with Philopœmen, and again with Diophanes, when in office as General of the Achæans,) his resentment never went far, nor did it ever break out into acts; but when it had vented itself in some citizen-like freedom of speech, there was an end of it. In fine, nobody charged malice or bitterness upon his nature, though many imputed hastiness and levity to it; in general, he was the most attractive and agreeable of companions, and could speak too, both with grace, and forcibly. For instance, to divert the Achæans from the conquest of the isle of Zacynthus, "If," said he, "they put their head too far out of Peloponnesus, they may hazard themselves as much as a tortoise out of its shell." Again, when he and Philip first met to treat of a cessation and peace the latter complaining that Titus came with a mighty train, while he himself came alone and unattended, "Yes," replied Titus, "you have left yourself alone by killing your friends." At another time, Dinocrates the Messenian, having drunk too much at a merrymeeting in Rome, danced there in woman's clothes, and the next day addressed himself to Titus for assistance in his design to get Messene out of the hands of the Achæans. "This," replied Titus, "will be matter for consideration; my only surprise is that a man with such purposes on his hands should be able to dance and sing at drinking parties." When, again, the ambassadors of Antiochus were recounting to those of Achæa, the various multitudes composing their royal master's forces, and ran over a long catalogue of hard names, "I supped once," said Titus, "with a friend, and could not forbear expostulating with him at the number of dishes he had provided, and said I wondered where he had furnished himself with such a variety; 'Sir,' replied he, 'to confess the truth, it is all hog's flesh differently cooked.' And so, men of Achæa, when you are told of Antiochus's lancers, and pikemen, and foot-guards, I advise you not to be surprised; since in fact they are all Syrians differently armed."

After his achievements in Greece, and when the war with Antiochus was at an end, Titus was created censor; the most eminent office, and, in a manner, the highest preferment, in the commonwealth. The son of Marcellus, who had been five times consul, was his colleague. These, by virtue of their office, cashiered four senators of no great distinction, and admitted to the roll of citizens all freeborn residents. But this was more by constraint than their own choice; for Terentius Culeo, then tribune of the people, to spite the nobility, spurred on the populace to order it to be done. At this time, the two greatest and most eminent persons in the city, Africanus Scipio and Marcus Cato, were at variance. Titus named Scipio first member of the senate;[10] and involved himself in a quarrel with Cato, on the following unhappy occasion. Titus had a brother, Lucius Flamininus, very unlike him in all points of character, and, in particular, low and dissolute in his pleasures, and flagrantly regardless of all decency. He kept as a companion a boy whom he used to carry about with him, not only when he had troops under his charge, but even when the care of a province was committed to him. One day at a drinking-bout, when the youngster was wantoning with Lucius, "I love you, Sir, so dearly," said he, "that, preferring your satisfaction to my own, I came away without seeing the gladiators, though I have never seen a man killed in my life." Lucius, delighted with what the boy said, answered, "Let not that trouble you; I can satisfy that longing," and with that, orders a condemned man to be fetched out of the prison, and the executioner to be sent for, and commands him to strike off the man's head, before they rose from table. Valerius Antias only so far varies the story as to make it a woman for whom he did it. But Livy says that in Cato's own speech the statement is, that a Gaulish deserter coming with his wife and children to the door, Lucius took him into the banqueting-room, and killed him with his own hand, to gratify his paramour. Cato, it is probable, might say this by way of aggravation of the crime; but that the slain

---

[10] *Princeps senatus, prince;* i.e. in the original meaning, nothing more than *first* of the senate, a title afterwards engrossed by the emperors, from whose use of it has arisen the modern acceptation.

was no such fugitive, but a prisoner, and one condemned to die, not to mention other authorities, Cicero tells us in his treatise On Old Age, where he brings in Cato, himself, giving that account of the matter.

However, this is certain; Cato, during his censorship, made a severe scrutiny into the senators' lives in order to the purging and reforming the house, and expelled Lucius, though he had been once consul before, and though the punishment seemed to reflect dishonor on his brother also. Both of them presented themselves to the assembly of the people in a suppliant manner, not without tears in their eyes, requesting that Cato might show the reason and cause of his fixing such a stain upon so honorable a family. The citizens thought it a modest and moderate request. Cato, however, without any retraction or reserve, at once came forward, and standing up with his colleague interrogated Titus, as to whether he knew the story of the supper. Titus answering in the negative, Cato related it, and challenged Lucius to a formal denial of it.[11] Lucius made no reply, whereupon the people adjudged the disgrace just and suitable, and waited upon Cato home from the tribunal in great state. But Titus still so deeply resented his brother's degradation, that he allied himself with those who had long borne a grudge against Cato; and winning over a major part of the senate, he revoked and made void all the contracts, leases, and bargains made by Cato, relating to the public revenues, and also got numerous actions and accusations brought against him; carrying on against a lawful magistrate and excellent citizen, for the sake of one who was indeed

[11] By the *sponsio* or wager; compare the story as told in the life of Cato, page 372.

his relation, but was unworthy to be so, and had but gotten his deserts, a course of bitter and violent attacks, which it would be hard to say were either right or patriotic. Afterwards, however, at a public spectacle in the theatre, at which the senators appeared as usual, sitting, as became their rank, in the first seats, when Lucius was spied at the lower end, seated in a mean, dishonorable place, it made a great impression upon the people, nor could they endure the sight, but kept calling out to him to move, until he did move, and went in among those of consular dignity, who received him into their seats.

This natural ambition of Titus was well enough looked upon by the world, whilst the wars we have given a relation of afforded competent fuel to feed it; as, for instance, when after the expiration of his consulship, he had a command as military tribune, which nobody pressed upon him. But being now out of all employ in the government, and advanced in years, he showed his defects more plainly; allowing himself, in this inactive remainder of life, to be carried away with the passion for reputation, as uncontrollably as any youth. Some such transport, it is thought, betrayed him into a proceeding against Hannibal, which lost him the regard of many. For Hannibal, having fled his country, first took sanctuary with Antiochus; but he having been glad to obtain a peace, after the battle in Phrygia, Hannibal was put to shift for himself, by a second flight, and, after wandering through many countries, fixed at length in Bithynia, proffering his service to king Prusias. Every one at Rome knew where he was, but looked upon him, now in his weakness and old age, with no sort of apprehension, as one whom fortune had quite cast off. Titus, however, coming thither as ambassador, though he was sent from the senate to Prusias upon another errand, yet, seeing Hannibal resident there, it stirred up resentment in him to find that he was yet alive. And though Prusias used much intercession and entreaties in favor of him, as his suppliant and familiar friend, Titus was not to be entreated. There was an ancient oracle, it seems, which prophesied thus of Hannibal's end:—

Libyssan earth shall Hannibal inclose.

He interpreted this to be meant of the African Libya, and that he should be buried in Carthage; as if he might expect to return and end his life there. But there is a sandy place in Bithynia, bordering on the sea, and near it a little village called Libyssa. It was Hannibal's chance to be staying here, and having ever from the beginning had a distrust of the easiness and cowardice of Prusias, and a fear of the Romans, he had, long before, ordered seven underground passages to be dug from his house, leading from his lodging, and running a considerable distance in various opposite directions, all undiscernible from without. As soon, therefore, as he heard what Titus had ordered, he attempted to make his escape through these mines; but finding them beset with the king's guards, he resolved upon making away with himself. Some say that wrapping his upper garment about his neck, he commanded his servant to set his knee against his back, and not to cease twisting and pulling it, till he had completely strangled him. Others say, he drank bull's blood, after the example of Themistocles and Midas. Livy writes that he had poison in readiness, which he mixed for the purpose, and that taking the cup into his hand, " Let us ease," said he, " the Romans of their continual dread and care, who think it long and tedious to await the death of a hated old man. Yet Titus will not bear away a glorious victory, nor one worthy of those ancestors who sent to caution Pyrrhus, an enemy, and a conqueror too, against the poison prepared for him by traitors."

Thus various are the reports of Hannibal's death; but when the news of it came to the senators' ears, some felt indignation against Titus for it, blaming as well his officiousness as his cruelty; who, when there was nothing to urge it, out of mere appetite for distinction, to have it said that he had caused Hannibal's death, sent him to his grave when he was now like a bird that in its old age has lost its feathers, and incapable of flying is let alone to live tamely without molestation.

They began also now to regard with increased admiration the clemency and magnanimity of Scipio Africanus, and called to mind how he, when he had vanquished in Africa the till then invincible and terrible Hannibal, neither banished him his country, nor exacted of his countrymen that they should give him up. At a parley just before they joined battle, Scipio gave him his hand, and in the peace made after it, he put no hard article upon him, nor insulted over his fallen fortune. It is told, too, that they had another meeting afterwards, at Ephesus, and that when Hannibal, as they were walking together, took the upper hand, Africanus let it pass, and walked on without the least notice of it; and that then they began to talk of generals, and Hannibal affirmed that Alexander was the greatest commander the world had seen, next to him Pyrrhus, and the third was himself; Africanus, with a smile, asked, "What would you have said, if I had not defeated you?" "I would not then, Scipio," he replied, "have made

myself the third, but the first commander." Such
conduct was much admired in Scipio, and that of
Titus, who had as it were insulted the dead whom
another had slain, was no less generally found
fault with. Not but that there were some who
applauded the action, looking upon a living Hannibal as a fire, which only wanted blowing to become
a flame. For when he was in the prime and flower
of his age, it was not his body, nor his hand, that
had been so formidable, but his consummate skill
and experience, together with his innate malice and
rancor against the Roman name, things which do
not impair with age. For the temper and bent of
the soul remains constant, while fortune continually
varies; and some new hope might easily rouse to a
fresh attempt those whose hatred made them enemies
to the last. And what really happened afterwards
does to a certain extent tend yet further to the
exculpation of Titus. Aristonicus, of the family
of a common musician, upon the reputation of being
the son of Eumenes, filled all Asia with tumults
and rebellion. Then again, Mithridates, after his
defeats by Sylla and Fimbria, and vast slaughter,
as well among his prime officers as common soldiers,
made head again, and proved a most dangerous
enemy, against Lucullus, both by sea and land.
Hannibal was never reduced to so contemptible a
state as Caius Marius; he had the friendship of a
king, and the free exercise of his faculties, employment and charge in the navy, and over the horse
and foot, of Prusias; whereas those who but now
were laughing to hear of Marius wandering about
Africa, destitute and begging, in no long time after
were seen entreating his mercy in Rome, with his
rods at their backs, and his axes at their necks. So
true it is, that looking to the possible future, we can

call nothing that we see either great or small; as nothing puts an end to the mutability and vicissitude of things, but what puts an end to their very being. Some authors accordingly tell us, that Titus did not do this of his own head, but that he was joined in commission with Lucius Scipio, and that the whole object of the embassy was, to effect Hannibal's death. And now, as we find no further mention in history of any thing done by Titus, either in war or in the administration of the government, but simply that he died in peace; it is time to look upon him as he stands in comparison with Philopœmen.

COMPARISON OF PHILOPŒMEN WITH FLAMININUS

FIRST, then, as for the greatness of the benefits which Titus conferred on Greece, neither Philopœmen, nor many braver men than he, can make good the parallel. They were Greeks fighting against Greeks, but Titus, a stranger to Greece, fought for her. And at the very time when Philopœmen went over into Crete, destitute of means to succor his besieged countrymen, Titus, by a defeat given to Philip in the heart of Greece, set them and their cities free. Again, if we examine the battles they fought, Philopœmen, whilst he was the Achæans' general, slew more Greeks than Titus, in aiding the Greeks, slew Macedonians. As to their failings, ambition was Titus's weak side, and obstinacy Philopœmen's; in the former, anger was easily kindled, in the latter, it was as hardly quenched. Titus reserved to Philip the royal dignity; he pardoned the Ætolians, and stood their friend; but Philopœmen, exasperated against his country, deprived it of its supremacy over the adjacent villages. Titus was ever constant to those he had once befriended, the other, upon any offence, as prone to cancel kindnesses. He who had once been a benefactor to the Lacedæmonians, afterwards laid their walls level with the ground, wasted their country, and in the end changed and destroyed the whole frame of their government. He seems, in truth, to have prodigalled away his own life, through passion and perverseness; for he fell upon the Messenians, not with that conduct and caution that characterized the movements of Titus, but with unnecessary and unreasonable haste.

The many battles he fought, and the many trophies he won, may make us ascribe to Philopœmen the more thorough knowledge of war. Titus decided the matter betwixt Philip and himself in two engagements; but Philopœmen came off victorious in ten thousand encounters, to all which fortune had scarcely any pretence, so much were they owing to his skill. Besides, Titus got his renown, assisted by the power of a flourishing Rome; the other flourished under a declined Greece, so that his successes may be accounted his own; in Titus's glory Rome claims a share. The one had brave men under him, the other made his brave, by being over them. And though Philopœmen was unfortunate certainly, in always being opposed to his countrymen, yet this misfortune is at the same time a proof of his merit. Where the circumstances are the same, superior success can only be ascribed to superior merit. And he had, indeed, to do with the two most warlike nations of all Greece, the Cretans on the one hand, and the Lacedæmonians on the other, and he mastered the craftiest of them by art and the bravest of them by valor. It may also be said that Titus, having his men armed and disciplined to his hand, had in a manner his victories made for him; whereas Philopœmen was forced to introduce a discipline and tactics of his own, and to new-mould and model his soldiers; so that what is of greatest import towards insuring a victory was in his case his own creation, while the other had it ready provided for his benefit. Philopœmen effected many gallant things with his own hand, but Titus none; so much so that one Archedemus, an Ætolian, made it a jest against him that while he, the Ætolian, was running with his drawn sword, where he saw the Macedonians drawn up closest and fighting hardest, Titus was standing still, and with hands stretched out to heaven, praying to the gods for aid.

It is true, Titus acquitted himself admirably, both as a governor, and as an ambassador; but Philopœmen was no less serviceable and useful to the Achæans in the capacity of a private man, than in that of a commander. He was a private citizen when he restored the Messenians to their liberty, and delivered their city from Nabis; he was also a private citizen when he rescued the Lacedæmonians, and shut the gates of Sparta against the General Diophanes, and Titus. He had a nature so truly formed for command that he could govern even the laws themselves for the public good; he did not need to wait for the formality of being elected into command by the governed, but employed their service, if occasion required, at his own discretion; judging that he who understood their real interests, was more truly their supreme magistrate, than he whom they had elected to the office. The equity, clemency, and humanity of Titus towards the Greeks, display a great and generous nature; but the actions of Philopœmen, full of courage, and forward to assert his country's liberty against the Romans, have something yet greater and nobler in them. For it is not as hard a task to gratify the indigent and distressed, as to bear up against, and to dare to incur the anger of the powerful. To conclude, since it does not appear to be easy, by any review or discussion, to establish the true difference of their merits, and decide to which a preference is due, will it be an unfair award in the case, if we let the Greek bear away the crown for military conduct and warlike skill, and the Roman for justice and clemency?

www.ingramcontent.com/pod-product-compliance
Lightning Source LLC
Chambersburg PA
CBHW020632230426
43665CB00008B/133